SPITBALLING

SPITBALLING

The Baseball Days of Long Bob Ewing

MIKE LACKEY

ORANGE*frazer* PRESS

Wilmington, Ohio

B
EWING

ISBN 9781939710055
Copyright©2013 Mike Lackey

WK

No part of this publication may be reproduced in any material form (including
photocopying or storing in any medium by electronic means and whether or not
transiently or incidentally to some other use of this publication) without the written
permission of the copyright holder except in accordance with the provisions of the
Copyright, Designs and Patents Act 1988.

Published for Mike Lackey by:
Orange Frazer Press
P.O. Box 214
Wilmington, OH 45177
Telephone: 800.852.9332 for price and shipping information.
Website: www.orangefrazer.com
www.orangefrazercustombooks.com

Chapter 4 was originally published, in a somewhat different form, in *Nine: A
Journal of Baseball History and Culture, Vol. 14, No. 1* (fall 2005). It is reprinted
by permission of the University of Nebraska Press.

Book and cover design: Brittany Lament and Orange Frazer Press
Cover art: Jeff Suntala
Baseball cards on back cover: These Bob Ewing baseball cards, from the T206
(white border) and T205 (gold border) series, were issued in 1910 and 1911 by the
American Tobacco Co. The author bought both for about $50. By comparison, a
rare Honus Wagner card from the T206 series was sold in 2007 for $2.8 million.

Library of Congress Control Number 2013940668

THIS BOOK IS DEDICATED TO HEINIE PEITZ,
ADMIRAL SCHLEI, NOODLES HAHN, STANLEY ARTHUR,
EMIL HABERER, RUNT WALSH, FRED ODWELL AND
ALL THE OTHER FORGOTTEN PLAYMATES OF LONG BOB
WHO PUT SO MUCH LIFE INTO THE DEAD BALL ERA.

ACKNOWLEDGEMENTS

THIS BOOK WAS MANY YEARS IN THE MAKING. Along the way the author incurred debts of gratitude almost too numerous to list. The greatest debt is owed to Tom Simon, the indispensable man without whom this book might never have become a reality. The founding chairman of the Deadball Era Committee of the Society for American Baseball Research (SABR), Tom is a subtle, sensitive and sharp-eyed editor who contributed his extensive knowledge of baseball history. He was a font of sound guidance and, equally important, of infectious enthusiasm.

Ray Nemec, one of the founding fathers of SABR, did prodigious research on the minor league records of dozens of players, many of them obscure, and devoted years to the epic pursuit of Tacks Latimer. Steve Steinberg kept his eyes open throughout his own broad research and sent along many useful nuggets, including the best quote yet discovered from the taciturn Bob Ewing. Gabriel Schechter was consistently helpful as a friend and SABR colleague as well as in his official capacity while employed at the National Baseball Hall of Fame. Norman Macht was uncommonly generous in sharing his vast research, particularly with regard to the spitball. Len Levin provided invaluable assistance as keeper of the SABR Research Exchange.

Most especially I want to express my deepest gratitude to the grandchildren of Bob and Nelle Ewing—Christine Frye Terkelsen, Coleen Bowersock, Carol Hickman, Charlotte Ewing-Preville, Clifford Ewing, Cindy Ewing Stechschulte, Connie Ewing Kantner and the late Christopher Ewing—for their generous help and extraordinary patience. Thanks also to Bob's niece Winifred Ewing Nelson and her grandson, Jason Nelson; to Bob's great-nephew Jim Morris; and to Nelle's friend Jim Bowsher.

Sadly, two of my dearest friends (and two avid and knowledgeable baseball fans) did not live to see the project completed. Both Dave Alm and Dave Gerwig read substantial parts of the manuscript, and their observations and suggestions helped to shape the final book. Alm also volunteered many hours of research in microfilm of Chicago newspapers. I should also give a nod in the direction of their wives, Kathie Gerwig and Sue Alm, who tolerated many hours of discussion of the life and career of Long Bob Ewing.

The book was enriched in numerous small ways by SABR members past and present, including Carlos Bauer, John S. Bowman, Paul Dickson, Eric Enders, Jan Finkel, Kathy Gardner, Ernest Green, Bob Hoie, John Husman, Bill Kirwin, Steve Lauer, R.J. Lesch, Fredric London, Jim Moyes, Rod Nelson, Dan O'Brien, Ron Selter, Tom Shieber, Trey Strecker, John Thorn and Rich Topp—whose inquiry about the burial places of former big league ballplayers got this ball rolling in the first place—and all the members of the Deadball Era Committee.

The Hall of Fame was a treasure trove of information; among its staff, Tim Wiles, Pat Kelly and Scot E. Mondore were particularly helpful. Jeff Suntala, whose work I have long admired, created the terrific cover art and was a pleasure to work with. So was Lindsay Steiner, who made a vital contribution with her photographs. Among my former co-workers at *The Lima* (Ohio) *News,* editor Jim Krumel, photo editor Craig Orosz and Rebecca Gratz merit special thanks. Also from the journalistic fraternity, thanks to Mike Philipps and Bob Hahn at the late, lamented *Cincinnati Post,* Steve Geitschier at *The Sporting News* and John Erardi at the *Cincinnati Enquirer.*

The book would not have been possible without patient and diligent help from the following individuals and libraries:

Corene Newby and Alice Hackett, Lima (Ohio) Public Library; Paul Logsdon, Heterick Memorial Library, Ohio Northern University; Richard Ryan, Marianne Reynolds and Victoria L. Norman, Public Library of Cincinnati and Hamilton County; Jerome Szpila and Lee Weinstein, Free Public Library of Philadelphia; Auglaize County District Public Library, Wapakoneta, Ohio; Katie Quinn, Albany (N.Y.) Public Library; Beth E. Oljace, Anderson (Ind.) Public Library; Pat Rothenberg, Atlantic City (N.J.) Free Public Library; Enoch Pratt Free Library, Baltimore; Bianca E.V. Kelley, Knowlton Library, Bellefontaine, Ohio; Boston Public Library; Patricia Monahan, Buffalo and Erie County (N.Y.) Public Library; Cleveland Public Library; Allen County Public Library, Fort Wayne, Ind.;

Kansas City (Mo.) Public Library; Mary Lou Johnson Hardin County District Public Library, Kenton, Ohio; Joan Murray, Minneapolis Central Library; New York Public Library; Putnam County District Public Library, Ottawa, Ohio; Larry Fickenwirth, Flesh Public Library and Museum, Piqua, Ohio; Marilyn Holt, Carnegie Library of Pittsburgh; St. Louis Public Library; Amos Memorial Public Library, Sidney, Ohio; Cathy S. Hackett, Clark County Public Library, Springfield, Ohio; James C. Marshall and Angela Kalinowski, Toledo-Lucas County (Ohio) Public Library; Greene County District Public Library, Xenia, Ohio; Jeffrey M. Flannery, Library of Congress; and Washington, D.C. Public Library.

Thanks also to Anna B. Selfridge and Charles Bates, Allen County (Ohio) Historical Society; Rachel Barber, Auglaize County (Ohio) Historical Society; Thomas J. Rieder, Ohio Historical Society; Arkansas History Commission and Archives; Linda Bailey, Cincinnati Historical Society; Frances Egner, Dearborn County (Ind.) Historical Society; Helen M. Casey, Delaware County (N.Y.) Historical Society; and Piriya Vongkasemsiri, Chicago Historical Society.

Dave Ross shared enlightening clippings from newspapers in Shelby County, Ohio; Kathy Meagher at the New Brunswick Sports Hall of Fame contributed to a more rounded picture of Larry McLean; and Kate Murphy helped with newspaper research in Boston. Various forms of assistance came from Zane L. Miller at the University of Cincinnati and Marlene Wasikowski at the University of Notre Dame; Irene Colbert and Barbara Wise at the Greene County (Ohio) Courthouse; Jack O'Connell and the late Jack Lang of the Baseball Writers' Association of America; and James Lee in the Ohio secretary of state's office.

And of course there would be no book without Marcy Hawley, Brittany Lament and Sarah Hawley at Orange Frazer Press.

Last but by no means least, I can't overlook Christina Ryan Claypool, who provided constant encouragement as a friend and wise counsel as a published author; and my sisters Lynne, Lara and Lu Ann Lackey for their steadfast and essential support in life and their occasional strategic (and necessary) prodding to finish the job.

TABLE OF CONTENTS

INTRODUCTION

WHEN LAWRENCE RITTER CRISSCROSSED North America interviewing old-time ballplayers for his book *The Glory of Their Times*, he marveled at the "near total recall" demonstrated by men in their 70s and 80s when recollecting the days of their youth. They painted word pictures that, when checked against contemporary accounts, proved time and again to be startlingly accurate.[1]

George Gibson was typical. Looking back on his major league debut, the durable old Pittsburgh Pirates catcher remembered the first time a runner tried to steal second on him. "I rocked back on my heels and threw a bullet," he told Ritter, "knee high, right over the base"—only to watch in horror as the ball whistled untouched into center field. Not anticipating the speed and precision of Gibson's throw, neither shortstop Honus Wagner nor second baseman Claude Ritchey had gotten over in time to cover the bag.

The date was July 2, 1905. Sixty years later, Gibson remembered that the Pirates were in Cincinnati, and he remembered clearly how he fared at the plate: "They had a spitball pitcher going against us and I didn't get any hits that day."[2]

The one thing Gibson didn't remember was the name of that spitball pitcher. For the record, he was a tall, slim right-hander named Bob Ewing. He disposed of Gibson and his mates in routine fashion, striking out six and walking one on the way to a 4–1 victory.

Today, the era that Ritter sought to illuminate has receded beyond the reach of living memory. Most of Gibson's contemporaries—those who aren't in the Hall of Fame and weren't fortunate enough to be interviewed by Lawrence Ritter—are forgotten except by their families, a dwindling circle of personal acquaintances and perhaps a handful of baseball history devotees. Bob Ewing lived his entire life in or near Wapakoneta, Ohio, 15 miles from my home. Yet after most of a lifetime as a baseball fan, everything I knew about him began and ended with a few lines of statistics in a baseball encyclopedia.

That began to change in August 1997, when I came across a notice about an effort to create a database of the burial places of all former major league ballplayers. I looked up some obituaries in the newspaper where I worked and sent along the information on a half-dozen players, including Ewing. Then one day, out of curiosity, I drove out to the little country cemetery where Ewing had been buried for more than half a century.

What I found started me thinking—about the gravestone at my feet, about that block of statistics in the baseball encyclopedia, and about the life that connected them. Bob Ewing had thrown his last pitch nearly 85 years earlier. He was all but forgotten, his achievements buried under decade upon decade of subsequent seasons. Even the ballparks where he played were long gone. At this late date, I wondered, how much could still be learned about a little-known ballplayer who hung up his glove before the sinking of the *Lusitania*? I figured that in six months, I would know everything that was possible to know. I could dash off a quick article that would be of passing interest in his hometown, then move on to something else.

Fifteen years later I was still learning.

WHEN I SET OUT IN SEARCH OF BOB EWING, I little imagined the trip I was about to take. Ewing effectively opened a door and became my guide to a fascinating era teeming with remarkable characters. Ewing's career largely coincided with what New York Giants manager John J. McGraw termed "one of the most interesting and important periods in major league baseball."[3] Ewing pitched through the heart of what is known as the dead ball era, when pitching was dominant, runs were scarce and the outcome of a given contest often turned on some fine point of "inside baseball." The Society for American Baseball Research defines the era as the years 1901 to 1919, or roughly from the turn of the 20th century to the Black Sox scandal.

At first, those times seemed distant and alien. The jargon of the game was strange and baffling. Pitchers were dealing an exotic assortment of inshoots, drops, outcurves and raise balls, with an occasional combination drop/outcurve—an "outdrop"—mixed in. But gradually it became clear that the concepts under discussion were the same ones that television commentators expound on today. Then as now, pitching was a matter of movement, changing speeds and location, location, location; Christy Mathewson's famous fadeaway was nothing more or less than a screwball. It became clear that despite mostly superficial changes, baseball in the early 21st century remains much as it was in Ewing's time. If Ewing were to come back today, he would certainly be struck by changes in the game—indoor playing fields, staggering salaries, the demise of the complete game, the proliferation of home runs at the expense of what is now classified under the somewhat dismissive term "small ball." But if he could amble out to the pitcher's mound one more time, he would understand immediately and completely everything that goes on between the white lines. The endlessly repeated duel of pitcher versus batter would be as intensely and intimately familiar to him as it was in 1910.

On the other hand, when Ewing began playing ball for a living the telephone was still a novelty to most Americans. In Detroit, Henry Ford was making refinements to his first gasoline-powered vehicle, with bicycle wheels and a two-cylinder, four-horsepower engine.[4] In Dayton, Ohio, the Wright brothers were busily building bicycles, riding the crest of the 1890s cycling boom; it would be another two years before Orville and Wilbur took their first serious step toward creation of a heavier-than-air flying machine.[5] While in the East the nation's population was shifting from the rural areas to the cities, further west blood was still being shed in clashes between Native Americans and the U.S. Army.[6]

At the same time, ballplayers were striving for respectability and the financial interests behind the game were about to embark on a systematic push to interweave their enterprise with the social fabric of the nation's cities and towns. Inevitably the story of baseball between the Chicago World's Fair and World War I is entwined with the political, economic and social changes that were taking place across America. While the game Ewing played was much the same as the one we know today, the world he played it in was in many ways vastly different.

For an Ohio farm boy born barely 25 years after his home county came into existence, Ewing saw a fair amount of that world. When Bob Ewing broke into professional baseball, the country had 45 states. Two more were added before he retired. During the intervening years, he visited at least 28 of them, nearly all as a direct consequence of his career. The country was growing and changing, and baseball allowed Ewing a unique opportunity to witness the process.

On the field, the game was dominated by such immortals as Ty Cobb, Christy Mathewson, Napoleon Lajoie, Honus Wagner, Walter Johnson and Cy Young. In such company, Ewing could easily fade into the background. Moreover, in an era almost overpopulated with colorful personalities, it would be easy to overlook one of the "quiet men" of the game.[7] While Ewing has receded into history, many of his teammates have secured lasting places in baseball lore, often for reasons that had little to do with their on-field accomplishments. One toured with his vaudeville-star wife and became a Hollywood movie actor. A pitcher who won fewer than one-third as many games as Ewing was remembered for decades because he once punched out John J. McGraw. A legendary carouser was elegized upon his death in Damon Runyon's nationally syndicated column. A lifetime .249 hitter had a monument erected in his honor at the Polo Grounds after being killed in World War I. Another teammate is often credited with prompting umpires to use hand signals for balls and strikes; as recently as the mid-1980s, his story was the inspiration for an off-Broadway play. Another was portrayed on the screen by Edward G. Robinson. Still another lives on as the answer to a classic baseball trivia question.[8]

Ten of Ewing's managers and/or teammates are in the National Baseball Hall of Fame.[9] Arguments, some stronger and some weaker, have been made for the enshrinement of a few others.[10] Unfortunately for Ewing, none of those in the Hall of Fame was honored primarily for anything he did while associated with him. Over time, his memory has not been enhanced by the fact that he never played for a pennant-winning team and spent nearly all of his major league career in Cincinnati; even in the 1900s, though the terms had not yet been invented, baseball had its "large market" and "small market" teams. In fact, Ewing offers a fair illustration of at least three factors that baseball analyst Bill James has identified as contributing to a player being underrated:

- *"Players who get stuck with bad teams are often underrated."*
- *"Players who play in smaller and less glamorous cities are sometimes underrated."*

- *"Players who are quiet are sometimes underrated."*[11]

Ultimately though, such factors do little to detract from the interest of Ewing's career. Being neither one of the major stars nor one of the flamboyant characters of his time, he is in many ways more representative of it. Ewing's life and career offer a case study of something not often studied—a typical professional baseball player of his day.

I use the word "typical" advisedly. While Bob Ewing was in many ways a typical player of the first decade of the 20th century, that is not to suggest that he was in any way average. He was much more than that. The Reds' winningest pitcher of the dead ball era, he was an all-star caliber talent before there was an All-Star Game. He also holds the unique distinction of being (by far) Cincinnati's most prominent spitball artist.[12]

Yet in assessing Ewing's career, the most obvious measurements might not be the most useful. If you crosscheck Ewing in the standard sources, the most impressive statistic you're likely to find is that he holds the Cincinnati franchise record for career earned run average at 2.37.[13] That would have been news to him. Although the notion of measuring a pitcher's effectiveness by the number of runs chargeable to his work was kicked around at least as far back as the 1880s, ERA did not become an official statistic until after Ewing retired. Though box scores in Ewing's day sometimes listed the number of "earned runs" scored by each team, those notations reflected only the individual scorekeeper's opinion of which runs were rightly the responsibility of each pitcher. There was in fact no universally accepted definition of what constituted an earned run. One stringent view, espoused by Henry Chadwick and others, was that the pitcher should be held responsible only for "runs scored by base hits alone."[14] In the absence of any agreement on such a system, pitchers were most often ranked on the basis of won-lost percentage. The search for "a truer test of a pitcher's general ability"[15] continued throughout Ewing's career. But, as *The Sporting News* sternly reminded official scorers who included "earned runs" in their box scores, that statistic was "not down in the rules."[16]

Ewing's earned run average was never calculated until after his death, as part of the massive research effort for Macmillan's original *Baseball Encyclopedia*, published in 1969. Once all the numbers were crunched, Ewing's career ERA—including his stints with Cincinnati, Philadelphia and St. Louis—came out to 2.49. One hundred years after his retirement, that figure still ranks 28th on the all-time list among pitchers who worked at least 1,500 innings. It's an impressive statistic. But even that merely goes to show that comparisons, besides being odious, are sometimes misleading. For while Ewing rates 28th on the all-time ERA list, he stands only 22nd among pitchers whose careers fell mainly within the dead ball era. Even in his best years, Ewing never ranked among the top five in the National League in ERA. His best single-season figure—1.73 in 1907—was only seventh best in the league. Outstanding as Ewing's earned run averages look when judged by modern standards, we must remember they were compiled during a decade when the National League established all-time lows for both earned run average and batting average. Impressive as Ewing's statistics are, they were merely good during the dead ball era, when most ERAs—as we now know—were dramatically low. All of this points us back to Bill James and another of his lists, this one of factors that can contribute to a player being overrated. "Pitchers from the dead ball era," James has concluded, "… are overrated."[17]

Certainly they can be, especially if the analysis leans too heavily on comparing earned run averages from the dead ball days to those of later (or earlier) periods. Even so, Ewing's statistics place him a lot closer to the front rank of major league pitchers than the middle of the pack. Some years ago I spent several days combing through more than 500 pages of small print in a baseball encyclopedia, examining the records of every man who ever pitched in the major leagues. At the time, they numbered somewhat more than 7,200. My resulting tabulations were rough and are now outdated. Still, a few telling facts emerged: Of all those pitchers, fewer than one-third retired with winning percentages of .500 or better. Fewer than 15 percent lasted 10 years in the major leagues. Fewer than 10 percent won as many as 100 games.[18]

Ewing did all three. Even disregarding position players who pitched only incidentally and setting aside the won-lost records of modern-day relief specialists, whose statistics are not readily comparable to Ewing's, a fair estimate would be that fewer than 7 percent of all the pitchers in baseball history have had careers as productive as his.

Ewing never led the National League in a major statistical category. But in 1907, he was second in innings pitched, complete games and strikeouts. In other years, he ranked as high as fourth in fewest hits per inning and fewest walks per inning. Even in his own time, long before the advent of sabermetrics, people recognized that Ewing's record was better than it appeared. A blurb on the back of a 1911 baseball card noted that while Ewing "has not been fortunate in being with teams that were consistent winners, ... his percentage of victories the last three years out of four has been greater than his club's."[19] If the writer had checked a little more deeply, he would have found that in fact Ewing's winning percentage had been better than his team's five years out of the past six. Over the course of his major league career, Ewing's won-lost record outstripped his teams' by 20 percentage points. Here, when we start comparing Ewing to his contemporaries, his earned run averages come into focus: Ewing's ERA was lower than the figure for the National League as a whole in every complete season he pitched. For his career, Ewing bettered the league average by two-fifths of an earned run for every nine innings. This despite pitching all his home games for 85 percent of his career in the best hitters' park in the league.[20]

In some ways, the more sophisticated the tools devised for analyzing statistics, the better Ewing looks. A good example might be Bill James' "win shares" system, unveiled in 2001. Win shares is a complex system which attempts to reduce the performance of every player for every season to a single number. The goal is to arrive at one objective measure by which to compare any two players, irrespective of position, era, league or other factors, such as ballparks or the relative strength or weakness of their teammates. For the most part, a starting pitcher's win shares will track pretty closely with his victories. As a rule of thumb, James says, if a pitcher accumulates more victories than win shares, that could suggest a mediocre player being carried along by a strong team. Conversely, if his win shares outstrip his victories, that's a sign of a good pitcher handicapped by a bad team.[21]

James' calculations for Ewing are revealing. For his career, Ewing is credited with 19 percent more win shares than victories. Based on win shares, Ewing was among the National League's top 10 pitchers four straight years, 1905 to 1908. In 1906, when Ewing went 13–14 for a Cincinnati team that won 64 games and finished sixth, win shares indicate he pitched better than Christy Mathewson, who was 22–12 for a New York Giants team that won 96 games and finished second.[22]

Ewing's career numbers in this regard come down quite close to those of Dean Chance. Ewing pitched 11 seasons in the big leagues, winning 124 games and losing 118. Chance pitched 11 seasons in the big leagues, winning 128 and losing 115. Chance also started two All-Star Games and won the Cy Young award in 1964. James credits both Ewing and Chance with a total of 148 win shares.

But enough of statistics. Ewing and his mates have long since, in the felicitous phrase of sportswriter Ren Mulford, "slid across the home plate of eternity."[23] At this remove, numbers can provide at best a pale reflection of the games they played, the blood and sweat they expended, and the vibrant lives they lived. While the feats of a few have been immortalized, cast in bronze and enshrined in Cooperstown, the struggles and triumphs of hundreds were written on water. Theirs was but the fleeting and uncertain celebrity of the sports pages, apportioned and reapportioned from one day to the next by Mulford and the other chroniclers who served as the Greek chorus to the great drama of baseball in its early days. With their help, we hope to return to those days. Our aim is to rediscover our subject in the context of his time and to try to understand him and the game as they were seen and understood more than 100 years ago, in the eventful baseball days of Long Bob Ewing.

ENDNOTES

1   Lawrence S. Ritter, *The Glory of Their Times: The Story of the Early Days of Baseball Told by the Men Who Played It* (New York: Macmillan Co., 1966), p. xviii.

2   Ritter, *op. cit.*, enlarged edition (New York: HarperCollins Publishers Inc., 2002), pp. 71-72.

3   John J. McGraw, *My 30 Years in Baseball* (New York: Arno Press, 1974 reprint of 1923 original), p. 194. McGraw was referring specifically to the years 1907 to 1912, essentially the second half of Ewing's big league career.

4   Douglas Brinkley, *Wheels for the World: Henry Ford, His Company, and a Century of Progress, 1903-2003* (New York: Viking Penguin, 2003), pp. 20-22.

5   This according to Wilbur Wright, quoted in Tom D. Crouch, *The Bishop's Boys: A Life of Wilbur and Orville Wright* (New York: W.W. Norton and Co., 1989), p. 161.

6   What David Traxler called "the last pitched battle in the centuries-long wilderness war between white man and red for control of the continent" took place Oct. 5, 1898 – at the conclusion of Ewing's first full year in professional ball – in north-central Minnesota. Six (or possibly seven) whites were killed and perhaps twice that many wounded in what is sometimes called the Battle of Sugar Point. Initial reports of the clash sparked panic in nearby settlements, and a wildly inaccurate front-page account in the *New York Times* headlined the "rumored massacre" of Gen. John M. Bacon and his entire 100-man detachment. See Traxler, *1898: The Birth of the American Century* (New York: Alfred A. Knopf, 1998), pp. 246-51; and *New York Times*, Oct. 6, 1898.

7   The description was applied to Ewing in *Sporting Life*, March 24, 1906.

8   Memorable teammates, in order: Mike Donlin toured the vaudeville circuit with his wife, Mabel Hite; he later appeared in some three dozen movies, most notably *The General* (1927) with Buster Keaton. Ad Brennan, who won 38 games in the major leagues, was remembered on his death nearly 50 years later as the fellow who decked the notoriously pugnacious McGraw in a post-game confrontation in 1913. Remembering Larry McLean, Runyon wrote, "Only his weakness for the merry-go-round of life prevented him from being the greatest catcher ever." Ivy League-educated infielder Eddie Grant, known as "Harvard Eddie," was a captain in the Army's 77th Division when he was killed by an artillery shell in the Argonne Forest on Oct. 5, 1918, barely a month before the end of the war. Outfielder Dummy Hoy, who was deaf and mute, was the subject of *The Signal Season of Dummy Hoy* (1987) by Allen Meyer and Michael Nowak. Hans Lobert was a scout for the New York Giants when he was portrayed by Edward G. Robinson in *Big Leaguer* (1953), Hollywood's attempt at an inside look at a baseball tryout camp. Harry Steinfeldt is the answer to the question, "Who played third base in the Chicago Cubs infield with Tinker, Evers and Chance?"

9   The 10 are managers Bid McPhee, Joe Kelley, Ned Hanlon, Clark Griffith and Roger Bresnahan; Cincinnati teammates Jake Beckley, Sam Crawford and Miller Huggins; Philadelphia teammate Grover Cleveland Alexander; and Addie Joss, a teammate at Toledo in the minor leagues. Only Alexander (1938) and Bresnahan (1945) were inducted in Ewing's lifetime. The list could also include Rube Waddell (inducted 1946) and Branch Rickey (inducted as an executive, 1967). Both Ewing and Waddell began the 1913 season on the payroll of the Minneapolis Millers, though neither appeared in a game for the team that year. Rickey, though he never signed a contract or played in a league game for the Reds, had a two-week tryout with them during the 1904 season.

10   See for instance the chapter on Mike Donlin in Brent Kelley, *The Case For: Those Overlooked by Baseball's Hall of Fame* (Jefferson, N.C.: McFarland and Co. Inc., 1992), pp. 188-95 ; and the ongoing push for Dummy Hoy, as mentioned in Barbara Oremland, "The Silent World of Dummy Hoy" in Walter Barney, ed., *A Celebration of Louisville Baseball in the Major and Minor Leagues* (Louisville, Ky.: Society for American Baseball Research, 1997), pp. 49-51. After analyzing the statistics, Andre Lower stated emphatically that Ewing's Philadelphia teammate Sherry Magee "did indeed compile a record worthy of the Hall of Fame." See Lower, *Auditioning for Cooperstown: Rating Baseball's Stars for the Hall of Fame* (Lexington, Ky.: Baseball by Positions. com, 2012), p. 87.

11   Bill James, *The New Bill James Historical Baseball Abstract* (New York: The Free Press, 2001), p. 546.

12   This interesting aspect of Ewing's career has been particularly overlooked. Lonnie Wheeler and John Baskin, in their estimable book *The Cincinnati Game* (Wilmington, Ohio: Orange Frazer Press, 1988), don't even include Ewing on their list of 12 "known and suspected Reds spitballers," legal and otherwise (p. 111). Besides Ewing, my research has turned up 12 pitchers who were identified at one time or another as employing the spitball and who could have thrown it legally for the Reds. Leaving aside Andy Coakley, who reportedly discarded the pitch after one disastrous game; Orval Overall, who didn't take it up until after he left Cincinnati; and Fred Toney, who didn't rely on it sufficiently to be grandfathered in when it was outlawed (although he remained in the National League through 1923), the other nine won a total of 67 games for Cincinnati to Ewing's 108.

13 Based on at least 1,000 innings pitched. Some sources, using a lower standard, credit the record to Fred Toney. Pitching for the Reds from 1911 to 1918, Toney compiled a 2.18 ERA for 999 innings.

14 Henry Chadwick, ed., *Spalding's Official Baseball Guide* (New York: American Sports Publishing Co., 1904), p. 101. In a similar vein, *The Sporting News* (Nov. 16, 1901) maintained that "runs earned solely by base hits are the only earned runs that form a criterion of a pitcher's effectiveness."

15 *The Sporting News,* Sept. 15, 1910.

16 *Ibid.,* Nov. 16, 1901.

17 James, *op. cit.*

18 These figures were taken from John Thorn, Pete Palmer and Michael Gershman, eds., *Total Baseball*, seventh edition (Kingston, N.Y.: Total Baseball Publishing, 2001), pp. 1,310-1,845.

19 "Robert Ewing" T205 (gold border) card issued by the American Tobacco Co., 1911.

20 Ronald M. Selter, *Ballparks of the Deadball Era: A Comprehensive Study of Their Dimensions, Configurations and Effects on Batting, 1901-19* (Jefferson, N.C.: McFarland and Co. Inc., 2008), pp. 67 and 77-78. On a scale where 100 is average, Selter calculates League Park's "dead ball era run factor" at 108, second-highest of any ballpark used in the National League between 1901 and 1919. The only higher figure goes to Weeghman Park in Chicago, first used by the Federal League in 1914 and by the NL Cubs starting in 1916 – after Ewing was retired. See also John Thorn and Pete Palmer, *Total Baseball*, first edition (New York: Warner Books Inc.), pp. 2,175-76. During Ewing's years with the Reds, more runs were scored in Cincinnati than anywhere else in the league. This was particularly true in the early years, when Cincinnati saw more run production than any other National League city every year from 1902 through 1906.

21 Bill James and Jim Henzler, *Win Shares* (Morton Grove, Ill.: STATS Inc., 2002), p. 217.

22 *Ibid.,* p. 292.

23 Ren Mulford, "The Ball Fields from 1876 to the Present Day" in Harry Ellard, *Baseball in Cincinnati* (Cincinnati: privately published, 1907), p. 249.

SPITBALLING

> "Ballplayers are born. If they are cut out
> for baseball, if they have the *desire*
> and the *ambition,* they will make it.
> That's all there is to it."
> —WALTER JOHNSON[1]

CHAPTER 1

The Auglaize Farmer Boy

BOB EWING GREW UP on a farm in western Ohio where, according to family lore, he started out pitching potatoes against a target painted on the barn.[2]

Professional baseball was in its infancy when Ewing was a boy and the country was barely 100 years old, having celebrated its centennial when he was 3. The National League began play the same year.

Towns and farms were still relatively new things in the Ewings' part of Ohio. Auglaize County was one of the last counties created in the state, carved out of two previously existing counties in 1848, 45 years after Ohio attained statehood. The county seat was established at Wapakoneta on the Auglaize River. As recently as 16 years earlier, the site had been occupied by a Shawnee Indian village. That changed after Congress passed the Indian Removal Act of 1830. The Shawnee were removed to a reservation in Kansas in 1832.

To the north of Auglaize County when pioneers began arriving was the forbidding Great Black Swamp, which made the northwest quadrant of Ohio the last part of the state to attract settlers. To the northeast was Scioto Marsh and to the southwest was the vast cranberry bog in Mercer County. Much of the area around where the Ewings lived was originally black muck soil. Not many years before Bob was born, an observer wrote, the landscape "was covered with water, good only for duck shooting."[3] Only a systematic program of ditching and drainage, still ongoing during Ewing's youth, made the land fit for cultivation.

Ewing's family lived in the southeastern part of the county, in Goshen Township, around the unincorporated hamlet of New Hampshire,[4] near the headwaters of the Scioto River. His mother, the former Alvira Bidwell, was regarded as coming from "pioneer stock" because her family had arrived in the township by 1840.[5] Her father, Josiah Bidwell, served as a justice of the peace in the 1850s and she taught school in Indiana and Ohio for several years prior to her marriage.

The Ewings came later. Bob's father, Edward H. Ewing, and Edward's parents, Robert and Nancy Campbell Ewing, were born in Pennsylvania and settled in Goshen Township sometime in the 1850s. The men were gone again within a few years, off to fight in the Civil War. Both Bob's father and grandfather enlisted at New Hampshire on the same day in July 1862, joining the 45th Ohio Volunteer Infantry regiment. Edward Ewing was 20 years old; his father was 41. Robert Ewing, possibly in deference to his years and presumed good sense, was soon promoted to the rank of sergeant.

The 45th had an eventful war. Placed on horseback and brigaded with two cavalry regiments, the foot soldiers functioned for more than a year as mounted infantry. They pursued the Confederate raider Gen. John Hunt Morgan on his daring dash across southern Ohio in the summer of 1863 and took part in the state's most significant Civil War battle, at Buffington Island on the Ohio River. Once they got their feet back on solid ground, they were plunged into the Atlanta campaign, seeing action at Resaca, Dallas, New Hope Church and elsewhere. Robert Ewing's active service ended in 1863 when he was "crippled by falling from [a] bridge."[6] He was transferred to the Veteran Reserve Corps and later discharged by reason of disability. Edward Ewing was wounded in the federal assault on Kennesaw Mountain, Georgia, on June 27, 1864. He survived to rejoin his regiment, which subsequently saw heavy fighting at Franklin and Nashville, Tennessee. He was mustered out of military service March 27, 1865.

The 45th OVI lost 339 men during the course of the war, but both Ewings returned home and resumed their lives in Auglaize County. Robert and Edward Ewing had owned some land in or near New Hampshire since before the war. The family apparently farmed on a small scale, planting a few acres and raising crops mainly for their own use while the men also took other work. In the 1870 census, both Robert and Edward Ewing are listed as carpenters; in 1880, Robert is listed as a carpenter, Edward as a teamster.

Edward Ewing and Alvira Bidwell were married February 27, 1869. Bob was the third of their four children. Older sister Jessie L., called Lulu, was born in late 1869; she died at age 11. Brother Alfred Maynard Ewing, always known by his middle name, was born in 1871. Younger sister Laura Florence Ewing was born in 1876.

The future pitcher was born April 24, 1873, and given the name George Lemuel Ewing. It is not known when or how he came to be called Bob; family sources suggest that from an early age, the young man simply did not care for the name George and adopted another that he liked better. One theory is that he chose his new name out of admiration for his grandfather. In any event, for most of his life, George Lemuel Ewing was known as Bob or Robert Ewing, not only among family and friends but even in official and semi-official documents such as legal papers and census records.

An 1880 map of New Hampshire shows a schoolhouse in the village, just two blocks from the Ewing home, but there was no high school in the township until around 1890. Young Bob's formal education ended with eighth grade.

Given his early fascination, it is reasonable to assume that young Ewing played as much baseball as he could while growing up, but he might not have envisioned the game as a career option. As a grown man, Ewing was still pitching only for the village team in New Hampshire. In the mid-1890s there was sufficient interest for the small community of no more than a couple hundred people to field a "first nine" and a "second nine." Ewing was a member of the first nine that remained unbeaten into mid-season 1895, but the caliber of play may be surmised from brief news items like one in the *Auglaize Republican* reporting that New Hampshire had defeated Lakeview 28–16. At age 22, Ewing had never tested his good right arm anywhere other than farm pastures and vacant lots within a few miles of New Hampshire.

Ewing played his "first game away from home," as he recalled it many years later,[7] on June 11, 1895, when the New Hampshire team was invited to play New Bremen at the county fairgrounds in Wapakoneta. The occasion was Maccabee Day, marking the anniversary of the founding of the Knights of the Maccabees, a fraternal benevolent society that at the time had 200,000 members in the United States. As many as 2,000 people, representing local Maccabee "tents" throughout Auglaize and neighboring Allen County, attended the picnic, and Ewing got to pitch in front of a genuine crowd for the first time. The New Hampshire team was a bunch of kids, Ewing remembered, while "New Bremen had a real club," led by future pros Whitey Guese and Bade Myers.

"We got beat, but it was a real game," Ewing recollected.[8]

Auglaize County was becoming a baseball hotbed. Over the span of Ewing's career, the rural county nurtured more than a half-dozen players who reached the major leagues and several others who played professionally in the minors. In such an atmosphere, it was inevitable that the tall, hard-throwing Ewing should eventually attract notice. The game at the fairgrounds was his first small step into the limelight. He took a larger step the following spring when he joined the team in the county seat.

Wapakoneta, Ohio, in 1896 was a growing little town of close to 4,000 people that boasted of having "more [baseball] rooters big and little than any town of its population on earth."[9] Borrowing from the city's past, the team was called the Indians or sometimes the Chiefs.[10] Ewing's teammates were mostly homegrown players, including Theodore "Whitey" Guese and his younger brother Otto "Red" Guese.[11] The team was followed by avid fans and a partisan press. At every home game, small boys and even grown men hung on the fence or climbed the trees east of the field in order to view the proceedings without paying admission. When the team didn't perform up to expectations, the newspapers were perfectly prepared to fire a broadside on the order of "the rankest game ever played on the grounds."[12] More often they were ready with an alibi for any defeat. When the Indians were beaten 16–12 in mud "several inches deep" at Piqua, the *Auglaize County Democrat* reported, "The game was lost by the [Wapakoneta] club simply because they refused to field the ball at the risk of their lives."[13]

Ewing quickly shouldered his share of the load. He beat the Page Fence Giants, the famous black barnstormers from Adrian, Michigan, and soon became a local favorite. When the club secretary wired little more than the 4–1 score and the winning battery from an out-of-town engagement, the *Democrat* lamented the paucity of details, then gushed, "What a game our farmer boy must have pitched!"[14]

Ball teams were a source of intense community pride and rivalries were hotly contested, often with substantial side bets between the competitors. The warmest series of games in 1896 pitted the amateurs of Wapakoneta against the supposedly "salaried club"[15] from the village of Ottawa. By late July, the teams had met twice in Ottawa and once in Wapakoneta, the home team winning each time. In every case, the losers decried one-sided umpiring and fan interference. By now, each side was convinced it would never receive fair treatment on the other's grounds. They decided to settle the matter by meeting one more time on a neutral site.

The logical place was Lima, halfway between the two contending towns. The game was arranged for a Tuesday afternoon on the diamond in Faurot's Park, the spacious private grounds of oilman and entrepreneur Benjamin C. Faurot.[16] The two clubs laid a $100 wager on the outcome. On the appointed day, 1,000 people gathered to see the contest. An estimated 125 followed the team from Wapakoneta, all "supplied with tin horns, which they used loud and often."[17]

Ewing allowed only six hits, got three himself, stole a base and scored a run. As the game reached a climax, "every man on the grounds was yelling [for] one of the two teams."[18] Clinging to a 4–3 lead with two men on base in the bottom of the ninth inning, Ewing got the final out on a long fly ball. Returning to Wapakoneta that evening on the train, the team was met at the depot by several hundred supporters. Most of the local band was out of town, but two members ran and got drums and the happy crowd "paraded Auglaize Street from one end to the other and yelled until almost exhausted."[19]

By now, the club was developing something of a reputation. Wapakoneta might not have had, as some enthusiasts insisted, "the best amateur team in the state,"[20] but when promoters went looking for a local nine to take on the Cincinnati Reds in an exhibition game, they invited the Indians. The game was set for August 10 at a spot out in the country about 35 miles south of Wapakoneta and 70 miles north of Cincinnati.

This remote location, several miles from the nearest town, was not chosen to suit the convenience of either ballclub. It was the site preferred by the Miami Valley Electric Railway Co. Incorporated in 1892, the Miami Valley system connected Sidney, 20 miles south of Wapakoneta, with Cincinnati. It was part of a burgeoning network of electric interurban railways that were spreading all across Ohio, bringing efficient, economical rail service to crossroads and hamlets too small to be effectively served by more costly steam locomotives. Drawing power from electric lines strung along the right of way, the interurban was quiet and smoke-free, a cross between the lightweight streetcars that were replacing horse-drawn

Bob Ewing first attracted serious notice while pitching for the Wapakoneta Indians in 1896 and 1897. The Auglaize County farm boy, the team's star pitcher, is seated on the ground, front left. *Photo: Courtesy of Charlotte Ewing-Preville.*

trolleys in urban areas and the bulky steam-powered trains that operated between cities. Each interurban car contained both motor and passenger compartments, becoming in effect a self-contained train. The interurban could make frequent runs and stop practically anywhere, and soon the western Ohio corridor between Toledo and Cincinnati developed one of the most extensive interurban networks in the country.[21]

But in 1896, the interurbans were concerned mainly with building a customer base. Some, not content to simply wait for passengers to come, set out to lure riders by creating destinations. One such was carved out of a grove of trees at a site known as Dead Man's Hollow. There, where the electric interurban paralleled the Miami River, the Miami-Erie Canal and the Cincinnati, Hamilton & Dayton Railroad, halfway between the cities of Piqua and Troy, the operators of the Miami Valley Electric Railway laid out Midway Park. The park opened in 1894 and soon had a dance hall and a 1,200-seat opera house; over the next few years, a bowling alley, shooting gallery, summer cottages and a roller coaster were added.

The baseball diamond was new in 1896 and the Cincinnati Reds were certain to draw a crowd. The Reds were a good club, on their way to third place among 12 teams in the National League. Some of the Reds' regulars took a day off against Wapakoneta's collection of small-town amateurs, but there were still a couple of great players in the lineup, plus some other very good ones. One of the greats was the remarkable deaf and mute center fielder William Ellsworth "Dummy" Hoy,[22] born about 30 miles from Ewing in Hancock County, Ohio. The other was Bid McPhee, who had held down second base for the Reds for 15 years. Also penciled in to face Ewing were veteran shortstop Germany Smith and left fielder Eddie Burke, in the middle of the best season of his career. Heinie Peitz, the Reds' regular catcher, played third base. The pitcher was the celebrated Billy Rhines, known for confounding opposing batsmen with his underhanded "upshoot."

The game attracted 1,500 spectators. The Indians knew before the first pitch that they were in over their heads, but they managed to put on an entertaining show. They batted Rhines around for 16 hits, earning him "a gentle roast"[23] from the Cincinnati sportswriters on hand. Ewing singled twice and drove in two runs. But the big leaguers had little trouble with Ewing's pitches. They scored five times on six hits in the second inning and led 10–6 after four. In the sixth inning, Ewing complained of illness and asked to come out of the game; the team captain, perhaps suspecting the problem was nothing more than an attack of nerves, told him to keep going. The Reds exploded for six more runs and went on to win 16–8.

But the day ended on a hopeful note. After the game, the Reds' manager called him over. This was Buck Ewing, the greatest catcher—and in the view of some, the greatest player[24]—baseball had yet seen. Back in the 1880s, when protective gear was primitive and catchers routinely played as much as 15 feet behind home plate, Ewing adopted a full crouch and moved up directly under the bat for each pitch. By now, at age 36, he had given up catching and was in his last year as an active player, as a part-time first baseman. But he still had an old catcher's interest in young pitchers, and he might have wondered whether this one was distantly related to him.[25] They talked briefly, Buck offering Bob some words of encouragement and a few pointers.

The following spring, Wapakoneta put together a considerably stronger club. Ewing and the Guese brothers were back, and the Indians were bolstered with more imported talent. Their lineup was composed almost entirely of men who would be playing professionally within a year or two. New faces included four Cincinnatians—Jim Honeyman, Harry Eichler, George Rohe and Jerry McDonough.

The additional talent proved welcome because the opposition was getting tougher. For one thing Lima, which had no team in 1896, had assembled a club that backers thought was strong enough to join Toledo, Dayton, Wheeling and Fort Wayne in the Inter-State League, should an opening occur. A spirited competition soon developed. Lima was four times the size of Wapakoneta. Wapakoneta considered it a triumph to defeat the bigger city; Lima considered it a disgrace to lose to the smaller one.

Ewing threw himself into the contentious rivalry. "He seemed to take special delight in winning from Lima,"[26] a newspaper reported. At the same time, Lima chafed at its defeats. When Ewing beat Lima 7–4 on his home field, the *Lima Times-Democrat* complained of "profanity and vulgar remarks" heaped on the Lima players, and of Wapakoneta players and fans who "seemed determined to win, fair or foul."

"Before Wapakoneta invites another club of gentlemen to play on their grounds," the reporter sniffed, "they should buy a book on etiquette."[27]

By the time the teams met again, the Lima paper acknowledged Ewing as Wapakoneta's "crack pitcher."[28] So when Lima handed Wapakoneta a 9–3 defeat, there was more than a little big-city condescension in the *Times-Democrat*'s gloating report that "the Lima players batted Farmer Ewing out of the business and he was forced to retire."[29]

For most of the summer, Lima, Wapakoneta and teams from other surrounding towns kept their fans entertained with a catch-as-catch-can schedule of games against whoever was available. Late in the season this loose network of local rivalries coalesced into the short-lived North-western Ohio League. The four members were all within 45 miles of each other—Lima at the northernmost extreme, Piqua the southernmost, Wapakoneta and St. Marys in between. The league was outside organized baseball, operating, as one of the players later wrote, "under no protection or agreement ... but its own."[30] The players were amateurs or at best semipros, playing for nothing but "board and railroad fare."[31] Yet the competition was surprisingly brisk. Of all the players in the four-team circuit, nearly one in five eventually reached the major leagues. Wapa-koneta had Ewing and Rohe, St. Marys boasted Jack Harper and Topsy Hartsel, and Piqua featured Nick Altrock. Lima was led by Jim Delahanty of the ballplaying Cleveland Delahantys[32] and an 18-year-old pitcher from Toledo, a son of Irish immigrants by the name of Roger Bresnahan.

Formation of the league was announced July 19. League play com-menced August 1, organizers hoping to get in a six-week season. To this point in the summer, Ewing and Bresnahan had faced each other twice, each winning once. They met for the final time August 9. The Indians trailed early but knocked Bresnahan out of the game with five runs in the eighth inning and won 10–6. Ewing, seeming to grow stronger as the game progressed, struck out six and allowed just five hits. He also singled three times, contributing to two Wapakoneta rallies.

By August 25, Wapakoneta had a 12–6 record and held first place by half a game over St. Marys. But the league was already unraveling as pro-fessional teams swooped in to raid the new organization for talent. Bres-nahan jumped directly to the National League. He joined the Washington Senators and made his debut August 27, beating the St. Louis Browns on a six-hit shutout. Toledo signed Jerry McDonough in mid-August and soon he was earning rave reviews for his play at third base. McDonough in turn recommended that Toledo's management take a look at Ewing.

Ewing made his farewell appearance in Wapakoneta on August 20. He beat St. Marys 6–5 in 12 innings, scoring the winning run himself after hitting a triple. The next day he was in uniform on the Toledo bench.

When Ewing arrived in Toledo, the Mud Hens were attempting to nail down their second consecutive Inter-State League pennant. The *Toledo Bee* immediately liked the looks of the "strapping youngster,"[33] and the Mud Hens didn't wait long to see what he could do. They threw him into action before a Sunday afternoon crowd on August 22, 1897. Toledo had an eight-game lead in the standings with 23 games to play, a cushion that was comfortable but hardly safe.

Ewing's opposition was seventh-place Springfield, a team Toledo had beaten in their last four meetings. Ewing had little difficulty making it five. Pitching on only one day's rest, he held the Governors to four singles—two of them described as "scratchy"[34]—while rapping two himself on the way to a 9–4 victory. He pitched scoreless ball except for the third inning, when Toledo committed three of its five errors. Despite such moments of "wretched support," the *Toledo Commercial* told its readers, the tall newcomer remained "as cool as the January weather in Alaska."[35] A headline the next day announced, "He Looks Like Another Find,"[36] and Ewing was on his way to establishing an image with the fans. "Ewing the iceberg," he was sometimes called.[37]

Ewing was still a long way from the major league, but Toledo must have seemed like the big time to the Auglaize "farmer boy." He had been in Toledo barely two weeks when James J. Corbett came to town amid much publicity to show off his baseball skills with the Mud Hens. Gentleman Jim had lost the world heavyweight boxing championship to Bob Fitzsimmons six months earlier and was now preparing to resume his intermittent theatrical career in *A Naval Cadet,* a comedy-drama in four acts tailored to his talents by Charles T. Vincent. The play would open in New York in October. In the meanwhile, Corbett traveled the country offering himself as a gate attraction for amateur and minor league baseball teams. Though these promotional appearances were often described as "benefits" for the ball clubs, Corbett always took a healthy cut of the gate, sometimes making more money in an afternoon than most ballplayers would earn all summer. By the time he reached northwest Ohio, Corbett was said to have "made a barrel of money playing first base this season."[38]

Corbett, a former bank teller from San Francisco, had played ball for the Alcazars club there in his younger days. He might even have considered becoming a professional ballplayer like his younger brother Joe, who pitched in the National League and later the Pacific Coast League. Now, just days past his 31st birthday, Gentleman Jim stood 6-feet-1 and weighed around 190 pounds—about Ewing's size, only heavier. To a reporter who observed him shortly after his Toledo performance, Corbett appeared "the very picture of the ideal man in a baseball player's uniform."[39] He cultivated the reputation of a fair hitter, but it's likely that his manager, theatrical producer William A. Brady, sometimes slipped the opposing pitcher "a little something" so he wouldn't make the ex-champ look bad.[40]

Coincidentally, Corbett's appearance in Toledo fell on September 7, 1897, five years to the day after he won the heavyweight championship from John L. Sullivan in the first world title fight conducted under the Marquess of Queensberry rules. Corbett marked the anniversary by playing errorless defense and hitting two singles in five at-bats as the Mud Hens gained a 2–1 victory over the Fort Wayne Indians. The newspapers watched his every move and compiled a mercilessly detailed scouting report. His two hits were discounted, "one being a fluke and the other a scratch."[41] At first base, he couldn't handle a low throw "and doesn't cover enough ground to make a groove."[42] Worse still, "he ran the bases like an old woman chasing hens out of a back yard."[43]

"Were Corbett a youngster from the woods looking for an engagement," the *Toledo Bee* concluded, "the verdict would be, 'He won't do.'"[44]

The turnout was estimated as high as 3,500 people. Corbett and Brady pocketed 12½ cents from each paid admission.

BOB EWING HAD EMBARKED on a dubious profession. Baseball in the 1890s, in the view of Bill James, "was evolving backward," becoming "a crude, violent game dominated as much by intimidation as by skillful play."[45] The year 1897, said the editors of *Reach's Official Baseball Guide,* "was notable for many disgraceful brawls upon the field, indicating a steady decline in the decorum of players."[46] A month before Ewing made his professional debut, an editorial in the *New York Times* deplored the influence of "degenerate baseball players"[47] on the nation's youth. Sportswriter Walter Camp surveyed the "once-popular pastime" and found it everywhere degraded by "rowdy ballplaying, abuse of umpires, profanity, and finally pandemonium among spectators, threats, offers of violence, and even actual assaults."

"Without reform, and serious reform," Camp warned, "... the National Game of America is going to disappear."[48]

At the moment, it's doubtful Ewing gave much thought to such talk. At age 24, not yet a month removed from the bush leagues, he was living for the first time in his life in an exciting big city, rubbing shoulders with one of the most famous men in America, and getting paid to play baseball.

1   Lee Allen, *The Hot Stove League: Raking the Embers of Baseball's Golden Age* (New York: A.S. Barnes and Co., 1955), p. 56.

2   Another potato-pitching story appeared in print when Ewing was at the height of his fame. A man who operated a farm just south of the Ewings' told a reporter that when Bob was young, he and other boys from the neighborhood used to hire out to pick up potatoes after they were dug. Ewing, the farmer said, would hold back "the best potatoes for throwing purposes" and wing them at his co-workers when they bent over, often triggering "a regular battle." The farmer, James Reams, said he eventually took to fining Ewing for every potato he threw. The story appeared in the *Bellefontaine Index* and was reprinted in the *Lima Daily News*, May 21, 1906.

3   William J. McMurray, ed., *History of Auglaize County, Ohio, Vol. 1* (Indianapolis: Historical Publishing Co., 1923), p. 429.

4   A county history says the village was named by an early settler in honor of his home state. See McMurray, *op. cit.*, p. 429.

5   Unidentified newspaper clipping, April 1922.

6   Whitelaw Reid, *Ohio in the War, Volume II: The History of Her Regiments and Other Military Organizations* (Cincinnati: Moore, Wilstach and Baldwin, 1868), p. 299.

7   *Wapakoneta Daily News*, undated clipping, February 1925.

8   *Ibid.*

9   *Auglaize County Democrat*, July 30, 1896.

10   The tradition continues. Today, Wapakoneta High School's teams are known as the Redskins.

11   A third color-coded brother, Adolph "Blackie" Guese, was not a member of the team.

12   *Auglaize County Democrat*, Aug. 6, 1896.

13   *Ibid.*, Aug. 27, 1896.

14   *Ibid.*, Aug. 13, 1896.

15   *Lima Times-Democrat*, July 25, 1896.

16   A large part of Faurot's Park was deeded to the city of Lima in 1904. It is now an 89-acre city park bearing the name of its former owner.

17   *Lima Times-Democrat*, July 29, 1896.

18   *Ibid.*

19   *Auglaize County Democrat*, July 30, 1896.

20   *Ibid.*, Aug. 13, 1896.

21   By 1902, the Western Ohio Railway was traversing Auglaize County, offering a round trip between Wapakoneta and St. Marys for 35 cents and making several runs daily. By 1904, the Western Ohio teamed with the Dayton & Troy Electric Railway to offer four runs daily between Lima and Dayton for a round-trip fare of $2. Covering the 80-mile distance each way in 2½ hours—with five intervening stops—the arrangement was touted as the fastest trolley service in the world. Carrying passengers, farm produce and some freight, providing same-day mail service and electric power along their routes, the interurbans would begin to break down what Scott D. Trostel called the "awful isolation" of Ohio's rural communities at the beginning of the 20th century. See Trostel, *The Lima Route* (Fletcher, Ohio: Cam-Tech Publishing, 1998), pp. 128, 130 and 177; and Joseph P. Schwieterman, *When the Railroad Leaves Town* (Kirksville, Mo.: Truman State University Press, 2001), p. xviii.

22   In the days before political correctness, "Dummy" was the standard nickname for any deaf and mute player. Ewing played with or against at least three—Hoy, pitcher Bill Deegan, and Luther Taylor, a frequent opponent who won 115 games

for the New York Giants between 1900 and 1908. Ewing also likely crossed paths with George "Dummy" Kihm, a longtime minor leaguer who lived for many years in Delphos, Ohio, about 20 miles from Wapakoneta. Hoy, who played 14 years in four different major leagues, managed to turn the derogatory nickname into a badge of honor. Late in life, he grew impatient with interviewers who delicately addressed him as William or Bill or Mr. Hoy. The old ballplayer delivered a sharp message: "Tell them to call me Dummy again, like always." See Barbara Oremland, "The Silent World of Dummy Hoy," in Walter Barney, ed., *A Celebration of Louisville Baseball in the Major and Minor Leagues* (Louisville, Ky.: Society for American Baseball Research, 1997), p. 49.

23 *Auglaize County Democrat,* July 30, 1896.

24 This assessment is based on the opinions of knowledgeable observers who saw all the greats up to Bob Ewing's time, including Clark Griffith, and Francis Richter and John B. Foster, editors respectively of the Reach and Spalding guides. See Bill James, *The Bill James Historical Baseball Abstract* (New York: Villard Books, 1986), pp. 33-35; Lee Allen, *The Cincinnati Reds: An Informal History* (New York: G.P. Putnam's Sons, 1948), pp. 53-54; and Irv Bergman, "William Ewing" in Frederick Ivor-Campbell, ed., *Baseball's First Stars* (Cleveland: Society for American Baseball Research, 1996), pp. 60-61.

25 When Bob made his major league debut, the *Chicago American* (April 20, 1902) reported that he was "said to be the youngest grandson of the esteemed Buck." It was sometimes more plausibly, but also erroneously, reported that Buck, born in 1859 in Highland County, Ohio, was Bob's uncle; see for example the *Philadelphia Bulletin* and *Philadelphia Record*, both Jan. 21, 1910. I have found no evidence of a genealogical link between the two ballplayers' families.

26 *Lima Times-Democrat,* Aug. 10, 1897.

27 *Ibid.,* June 26, 1897.

28 *Ibid.,* July 10, 1897.

29 *Ibid.,* July 16, 1897.

30 W.C. Harris, *The Sporting News,* Feb. 9, 1901.

31 *Lima Times-Democrat,* Aug. 28, 1897.

32 Five Delahanty brothers – Ed, Tom, Joe, Jim and Frank – played in the major leagues. A sixth, Bill Delahanty, was a minor league infielder from 1905 to 1912.

33 *Toledo Bee,* Aug. 22, 1897.

34 *Ibid.,* Aug. 23, 1897.

35 *Toledo Commercial,* Aug. 23, 1897.

36 *Toledo Bee,* Aug. 23, 1897.

37 Unidentified Toledo newspaper clipping.

38 *Lima Times-Democrat,* Sept. 24, 1897. One estimate placed Corbett's baseball earnings for 1897 at $17,000. See "Jim Corbett Playing First Base," *Baseball Research Journal,* No. 12 (1983), p. 185.

39 *Lima Times-Democrat,* Sept. 24, 1897.

40 Patrick Myler, *Gentleman Jim Corbett: The Truth Behind a Boxing Legend* (London: Robson Books Ltd., 1998), p. 131. Researcher Ray Nemec has determined that between 1895 and 1900, Corbett played in 37 official games with 23 different minor league teams, compiling a batting average of .274.

41 *Toledo Blade,* Sept. 8, 1897.

42 *Toledo Bee,* Sept. 8, 1897.

43 *Toledo Blade,* Sept. 8, 1897.

44 *Toledo Bee,* Sept. 8, 1897.

45 Bill James, *The Bill James Guide to Baseball Managers from 1870 to Today* (New York: Scribner, 1997), pp. 31-32.

46 *Reach's Official Baseball Guide* (Philadelphia: A.J. Reach Co., 1898), p. 40.

47 *New York Times,* July 20, 1897.

48 Walter Camp, "Our National Game—Save the Mark!" *Collier's* (April 4, 1899). Writing in the spring of 1899, Camp was looking back over "the last two or three seasons."

"Big Bob Ewing [is] probably
the *next* to step out
of this league."
—W.C. HARRIS[1]

CHAPTER 2

The Minor Years

WHEN BOB EWING ARRIVED IN TOLEDO, Ohio, it was a city of some 125,000 people—more than three times as many as in all of Auglaize County—and was entering one of the most interesting periods in its history.

The same year that Ewing first donned the uniform of the Toledo Mud Hens, the city's voters chose for their mayor an eccentric capitalist and former oil-field roustabout named Samuel M. "Golden Rule" Jones. Getting in on the ground floor after the 1885 discovery of oil in Lima, Jones had started a successful drilling company which he soon sold to John D. Rockefeller and Standard Oil. By the mid-1890s Jones was established in Toledo as head of the Acme Sucker Rod Co., manufacturing an oil-well pump of his own design. Taking as his mission statement the Golden Rule, Jones paid his employees more than the prevailing wage, implemented an eight-hour workday when 10 was standard, and instituted paid vacations and profit-sharing. Emblazoned on the exterior of his factory was a quotation from the proprietor: "Every man who is willing to work has a right to live. Divide the day and give him a chance."[2]

Jones, in other words, was a radical. In the assessment of historian Melvin G. Holli, the benefits Jones freely granted in the 1890s "encompassed the very issues that industrial workers and their unions would spend the first third of the 20th century fighting to attain."[3]

Elected as a Republican, Jones promptly broke with party bosses and was subsequently re-elected as an independent. As mayor, he created city parks and campaigned for a 3-cent fare on the street railway during the hours when workingmen were going to and from their jobs. He brought down the wrath of local clergy by refusing to enforce the city's blue laws. Jones took the view that saloons were poor men's clubs and that they should be allowed to operate on what was most patrons' only day off. Confronted with complaints that saloons were allowed to "run wide open on Sunday," the mayor issued assurances that most such establishments had their front doors closed and only the back and side doors open.[4]

While Golden Rule Jones was running the city, an almost equally interesting character was running the Mud Hens. A few years earlier, Charles J. Strobel had been ensconced in Findlay, a small city 45 miles south of Toledo. Business directories listed him as a confectioner and dealer in cigars and fireworks. At the same time, Strobel managed a strong independent baseball team that was unusual for its time and place. While organized baseball was solidifying its color barrier and systematically squeezing out such black players as George Stovey, Frank Grant and former Toledo standout Fleet Walker, the Findlay Sluggers were openly and to all appearances happily integrated. In 1894, Strobel's two best players were Bud Fowler and Findlay native Grant "Home Run" Johnson. Fowler, at age 36, was entering the twilight of a long and variegated career as the first black professional baseball player. Johnson, at 19, was at the dawn of a 38-year odyssey that would take him from barnstorming teams to the Cuban winter league to a long run as player and manager in the Negro Leagues. In 1895, the two combined to launch the Page Fence Giants with Fowler as player-manager and Johnson as team captain.

At some point Strobel, like Jones, got an economic boost from the oil and natural gas boom northwest Ohio experienced in the 1880s and '90s. By the time he set up shop in Toledo at age 32, his occupation was listed as "oil magnate."[5] This newfound prosperity enabled him to pursue his interest in baseball on a larger scale. He bought the Toledo ballclub in mid-season 1896 and proceeded to win the Inter-State League pennant. Strobel's takeover ushered in what one team history characterizes as a new era of "stable and committed leadership ... and a newly established winning attitude."[6]

It was also during Strobel's administration that the Toledo franchise, formerly known as the Swamp Angels, adopted one of the minor leagues' most distinctive and enduring nicknames. In the years prior to Ewing's arrival, the team had played at the coincidentally-named Ewing Street Park, a location selected because it was served by four trolley lines. But the park was in the middle of a residential neighborhood and residents complained about the noise and traffic generated by Sunday crowds. So in 1896 the club built a new park outside the city limits for weekend games. Bay View Park was in a marshy area inhabited by numerous American coots, commonly known as mud hens. When Strobel took over, he decided the ball-playing denizens of Bay View should also be known as Mud Hens.

Strobel had many interests aside from baseball. He promoted circuses, invested in hot-air balloon exhibitions, built dirigibles and later airplanes. He conducted his own 50-piece marching band, sometimes leading parades on Opening Day of the baseball season. Strobel also encouraged his players to get involved in musical recreations, possibly in hopes of keeping them out of the city's "wide open" saloons. Within a couple years after Ewing joined the Mud Hens, Strobel was applauded for having assembled "such a nice looking lot of gentlemanly and jolly boys." Ewing was among several Mud Hens who had become members of the Crescent Club and were "making themselves very popular with their musical accomplishments." Outfielder Billy Smith and pitcher Lew Wiltse in particular were said to be "very clever in both song and dance."[7]

Ewing had pitched in four games at the end of the 1897 season, winning two and losing one. From his first appearance, he had "proved to be all the specifications called for."[8] By season's end he was receiving lavish praise from Strobel and even a brief mention in a national sporting publication as "pitcher Ewing, the 'Wapak Wonder.'"[9] Toledo had finished the regular season 8½ games ahead of the Dayton Old Soldiers, then sealed the triumph by beating them four games to two in a post-season playoff. As Ewing began his first full season in professional baseball, he found himself at least partially surrounded by familiar faces. His Wapakoneta teammate Jerry McDonough had established himself at third base for the Mud Hens. At first was Bade Myers, the reigning Inter-State batting champion, who had played against Ewing at the Auglaize fairgrounds in 1895. Also on hand was Ewing's erstwhile Northwestern Ohio League rival, Roger Bresnahan.

Bresnahan had concluded the 1897 season in spectacular fashion. After going to Washington, he won four games without a defeat. Veteran catcher Deacon McGuire pronounced him possessed of "the right stuff."[10] But Bresnahan parted company with the Senators in a contract dispute and as a new season approached, he found himself unemployed and back in his hometown. He caught on with the Mud Hens and pitched four early-season games, going 2–2. He then headed west for another brief trial with Minneapolis in the Western League. Soon the one-time phenom dropped clear out of organized baseball. He would spend most of the next three seasons wandering through a succession of what he called "gas tank" leagues.[11]

Toledo's team captain was 33-year-old Bob Gilks, a former major league outfielder who would eventually spend 45 years in baseball, mostly as a scout and minor league manager. Gilks had scouted Ewing in the Northwestern Ohio League. Though Strobel appropriated for himself the title of manager and sat on the bench during games, it was Gilks who handled the day-to-day responsibilities of managing the Mud Hens.[12]

Another teammate who would play a role in Ewing's development was Stanley Arthur. Arthur was behind the plate when Ewing made his professional debut and he would remain Ewing's regular catcher throughout his three-plus years in Toledo. He would guide Ewing through more victories than any other catcher he ever worked with.

Arthur was a little guy and no great shakes as a hitter. In five seasons with Toledo, he never batted higher than .252. But he was a good defensive catcher and said to be capable of throwing to second base without coming out of his crouch. He was also tough: At a time when most major league catchers were good for no more than 95 games a year, Arthur averaged more than 115.

Ewing and Arthur were almost precisely the same age, born two months apart. But where Ewing was a newcomer to "league" ball, Arthur was a seasoned veteran, having played professionally since at least 1894. The two also shared other interests besides baseball. Both were Ohio country boys. During their off-seasons, while Ewing worked around the farm in his hometown of New Hampshire, Arthur raised poultry 85 miles away near New Vienna.

Teamed with Arthur in 1898, Ewing put forth more effort on the baseball diamond than he had expended in his entire life prior to that point. Gilks put him into harness alongside another workhorse, Charlie Ferguson, and between them, they pitched more than half of the Mud Hens' innings. They also accounted for 60 percent of the team's victories. Bidding for their third straight pennant, the Hens claimed first place late in June and remained at or near the top of the standings until mid-September. Ultimately the race came down to a series at Dayton on the last weekend of the season, and the home team clinched the championship by winning three of four games. Ewing pitched the first game of the series, battling down to the last out in the ninth inning before losing 4–3. At season's end, Ferguson led the league in innings pitched with 367. Ewing was close behind with 349. They tied for the league lead in victories with 25 each.

The campaign was completed in time for Ewing to get home and harvest his corn crop. Ewing enjoyed his time on the farm. "There's heaps of work there," he told a Toledo reporter cheerfully,[13] and he always kept busy during the winter. One December during his tenure with Toledo, the New Hampshire correspondent for the *Auglaize Republican* reported that Ewing was in the midst of harvesting an "ice crop" seven inches thick.[14] The same year he bought a small restaurant in town; the correspondent predicted "a liberal patronage."[15] When not occupied with farm chores or business obligations, Ewing could often be found tramping the woods and fields with a gun, hunting rabbits and quail. Among teammates who journeyed to Auglaize County to join him was Bob Gilks.

The 1899 season presented a test of a different kind for Ewing. Toledo went through most of the season with only 13 players. In addition to pitching 21 victories, Ewing—whose .308 batting average was second-best on the team—was pressed into service as the club's utility outfielder. This was not an alien role for Ewing, who had regularly played the outfield for Wapakoneta on his "days off." The newspapers were soon lauding him not only for his pitching but also his hitting and all-around play.

Gilks and his little band strove valiantly to stay in the pennant race. For the second year in a row, Arthur caught almost every day. At one stretch, the Mud Hens won 17 straight games. Among them was a 3–2 verdict over Wheeling, won by Ewing on his own home run. Toledo climbed into first place around July 1 and held on for more than half the season. But the team collapsed in the final three weeks and finished third.

AS THE TEAM GATHERED AGAIN in the spring of 1900, the players were still trying to get over an off-season tragedy. Jerry McDonough, who had batted .283 in 1899 and led the league in stolen bases, had died of accidental asphyxiation in his Toledo apartment shortly after the season ended. Just 21 years old, McDonough had already started attracting attention from major league clubs.[16] The sense of loss was acute for Ewing, a long-time teammate who remembered McDonough's help in getting him started in professional ball. But the shock was felt by everyone. After all, most of the regulars—Ewing, Arthur, second baseman Erve Beck and outfielders Gilks, Billy Smith and William "Skeeter" Hartman—had been together since McDonough's first year with the club in 1897.

Gilks tried a succession of third basemen as he searched for a satisfactory replacement. But the team got some help elsewhere, in the form of another tall, hard-throwing right-hander. Twenty-year-old Addie Joss had been pitching for town teams in his native Wisconsin for the past three years. Another new pitcher was built along different lines: Elmer Stricklett, 5-feet-6 and 140 pounds, was sometimes called the Little Fox.

Ewing's season was studded with sensational performances. On July 25 he pitched 16 innings, holding Mansfield scoreless over the last 12 en route to a hard-earned 5–2 victory. Four days later he defeated Wheeling 11–0, allowing just one hit. Ewing's bid for a no-hitter was spoiled by a single off the bat of Bob Rothermel, a much-traveled infielder who had reached the major leagues long enough, in his own words, to have "a sandwich and coffee with [John] McGraw in Baltimore in 1899."[17] By this time, thanks in part to the relaxed attitude of Mayor Jones, Toledo permitted Sunday games, as Strobel bragged, "right under the shadow of its office buildings."[18] The decorous Sunday afternoon crowd at downtown Armory Park greeted Ewing's performance with polite applause.[19]

Consistently held out to face the strongest teams in the league, Ewing had another 21–win season. On the whole, however, the year was not very satisfactory. The Mud Hens were in and out of first place for several weeks early in the season, then settled into second for a time. Early in August, they dropped to third, and that's where they finished. Fans grew progressively less polite. They became restive and finally downright hostile. A trip to the ballpark, Toledoans were advised, "will expand your notion of the English language."[20] "Obscene epithets" rained down from the bleachers, keeping the home team "on the keen edge of a nervous strain all the time they are on the grounds."[21]

The team's problems were aggravated when several players were felled by injuries. The seemingly indestructible Stanley Arthur was knocked out of action and failed to play 100 games for the first time in five years. Elmer Stricklett, after giving good service most of the summer, "was taken sick and unfitted for work"[22] for seven weeks. Even Ewing, in the midst of a stellar season, "got a trifle stale … [and] was sent to his home in the country for several weeks to recuperate."[23]

He still managed to pitch 290 innings. According to tabulations by a correspondent for *The Sporting News,* Ewing completed 16 games in which he allowed six hits or fewer, four of those games going extra innings. The Mud Hens won only six games from first-place Dayton while losing 14, but Ewing accounted for four of the victories. He put an exclamation point on his season in September by beating the front-runners twice in three days. The second of those decisions was a two-hit shutout.

"Other pitchers have won more, and lost less games than Bob Ewing," the *Sporting News* man acknowledged, "but the team behind a pitcher has more to do with his effectiveness … than anything else, and … the only pitchers ahead of Bob are Dayton and [second-place] Fort Wayne men." After three-plus years with Toledo, Ewing had proven himself "certainly too fast for the Inter-State League."[24]

Strobel had received several offers for Ewing, but was not eager to sell. And he didn't have to. Under the reserve system that had developed in baseball since the 1870s, a player once signed by a given club could be held over or "reserved" by that club even after the expiration of his contract. A clause to that effect was contained in the standard player's contract and, since the provisions of the reserve clause could be carried over indefinitely from one year to the next, the player was effectively bound to the same team for as long as the club desired, with no means of escape. Once under contract, a player could be retained indefinitely, until such time as he was sold, traded or released—or, in the case of a minor league player, until he was drafted by a major league club. So, despite the belief that Ewing would "surely command a good sum,"[25] it was considered quite likely that he, Stricklett and Joss, who had won 19 games, would all be back with Toledo in 1901. As always, Strobel was looking to build a winner, and money was a secondary consideration. Shortly after he took over the team, it was said that Strobel had turned down offers of $1,850 for both Erve Beck and Bade Myers, and the move had won him a pennant.

But by 1900, Strobel's dreams reached beyond the Inter-State League. He longed to return Toledo to the major league status it had enjoyed in 1884 and 1890 as a member of the American Association. He rankled at being stuck in a circuit with towns like Mansfield, Ohio, and New Castle, Pennsylvania. He toyed with the idea of forming a new league, and explored the possibility of abandoning the Inter-State for a proposed new American Association or for Ban Johnson's soon-to-be major, the American League. When these schemes fell through, Strobel was undismayed. Never mind, he told an out-of-town reporter, it wouldn't be long before "some of the major organizations are going to realize that Toledo is a great ball town that has been overlooked."[26] *The Sporting News* came to regard Strobel as "a disturbing factor" in the Inter-State League.[27]

About this time, the fate of the entire league dropped into Strobel's hands. Charles B. Power resigned as the league's president at the end of the 1900 season. Strobel, as vice president, was left in temporary charge of the Inter-State's affairs. Within weeks, the league had ceased to exist.

It's not entirely clear how this came about. Somehow, perhaps through confusion or oversight during the transition, the league failed to submit its annual payment as required under baseball's National Agreement. When they realized payment hadn't been made, several club owners scrambled to send in checks of their own, but the board that monitored compliance with the agreement insisted on the letter of "baseball law." The deadline had been missed and the Inter-State's protection under the agreement, by which all clubs in organized ball were bound to honor each other's contracts and respect each other's reserve lists, was determined to have lapsed. Overnight, every player in the league who hadn't already signed a contract for the 1901 season became a free agent.

Blame for the wreck of the Inter-State fell squarely on Strobel. An editorial in *The Sporting News* charged that he "neglected [the league's] interests in trying to promote [his own] selfish purposes."[28] Other operators rushed in to take advantage of the Inter-State League's going-out-of-business sale. Among the first on the scene was George "White Wings" Tebeau, a former major league outfielder and now owner of the new Kansas City franchise in the Western League. In short order, he signed 10 newly-liberated laborers off Inter-State rosters. Ewing agreed to a Kansas City contract in February. Also in Toledo, Tebeau collected the autographs of Skeeter Hartman, pitcher Ike Butler and catcher Monte Beville, who had joined the Mud Hens in time to work with Ewing in one late-season game. Around the league, Tebeau swept up first baseman Norman "Kitty" Brashear from Fort Wayne as well as pitcher Bill "Barney" Wolfe and infielder Clyde "Rabbit" Robinson from the Anderson, Indiana, club.[29] Stanley Arthur also got a shot in the Western League, signing on with the Omaha Omahogs. Elmer Stricklett headed for the West Coast after accepting an offer from Sacramento.

W.C. Harris, Toledo correspondent for *The Sporting News,* expressed "great surprise" at this exodus, and seemed particularly pained by the "defection" of Ewing. "Ewing was always appreciated in Toledo and a greater favorite never stepped in baseball shoes," Harris wrote. Moreover, "His money was always forthcoming."[30]

But in addition to better pay, Kansas City held out the promise of stronger competition, an opportunity to move up in baseball and take a step toward a chance in the major leagues. On the other hand, Ewing had placed himself in the employ of a man many ballplayers found difficult to work for. The sporting press often condemned Tebeau as a ruffian and a troublemaker. There were numerous instances of players balking at playing for Tebeau. When he owned the Louisville club, it was infected with "great dissatisfaction" and players "openly boasted that they did not intend to hurt themselves" for Tebeau's benefit.[31] Harry Arndt, returned to Louisville after a tryout with the Cincinnati Reds, refused to report and instead jumped to an outlaw league, risking permanent banishment from organized baseball. Tebeau, looking to recoup his investment, simply resold the recalcitrant ballplayer, who landed happily back in the big leagues with the St. Louis Cardinals. Still, it was said in locker rooms throughout baseball that when Tebeau's former employees said anything good about him, they crossed their fingers.[32] Rabbit Robinson, surveying his job prospects four full years after leaving Kansas City, made it clear that he "preferred the outlaws to Tebeau."[33]

To make matters worse, Tebeau was stepping into an unsettled situation in Kansas City. Before 1901, the Blues had been members of the American League. Now president Ban Johnson was leading the AL in a great eastward shift, invading the big eastern markets in a bid to challenge the National League's status as baseball's one and only major league. Already in 1900 Johnson had established franchises in Cleveland and Chicago. Now he was moving into Philadelphia, Baltimore and Washington. When all the moves were completed, the American League had occupied three of the cities the National League deserted when it contracted from 12 teams to eight after the 1899 season. Kansas City, the American League's westernmost outpost, was one of the cities abandoned in the reorganization. Johnson persuaded franchise owner Jimmy Manning to give up his comfortable situation in Missouri and move to Washington, D.C., to run the new American League club there.

Kansas City had a population of nearly 165,000. Like Toledo, Kansas City had sampled life in the big leagues in the 1880s, spending a year near the bottom of the National League and fielding teams at other times in the American Association and the short-lived Union Association. With the departure of the American League, the prospect of playing in the Western League was viewed as a decided comedown.

"Kansas City is too good a town to be classed with such dead ones as St. Joseph and Omaha," grumbled D.M. "Doc" Shively, local correspondent for *The Sporting News*.[34] Besides, he added, "Nobody here wants George Tebeau."[35]

Regardless what anybody thought of him, Tebeau cobbled together a good ballclub for Kansas City. Team captain was Canadian-born second baseman Johnny O'Brien, a veteran who had spent most of the 1890s in the National League. Brashear and center fielder Fred Ketchum also had brief major league experience, as did Tom Messitt, who would help Beville with the catching. Also on board was left fielder Dakin Miller, who had helped Tebeau win the Western League pennant for Denver the year before. An early-season deal added another player from that team, shortstop Ed "Kid" Lewee. With Robinson at third and Hartman, a former Inter-State batting champion, in right, it was a solid lineup.

But the strength of the club was its pitching. After sending Ike Butler to Denver in mid-May, Tebeau was left with a four-man staff that carried the team all season with precious little additional help. Besides Ewing and Barney Wolfe, the foursome included a third right-hander and a left-hander. The righty was Norwood Gibson, a chemistry major from the University of Notre Dame. The lefty was Tornado Jake Weimer, a former cigar maker from Ottumwa, Iowa. Among them, the four logged well over 1,000 innings and pitched 103 complete games.[36]

Ewing lost his first start for Kansas City but won his next four decisions as the Blues got off to a 22–8 start and jumped out to an early six-game lead. By late June they were far enough in front to absorb a seven-game losing streak without being seriously threatened. But despite the team's performance, the city never really warmed to its new club. Attendance in the "old, half-ruined stands"[37] at Exposition Park was disappointing; the same story was repeated in Minneapolis, another city taken in by the Western League after being dropped by the American. Fans never got over the sense that they "were getting second- or third-class ball."[38]

Ironically, the situation was only made worse by the fact that from Opening Day forward, Kansas City outclassed the rest of the league. The season was only weeks old when *The Sporting News* expressed concern that Kansas City's clear superiority would kill all interest in the Western League race. "The new Blues have already distanced many of their rivals and … will in all probability soon secure so great a lead that the race will be a runaway with Kansas City first and the rest nowhere," the paper editorialized.[39] Tebeau, having produced a winner his first year in the city, resigned himself to barely breaking even financially. Still, and to their credit, the players went out "and played the hardest kind of ball in the face of the most discouraging circumstances."[40]

By August 14, when Ewing shut out Colorado Springs 6–0 on four hits, the writers had all but conceded the pennant to Kansas City. The consensus, expressed by a scribe in Omaha, was that the Blues were "too fast for the Western League as it is now constituted."[41] On August 29 at Des Moines, Ewing surrendered three runs in the first inning, then held the Hawkeyes without another score until the sun went down to escape with a 12-inning 3–3 tie. Three days later he struck out 10 in a 10–4 victory over St. Joseph, then rested two days and beat the Saints again, 5–4. Having pitched 30 innings and struck out 27 batters in eight days, he sat back and watched while his teammates clinched the championship with a week left on the schedule.

In the final tally, Kansas City finished 10 games ahead of runner-up St. Paul. Ewing, Wolfe and Weimer combined for 64 victories. Ewing, with a 21–5 record, led the league in winning percentage, but Weimer, 23–9 with 180 strikeouts, was generally regarded as the circuit's outstanding pitcher. Doc Shively rated Weimer, Dakin Miller and Rabbit Robinson as the team's best major league prospects.

BACK HOME WITH THE PROSPECT of a few more weeks of good weather before winter set in, Ewing hooked up with an independent club in Sidney, Ohio. Sidney had booked a series of games with a team from Washington Court House for what was billed as "the amateur championship of Ohio."[42] This was merely drumbeating to pump up the gate. In actuality the series carried no prize beyond bragging rights between the two communities. The *Cincinnati Enquirer,* tongue firmly in cheek, referred to the games as the "monthly championship series."[43] And the teams—at least Sidney's—could hardly be classified as amateurs. With the end of the league season, Sidney had strengthened its lineup considerably with hired guns. Besides Ewing, the reinforcements included Whitey Guese, who had spent most of the season in the Western Association and had a trial with the Cincinnati Reds, and Fred "Lefty" Houtz, former Texas League batting champion who had also played briefly with the Reds in 1899.

Ewing quickly became the team's star. He pitched three games against Washington Court House, winning two, and played right field the rest of the time. Either pitching or hitting, he had a hand in every game Sidney won. Sidney claimed the championship by virtue of winning both three-game series that were played on its grounds, but in fact Washington Court House, thanks to a sweep of its three home games, won five of nine overall.

Minor leaguers like Ewing weren't the only ballplayers roaming Ohio in the autumn of 1901 in search of a couple more paydays before the snow flew. After the National League season ended, a number of the Cincinnati Reds got together and planned a one-week barnstorming tour. One of the dates they scheduled was October 10 in Sidney. At least five other pitchers were available to the home team but Ewing, the best of the bunch and a favorite with the fans, was the clear choice to draw the assignment. After four straight 20-win seasons in the minor leagues, he was getting a chance to showcase his skills against major leaguers.

The Reds had already had one opportunity to evaluate Ewing in 1901. During the season, they had sent out Ted Sullivan, one of the most respected scouts of the day, in search of talent. He made a swing through the Western League, but either didn't see Ewing or caught him on one of his rare off days. Sullivan, a former big league manager and longtime minor league organizer, came back with a recommendation that the Reds go after Barney Wolfe, a half-brother of Cincinnati pitcher Bill Phillips.[44] It came out later that Bid McPhee, who had succeeded Buck Ewing as manager of the Reds, had also written to inquire about the possibility of signing Jake Weimer, but the letter apparently went astray and nothing came of it.[45]

On the appointed day, the Reds were expected in Sidney at 11 a.m. but they missed their train at Piqua. Forced to fall back on horse-drawn transportation, they didn't arrive until after 3 p.m. Throughout the day, the anticipation mounted. Certainly Ewing must have thought back to the first time he pitched against the Reds, surrendering 16 runs at Midway Park in 1896. This time he had a better team behind him. More importantly, he was no longer the raw farm boy he had been five years earlier. Twenty-eight years old, having traveled as far west as Denver and amassed more than 1,100 innings in professional baseball, he was a confident, mature adult and well on his way to becoming a polished pitcher.

Then there was the matter of the afternoon's opposition. As major league teams go, the 1901 Cincinnati Reds were nothing to brag about. They had finished last in the National League. Owner John T. Brush was still smarting financially from the cost of rebuilding a grandstand that had burned down in 1900. When it became clear that the 1901 club was going nowhere, Brush decided he wasn't going to throw good money after bad by shelling out for a lot of new talent. Trying to assemble a respectable roster on a bargain-basement budget, McPhee tried out more than 20 rookies. Such desperation gave rise to some bizarre episodes. McPhee resurrected Harley "Doc" Parker, who had last pitched in the big leagues in 1896, and sent him out to try his stuff one afternoon in Brooklyn. In his only appearance with the Reds, Parker absorbed one of the worst beatings in baseball history, giving up 26 hits in a 21–3 drubbing. McPhee also took a flier on 18-year-old Dick Scott from neighboring Clermont County, signed on the strength of a local newspaper's glowing accounts of his pitching prowess. It turned out young Scott had written the notices himself. When injuries struck late in the season, McPhee was reduced to scouring Cincinnati's sandlots in order to field a team.

For all that, the barnstormers who showed up in Sidney were mostly legitimate major leaguers. The lineup included Johnny Dobbs, Dick Harley, Tommy Corcoran, George Magoon and Bill Bergen. Heinie Peitz, who had ripped Ewing for a double and a triple five years earlier, batted fourth and held down first base. The game finally got under way at 4 p.m. on the Miami Avenue ball grounds, along the banks of the Great Miami River. Opposing Ewing was another aspiring right-hander whom the Reds had picked up in Cincinnati to help with pitching duties on the tour. Twenty-two-year-old Matty Schwab had pitched a little minor league ball. He also had worked since his mid-teens on the grounds crew at Cincinnati's League Park, where his father, John Schwab, was head groundskeeper.

A historical marker in Sidney, Ohio, commemorates the day Bob Ewing earned his crack at the major leagues by pitching a local team to a 3–3 tie with the Cincinnati Reds. The marker, unveiled in 2001, is at Custenborder Field, approximately a half-mile north of where the 1901 game was played in what is now Berger Park. *Photo: Lindsay Steiner.*

The game was tight from the start. Sidney suffered a setback in the fourth inning, when catcher Pete Garvey was forced to leave the game with a broken finger. Ewing, batting sixth, doubled twice off Schwab but was stranded both times. Cincinnati scored two unearned runs and led 2–1, but with two men on in the eighth inning, Houtz tripled to the center-field fence, putting Sidney ahead 3–2. In the gathering gloom of the late afternoon, the Reds tied the score 3–3 in their half of the inning on Dobbs' single, two misplayed sacrifice attempts and a throwing error. That's where it stood when the game was called because of darkness. Ewing had struck out seven, walked none and held the big leaguers for eight innings without an earned run. The *Cincinnati Enquirer* credited the Reds with eight hits; the *Sidney Daily News* counted only six.

Reds players, particularly Corcoran and Peitz, fairly ran back to Cincinnati and told McPhee he should waste no time in obtaining this rangy pitcher from Auglaize County.[46] The formalities were accomplished with little fanfare, and without so much as a by-your-leave in the direction of George Tebeau and the Kansas City club. The National League, finding itself suddenly locked in a battle for survival with Ban Johnson's upstart American League, had abruptly abandoned its role as the guardian of baseball law and unilaterally abrogated the National Agreement which had governed relationships among different organizations within organized baseball for nearly 20 years. In the fall of 1901, anarchy reigned. The American League vigorously raided National League rosters, the National League fought back any way it could, and both major leagues helped themselves to talent from the unprotected and largely helpless minor leagues, often without compensation.[47]

Ewing's former employer was among the victims. Eight days after the game in Sidney, Ewing took the morning train to Cincinnati, signed a contract before noon and returned home the same day. "The Reds Secure Another Ewing," trumpeted one optimistic headline. The accompanying story recounted that Ewing had arrived "from the good old town of Wapakoneta" and was found on the street "looking at the skyscraper."[48] The reporter was having some fun at the expense of country boy Ewing, but he probably did pause on the street to do a little gawking. Cincinnati was in the midst of a construction boom and the city's first acknowledged skyscraper, the 18-story Bartlett Building at 36 E. Fourth St., was completed in

1901 within a few blocks of the Reds' offices. Ewing's contract negotiations amounted to only "a few minutes' chat" with McPhee.[49]

News of the signing was greeted with enthusiasm everywhere Ewing had played. At his latest stop, a local paper toasted the success of "Bob Ewing, Sidney's popular pitcher."[50] Jim Honeyman, who played with Ewing in Wapakoneta and against him in the Western League, pronounced him "the best pitcher in the business when men are on base," and added, "Cincinnati has certainly secured a corker."[51] From Toledo, W.C. Harris summed up the reaction: "He has no enemies and his many friends in northwestern Ohio are more than pleased to hear of his rise in the baseball world."[52]

It hadn't been a rapid rise or an easy one. But 20 years after he used to pitch potatoes against the barn, Bob Ewing was going to the big leagues.

ENDNOTES

1 *The Sporting News*, Nov. 20, 1900.
2 Melvin G. Holli, "Toledo's Golden Ruler," *Timeline*, Vol. 17, No. 4 (July/August 2000), p. 43.
3 *Ibid*.
4 *Ibid*., p. 45.
5 Ralph Lin Weber, *The Toledo Baseball Guide of the Mud Hens, 1883-1943* (Rossford, Ohio: Baseball Research Bureau, 1944), p. 233.
6 John O'Brien and Jerry DeBruin with John Husman, *Mud Hens Memories* (Perrysburg, Ohio: BWD Publishing, 2001), p. 8.
7 *The Sporting News*, April 21, 1900.
8 *Toledo Commercial*, Aug. 23, 1897.
9 *Sporting Life*, Oct. 9, 1897.
10 Cappy Gagnon, "The Debut of Roger Bresnahan," *Baseball Research Journal*, No. 8 (1979), p. 41.
11 *The Sporting News*, Feb. 27, 1908.
12 Lin Weber, *op. cit*., p. 71.
13 *The Sporting News*, Oct. 6, 1900.
14 *Auglaize Republican*, Dec. 15, 1898.
15 *Ibid*., Oct. 6, 1898.
16 *Sporting Life*, Oct. 21, 1899. Evidence indicated that McDonough, probably half asleep, inadvertently opened one gas jet while meaning to close another.
17 Bob Rothermel, letter to August Herrmann, July 20, 1912. The letter is on file at the A. Bartlett Giamatti Research Center at the National Baseball Hall of Fame.
18 *Cincinnati Commercial Tribune*, reprinted in *The Sporting News*, Jan. 26, 1901.
19 *Toledo Bee*, July 30, 1900.
20 *Toledo Bee*, reprinted in *The Sporting News*, Dec. 15, 1900.
21 *Toledo Blade*, reprinted in *The Sporting News*, Dec. 1, 1900.
22 *The Sporting News*, Sept. 22, 1900.
23 *Ibid*., Nov. 17, 1900.
24 *Ibid*., Sept. 15, 1900. In fact Ewing, with a career record of 69-33, had won more games than any other pitcher to date for the Toledo franchise, which had been in organized baseball 15 seasons since 1883. His victory total was surpassed

in 1910 by James Hiram "Hi" West, who pitched for the Mud Hens from 1907 to 1912 and compiled a record of 85-61. West pitched in the major leagues with Cleveland in 1905 and 1911.

25   *The Sporting News,* Sept. 15, 1900.

26   *Cincinnati Commercial Tribune,* reprinted in *The Sporting News,* Jan. 26, 1901.

27   *The Sporting News,* Sept. 22, 1900.

28   *Ibid.,* April 6, 1901.

29   The Inter-State team that finished the season in Anderson, Ind., had functioned most of the summer as the Columbus (Ohio) Senators; see *Sporting Life,* Sept. 29, 1900.

30   *The Sporting News,* March 2, 1901.

31   *Ibid.,* Oct. 22, 1904.

32   *Ibid.,* Oct. 1, 1904.

33   *Ibid.,* May 12, 1906.

34   *Ibid.,* Dec. 15, 1900.

35   *Ibid.,* Dec. 8, 1900.

36   Nearly all the regulars from the 1901 Kansas City Blues eventually reached the major leagues. The only exceptions were Hartman and Lewee, who both played in the neighborhood of 2,000 games in the minors.

37   Unidentified Kansas City newspaper, 1902, quoted in Rex Hamann, "Kansas City's American Association Ballparks, Part 1," *The American Association Almanac,* Vol. 4, No. 3 (summer 2005), p. 2. Hamann describes Exposition Park, from its construction in 1888, as "a very humble all-wooden affair." The sense that the Blues were overdue for a new ballpark is indicated by the fact that, although Exposition Park remained in use until the spring of 1903, as early as 1900 the site was platted for redevelopment as a residential neighborhood. See Hamann, *op. cit.,* pp. 1 and 11.

38   *The Sporting News,* Aug. 24, 1901.

39   *Ibid.,* June 8, 1901.

40   *Ibid.,* Aug. 24, 1901.

41   *Ibid.,* Sept. 21, 1901.

42   *Sidney Daily News,* Sept. 24, 1901.

43   *Cincinnati Enquirer,* Oct. 15, 1901.

44   *The Sporting News,* Oct. 19, 1901.

45   *Ibid.,* Nov. 11, 1905.

46   *Cincinnati Enquirer,* Oct. 19, 1901.

47   Harold Seymour and Dorothy Seymour Mills, *Baseball: The Early Years* (New York: Oxford University Press, 1960), p. 315: "The chief victims of player-snatching were the minor leagues, which were raided by both the American and National leagues. The American League, as an 'outlaw' league ..., could be expected to pirate minor leaguers. But the National League, as the reputed defender of the National Agreement and stability in baseball, might have been expected to follow 'baseball law.' Instead, thinking only of its own interests, it renounced the National Agreement, leaving the minors without protection at a time when they badly needed it." See also Albert G. Spalding, *America's National Game: Historic Facts Concerning the Beginning, Evolution, Development and Popularity of Baseball* (Lincoln, Neb.: University of Nebraska Press, 1992 reprint of 1911 original), pp. 305 and 329.

48   *Cincinnati Commercial Tribune,* Oct. 19, 1901.

49   J. Ed Grillo, *The Sporting News,* Oct. 26, 1901.

50   *Shelby County Democrat,* Oct. 25, 1901.

51   *Cincinnati Enquirer,* Oct. 21, 1901.

52   W.C. Harris, *The Sporting News,* Oct. 26, 1901.

"The fact is plainly in evidence that the instructions
on how to play baseball *scientifically*,
which the chapters in the Guide have
contained, year *after* year, ... have
brought forth good fruit."
—HENRY CHADWICK[1]

CHAPTER 3

Dead Ball Days

BASEBALL WAS STILL EVOLVING when Bob Ewing arrived in the major leagues in 1902. At the start of his career, home plate was a 12-inch square; 1900 saw the introduction of the five-sided plate with a 17-inch front edge, increasing the size of the strike zone by 42 percent. Starting in 1899, rules were modified to require the catcher to set up directly behind the plate at all times. The National League adopted the foul-strike rule in 1901, charging the batter with strikes on his first two foul balls. The pitcher's mound was also a recent innovation, having developed through the 1890s; there was no set standard as to the construction of the mound until 1903, when its height was capped at 15 inches.[2]

Such changes consistently worked to the advantage of the pitcher. At the same time, the development of larger and better gloves allowed fielders to routinely make plays that had been all but impossible a decade earlier. Scoring was on the decline, a trend that would continue for most of Ewing's career. By 1908, the average number of runs in a major league game was less than half what it had been in 1894. Though, officially at least, the ball itself remained unchanged, baseball had entered what came to be known as its "dead ball" era.

As every run became more and more precious, baseball was becoming an increasingly subtle, strategic game. Instead of swinging away and hoping for a big inning, teams were forced to scratch and scrape for one score at a time. With a runner on first base and none out, according to Bill James, the sacrifice bunt eventually became so automatic that some managers didn't even have a sign for it.[3] As impressive batting averages became less common, they almost threatened to go out of style. Henry Chadwick, who had written about baseball since the 1850s and had a major hand in refining and standardizing the game's rules, denigrated the pursuit of high averages as "mere 'record batting.'" A better system, argued the man called the Father of Baseball, would be to rank hitters by their success rate in advancing base runners, which he called "the true criterion of 'teamwork at the bat.'"[4] Even Billy Sunday, the 1880s outfielder who quit baseball to become America's most famous evangelist, came to scoff at the game he used to play as nothing more than a "batting fest."[5] The fashion of the day was what Christy Mathewson described as "the hand-raised, cultivated, hothouse form of baseball."[6]

The term that was coming into vogue for this style of play, which placed a premium on brains, teamwork and a thorough awareness of the fine points of the game, was "inside baseball."[7] The phrase conjured up the notion of a contest of deep psychological subtlety and arcane tactical intricacy—in the words of baseball historian Harold Seymour, an "esoteric amalgam of psychology, science, and mental prowess ..., supposedly so complex as to be beyond the ken of most fans, however well informed they were."[8] Within a few years, the term became laughably overused. *Spalding's Official Baseball Guide* ultimately concluded that most of the "inside baseball" fans read about was played only inside the heads of over-enthusiastic sportswriters.[9] Even John J. McGraw, one of the most celebrated practitioners of the inside game, eventually admitted, "So-called inside baseball is mostly bunk."[10]

Still, the prevailing view at the outset of Ewing's major league career was that the modern game, with its pitching duels and heavy reliance on strategy, represented the highest expression baseball had yet achieved. Most boosters would have agreed with umpire Silk O'Loughlin when he said, "The games that make new fans and bring the old ones out the next day are the 1–0, 2–1 and 3–2 contests in which, from start to finish, a hit or a brilliant fielding play will turn the tide of victory or defeat."[11] Baseball prided itself on being not only subtle but scientific. Chadwick extolled the advancement of base runners as "the acme of scientific batting."[12] Billy Sunday rhapsodized over the reduction of baseball teamwork to "a perfect science."[13] Johnny Evers of the Chicago Cubs believed that the constraints of the dead-ball game—the need "to advance runners and score runs rather than … get base hits"[14]—reduced many a potential .300 hitter to a .250 hitter. Even so, he maintained, "The batters of the modern game are better hitters, more scientific, and more effective than those of 20 or 10 years ago."[15]

This insistence on baseball as a scientific enterprise put the sport right in step with the national mood at the dawn of the new century. It was a time of optimism, founded in no small part on the technological marvels that dazzled millions of visitors to the Pan-American Exposition at Buffalo, New York, in 1901 and the St. Louis World's Fair, which Ewing and his teammates visited in 1904. The imprimatur of science also dovetailed nicely with baseball's efforts to erase lingering impressions from the raucous 1890s and to present itself in a new light, not only as socially acceptable entertainment but as a positively constructive influence in American life. The game was promoted through what historian Steven A. Riess called "a vigorous public relations campaign waged by baseball magnates" with the aid of a cooperative press. Aim of the campaign was to convince the public "that participation in the rituals of baseball contributed to both individual self-improvement and national betterment."[16]

According to what Riess termed the official ideology, baseball typified and reinforced our highest ideals and contributed to the advancement of specific socially desirable goals. "Two of the principal functions ascribed to baseball," Riess found, "were that it would teach children traditional American values and that it would help newcomers assimilate into the dominant WASP culture."[17] Baseball largely believed its own publicity. By the end of the decade, Evers and his collaborator, sportswriter Hugh Fullerton, could state without irony that professional ballplayers, regarded only a few years earlier "as ruffians or at best itinerant ne'er-do-wells," were now engaged in "an established and honorable trade."[18] Players at the highest level of this admirable and beneficial profession, Evers and Fullerton asserted, had "reached the post-graduate course of a moral and physical training school."[19]

Often there was a wide gap between baseball's image and its reality. In practice, Ewing's teammate Sam Crawford told Lawrence Ritter years later, "Baseball players weren't too much accepted in those days." They were "considered pretty crude" and weren't generally welcome at the best hotels.[20] In 1904, the Reds were turned away from a hotel in Rochester, Pennsylvania, by a desk clerk who informed them that her establishment did not cater to a sporting crowd, and certainly not to ballplayers. Carrying their luggage, the players trudged off in the rain to seek other lodgings, looking, in the words of a writer who shared the experience, as if they had been "refused at the morgue."[21]

Still, Riess wrote, the owners' authorized version "was accepted unquestioningly by the public and became the conventional wisdom." One element of the conventional wisdom was that baseball was a democratic institution, "open to anyone with talent and perseverance."[22] A glaring but universally ignored exception involved black players, who were as thoroughly marginalized during this period as at any time in baseball history. Though more than 70 blacks played in the minor leagues (and at least two in the majors) in the 19th century, the last of them had disappeared from organized ball by 1900,[23] and the Negro Leagues would not materialize until the 1920s. Ewing, who had pitched against the Page Fence Giants as an amateur in 1896, never again stepped onto the same field with black players during the rest of his career.

Up to the time of Ewing's entry into the professional ranks, the game was dominated by second-generation Irishmen and Germans. Sportswriters commonly found off-season column fodder in arguing whether the Irish or the Germans had performed better during the past campaign. In the early 1900s, these two groups continued to predominate, along with a third general class of players, still white and mostly of northern European ancestry, who have been categorized as "old-stock Americans."[24] These last would have included Ewing, who represented at least the fourth generation of his family in America.[25]

Early on, most players came from states in the heavily populated Northeast. Ballplayers from the Deep South remained something of a novelty throughout much of Ewing's career, perhaps partly as a reflection of regional divisions that still lingered 35 years after the end of the Civil War. Ohio, where the relatively urbanized Northeast met the more rural Midwest, was producing a lot of ballplayers by the 1890s. In 1896, the Buckeye State ranked behind only Pennsylvania and Massachusetts in the number of native sons in the National League[26] and the game's center of gravity was shifting westward. By 1905, some saw the Midwest taking over as the incubator of most of the nation's baseball talent. Marking off boundaries passing through Cleveland in the north, Cincinnati in the south, Harrisburg, Pennsylvania, in the east and following the Ohio-Indiana line in the west, an anonymous Chicago-based writer claimed that "at least three-fifths of the men now playing ball in the large leagues hail from towns and villages within the limits of that rectangle."[27] Even allowing for the article's lack of hard figures and possible regional bias, the writer was probably onto something. By 1910, Bill James found, baseball was becoming "to a considerable extent the property of midwestern farm boys" who started out playing Sunday afternoons in cow pastures.[28]

Whether anyone realized it or not, Bob Ewing was practically the definition of what major league teams were buying in 1902, the prototypical pitcher of the coming decade. The Auglaize farm boy was tall and rangy, carrying only 170 pounds on his 6-foot, 1½-inch frame, and he came already fitted with an appropriate nickname. He was sometimes referred to as "Buck" Ewing, a sobriquet simply borrowed from the illustrious earlier Ewing, but that handle never caught on in Cincinnati, where the original Buck Ewing was still a familiar figure in baseball circles. The writers, probably seeing two Buck Ewings in the same town as a formula for confusion, were quick to jettison the hand-me-down nickname in favor of another and more descriptive one Bob had acquired in Kansas City. For most of his career, the lanky right-hander was most commonly known as Long Bob.[29]

The nickname was descriptive in more ways than one. Ewing's tall, slim physique was accentuated by long arms and even long fingers, heightening the overall impression. Reporters sizing him up sometimes took him to be 6-foot-3. Physically, Ewing was of the same design as many of the era's top pitchers. Like Ewing, Walter Johnson (6-foot-1, 200 pounds) was tall and had long arms, physical attributes he used "to great advantage" working off the elevated pitcher's mound.[30] The same was true of Ewing's former Toledo teammate Addie Joss (6-3, 185), who in 1902 was beginning a brilliant career with Cleveland in the American League. Other notable contemporaries of Ewing's who came out of the same mold included Rube Waddell (6-1½, 195), Christy Mathewson (6-1½, 195), Chief Bender (6-2, 185) and, coming along a few years later, Rube Marquard (6-3, 180) and Grover Cleveland Alexander (6-1, 185).

Pitchers had been growing bigger, and especially taller, ever since 1893, when the pitching distance was increased from 50 feet to 60 feet, 6 inches. Ballplayers, like the population in general, were smaller than they are today.[31] But increasingly, the biggest men in the game were mostly pitchers. By 1908, the average pitcher was 5-foot-11 and 180 pounds, 1½ inches taller and nine pounds heavier than the average position player.[32] Tall pitchers were greatly sought after. Reading the sports pages, one could almost get the idea that height was all a pitcher needed to succeed. Writers invariably commented favorably on Ewing's size. When he signed with Cincinnati, J. Ed Grillo's assessment was brief and to the point: "He is a 6-footer and looks like he can deliver the goods."[33] When the Reds landed right-hander Orval Overall a few years later, a writer exulted—happily but inaccurately—over the acquisition of "the tallest player in the country."[34]

As Ewing or any other knowledgeable baseball man realized, there was more to it than that. The pitcher was responsible for the most complex, most critical aspect of the game. It is not too much to say that the man on the mound was universally recognized as the central figure in the drama on the field. Evers and Fullerton represented the generally-held view:

> Pitching is the most highly developed, most skillful and most important part of baseball, requiring more thought, more strength and more brains than any other position demands. Good pitching is the absolute essential to victory, and, considered in relation to the "inside game," is vital, for unless the pitcher understands every move of his fellow players, and adjusts his pitching to the plan, the "inside game" becomes worse than useless.[35]

The more sophisticated the game became, the clearer it was that being big and throwing hard weren't sufficient to make a pitcher. While Henry Chadwick acknowledged that "speed in delivery" could be "of great effect when judiciously used," he listed speed only second among his seven "essentials for strategic skill in pitching." First was the ability to locate pitches "just as the pitcher's knowledge of the strong and weak points of the opposing batsmen may suggest." Further, the pitcher must demonstrate full control of "various curves," the endurance to last the full game and "the nerve and pluck to discharge [his] onerous duties" even in adverse circumstances. Moreover, Chadwick stressed, the pitcher must always control his temper and refrain from "kicking" against the umpire's decisions. Such disputation,

Father Chadwick preached, "implies either dishonesty or misjudgment on the part of the umpire, and naturally forces him to deprive the offending pitcher of the benefit of the doubt he would otherwise have profited by."[36]

Temperamentally, Ewing was—or would become—something close to the Chadwickian ideal of the perfect pitcher. Already he had many of the physical tools. "Ewing is a tall, rangy fellow with lots of speed and a change of pace and a motion so graceful that…he [could] be mistaken for [former Reds pitcher] Ed Scott," one scribe wrote.[37] The control so prized by Chadwick was regarded as one of Ewing's strong points.[38] Joe Schrall, who faced Ewing in the Western League, told the *Cincinnati Enquirer* he had "a splendid curve and a deceptive motion."[39]

LONG BOB HAD THE MAKINGS of a major league pitcher. Whether he could live up to that potential remained to be seen. In the meantime, Reds owner John T. Brush wasn't going to gamble a lot of money on an unproven newcomer. As a rookie, Ewing started at the very bottom of the Cincinnati pay list. His first major league contract called for a salary of $1,800.[40]

At the other end of the scale, Frank "Noodles" Hahn, the National League's premier left-hander, was pulling down more than $4,000. In 1901, Hahn had won 22 games for a last-place team. He completed 41 of 42 starts, pitching 375 innings. He also led the league with 239 strikeouts. In the winter of 1901-02, a player of Hahn's stature was in a strong position in contract negotiations. For the first time since the demise of the Players League and the dissolution of the American Association in rapid succession in 1890-91, the National League had serious competition. More than a year after declaring itself a major league, the American League continued busily recruiting and signing National League talent. While American League president Ban Johnson officially eschewed the signing of "contract jumpers," he claimed the right to make competitive offers to National League players once their contracts had expired. In other words, any player bound to his National League team only by the reserve clause was considered fair game.[41] The Reds initially offered Hahn $3,500. He held out for $3,600 and they eventually acquiesced. But Hahn balked at signing, having by then reportedly received an offer of $4,000 from the American League. The Reds, faced with a choice of either topping that offer or losing their star pitcher, finally agreed to a figure variously reported at $4,100 or $4,200.[42] Under these "wartime" conditions, the Reds' payroll increased by more than 60 percent from 1900 to 1902.[43]

In this atmosphere, even Ewing might have been able to make a better deal had he been willing to push his contract talks beyond a few minutes of friendly conversation. Other National League clubs were interested in him and it couldn't have been too difficult to stir up a little American League interest, too. On the other hand, $1,800 was a considerable sum of money in 1902—more than three times the income of the average American worker.[44] And Ewing had made it clear that he preferred to play close to home.[45]

Cincinnati was the place for him.

ENDNOTES

1   Henry Chadwick, ed., *Spalding's Official Baseball Guide, 1904* (New York: American Sports Publishing Co., 1904), p. 79.

2   Even so, the height and construction of pitcher's mounds varied widely from ballpark to ballpark. There was no rule mandating a standard height for mounds until 1950. See Peter Morris, *Level Playing Fields: How the Groundskeeping Murphy Brothers Shaped Baseball* (Lincoln, Neb.: University of Nebraska Press, 2007), pp. 57-59.

3   Bill James, *The New Bill James Historical Baseball Abstract* (New York: The Free Press, 2001), p. 72.

4   Chadwick, *op. cit.*, p. 101.

5   Rev. W.A. "Billy" Sunday, "All-America Baseball Team," *Collier's* (October 1908), in Tom Meany, ed., *Collier's Greatest Sports Stories* (New York: A.S. Barnes and Co., 1955), p. 40.

6   Christy Mathewson, *Pitching in a Pinch, or Baseball from the Inside* (New York: Stein and Day, 1977 edition of 1912 original), p. 287.

7   The term "inside baseball" may have first appeared in *Sporting Life,* April 26, 1902. See Paul Dickson, *The Dickson Baseball Dictionary* (New York: Facts on File, 1989), p. 221.

8   Harold Seymour and Dorothy Seymour Mills, *Baseball: The Golden Age* (New York: Oxford University Press, 1971), p. 94.

9   *Ibid.* See also Dickson, *op. cit.*

10 John J. McGraw, *My 30 Years in Baseball* (New York: Arno Press, 1974 edition of 1923 original), p. 14.

11 *Sporting Life,* June 27, 1908.

12 Chadwick, *op. cit.*, p. 101.

13 Sunday, *op. cit.*

14 John J. Evers and Hugh S. Fullerton, *Touching Second: The Science of Baseball* (Chicago: Reilly and Britton Co., 1910), p. 156.

15 *Ibid.*, p. 154.

16 Steven A. Riess, *Touching Base: Professional Baseball and American Culture in the Progressive Era* (Westport, Conn.: Greenwood Press, 1980), p. 13.

17 *Ibid.*, p. 7.

18 Evers and Fullerton, *op. cit.*, p. 25.

19 *Ibid.,* p. 41.

20 Lawrence S. Ritter, *The Glory of Their Times: The Story of the Early Days of Baseball Told by the Men Who Played It* (New York: Macmillan Co., 1966), p. 51.

21 *Cincinnati Commercial Tribune,* May 26, 1904.

22 Riess, *op. cit.,* p. 7.

23 Dick Clark and Larry Lester, *The Negro Leagues Book* (Cleveland: Society for American Baseball Research, 1994), pp. 15-17.

24 John Bowman and Joel Zoss, *Diamonds in the Rough: The Untold History of Baseball* (New York: Macmillan Publishing Co., 1989), p. 122.

25 The origins of Bob Ewing's family haven't been systematically traced. Most Ewings in the United States are of English or Scotch-Irish ancestry.

26 *Reach's Official Baseball Guide for 1897* (Philadelphia: A.J. Reach Co., 1897), pp. 104-05.

27 Syndicated article, source not identified, *The Lima News,* June 29, 1905.

28 James, *op. cit.,* p. 95.

29 Origin of the nickname hasn't been systematically traced, but the first place the author has seen "Long Bob" was in the *Kansas City Star,* Sept. 3, 1901. After that, it quickly started popping up everywhere – the *Cincinnati Enquirer,* Oct. 19, 1901; the *Lima Times-Democrat,* Oct. 21, 1901; *The Sporting News,* Oct. 26, 1901, in a dispatch dated Oct. 21; and the *Shelby County Democrat,* Oct. 25, 1901.

30 David W. Anderson, *More than Merkle: A History of the Best and Most Exciting Baseball Season in Human History* (Lincoln, Neb.: University of Nebraska Press, 2000), p. 57.

31 The 1904 New York Giants were declared to live up to their name after it was calculated that they averaged 5-feet-10 and 171 pounds; *Sporting Life,* April 23, 1904. Bill James found that the regulars on the 1906 Chicago Cubs, who won 116 games, averaged 5-feet-9 and 174 pounds, and that there was "a consistent increase" in players' size throughout the 20th century; James, *The Politics of Glory: How Baseball's Hall of Fame Really Works* (New York: Macmillan Publishing Co., 1994), p. 239.

32 Benjamin G. Rader, *Baseball: A History of America's Game* (Urbana, Ill.: University of Illinois Press, 1994), p. 89.

33 *The Sporting News,* Oct. 26, 1901.

34 *Sporting Life,* April 15, 1905. Like much of his advance publicity, Overall's height was exaggerated: At 6-2 and 215 pounds, he was only half an inch taller than Ewing, though considerably heavier.

35 Evers and Fullerton, *op. cit.,* p. 100.

36 Chadwick, *op. cit.,* pp. 79-81.

37 *The Sporting News,* April 12, 1902. Scott, a 6-foot-3 right-hander, had a 17-20 record with the Reds in 1900, his only full season in the major leagues.

38 *Cincinnati Times-Star,* April 21, 1902.

39 *Cincinnati Enquirer,* Oct. 21, 1901.

40 *Sporting Life,* Aug. 23, 1902. In terms of purchasing power, Ewing's $1,800 salary for six months' work in 1902 would have been the equivalent of more than $48,000 in 2011.

41 Eugene C. Murdock, *Ban Johnson: Czar of Baseball* (Westport, Conn.: Greenwood Press, 1982), pp. 47-48.

42 *The Sporting News,* Nov. 16, 1901; *Sporting Life,* Aug. 23, 1902.

43 For comparison, see figures in *The Sporting News,* March 2, 1901, and *Sporting Life,* Aug. 23, 1902.

44 Scott Derks, ed., *The Value of a Dollar: Prices and Incomes in the United States, 1860-1999* (Lakeville, Conn.: Grey House Publishing, 1999), p. 52.

45 *Shelby County Democrat,* Oct. 25, 1901.

CHAPTER 4

Playing the Palace

CINCINNATI, perched on a bend in the Ohio River, had become in the 19th century an important terminus of western migration. The self-styled Queen City of the West had also become an early center of the meatpacking industry, "the nation's premier hog-slaughterer and supplier of cured hams."[2] In Bob Ewing's day, Cincinnati was still nicknamed Porkville or Porkopolis, and the ballclub the Porkers or Porkopolitans.

In 1902 Cincinnati, with just over 325,000 people, was the second-smallest city in the National League. Though the population increased by nearly 12 percent over the next several years, Cincinnati would be outstripped by Pittsburgh and by 1910 would be by far the smallest city in the league. But no city had a longer or more vigorous history in baseball. Cincinnati was home to the first all-professional nine, the illustrious 1869 Red Stockings, and was a charter member of the National League. Expelled from the league in 1881 for refusing to give up Sunday ball and beer sales at the ballpark, Cincinnati spent nearly a decade in exile in the American Association—otherwise known as the Beer and Whiskey League—before returning to the fold in 1890.

Beer was part of the culture in heavily German Cincinnati. German immigrants and German-Americans made up the largest identifiable segment of the population. The city had dozens of German labor unions, social organizations, cultural associations and charitable societies, extensive German-language instruction in the public schools, two major German-language newspapers—and 26 breweries, producing 1.4 million barrels of beer annually.[3] In the 1890s, it has been calculated that Cincinnati had one saloon for every 37 adult males, and the city's per capita beer consumption was 2½ times the national average.[4]

Nowhere was a ballclub more representative of its community. So many players of German ancestry performed for the Reds that they were sometimes called the Heinies.

"Where in the world does the Cincinnati club get these fellows with the funny names?" asked former National League manager Tom Loftus. "When I look at a scorecard in Cincinnati, I always feel as if I was looking over a brewery payroll. They get more Steins, Bachs, Stimmels, Gueses, Peitzes, and other noodle soup names on the scorecard here than any other town in the world."[5]

Much of the team's talent was homegrown, or at least harvested nearby. Throughout the dead ball era, Cincinnati was fertile ground for baseball ability. Only St. Louis produced slightly more major leaguers relative to population, with Cincinnati and Cleveland in a virtual dead heat for second place.[6] Ewing, though not a native, typified the regional nature of the team's scouting. Over his eight years with the Reds, 25 percent of all spots in the Opening Day lineup were occupied by players born within 100 miles of Cincinnati's League Park—18 percent by players born within 35 miles.

Ewing's first major league manager was John Alexander "Bid" McPhee. McPhee was an institution in Cincinnati. He had played second base for the Reds, first in the American Association and then in the National League, from 1882 to 1899. The major leagues' last barehanded infielder—a choice that enabled him to catch and throw with either hand—he never wore a glove until 1896, when forced to do so because of an injury. Even without a glove, he was the finest second baseman of the 19th century; when he finally put one on, he established a record for fielding percentage at his position that stood for more than 20 years.

In contrast to many of his contemporaries, McPhee was "sober and sedate, always in prime physical condition."[7] His personal dignity shone through when he announced his retirement as a player, after batting .279 at age 39. Fans begged him to stay on, but McPhee stuck to his decision.

"I know what I'm doing," he said. "The fans are never going to have a chance to urge that I be benched, or traded, or asked to retire. I'm going out while I can still play ball."[8]

Having played through one of baseball's most rough-and-tumble eras, McPhee was proud of the fact that he had never been ejected from a game.

Going into the 1902 season, McPhee's first concern was merely to lift the team out of last place. He didn't expect a lot more.

"There is nothing for us to do but hustle and hope," he said.[9] Beyond that, the best the writers could distill from McPhee's pre-season comments was a rather lukewarm pledge that "the Reds would certainly do the very best they know how."[10]

McPhee was eager to go south for a good look at his prospects, but that decision was out of his hands. Though the Reds had worked themselves into shape in New Orleans as recently as 1900, owner John T. Brush had lately found it convenient, and financially advantageous, to align himself with those who believed it more beneficial for players to do their training at home.

Such views were not uncommon in the first years of the 20th century. Some critics maintained that southern trips served only to increase susceptibility to colds and charley horses when players returned to their chilly home cities. Others cited the dangers of malaria, which was said to be prevalent "in all the southern latitudes." Then there was the tendency of ballplayers to regard a spring junket as merely an excuse for all manner of overindulgence, from gambling to late hours to liquor.[11] Brush, still rebuilding after his 1900 grandstand fire, was only too glad to join the chorus.

"I see no reason why it is not possible to get into shape in the same climate in which you have to play your games," he informed one reporter.[12] To another, he added, "I do not believe in the New Orleans idea. There is a great deal in the Crescent City to draw the players away from the work of preparation."[13]

The Reds were ordered to report to League Park on April 1, just 2½ weeks before Opening Day. The deadline came and went with snow on the ground as the players straggled into town. A week later, there had been little opportunity to work out. When the players did get onto the field, they went through their drills with an air of grim resignation. None of the pitchers got much work, but Ewing and another right-hander, Clarence Currie, emerged as the most promising newcomers. When Long Bob breezed through an outing against the minor league Columbus Senators, facing only nine men in three innings, the *Cincinnati Commercial Tribune* concluded, "Ewing, the Reds' new pitcher, seems to be the real article."[14]

As the season approached, Ewing remained in the dark as to when he would get his first test in major league competition. The notion of a fixed pitching rotation wouldn't begin to take hold until after Ewing retired; for now, if McPhee had laid any plans, he was keeping them to himself.[15] Right up to Opening Day, April 17, the morning papers were speculating about who would draw the pitching assignment that afternoon against the Chicago Cubs.

With veterans Noodles Hahn and Bill Phillips slow to round into shape in the cold weather, McPhee decided to entrust the first three games of the season to youngsters. First out of the box was Len Swormstedt, a 23-year-old right-hander who, like Ewing, had pitched in the Western League in 1901 before showing up well in a late-season tryout with the Reds. Swormstedt was also a Cincinnati native, a product of the Hilltops[16]—local code for the city's more affluent neighborhoods.

At 12:30 p.m. on the big day, the Reds and Cubs, in full uniform, boarded special trolley cars at Fountain Square and were paraded through downtown Cincinnati for an hour behind a marching band before heading out to the ballpark for a pre-game concert and a speech by a local judge. Once the game started, the Cubs experienced little difficulty with Swormstedt. Finding him "easy meat,"[17] the visitors pounded out 11 hits and walked off with an effortless 6–1 victory.

Next up was Martin Glendon. He had won 21 games the previous year in the Pacific Northwest League. He was 25, to all appearances "full of sassafras, tea and ginger" and, in the words of writer Ren Mulford, wanted nothing in the world except a chance to "make Frank Hahn look like counterfeit money."[18] Glendon got through two innings against the Cubs. Then, in the third, he surrendered four hits, walked a batter and made a critical throwing error. Five runs crossed the plate, Chicago was on its way to a 5–2 triumph and Glendon's day was finished.

One of the local papers published a rather unflattering review of Glendon's work and he "took the joshing very much to heart."[19] Within 48 hours—and without a word to McPhee—Glendon caught a train for the West Coast, where he soon resurfaced with the San Francisco club of the

California League. Technically he was jumping his contract and the Reds could have raised a howl, but they released him without a murmur.

"If Martin Glendon's backbone is tinted with ochre, then Cincinnati is fortunate in his going," Mulford wrote.[20]

That is how things stood on April 19, 1902. The Reds had taken the field twice behind two inexperienced pitchers, "and before the season was two days old they had both eyes beautifully blacked."[21] It was at this gloomy juncture, five days before his 29th birthday, that Bob Ewing was tapped to make his major league debut. The weather was still frosty and although it was a Saturday afternoon, the crowd for the third game of the Reds-Cubs series was a fraction of the estimated 10,000 who had turned out Thursday for the opener.

The Cubs had finished sixth in 1901 and were a team in transition. New manager Frank Selee was systematically assembling the club that would dominate the National League through the second half of the decade. But most of those players had not yet established themselves in April 1902. Of those who would be mainstays of the Chicago dynasty in the years to come, the lineup facing Ewing included only center fielder Jimmy Slagle, Frank Chance behind the plate and rookie shortstop Joe Tinker, who had made his debut two days earlier when the Cubs' only double play went Tinker to Lowe to O'Hagen. On the mound for Chicago was right-hander Jim Gardner, known as Barrister Jim because he practiced law in the off-season. Though he was 15 months younger than Ewing, Gardner had been in and out of the National League since 1895; the Commercial Tribune dismissed him as "a pitcher who was supposed to have been placed on the retired list some years ago."[22]

Ewing's day started off well enough. He walked Slagle leading off, but fanned Dakin Miller, his old Kansas City teammate, on a 3–2 pitch. Then he struck out Charlie Dexter and got Germany Schaefer on a ground ball to shortstop. The Cubs went out in order in the second inning and also in the third, and when Ewing retired Miller again to open the fourth, he had set down 10 batters in a row. Meanwhile, the Reds had scored twice in the first inning and held a 2–0 lead.

Then everything went wrong. Suddenly Ewing "could not have pitched the ball over a washtub, much less the regulation-size home plate."[23] He walked Dexter and Schaefer. Chance popped up for the second out of the inning, but Ewing walked Bobby Lowe to load the bases and ran the count full on Hal O'Hagen. On the next pitch, O'Hagen "stooped like a hunchback"[24] and umpire Bob Emslie called ball four, forcing home a run. From the sidelines, Chicago's Jack Taylor "kept up a running fire of caustic shots" at the struggling pitcher.[25] The Reds infielders and catcher Bill Bergen countered with shouts of encouragement, but Ewing couldn't find the strike zone. The ball was moving all over the place on him. He walked Tinker on four pitches, forcing in another run and tying the score.

Gardner, the opposing pitcher, finally saw a pitch to hit and lifted a tantalizing little looper over first base. It fell for a single, scoring two more runs. Ewing delivered three balls to Slagle, then uncorked a wild pitch, sending him to first base while Tinker scampered home from third. After a passed ball moved the runners to second and third, Miller walked to once again load the bases. But Dexter grounded into a force play, finally bringing the nightmare inning to a close.

All told, Ewing had allowed five runs on just one hit. He had tied an ignominious National League record by walking seven batters in a single inning.[26] McPhee wondered whether the rookie had had enough and asked if he wanted to come out of the game. No, Ewing replied, he was fine and would just as soon go on.[27]

As suddenly as Ewing's control had deserted him, it returned. The Cubs went out one-two-three in the fifth inning. They added another run in the sixth on a walk, two infield outs and an error, but Ewing held steady and the Reds battled back. Ewing doubled and scored in the fifth, and the Reds came within a foot of tying the game in the seventh when Erve Beck lined into an inning-ending double play. After eight innings, Chicago led 6–4. Ewing had still given up only one hit.

But he had thrown a lot of pitches. In the last inning, the Cubs got to him for four hits and three runs. The final score was 9–5.

In his first game with the Reds, Ewing had surrendered nine runs, walked 10 batters and thrown a wild pitch. At the end of the day, Cincinnati was in last place with an 0–3 record. But the newspapers, usually unforgiving toward players who failed to measure up, were encouraged, even pleased, by his performance. True, the *Cincinnati Times-Star* acknowledged that Ewing's walk total amounted to "an alarming bunch."[28] The *Enquirer,* bemoaning Ewing's generosity to the Cubs, dubbed him "the new Santa Claus at the slab."[29] But McPhee defended his pitcher, asserting that if he had gotten the third strike call he should've gotten on O'Hagen in the fourth, he would have been out of the inning without a run scored.[30]

"Ewing proved to me today that he can pitch," McPhee said. "Cut out that fourth inning, when he could not locate the plate, and he did splendid work. Ewing had good control during the exhibition season, but he was not letting his arm out then. He cut loose today and the result was that his fastball was taking all kinds of shoots."[31]

All things considered, the *Commercial Tribune* pronounced Ewing "some pumpkins as a pitcher."[32] J. Ed Grillo, writing in *The Sporting News*, dismissed Ewing's wildness as understandable and declared, "He showed … that he is a great pitcher."[33]

Well, maybe someday. For now, Ewing was an apprentice pitcher with a lot to learn. He got some rough handling in his next two starts and endured more bouts of wildness. The team staggered. As the deadline neared for cutting down to the 16-man roster limit, the Reds shipped Swormstedt and another Cincinnati native, left-hander Crese Heismann, back to the minor leagues. But McPhee didn't lose faith in Ewing. The manager liked the way Ewing had kept his head in the midst of disaster against the Cubs. Maybe the manager also saw something of himself in Ewing's quiet manner and gentlemanly demeanor.

On May 15, Cincinnati had a 7–16 record and was mired in seventh place. Ewing was 0–3; in three starts, he had been charged with 27 hits, 22 walks and 26 runs. That morning, the Reds released pitcher Archie Stimmel, who had been a regular starter for half of the 1901 season. Then McPhee sent Ewing out to face the visiting Philadelphia Phillies. This time Ewing scattered seven hits and contributed to Cincinnati's offense with a run-scoring single. The fact that he issued six more walks went almost unnoticed as the Reds won 8–4.

Having at last "broke[n] into the society of winners,"[34] Ewing could relax a bit. The next day he was an interested spectator at one of the big events of Cincinnati's 1902 season—the official dedication of the ornate new grandstand that had been built to replace the one that burned in 1900. In the interim, the Reds had continued to play on the same grounds, home to professional baseball in the city since 1884. After the fire, the playing field had been temporarily turned around, home plate situated in right field so the surviving outfield pavilion could serve as the main grandstand.

The new grandstand, under construction for more than a year, had been in use since Opening Day, but work was still being completed. Built at a cost of more than $35,000[35]—equal to about 80 percent of the Reds' payroll for 1902—the stand was the second in the major leagues constructed of concrete and steel and was said to be absolutely fireproof.[36] It was the first to make a conscious attempt at architectural style. Inspired by the neoclassical architecture of the 1893 Chicago World's Fair, the reconfigured ballpark now featured an elaborate arch over the main entrance off Findlay Street. Inside, the roof of the grandstand was supported by 22 hand-carved Corinthian columns, topped in the center by a peaked cornice looking out to center field with *CINCINNATI* chiseled into its glowing white face. Directly behind home plate and extending toward first and third bases were 19 "fashion boxes," filled for the occasion with Queen City society and visiting dignitaries. Sportswriters had christened the new grandstand the Palace of the Fans.[37]

Ren Mulford deemed the Palace "the most magnificent edifice ever dedicated to baseball" and likened it to the Colosseum in Rome.[38] Judge Howard Ferris, in his pre-game oration, evoked instead the ancient ruins of Athens, with one important difference: "The ravages of time," he predicted, "will make little or no change in the buildings that are now dedicated to the national sport."[39] Other observers were more restrained, but even *The Sporting News* acknowledged that Cincinnati now offered "the handsomest and most comfortable accommodations" any ballclub had ever provided for its patrons.[40]

Even with the opening of the Palace of the Fans, seating capacity at League Park[41] was less than 10,000. Before the 1903 season, concrete "wings" would be added onto the grandstand; with the surviving bleachers and pavilion, that would push the total number of seats to around 12,000.[42] The best seat in the house cost $1; the "sun gods" in the bleachers could see the game for 25 cents. For hard-core fans, 50 cents would secure a place on a wooden bench under the grandstand at ground level, along what was known as Rooters Row.[43] Beers were 12 for a dollar[44] and the rooters were close enough to the field to exchange pleasantries—or unpleasantries—with the players, separated only by a three-foot wall and a chicken wire screen.

Dedicated in May 1902, the Palace of the Fans boasted "the handsomest and most comfortable accommodations" ever provided for baseball fans. The roof garden boxes on either side of the central cornice were a later addition. *Photo: Cincinnati Historical Society Library.*

While the paying customers were assiduously catered to, the hired help received no such coddling. Players still sat on bare benches out in the open; covered, in-ground dugouts would begin to appear around the league later in the decade.[45] The Reds' new clubhouse, under the stands, was a cramped, damp, concrete box that inspired considerable grumbling before it was replaced the following year with "a picturesque little cottage" offering a choice of baths—plunge, shower or steam—plus a lounge for reading or smoking.[46] No such amenities were yet provided for visiting players. They had to dress at their downtown hotel and ride two miles or more to the ballpark, typically in open wagons, running the risk of being pelted with fruit by small boys on the way to work and abused by hostile fans on the way back. When the new visitors' clubhouse was opened in 1907, Pittsburgh manager Fred Clarke expressed appreciation, saying his players were particularly grateful to "escape the long ride through the streets, especially after a game."[47]

Five thousand people came out for the dedication of the Palace of the Fans. Those close enough to hear listened to the pre-game speeches, then all watched as the New York Giants scored five times in the ninth inning to beat Noodles Hahn 5–3. The ballpark was a grand success but the team, 13 games out of first place after only a month of play, was starting to look like "a great disappointment."[48]

The Reds spent the first six weeks of the season getting accustomed to their renovated ballpark. The schedule included quick forays to Pittsburgh, Chicago and St. Louis, but McPhee's charges played three-quarters of their games at home. Ewing had plenty of time to settle into his new life as a big league ballplayer. Then, in early June, the club left on its first protracted road trip—a two-week tour of Boston, New York and Philadelphia.

Ewing had never seen the East before and the trip was an eye-opener. He passed up the steamed Duxbury clams at the Quincy House in Boston but plunged eagerly into other new experiences, including a ride on the nation's first subway, opened in Boston less than five years earlier. As the train clattered along beneath the streets, propelled by "pent-up lightning,"[49] Charles Webb Murphy of the *Cincinnati Times-Star* triggered a brief commotion by suddenly shouting, "Oh, look at the cow on the track!"[50]

Along Broadway in New York, many of the players bought stylish Panama hats "right from Ecuador."[51] Ewing saw all the sights—Grant's tomb,

Central Park, the aquarium in Battery Park, and the Metropolitan Museum of Art. At the Hall of Fame for Great Americans in the Bronx, dedicated just a year before, he strolled the 630-foot open-air colonnade, designed by architect Stanford White. Looking around a lavish theater with plush carpets and tiers of private boxes ornamented with gold leaf, Clarence Currie—another first-timer in the big city—allowed that this was considerably more impressive than the town hall in Appleton, Wisconsin.

"It also has the Valentine, at Toledo, beaten a few blocks," Ewing replied, recalling an impressive theater in that city.[52]

Ewing pitched well on the trip, winning back-to-back starts in Philadelphia and New York. With some help, he was beginning to get comfortable. Ewing had been teamed in most of his early outings with catcher Bill Bergen. Bergen was an outstanding receiver with an exceptional arm. His skills behind the plate were so greatly prized that they kept him in the National League for 11 years and nearly 950 games—this despite the fact that Bergen was one of the worst hitters ever, with a lifetime batting average of .170. But it was becoming obvious that Ewing worked more effectively with the Reds' No. 2 catcher, Heinie Peitz. Just two years older than Ewing, Peitz had been in the league for a decade. In St. Louis in the early 1890s, he had formed the famous "pretzel battery" with pitcher Ted Breitenstein. Peitz came to Cincinnati in 1896 in a five-player trade—the franchise's first such blockbuster deal.[53]

The German Baron, as Peitz was known, was a native of St. Louis, a graduate of the Goose Hill neighborhood on the city's north side that had produced such rough-and-ready ballplayers as Scrappy Bill Joyce, Rowdy Jack O'Connor and the Tebeau brothers, George and Patsy.[54] Peitz, it was said, "possesses neither polish nor intellectuality."[55] On the field, he was brainy and bold and "not overscrupulous about the tactics he employed."[56] He was also a merciless bench jockey who was frequently mentioned by name when complaints were raised about the ungentlemanly practice of noisy base coaching, the kind intended mainly to rattle the opposing pitcher.

Temperamentally, Ewing and Peitz might have been something of an odd couple. On the other hand, Peitz had been one of Ewing's earliest boosters, going back to the exhibition game in Sidney. For all his lack of refinement, Peitz was a man of "rare good nature"[57] and he knew baseball "in all its phases, its tricks and its fine points." He was a master "in finding

Catcher Heinie Peitz, "the German Baron," was Bob Ewing's temperamental opposite, but they quickly formed an effective battery and became lifelong friends. Peitz had a reputation for getting the best out of young pitchers. *Photo: Chicago Historical Society, SDN-003037.*

the flaws in a batsman and in steadying a pitcher."[58] With the Reds, Peitz had been behind the plate for two no-hit games. He had a particular reputation for "jollying" young pitchers—that is, gently bringing them along and coaxing the best out of them. In the opinion of Ren Mulford, "a man of better judgment never stood behind a young pitcher."[59]

Ewing's control problems virtually vanished once he began working regularly with Peitz, and he began to attract good notices. *Sporting Life*, rather cautiously, listed him among the promising rookies of the year. After the Reds returned from their eastern trip, Ewing found a hero's welcome waiting for him when, on June 27, the club took advantage of an open date on the schedule to book another exhibition in Sidney. Before television or radio, when the only way to experience a ballgame was to see it in person, such appearances were a way for major league teams to generate fan interest in outlying areas. Exhibitions also provided safe opportunities to try out new prospects or to test the progress of players recovering from injuries. Above all, Cincinnati business manager Frank Bancroft was a great believer in never letting players lie idle when there was a chance to make a few dollars. Bancroft was particularly alert for any opportunity to take the team to a player's hometown or anywhere there might be a connection that would assure a good turnout.

For a small community like Sidney, a visit by a big league baseball team was like the day the circus came to town. With Ewing's triumphs the previous fall with the local team still fresh in memory, enthusiasm for his return ran high. When the Reds arrived, they found a great streamer across the front of the Wagner House hotel proclaiming "Ewing Day at the Ball Park." Businesses closed for the afternoon and Sidney "put on a carnival appearance."[60] Fans came by rail and carriage from 35 miles around. Among the sizable delegation from New Hampshire were Ewing's parents, his brother and sister, "and a hundred and one other relatives."[61]

"Ewing … was a bigger man than President Roosevelt for the time being," wrote Fred J. Hewitt in the *Cincinnati Post*. "… He was it, with a capital 'I,' and the rest of the Red outfit were not given a thought. The town baker made Ewing pies, the bartenders served Ewing highballs, while the ladies visited the soda water fountains and called for a Ewing flip."[62]

At the ballpark beside the Great Miami River, where Ewing had held the Reds to a 3–3 tie barely eight months earlier, the grandstand was filled an hour before game time and the crowd of 2,000 spilled onto the field. The throng "gave Ewing the glad hand," but once the game started, they rooted for the hometown boys to beat him.[63] That wasn't going to happen. It soon became evident that the only pitch the home team could hit was Ewing's change-up. Sidney, "attacked by the rattles,"[64] gave away three early runs and Cincinnati soon had a comfortable 5–0 lead.

Ewing didn't completely stifle his old mates. He passed out eight hits and Sidney broke the shutout in the eighth inning, when Harry Eichler tripled over the head of Clarence Currie in left field and scored on Pete Garvey's slow roller to shortstop. The Reds won the contest 6–1 but the crowd went away happy, the home team having preserved its record of not having been held scoreless all season. The game took just 68 minutes and an hour later the Reds were on a train back to Cincinnati. Ewing was given permission to remain behind "to participate in the evening's celebration in his honor."[65]

In Cincinnati, there wasn't much to celebrate. The Reds were barely hanging onto sixth place. Team captain Tommy Corcoran was said to be aloof and uncommunicative with his teammates. Individually, the players were "all good fellows," the *Post* acknowledged, but "the combinations are bad, and the team does not work well together."[66] Disgruntled fans were walking out in the middle of games. Even Bid McPhee was getting fed up. After more than a month of speculation about his future, McPhee resigned. He had been "an honor to his profession"[67] for more than two decades. But on July 11, he handed the club over to Frank Bancroft and retired to look after his "extensive mining interests" in the West.[68] *The Sporting News* regretted McPhee's passing from the scene, but at the same time pronounced him "a managerial failure" who should have stepped down sooner. In the end, the newspaper sniped, "He thought more of the salary than his professional reputation."[69]

McPhee subsequently did some scouting for the Reds for a few years, but got out of baseball altogether after 1909.

While King Bid's resignation made headlines, events were taking place behind the scenes that would have an even more dramatic impact on baseball in Cincinnati. Three ambitious men were looking to change their circumstances. In New York, Andrew Freedman, the contentious owner of the Giants, was looking to get out of baseball after a string of losing seasons both on and off the field. In Baltimore, John J. McGraw, the pugnacious player-manager of the Orioles, was looking to get out from under the thumb of Ban Johnson, the strait-laced president of the American League. And in Cincinnati, John T. Brush, the Reds' unpopular absentee owner, was looking for a more lucrative market in which to pursue his baseball aspirations. When the three got together, the results would alter the game's economic and competitive balance of power for the rest of Bob Ewing's career and beyond.

McGraw had come up through a rough school in baseball. He had played for the old Orioles in the 1890s, when they dominated the National League through a combination of speed, brains and intimidation. In the American League, it was inevitable that McGraw's umpire baiting and take-no-prisoners tactics should bring him into conflict with the equally strong-willed Johnson, who was determined to purge his new organization of rowdyism. By mid-1902 McGraw was ready for a change of scenery. In fact, he was under suspension by Johnson when it was announced on July 9 that he had signed to return to the National League as manager of the New York Giants at a salary of $10,000 a year.

McGraw next had to get free of Baltimore and secure some players to build up his new team, which was currently in last place. McGraw, who was also part-owner of the Orioles, arranged a transfer of his stock, along with that owned by outfielder Joe Kelley, to local politician John J. "Sonny" Mahon, another part-owner who was also Kelley's father-in-law. This gave Mahon a majority of Baltimore's stock, which he promptly sold to Andrew Freedman. Freedman in turn released McGraw and most of Baltimore's top players. Joe McGinnity, Jack Cronin, Dan McGann and Roger Bresnahan followed McGraw to New York. John T. Brush, an old ally of Freedman's in league politics and long a minority stockholder in the Giants, also received a share of the spoils: He signed Kelley, who was rewarded with the manager's job in Cincinnati, and outfielder Cy Seymour.

Having successfully gutted the Baltimore franchise, Freedman and Brush carried out the final steps of the plot. Brush sold the Reds to a group of local investors and stepped into a new role as "managing director" of the Giants; before season's end, he formally ascended to the presidency of the New York club and Freedman was off on a well-earned European vacation.

Kelley and Seymour strengthened the Reds considerably. Kelley, who would play left field and also relieve Corcoran of the captain's duties, was another old Oriole who had hit over .360 four straight years during the team's glory days. The son of Irish immigrants born Joseph James Kelly, he had been awarded the second "e"—viewed as a sign of higher social status—by sportswriters in Baltimore, and he decided to keep it. Kelley was regarded as a fine figure of a man, and was vain enough about his appearance to carry a mirror in his pocket on the field. James Bentley Seymour, who would take over in center, was an erratic talent whose career presaged, on a smaller scale, that of Babe Ruth: Like Ruth, Seymour batted and threw left-handed, and ate and drank with both fists. Also like the Bambino, he was a converted pitcher—a 25-game winner for the Giants in 1898—who became, for a time, the preeminent slugger in the game.

Not long after Kelley and Seymour joined the team, another ex-Oriole also came aboard. Mike Donlin—known, because of his strutting manner, as Turkey Mike—was a hard hitter and a hard drinker, in his own words a guy who "could get into trouble easier than the man who invented it."[70] Already, at 24, he trailed a long record of "rowdy acts upon the field and nasty brawls in private";[71] a knife scar running from his left cheek down to his jaw was a souvenir of one such episode. Donlin had signed a Cincinnati contract while sitting in a Baltimore jail, where he was serving six months for beating up a chorus girl on the street. *Sporting Life* called for his banishment from baseball and *The Sporting News* said any club that took him in "should be boycotted by decent people."[72] But Donlin had batted .340 for Baltimore in 1901 and Reds fans were inclined to be forgiving. While his signing stirred some unfavorable comment, J. Ed Grillo wrote at the time, "most of the patrons of the game seemed to think that Donlin is a good player and his present [jail] experience will do much to make him a good boy."[73]

The greatest rejoicing in Cincinnati, however, was over the club's change in ownership. Brush had operated the Reds since 1891 but had continued to live in Indianapolis, where he owned a clothing store and for several years ran a minor league team. It was said he expected a report of the Reds' daily gate receipts as soon as they were counted, but was content to wait and read the result of the game in the next day's paper. Critics accused him of busily promoting his other baseball interests while turning Cincinnati into "a baseball cemetery."[74] In 1900, after the Giants withdrew a $2,000 offer to buy a minor league pitcher they had borrowed for a tryout, Brush drafted the same player for $100 and traded him back to New York. As their end of the deal, the Reds received Amos Rusie, the so-called Hoosier Thunderbolt. Rusie had been a big star through the mid-'90s but hadn't pitched in two years as a result of a dispute with Freedman over money. Rusie never won another game and was out of baseball permanently after pitching three times for Cincinnati. The minor leaguer, a 20-year-old college boy named Christy Mathewson, quickly blossomed into a 20-game winner for the Giants. *The Sporting News* denounced Brush for his role in "one of the most questionable transactions within the game's history"[75] and some in the Queen City came to believe he found it "more profitable ... to see New York succeed than Cincinnati."[76]

Brush's sale of the Cincinnati club to a combine of local businessmen and power brokers was widely hailed as a positive development. Francis C. Richter, editor of *Sporting Life,* wrote hopefully of the end of "11 years of alien ownership."[77] While *The Sporting News* discerned in Brush "none of the traits which commend themselves to sportsmen,"[78] it lauded the new owners as "public-spirited gentlemen" motivated solely by civic pride and "a desire to give the patrons a higher grade team than they are accustomed to."[79] News of the sale touched off a night of celebrations with music, bonfires and a long procession of cheering fans through downtown Cincinnati.

But while things were starting to look up for the Reds, Ewing's season was unraveling. Just as he was beginning to find himself as a big league pitcher, he ran into a string of injuries. First he strained a knee and was sent home for several days to rest. A few weeks later he left a game with what was initially reported as an injured hand. In fact, the situation was considerably more serious. Ewing's pitching arm, in the current phrase, had "gone back on him." Ewing had first hurt the arm in Philadelphia in mid-June, but didn't say anything about it for three weeks. The team already had a rash of sore arms, he said later, and in any case, he thought he "had merely taken a little cold."[80] What the rookie pitcher didn't say was that he was probably reluctant to admit that his arm had gone sour, for fear the ballclub might decide he was expendable. When the trouble became known, Ewing and his ailing wing were turned over to Gene Lutz for massage treatments at his "school of physical culture."[81]

For two months, Ewing was in a sort of limbo – still a member of the team but not truly part of it. By the end of July, when Joe Kelley took over from interim manager Frank Bancroft, Ewing had pitched only twice in six weeks. He played some outfield when the team was shorthanded, and was used occasionally as a pinch hitter. Again he was sent home to recuperate. The medical report wasn't promising: "Long Bob Ewing's soup bone is in none too good shape."[82]

Finally on August 3, an open date offered an opportunity to test the progress of his rehabilitation. The Reds had a Sunday afternoon exhibition scheduled against a local team on St. George's cricket grounds in Hoboken, New Jersey. Three thousand people came out to see Ewing matched against Bill "Dummy" Deegan, formerly of the New York Giants. The Hobos quickly jumped on Ewing. As his pitches floated across the plate, the crowd hissed and shouted "fake!" After two innings, the home team led 3–0 and was complaining loudly at the Reds' failure to put up anything like a major league pitcher. Henry Thielman was brought in to pitch and Ewing banished to left field, where his eighth-inning throwing error sealed Cincinnati's 6–5 defeat.

The Reds, who started the game with only three everyday players in their regular positions, took considerable heat in the press for giving a poor account not only of themselves but of National League ball generally. The Cincinnati writers defended Ewing's honor, if not his pitching. He wasn't a malingerer, the *Enquirer* insisted, merely "a broken-down sport."[83] Either way, Ewing's performance had "revealed his absolute helplessness" on the mound. If he had offered up the same stuff against hitters even approaching major league caliber, one witness wrote, "he'd be among the hollyhocks near Wapakoneta today."[84]

Twelve days after "the Hobo farce,"[85] Ewing tried again against an amateur team in Homestead, Pennsylvania. This time both he and the Reds put on a considerably better show. Summoning up an occasional fastball, Ewing went the distance and won 3–2. But most of the time he was still careful and tentative. Two league tests over the following week—pitching relief in losses to Boston and Brooklyn—showed no improvement.

On September 2, having rallied impressively under their new leadership, the Reds nosed into fourth place. Two days later they nudged their record up to .500 for the first time all season. They managed to hold onto both of those tenuous perches at season's end. By then, the sore-armed rookie had cleaned out his locker in the dank little clubhouse under the stands at League Park. On August 30, *Sporting Life* reported that Cincinnati had released pitcher Bob Ewing.

The report was erroneous. In fact the new owners had "paid him in full and sent him back to the farm ... in old Auglaize."[86] Before departing, Ewing had signed a contract for 1903 at what his hometown paper described as "quite an enlarged salary."[87] But the contract offered Ewing no security over the cold winter months: He would collect the "enlarged salary" only if his arm came back to life sufficiently for him to regain his place on the roster in the spring.

As the leaves began to turn in the fall of 1902, his prospects were anything but encouraging.

ENDNOTES

1   *Sporting Life*, May 31, 1902.
2   R. Douglas Hurt, *The Ohio Frontier: Crucible of the Old Northwest, 1720-1830* (Bloomington, Ind.: University of Indiana Press, 1996), p. 354.
3   *Cincinnati Post*, July 20, 2001.
4   Stephen Z. Starr, "Prosit! A Non-Cosmic Tour of the Cincinnati Saloon," in Don Heinrich Tolzmann, ed., *Festschrift for the German-American Tricentennial Jubilee: Cincinnati, 1983* (Cincinnati: Cincinnati Historical Society, 1982), pp. 47-49.
5   *The Sporting News*, Aug. 24, 1901.
6   Steven A. Riess, *Touching Base: Professional Baseball and American Culture in the Progressive Era* (Westport, Conn.: Greenwood Press, 1980), p. 182.
7   A.D. Suehsdorf, "John Alexander McPhee," in Robert L. Tiemann and Mark Rucker, eds., *19th Century Stars* (Kansas City, Mo.: Society for American Baseball Research, 1989), p. 91.
8   Lee Allen, *The Cincinnati Reds: An Informal History* (New York: G.P. Putnam's Sons, 1948), p. 65.
9   *The Sporting News*, Nov. 30, 1901.
10 *Cincinnati Enquirer*, April 17, 1902.
11 Timothy Sharp, *The Sporting News*, Dec. 17, 1904; see also B.F. Wright, *The Sporting News*, Dec. 31, 1904.
12 *Sporting Life*, March 22, 1902.
13 *The Sporting News*, March 8, 1902.
14 *Cincinnati Commercial Tribune*, quoted in *The Sporting News*, April 19, 1902.
15 Teams had experimented with fixed four- and five-man rotations as far back as the 1880s but Frank Vaccaro, after studying the matter, concluded that managers in Ewing's day apparently "used tea leaves and magic dice to pick a pitcher for a day's game." Vaccaro, "Origins of the Pitching Rotation," *The Baseball Research Journal*, Vol. 40, No. 2 (fall 2011), p. 32.
16 *Sporting Life*, Oct. 4, 1902.
17 *Ibid.*, April 26, 1902.
18 *Ibid.*, May 3, 1902.

19 *The Sporting News,* April 26, 1902.

20 *Sporting Life,* May 3, 1902. Glendon pitched minor league and independent ball for several more years. He returned to the majors only briefly, with Cleveland in 1903, winning one game and losing two.

21 *Sporting Life,* April 26, 1902.

22 *Cincinnati Commercial Tribune,* April 20, 1902.

23 *Ibid.*

24 *Cincinnati Enquirer,* April 20, 1902.

25 *Ibid.*

26 Ewing still shares the National League record of seven walks in an inning. The record was set by George Keefe of Washington in 1889 and tied by Tony Mullane of Baltimore in 1894. The major league record was established Aug. 28, 1909, when Washington's Bill "Dolly" Gray walked eight Chicago White Sox, including seven in a row, in the second inning of an American League game. Gray pitched a one-hitter and held Chicago scoreless except for that one inning, but lost the game 6-4. All told, he walked 11. Craig Carter, ed., *Complete Baseball Record Book,* 2003 edition (St. Louis: The Sporting News, 2002), p. 90.

27 *Cincinnati Commercial Tribune,* April 20, 1902.

28 *Cincinnati Times-Star,* April 21, 1902.

29 *Cincinnati Enquirer,* April 20, 1902.

30 *Ibid.*

31 *Cincinnati Commercial Tribune,* April 20, 1902.

32 *Ibid.*

33 *The Sporting News,* April 26, 1902.

34 *Cincinnati Enquirer,* May 16, 1902.

35 *The Sporting News,* Nov. 23, 1901. The 1902 cost of the grandstand was the equivalent of approximately $950,000 in 2011.

36 Note that this claim applied only to the new grandstand, not to the entire ballpark. Philadelphia's Shibe Park, opened in 1909, is generally credited as the major leagues' first all-steel and concrete stadium. See Peter Morris, *Level Playing Fields: How the Groundskeeping Murphy Brothers Shaped Baseball* (Lincoln, Neb.: University of Nebraska Press, 2007), p. 117; and Philip J. Lowry, *Green Cathedrals: The Ultimate Celebration of Major League and Negro League Ballparks* (New York: Walker and Co., 2006), p. 176.

37 The name was established before the grandstand was completed. As early as Sept. 24, 1901, a brief item in *The Sporting News* promised that the new grandstand in Cincinnati would be "a veritable palace for the fans."

38 *Sporting Life,* May 24, 1902. Charles Webb Murphy of the *Cincinnati Times-Star* made the same comparison in an article for the program for the dedication of the new grandstand; see Mark Stallard, ed., *Echoes of Cincinnati Reds Baseball: The Greatest Stories Ever Told* (Chicago: Triumph Books, 2007), p. 159.

39 *Cincinnati Enquirer,* May 17, 1902.

40 *The Sporting News,* May 17, 1902.

41 Modern sources typically refer to the Cincinnati ballpark of 1902-11 as the Palace of the Fans, to differentiate it from earlier configurations of the park on the same site, but contemporary sportswriters applied that name only to the ornate main grandstand. The ballpark itself continued to be called League Park. See for example the *Cincinnati Enquirer,* April 17, 1902: "Chicago's Fledglings will be the opponents of Cincinnati's Redlegs at League Park. ... The Cincinnati boys will leave League Park in a trolley tourist car at 12:30,

meeting the Chicagoans at Fountain Square. ... Until 3 [p.m.] a concert will be given at the Palace of the Fans." Also *Sporting Life*, Jan. 3, 1903: "All the surroundings of the Palace of the Fans will be in keeping with that handsome structure next season. ... As a result of an official inspection of League Park all plans for improvements ... were completed and orders given to rush the work"; and *Sporting Life*, April 25, 1903: "The Palace of the Fans, as the concrete grandstand in Cincinnati is known, has been painted white and green."

42 *Sporting Life,* March 21, 1903.
43 *Ibid.,* April 5, 1902.
44 Allen, *op. cit.,* p. 71.
45 See for instance the *Brooklyn Eagle,* April 13, 1908, commenting on "new-fangled" dugouts; quoted in G.H. Fleming, *The Unforgettable Season* (New York: Holt, Rinehart and Winston, 1981), p. 39.
46 *Sporting Life,* March 21, 1903.
47 *Cincinnati Enquirer,* April 13, 1907.
48 *Sporting Life*, May 24, 1902.
49 *Boston Globe,* Sept. 1, 1897.
50 *Sporting Life,* June 21, 1902.
51 *Ibid.*
52 *Cincinnati Times-Star,* reprinted in *Sporting Life,* April 11, 1903. The Valentine Theater, built at a cost of $300,000 and opened eight months before Ewing joined the Mud Hens – on Christmas Day, 1896 – is still a landmark in downtown Toledo. After a period of decline led to its closing in 1974, the Valentine reopened in 1999 following a $28 million restoration. It is now home to the Toledo Cultural Arts Center.
53 Allen, *op. cit.,* p. 57. The Reds obtained Peitz and pitcher Red Ehret from St. Louis in exchange for pitcher Tom Parrott, catcher Morgan Murphy and third baseman Arlie Latham.
54 A slightly later product of the neighborhood was Ewing's contemporary, infielder (and later manager) James Timothy Burke, sometimes referred to as Goose Hill Jimmy. See *New York American*, June 16, 1919, reprinted in Damon Runyon, edited by Jim Reisler, *Guys, Dolls and Curveballs: Damon Runyon on Baseball* (New York: Carroll and Graf Publishers, 2005), pp. 387 and 392.
55 *The Sporting News,* Dec. 29, 1906.
56 Unidentified newspaper clipping, Dec. 24, 1904, on file in the A. Bartlett Giamatti Research Center at the National Baseball Hall of Fame.
57 *Sporting Life,* Dec. 29, 1906.
58 *The Sporting News,* Dec. 29, 1906.
59 *Sporting Life,* Dec. 29, 1906.
60 *Cincinnati Post,* June 28, 1902.
61 *Ibid.*
62 *Ibid.*
63 *Sidney Daily News,* June 28, 1902.
64 *Cincinnati Enquirer,* June 28, 1902.
65 *Cincinnati Post,* June 28, 1902.
66 *Cincinnati Post,* reprinted in *The Sporting News,* May 24, 1902.
67 *Cincinnati Enquirer,* April 17, 1902.
68 *The Sporting News,* July 19, 1902.
69 *Ibid.*
70 Bill James, *The New Bill James Baseball Abstract* (New York: The Free Press, 2001), p. 757.

71   *Sporting Life,* March 22, 1902.

72   *The Sporting News,* March 22, 1902.

73   *Ibid.,* May 24, 1902.

74   *Ibid.,* July 26, 1902.

75   *Ibid.,* Feb. 20, 1904. Questions have been raised as to whether an actual Mathewson-for-Rusie trade ever took place, but observers at the time took for granted that some sort of *quid pro quo* was involved. See Steven A. King, "Rusie for Mathewson: The Most Famous Trade that Never Happened," *Base Ball: A Journal of the Early Game,* Vol. 6, No. 2 (fall 2012), pp. 83-101.

76   *Ibid.,* Jan. 4, 1902.

77   *Sporting Life,* Aug. 23, 1902.

78   *The Sporting News,* Sept. 27, 1902.

79   *Ibid.,* Nov. 8, 1902.

80   *Ibid.,* Oct. 18, 1902.

81   *Cincinnati Enquirer,* July 12, 1902.

82   *Sporting Life,* July 26, 1902.

83   *Cincinnati Enquirer,* Aug. 4, 1902.

84   *Ibid.*

85   *Sporting Life,* Aug. 16, 1902.

86   *Ibid.,* Feb. 18, 1905.

87   *Auglaize Republican,* Sept. 4, 1902.

"Long Bob hasn't
much *chance* to
stick another year."
—REN MULFORD[1]

CHAPTER 5

Working for the Boss (and Garry)

THE REDS' NEW OWNERS had paid John T. Brush $60,000 in cash and
agreed to assume an additional $90,000 in outstanding debt. The $150,000
total was regarded as far more than the franchise was worth, and the will-
ingness to pay such a price was seen as evidence of the civic-mindedness
of Bob Ewing's new employers. On the other hand, the large outlay might
simply indicate that these were men who had money and were accustomed
to getting what they wanted. To them, it probably seemed only logical that
they should run the ballclub; after all, they already ran the city.

The new men in charge were George Barnesdale Cox, August
Herrmann and brothers Max and Julius Fleischmann. Cox was head of
the local Republican Party machine and Herrmann his right-hand man.
The Fleischmanns were distillers and heirs to the Fleischmann's yeast fortune; Julius was also mayor of Cincinnati. Sportswriters paid obeisance to
the new owners in print by referring to them collectively as the Reds'
Big Four.

By any measure, the biggest of the Big Four was Cox, indisputably the
biggest man in Hamilton County, Ohio. Gruff, cigar-chomping, weighing
in at 225 pounds, Boss Cox was the antithesis of Toledo Mayor Samuel M.
"Golden Rule" Jones. Preoccupied as he was as he worked his way up from
the minor leagues to the majors, Ewing might not have paid much attention

to the political nuances of life in his new city. But if he stopped to consider, he would have recognized that Cox was the very embodiment of everything reformers like Jones were fighting to eliminate.[2] Son of an English immigrant father who died when he was 8, Cox had worked from childhood as a newsboy, bootblack, lookout for a gambling joint and later as deliveryman, tobacco salesman and saloonkeeper. He entered politics in the 1870s and served two terms on city council. But he soon realized he could wield the greatest influence not by holding office himself but by working behind the scenes to determine who would. By the mid-1890s, barely 40 years old, he was the most powerful man in what had become Cincinnati's dominant political party.

The Republicans held power locally through a complicated system of patronage and kickbacks, all sustained by fear, self-interest and a universally accepted "code of honor."[3] Even Cox's detractors acknowledged his good qualities. Wrote one: "He never broke a promise, never went back on a henchman who served him well, and always delivered the promised goods in lucrative city jobs,"[4] of which he controlled some 2,000. Once Cox and his friends took over the Reds, they often provided off-season sinecures for ballplayers. Among the first beneficiaries was Heinie Peitz, who was handed a $3.50-a-day job as "inspector of streets." One wag assured Cincinnatians that if they should happen to see the German Baron "walking with wrinkled brow on some winter day," they must not assume he was loafing: "He will only be inspecting."[5] Peitz bought into the system. He worked on election campaigns, marched in GOP parades, and was soon accounted "a strong man in his ward."[6]

The Cox organization was once commonly denounced as "possibly the most corrupt government that ever infested a municipality."[7] Modern scholars allow that the machine functioned mainly within the law, if barely; one describes a system of "law and order, discriminately applied."[8] One story, though almost certainly apocryphal, was repeated for decades to illustrate how the machine did business. When Cox determined to buy the ballclub, so the story goes, his people went to Brush and named a price. Then they told him that if he didn't accept their offer, they would build a street (or a streetcar line) through the middle of his ballpark.[9] Perhaps the most telling assessment of the machine came from a contemporary observer, muckraking journalist Lincoln Steffens, for whom Cincinnati inspired a wave of repugnance intermingled with a dash of grudging admiration. Under Cox, Steffens wrote, the city was "all one great graft." At the same time, he acknowledged, the Cox machine was "the most perfect thing of its kind in this country."[10]

Whatever else he was, Cox was an able and efficient leader. He found ways to turn enemies into allies and provided effective administration for a fast-growing and increasingly diverse city. When Ewing arrived in Cincinnati, Cox was at the apex of his power. Under his direction, by the early years of the 20th century, Hamilton County's numerous and disciplined Republicans "practically controlled the politics of Ohio."[11]

The job of running the ballclub was delegated to Herrmann. He was the natural choice. The ablest of Cox's lieutenants, he was a first-class administrator and a tireless workhorse with a remarkable head for figures. Grasping facts quickly, making decisions and then moving on, he had a knack for doing several jobs at once. He also possessed a useful talent for ingratiating himself with the press.

The son of German immigrants, Herrmann was born in 1859 in Cincinnati's distinctively German Over-the-Rhine district and lived all his life in or near his old neighborhood. He received little formal education, going to work at age 11 as a printer's devil to help support his widowed mother. According to Herrmann, the shop foreman was determined that the youngster have a nickname. Seeing young August in his father's outsized hand-me-down coat with its brass buttons, the foreman thought something military might fit the bill and initially suggested the appropriately Germanic "Bismarck." Reminded that the shop already had a Bismarck, the foreman decided instead to call Herrmann "Garibaldi," after the Italian soldier and patriot. Herrmann enjoyed the joke as much as anyone. The name was soon shortened to Garry, to which Herrmann happily answered for the rest of his days.

Herrmann started early in politics, winning election to the school board in 1882. He was later appointed assistant clerk of the police court and then a member of the influential board of public works. Ultimately Herrmann became the man who ran city hall for Cox, doling out patronage jobs and acting, in effect, as Cincinnati's first city manager. He also oversaw the collection of campaign funds and served as Cox's ambassador to the German community.

In 1897 Herrmann was tapped to head the commission that was building Cincinnati's new waterworks. The project came to be remembered as his greatest civic achievement. Supporters of the machine pointed out that the system, built for $11 million, was later independently appraised at $20 million;[12] what supporters didn't mention was that the annual operating costs were three times those of a much larger facility in Cleveland.[13] When not occupied with baseball or city government, Herrmann kept busy helping to determine who would get Cox's support for the governorship of Ohio, a seat in the Senate or the Republican nomination for president. U.S. Sen. Joseph B. Foraker, a longtime ally and occasional rival of Cox, complained of having his presidential aspirations derailed when he was "double-crossed by occult methods" engineered by Herrmann.[14]

Damon Runyon, creator and collector of colorful characters, recalled Herrmann as "portly, florid, and very active."[15] He was fond of loud suits and silk underwear, and sported diamond rings on both hands. He was an inveterate joiner who was elected president of the American Bowling Congress and Grand Exalted Ruler of the Benevolent Protective Order of Elks. He gave away $1 cigars by the box, and when he traveled, it was by private Pullman stocked with his favorite sauerkraut, sausage and lager beer. "Happy only in a crowd of boon companions,"[16] he threw legendary parties and always picked up the tab. Herrmann conducted much of his business at Weilert's Over-the-Rhine beer garden and often stayed out socializing and making merry until long after midnight, but was always in his office by 9 a.m. and ready to go to work.

Under Herrmann and the other new owners, baseball became an extension of politics in Cincinnati. Perhaps this represented a conscious strategy or perhaps it was merely a case of politicians doing what comes naturally. Either way, baseball and politics were not unusual bedfellows in the first decade of the 20th century. Throughout the major leagues, in the words of Steven A. Riess, "baseball was ... ruled by men deeply involved in urban politics."[17] Political connections enabled baseball magnates to protect their investments and to secure preferential treatment from municipal governments. Baseball also made for good public relations. Politicians found that by investing in and rooting for the home team, "they could be seen by their public as regular fellows ..., making them more identifiable with the electorate."[18]

August "Garry" Herrmann became president of the Reds in 1902 and held the position for 25 years. He was instrumental in making peace between the National and American leagues, and in making the World Series an annual event.
Photo: National Baseball Hall of Fame Library, Cooperstown, N.Y.

In Cincinnati, the Fleischmann brothers curried favor with potential voters by providing uniforms for local amateur teams. They also operated—and sometimes played for—a semipro team that performed each summer for the entertainment of the guests at fashionable resorts in New York's Catskill Mountains.[19] As far back as the 1880s, the Fleischmann family had been the "first of the very rich to become conspicuous independent householders" in that neighborhood. Led by Max and Julius' father, Ohio state Sen. Charles L. Fleischmann, they created a resort offering "luxury unheard of in the Catskills" near a little crossroads called Griffin's Corners;[20] by 1913, when the place was incorporated, the family had achieved such local prominence that the village was renamed Fleischmanns.

Ballplayers representing the Fleischmanns' resort were paid enough to deter offers from professional clubs and were kept in big league style—put up in first-class hotels and outfitted in "gorgeous" made-to-order uniforms.[21] When they traveled, it was in the Fleischmanns' own elegant horse-drawn four-in-hand tallyho or, for longer excursions, by chartered Pullman sleeping car. Much of the talent was recruited in and around Cincinnati and several members of Fleischmanns' Mountain Tourists, including Ewing's former Wapakoneta teammate George Rohe, eventually reached the major leagues. Though some baseball insiders scoffed,[22] the Fleischmanns enjoyed a reputation in the sporting press as men who "possess a true love for the game, which they thoroughly know and enjoy."[23]

From the outset, the new owners cultivated the goodwill of the players. Cy Seymour received a pay raise when he arrived in Cincinnati and was immediately signed for the following season at another increase. Pitcher Bill Phillips was invited to Herrmann's office and presented with a 1903 contract that increased his salary by two-thirds. Infielder George Magoon, sidelined much of the 1902 season with "severe rheumatism,"[24] was not only paid in full but sent to a private sanitarium for treatment at the club's expense. After Magoon agreed on a pay hike for 1903, Herrmann voided that contract and produced a new one calling for an additional $500. "These Cincinnati people can't do enough for a man," Magoon marveled.[25]

Ewing, having similarly witnessed (if not actually profited from) the largess of the new regime, had done some duck hunting in Louisiana and spent the off-season finding ways to keep himself occupied around the farm. He built a barn for three horses he had acquired and, with brother Maynard, bought 80 acres of farmland. Maynard's role was probably just to help secure financing; a year later, Bob would buy out his brother's interest for $1. He also played a little ball after being sent home, but he made no attempt to pitch. His appearances with the Wapakoneta team were limited to playing first base.

"I did just enough work after leaving the Reds to know that my arm is better," he told a reporter.[26]

While Ewing was "rusticating at his home at New Hampshire,"[27] baseball was experiencing a busy winter. Garry Herrmann, having early on declared himself in favor of peace between the National and American leagues, quickly took it upon himself to resolve the costly 2-year-old war. An old acquaintance of Ban Johnson, who had once been a Cincinnati sportswriter, Herrmann got together with the American League president and worked out ground rules for a peace conference, which opened January 9, 1903, at Cincinnati's St. Nicholas Hotel. Herrmann not only volunteered to host the conference, he even offered to provide accommodations for both leagues' peace commissioners—and the out-of-town press—at his own expense.

Herrmann set the tone for the conference when he relinquished Cincinnati's claim to Sam Crawford, the slugging young outfielder who had batted .333 for the Reds in 1902 with a league-leading 22 triples. While Herrmann's gesture was applauded as a selfless overture of peace, it might simply have been the pragmatic act of a seasoned political operator who knew how to pick his battles. Crawford, 22 years old and fairly launched on an outstanding 19-year major league career, had played various clubs off against each other before being approached in mid-1902 and offered a reported $4,500, plus a $1,000 signing bonus, to play for the American League's Detroit Tigers in 1903.[28] Crawford eventually signed 1903 contracts with both Cincinnati and Detroit, but he signed the Detroit contract first. Herrmann could have contested that signing, but if the matter ended up in court, the Reds' case would rest solely on a prior claim based on the reserve clause in Crawford's 1902 contract.

Herrmann knew that would be a chancy proposition. In previous court tests, the reserve clause had met with a decidedly mixed reception. In May 1902, the National League's St. Louis franchise had sought to block three former Cardinals—one of them was Jack Harper, who had pitched against Ewing in the short-lived Northwestern Ohio League—from moving across town to the American League Browns. Instead, Judge John A. Talty lambasted the older league for violating the players' rights to equal protection and due process, as guaranteed by the 14th Amendment to the Constitution, and for engaging in restrictive labor practices contrary to the Sherman Antitrust Act. Herrmann could take Crawford and the Tigers to court, but he was liable to lose. Worse, if the issue ever landed before a federal judge, there was a chance the entire reserve system would end up being declared unconstitutional, leaving all the owners in a permanent state of unrestricted competition and spiraling player salaries.

Facing the prospect of losing Crawford either way, Herrmann made the best of his situation. Then, having demonstrated his magnanimity, and at one point walking out of the room when the discussion threatened to turn nasty, Herrmann steered the conferees to an agreement that would lead to 50 years of stability in baseball. After only two days of talks, the rival organizations agreed to function as separate and equal major leagues with a common set of rules and non-conflicting schedules. Most importantly Ban Johnson, who had previously held the reserve system to be illegal,[29] now accepted the reserve clause as part of the standard player contract to be used by both leagues. The settlement paved the way for a new National Agreement with protections for the minor leagues, and a minor league player draft. As a forum for settling disputes, a further agreement was soon reached creating a National Commission to oversee all of organized baseball.[30] The commission would comprise the presidents of the two major leagues, plus a mutually acceptable third party who would serve as chairman. That post went to Herrmann, who would hold it until 1920, the year the panel's functions were turned over to Judge Kenesaw Mountain Landis, the first holder of the one-man office of baseball commissioner.

Herrmann was applauded on all sides. In the opinion of *The Sporting News,* "A more equitable or comprehensive plan for securing permanent peace and prosperity to the leagues directly interested and to the game in general could not have been devised."[31] He was extolled as "the soul of sportsmanship and the embodiment of firmness and honesty," and his elevation to the highest place in baseball's "supreme court," it was said, "marks the end of distrust and trickery ... among the magnates of the game."[32]

AMID ALL THIS NEWFOUND HARMONY and good cheer, Ewing reported to Cincinnati on March 14 to join the team for his first real spring training trip. Under their new management, the Reds had secured facilities at Augusta, Georgia, and were going south for a month. Players would receive only room and board until the season started. But even without pay, Ewing was raring to go. He was convinced his arm trouble had resulted from training in the northern cold the year before.[33] Now his arm was better and, as he told Ren Mulford, he was eager to get back into uniform and "prove how grateful he was for the Cincinnati club's kindness to him."[34]

The Reds' pitching situation was a bit up in the air at the start of the 1903 season. Gone from the 1902 squad were Clarence Currie, sold to St. Louis after complaining that he wasn't getting enough work, and Henry Thielman, briefly hailed as "the idol of Redland,"[35] cut loose after getting into a fistfight with Cy Seymour during a late-season exhibition game in Indianapolis.

There was no shortage of candidates to fill the vacancies. Besides holdovers Noodles Hahn, Bill Phillips and Ed Poole—a former Inter-State League rival of Ewing's who had gone 12–4 after being purchased from Pittsburgh—pitchers in camp included Cincinnatian Jack Sutthoff, getting his second shot with the Reds after winning 24 games in the minor leagues for Indianapolis; 6-foot-4 Jim Wiggs, reputed to be one of the hardest throwers in baseball; Bill "Cy" Hooker, called up the previous September from Buffalo; and Jack Harper, who had remained only one season in the American League before signing with the Reds prior to ratification of the peace agreement. J. Ed Grillo of the *Cincinnati Commercial Tribune* had acted as the Reds' intermediary in the signing of Harper, a 15-game winner for the Browns; the contract was for $4,000, with half of the money up front.[36]

For a time, the Reds feared they had lost another pitching prospect. They received news that Harry Allemang, winner of 19 games for Little

Rock in the Southern Association and "regarded as a very promising young player,"[37] had been fatally shot in Mason, West Virginia, during a robbery in which his assailants made off with $980. Two weeks later Garry Herrmann received a letter assuring him that reports of Allemang's death were considerably exaggerated. In fact, Allemang wrote, he had been robbed of $9.80 and was recovering nicely from his wounds. A bullet had passed through the pitcher's right lung and had lodged in the muscles of his shoulder. The slug was still there when he showed up for spring training, but Allemang claimed to feel no ill effects. From then on, the writers gleefully referred to him as "Bullets" Allemang.

The same writers had been writing Ewing off ever since the previous August. Now, among the hopefuls for 1903, he was listed as one of Cincinnati's "surplus pitchers,...destined for the farm for a year at least."[38] Joe Kelley, who had seen Ewing only after his arm went bad, had already attempted to unload him. Ned Hanlon, once Kelley's boss in Baltimore and now manager of the Brooklyn Superbas, had tried to get Ewing before he signed with the Reds. After Ewing's rookie year, Kelley offered Brooklyn any two of the Reds' young pitchers, holding back only Poole, and urged Hanlon to take Ewing as one of them.[39] Hanlon passed on Ewing and instead bought Thielman and Rube Vickers.

So Ewing boarded the train for Augusta with the rest of the Reds. The perennial anticipation of the new season was evident all along the route. When the train stopped for 30 minutes at Erlanger, Kentucky, "a crowd of cheering boys and men...yelled themselves hoarse" the entire time, calling the players by name and showing themselves "as familiar with their ability and traits as anyone in the [Reds'] party."[40] Still, if Ewing was optimistic about what the coming season held for him, other observers weren't.

"I don't think Long Bob Ewing has much chance," Mulford wrote. "... In his work [last season] he impressed manager Kelley as lacking the ginger and ambition that a player must possess to reach his ideal of a winner."[41]

Kelley had definite ideas about what constituted a winning ballplayer. Between 1894 and 1900, he had played for Hanlon on five pennant-winners, three in Baltimore and two in Brooklyn. Along with John McGraw, Hughie Jennings and Wee Willie Keeler, Kelley had formed the "Big Four" of Hanlon's Baltimore teams that dominated the National League for much of the 1890s and carved out a unique niche in baseball lore.

John Heydler, a former umpire and future National League president, said the old Orioles "were mean, vicious, ready at any time to maim a rival player or an umpire, if it helped their cause. The things they would say to an umpire were unbelievably vile, and ... the worst of it was that they got away with much of their browbeating and hooliganism."[42] Kelley brought the spirit of the old Orioles to Cincinnati. One of his first moves was to dispense with the Reds' policy of levying a $25 fine against any player ejected from a game; instead—like his mentor, Hanlon Kelley would encourage his players to "stick up for their rights."[43] Kelley was always primed for a confrontation, and he wanted players who were the same way, on the field or on the bench. Baseball, he said, "is mimic war," and he liked to stir up an occasional "verbal scrap" among his own men, aiming to keep the team "on edge all the time."[44]

"Take a team where all is harmony among the men, where mistakes are glossed over and poor playing is met with sympathy instead of roasts, and there is but little hope for success," Kelley insisted. "... There is nothing that Hanlon hates so much as to see all his men sitting on the bench all satisfied with each other."[45]

Kelley's goal in spring training was to cull from the roster any man who was too slow, either mentally or physically, for Baltimore-style inside baseball. He had little use, he said, for "these fellows who can hit, but cannot play the game."[46] Writers covering the team had long ago gotten the impression that the methodical, even-tempered Ewing didn't match up very well with the manager's notion of a player. "His movements are too slow to suit manager Kelley," wrote one.[47]

The odds on Ewing's future in baseball weren't improved any by Kelley's plans for the pitching staff. A decade after the lengthening of the pitching distance, many in baseball still agreed with Henry Chadwick that "a corps of four pitchers amply suffices to do the full season's 'box' work" for a team.[48] Father Chadwick scoffed at modern pitchers who complained of being overworked "by going in the box every other day or so." The actual work of pitching a nine-inning game, Chadwick reasoned, typically represented no more than an hour's labor, "and it is absurd to claim that an hour's work in the box during each day is either trying to [a pitcher's] physique or to his powers of endurance."[49] Kelley followed the same line of thought.

"Four men should be able to do all the work," he said, allowing for a fifth to be held in reserve in case of emergencies.[50]

The Reds arrived in Augusta after a 25-hour train trip. Once there, they soon found that Kelley didn't run the most rigorous pre-season camp; he said he didn't regard it as necessary or even advisable for a player to get down to his ideal playing weight by Opening Day. Still, the players could expect several weeks of strenuous workouts including gymnastic exercises and long runs or jogs. There were also brisk sessions of high-low, in which several men stood in a large circle and flipped a ball rapidly back and forth, shooting each quick throw high, low or wide, forcing the receiver to stretch to make the catch. "High-low isn't a game, properly speaking," said Johnny Evers, "it is a torture."[51]

Other conditioning programs of the time were less conventional. Players were slathered with "a thousand kinds of rubbing oils," everything from patent medicines and horse liniment to "oil made by boiling down fishing worms." Evers described players having 20-pound cannonballs rolled across their stomachs to firm up abdominal muscles, and limbs being subjected to "arm bakers…superheated with electricity."[52] Cy Seymour recalled that when the Giants trained in Lakewood, New Jersey, in 1897 and 1898, the entire squad was required to play leapfrog all the way around Lake Carasaljo.[53]

Evenings in spring training were whiled away in swapping tales, singing songs and, in the words of Christy Mathewson, "kicking about the grub." It was always good to have a few new faces in camp to offer some fresh yarns; most of the conversation, Mathewson said, consisted of "the same old stories that creep out of the bushes on crutches year after year."[54] In 1903, Ewing and a few teammates filled some of their off hours with a little fishing.

Within days, the team fell into a routine of morning workouts followed by afternoon intrasquad games. Club secretary Max Fleischmann had been fitted for a uniform and joined the Reds in Augusta, hoping to break into a few games as an outfielder. Ewing attracted attention the first morning when he turned out wearing a ragged hand-me-down sweater, variously described as yellow and brown or orange and black, that "Noah might have worn when he pitched the ark."[55] The sweater looked "as if numerous members of the family had taken turns mending it, and used every possible variety of yarn to do it."[56] Two days later, while Ewing shagged flies in the outfield, the "garment of many patches" disappeared behind the grandstand and went up in smoke.[57] Mike Donlin, a notorious practical joker, was suspected, and Ewing vowed to get revenge. But no reprisals were reported and Ewing thereafter warded off the morning chill with a new sweater borrowed from Cy Seymour.

In his first spring games, Ewing was penciled in at first base or in center field for the recruits against the regulars, but within a week he was "showing as much speed as any pitcher of the nine" in camp and impressing his manager with, in Kelley's words, "more get-up and get-down here than he possessed last year."[58] As Ewing's star rose, others began to set. Bullets Allemang lost to the regulars when he pitched for the recruits and to the recruits when he pitched for the regulars. Jim Wiggs revealed a penchant for tripping over his feet in fielding bunts and finally came down with a sore arm. Some observers thought Cy Hooker had more talent than any of the other young pitchers but he demonstrated, in the words of one Cincinnati writer, "no more ambition than a South Carolina darkey."[59]

Ewing experienced a brief but worrisome bout of soreness, but worked his way through it and soon emerged as one of the bright spots of Kelley's first spring with the Reds. On April 9 in Birmingham, Alabama, Ewing allowed only two hits in five innings, combining with Jack Sutthoff for a 5–0 shutout of the local Southern Association club. By this time, sportswriters were noticing that Kelley was becoming increasingly "sweet on Long Bob Ewing."[60] For himself, Kelley seemed both surprised and pleased. He alerted fans to keep their eyes open when the club got home: "There will be lots of interest in Ewing's work," he predicted.[61]

Back in Cincinnati, his position secure for the time being, Ewing settled into the Gerdes Hotel, the summer home of many of the Reds' unmarried players, and looked forward to the season. The Gerdes was on West Fifth Street, about a block from Fountain Square. There Ewing could catch a streetcar which, for a few cents, would carry him two miles to the ballpark at Western Avenue and Findlay Street, in a neighborhood of row houses, factories and saloons on the city's west side.

Ewing's bachelor lodgings were just off Vine Street, described as "the spinal column of the city."[62] In the 1890s Vine Street, with its music halls, burlesque houses and beer gardens that never closed, had helped to give Cincinnati its reputation as "the 'wettest' city between New York and Chicago."[63] The neighborhood was a magnet for entertainers, sportsmen, politicians and gamblers. As the century turned, the flamboyant conviviality of the '90s was perhaps beginning to fade, but only just. In 1901, saloon-smasher Carry Nation paid a visit to Vine Street but departed without striking a single blow with her famous hatchet. Surveying all the drinking establishments lining the avenue, sometimes 20 or more in a single block, the formidable temperance crusader knew she had met her match. "I would have dropped from exhaustion before I had gone a block," she said.[64]

Many of Ewing's teammates were familiar figures up and down Vine Street. The previous management had sometimes attempted to enforce a sobriety clause in its contracts but Herrmann and Kelley, no teetotalers themselves, ran a considerably more relaxed operation. Hans Lobert, who joined the club a few years after Ewing, recalled the Reds as "beer drinkers" and a "pretty rough" bunch of boys.[65] Ewing, however, took little part in the nightlife. From early in his career, it had been clear that Long Bob did not fit the common image of a ballplayer. When he first signed with the Reds, one hometown observer wrote, "He is ... a pitcher and, strange to say, a young man of exemplary habits."[66]

"I can't drink, for I don't like it, only sometimes a little beer," he wrote in a letter three years after coming to Cincinnati. "I saw enough drinking to know that they isn't nothing in it."[67] On nights before he pitched, he made a point to be in bed by 10 p.m.

With or without a sobriety clause, it paid for Ewing to keep himself in top playing condition. He knew that his performance on the field, and his conduct off it, would be minutely scrutinized and commented on. Newspapers generally were becoming more ambitious and more aggressive in their coverage of sports, and Cincinnati was particularly baseball-crazy— a town where, in the words of Ren Mulford, "baseball news is ground out by the yard, summer and winter."[68]

For the players, the town's pervasive enthusiasm for the game could be a double-edged sword. When things didn't go well, the reconfigured League Park could be an especially unforgiving place to play. A combination of factors—fervor, proximity and alcohol—made Rooters Row an ever-present, often unpleasant, part of the game. Interactions between spectators and participants ranged from the comedic to the terrifying. Giants manager John J. McGraw triggered a small tempest when he was heard to call some Cincinnati supporters "fatheaded bums."[69] More seriously, after two different games in 1904, police had to rescue umpires from mobs of incensed fans.[70] In the middle of another game the same year, Giants catcher Frank Bowerman was arrested after punching a fan in the face.[71] On more than one occasion, management felt compelled to increase ballpark security. A special officer was stationed near the visitors' bench for the mutual protection of athletes and fans. Two years later, Herrmann hired five more men to enforce a crackdown on "personal or profane comments" directed toward the players; offenders were to be "promptly ejected from the grounds."[72]

Hometown players received only slightly gentler treatment than the opposition from what Ren Mulford came to call "Roasters Row."[73] The vociferous "half-stewed bugs" were eventually perceived as a peculiar sort of home-field disadvantage for Cincinnati.[74] Certain players—among them Harry Steinfeldt and Hans Lobert, whose lot it was to play within earshot of the grandstand at third base—came in for a particular hammering from the "anvil chorus" along the row. Outside observers placed much of the blame for this supercharged atmosphere on the local press which, rightly or wrongly, had a reputation for annually pumping up unrealistic hopes, then turning on the players when they inevitably failed to live up to the fans' over-inflated expectations.

By Ewing's time, this chronic gap between anticipation and fulfillment was a source of longstanding irritation. "More unredeemed promises have been made for the Reds than any other team in the country," *The Sporting News* stated.[75] The situation didn't improve during Ewing's tenure. Late in Long Bob's career, Christy Mathewson remarked that the players who had been run out of Cincinnati in the past decade would almost make a championship club. "I believe the local newspapers have done as much as anything to keep a pennant away from that town," he added.[76]

Joe Vila of the *New York Sun,* commiserating with Joe Kelley, wrote, "I've said all along that to be the manager of the Porkville team a man must be deaf, dumb and blind, else the journalistic shafts from the overheated press box could not fail to drive one to the booby hut." The best thing for baseball in Cincinnati, Vila maintained, would be for the newspapers to suspend publication.[77]

Ewing largely escaped both the exaggerated buildup and the dramatic fall from grace that was the fate of many players. Perhaps his unobtrusive personality and steady work habits gradually won over the writers and fans. Or perhaps he was simply too lacking in bravado to attract much attention. The chroniclers and the cranks, ever searching for new and shining Red hopes, tended to look past him. Still, if he was sometimes under-appreciated or taken for granted, at least he was spared the wrath that could come down on a player of whom much was expected, and who failed to deliver.

Turning 30 at the start of his second major league season, Ewing was already beginning to be treated as something of an elder on the ballclub. A reliable or at least predictable performer, he was accepted with a comfortable familiarity befitting an unpretentious farm boy from familiar, unpretentious Wapakoneta, Ohio. While other players made news with their run-ins with umpires, managers and sometimes even the law, Ewing rarely uttered a peep.[78] In an era when star players were often adorned with elaborate or imposing nicknames,[79] Ewing always seemed better suited to plain old everyday Long Bob—or, on occasions that seemed to demand a bit more formality, Elongated Robert. Other sobriquets the writers were constantly spinning out always had a certain homely quality, invariably emphasizing his country-boy origins and small-town roots. Later in his career he was sometimes called the Wapakoneta Horseman or the Sage of Wapakoneta. Already by 1903, Ren Mulford had taken to referring to him as "Old Wapak"[80] or sometimes, simply and affectionately, as "good old Bob."[81]

THE REDS GOT OFF to a slow start in 1903. They lost eight of their first nine games, and their first six at home, before Ewing beat Chicago 9–4 on April 28. Within two weeks the club was at .500. On June 2, Ewing held Boston hitless through seven innings and eventually won the game 4–1 on a two-hitter. In just six weeks, Fred J. Hewitt wrote in the *Cincinnati*

Post, "Long Bob Ewing ... has developed from an experiment into a star of the first water."[82] Six weeks later he was in the midst of a four-game losing streak.

The season was full of such ups and downs. Golden moments granted to grown men paid to play a boys' game alternated with stark reminders of the world that existed beyond the foul lines. An off day found the Reds in Wilmington, Delaware, where they overcame a local team 4–3. Six days later, while the Reds were in New York to play the Giants, they read the horrific headlines as Wilmington made news all over the country. A black man named George White, accused of raping and murdering a 17-year-old white schoolgirl, had been dragged out of jail by a mob of 2,000 people and burned at the stake. Some accounts said White's bones were later sold on the street as souvenirs.

In August, a scheduled series in Philadelphia had to be postponed after some rotted timbers gave way and a balcony collapsed at the ballpark. Twelve people were killed and more than 200 injured. Tragedy in Philadelphia meant a paid vacation for the Reds. They arranged a couple of exhibitions in Atlantic City, New Jersey, where a large crowd watched Ewing dispatch a team of college boys 11–2, and the ballplayers spent three days sampling the good life at one of America's favorite playgrounds. They lounged on the wide, white beach, cavorted in the surf, and those not encumbered by wives flirted with "the summer girls."[83] Jake Beckley and Heinie Peitz rented one of the famous rolling chairs and were pushed up and down the boardwalk like gentlemen of leisure.

Also in Atlantic City, the Reds risked a peek on the other side of baseball's color barrier, agreeing to a game against the Cuban X-Giants. Despite rigid segregation, and nearly 20 years before the organization of the Negro Leagues, black baseball was flourishing on its own terms, generating legendary players, spirited rivalries and great teams that occasionally attracted notice even from white fans and writers. The X-Giants, led by the great Rube Foster, were acknowledged as the top team in "colored" baseball. Many people regarded them as "the equal of many of the major league teams," the local newspaper noted, and a match with the Reds would go a long way toward proving or disproving that contention.[84]

It was rare, if not unheard of, for the Reds to take the field against a black team, and the prospect generated considerable anticipation, not to say apprehension. For their part, the X-Giants were said to be "quite confident of [their] ability to defeat the leaguers."[85] No such self-assured pronouncements issued from the Cincinnati camp. The Reds players probably weren't especially keen to play the game; the "leaguers" had little to gain from winning and considerable prestige at stake should they lose. But the matchup promised to draw a good crowd and Frank Bancroft, having lost the anticipated receipts from the Philadelphia series, was in no position to pass up the chance for a sizable payday.

How seriously the Reds took the challenge is reflected in their announced plans to start their best pitcher, Noodles Hahn, against the X-Giants' crafty left-hander, Dan McClellan. But after the big buildup, the day came, the skies opened up and the game was rained out. The Reds resumed their National League schedule and the Cuban X-Giants returned to the world of black baseball, where they cemented their claim of supremacy at season's end by winning four of six games in a championship series against Sol White's Philadelphia Giants. For the rest of Ewing's career, black and white baseball would remain alternative universes that rarely intersected.

The Reds, with Ewing settling in behind Hahn and Jack Sutthoff as the team's third most reliable pitcher, climbed—a little unsteadily—in the standings. On August 18, with Cincinnati parked in fourth place, Ewing found himself matched against the New York Giants' Joe McGinnity in the finale of a four-game series at the Polo Grounds. The last time the two pitchers had faced each other, on June 11 in Cincinnati, they had battled through 10 scoreless innings before errors by all three Reds outfielders opened the door for a 2–0 New York victory. This time, on a Tuesday afternoon before "many more vacant seats than full ones,"[86] Ewing and McGinnity picked up where they'd left off, stringing together more goose eggs in "a wildly exciting slab duel."[87]

"For five innings...the game looked to be a give-and-take affair that might last almost indefinitely," the New York Herald reported.[88]

For Ewing, it was one of those rare and glorious days in a pitcher's life when everything was working. His control was flawless and his breaking pitches "presented a series of irritating puzzles which the local men were quite incapable of solving."[89] And speed! Ewing had so much speed, the New York World declared, "that Peitz could barely hold him."[90]

Scarcely a ball was even hit solidly off Ewing. George Browne, leading off the game for New York, hit a fastball "square in the nose,"[91] but it rolled harmlessly to Tom Daly at second base. Third baseman Harry Steinfeldt made a "grand stop"[92] on Charlie Babb's hot grounder in the second inning. Otherwise, Ewing was completely in charge. Cincinnati broke on top with single runs in the sixth and seventh, then knocked McGinnity out of the box in the eighth when four consecutive hits ignited a five-run rally.

Meanwhile, for the second time in 2½ months, Ewing sailed through seven innings without allowing a hit. Even the New York fans cheered his performance. He struck out five; the Giants' best hitter, Roger Bresnahan, was victimized three times. Only two Giants reached base, both on throwing errors by Steinfeldt. Dan McGann's bounder in the seventh inning looked like trouble for a moment when Ewing, stretching to make the play, was only able to deflect the ball. But Daly managed to collect it in time to throw McGann out at first base.

Then, with one out in the eighth inning, the Giants' Jack Dunn stepped to the plate for the third time. Eleven years later, as owner and manager of the Baltimore club in the International League, Dunn would secure a permanent place in the annals of the game by signing 19-year-old George Herman Ruth to his first professional contract. But on this day in 1903, Dunn was in the lineup only because New York's regular second baseman, Billy Gilbert, had been plunked the day before by a pitch from Jack Sutthoff.

In his first two tries against Ewing, Dunn had grounded out and popped up. This time, he slashed a sharp two-bouncer deep in the hole between short and third. Tommy Corcoran sprang to his right, speared the ball and launched it hurriedly in the direction of first base. On the other side of the diamond, Jake Beckley stretched for the throw "with legs spread out like a pair of tailor's shears."[93]

For a fraction of a second, the Reds thought they'd gotten the out, but umpire Gus Moran called Dunn safe. Beckley, in a fit of anger, threw the ball on the ground and turned on Moran. While Beckley argued, the ball rolled into right field; Dunn alertly rounded first base and kept going. By the time order was restored, Dunn was on second base and Ewing's bid for a no-hit game was history. In the press box, official scorer Sam Crane, an old-time infielder and longtime sportswriter for the *New York Journal,* pronounced the play a single, with a subsequent error on Beckley allowing Dunn to advance.

Ewing got out of the inning on a ground ball and a long fly out. The Giants' final four outs required "two splendid running catches"[94] by Seymour in center field—the first off Jack Cronin to close the eighth inning, then off McGann to end the game—but Ewing completed the job without further incident, winning 7–0. He had faced only 30 batters, walking none and extending himself to a three-ball count only twice. The Cincinnati papers heralded the most brilliant pitching effort of the season. The *Commercial Tribune* could detect "not the semblance of a wabble" in Ewing's work; the Giants' heavy hitters "looked like pygmies before the giant from Wapakoneta."[95] Even in New York it was acknowledged that the Giants had been "shut out as completely as if they never existed."[96]

Before the game was over, the controversy had begun. The Reds and their supporters weren't united on whether Dunn was out or whether he had reached on an error. Either way, they argued, Ewing deserved credit for a no-hitter. Corcoran insisted his throw had beaten Dunn by 10 feet.

"It is an outrage to call that drive a hit," Corcoran said. "… If the man wasn't out, it was a wild throw."[97]

One witness in the press corps maintained that dozens of New York spectators—in fact "everybody in line of first base," with the crucial exception of Moran—were unanimous in the opinion that Dunn was out.[98] Kelley tried every possible argument, claiming that Moran's decision "was clearly wrong" and that Dunn "was out by at least a step." But even if he wasn't, Kelley added, it was because the throw was wide and drew Beckley off the base—which didn't matter anyway because Beckley got back before Dunn arrived.[99]

Moran defended his call but, at least when confronted by the Cincinnati writers, he sided with those who believed Ewing was entitled to a no-hitter. The umpire told reporters that Beckley's foot was off the bag.

"How can that be scored a hit?" Moran asked. "It was a wild throw."[100]

The Cincinnati press howled long and loudly. The *Enquirer* brazenly headlined Ewing's "runless and hitless defeat" of the Giants;[101] only halfway down the column was it made clear that, officially, Ewing hadn't pitched a no-hit game. Other papers weren't even that fastidious with the facts. Closer to Ewing's home, the headline in the *Lima Times-Democrat* had New York "shut out without a run or a hit."[102] The paper then reprinted the first two paragraphs of the *Enquirer* story without the subsequent disclaimer, leaving the uncontradicted impression that the game was a no-hitter.

Severe criticism fell on both Crane and Moran. Ren Mulford fumed that Crane had "skinned [Ewing] out of all the credit due him" on "a mere matter of opinion."[103] The *Cincinnati Post* gave prominent play to contentions that Ewing had been both "cheated" and "robbed" by Moran.[104]

Ewing was deeply upset. As usual, he let his teammates do most of the talking, but he did express an opinion of Sam Crane's scorekeeping. "A man ought to be arrested for giving a hit on that rap of Dunn's," he told Mulford.[105]

But there was nothing to be done for it. "Sam Crane ... chalked up a hit for Dunn," Mulford concluded, "and that is the way the returns will reach headquarters."[106]

In Ewing's mind, though, the game was a no-hitter, and he regarded it as such for the rest of his life.[107]

THE REDS CONTINUED TO WIN more than they lost and remained securely in fourth place. But they gradually slipped farther behind the front-runners, ultimately finishing 16½ games off the pace set by the Pittsburgh Pirates, who won their third straight National League pennant, and 8½ games behind the third-place Chicago Cubs. Ewing, in his first full season in the big leagues, was about as good as the team, winning 14 games and losing 13. At season's end, based on a handshake agreement between owners Barney Dreyfuss and Henry Killilea, the Pirates and the Boston Americans, winners of the American League, met in a best-of-nine series for the "world's championship" of baseball. Pittsburgh won three of the first four games but Boston came back to take the next four straight and win the first modern World Series, five games to three.

The league champions weren't the only players who remained active after the regular schedule was completed. Challenges sprang up all over the country, looking to exploit natural rivalries between the two now-friendly leagues. National and American rivals faced off in city series in Chicago, Philadelphia and St. Louis. In Ohio, Cincinnati arranged a series of meetings with the Cleveland club, sometimes called the Naps in deference to their celebrated slugger, Napoleon Lajoie. Cleveland had captured third place in the American League, and Lajoie had won the batting title with a .344 average.

The "Ohio championship" commenced October 3 in Cleveland with the home team's Red Donahue out-dueling Jack Sutthoff, 2–1. The series switched to Cincinnati the next day with Ewing matched against 20-game-winner Earl Moore. Even on the Reds' home turf, Lajoie was a big attraction, "surrounded by a mob of kids" off the field and roundly cheered when he stepped to the plate.[108] Ewing went into the game as something of a question mark. He had been hit hard in his final regular-season start, a 10–7 loss to Brooklyn, and had suffered the most embarrassing drubbing of his career in a tune-up for the Cleveland series: Returning once again to Sidney, the scene of previous triumphs and a town where he could always count on a warm reception, Ewing was batted around unmercifully as the local amateurs humiliated the Reds 14–2, pounding out 22 hits. All in all, Ren Mulford observed as the series began, Long Bob's recent performances "are not calculated to boom faith in him."[109]

Ewing restored some of that faith by scattering 12 hits and holding Lajoie hitless in four at-bats, evening the series with a 7–3 victory. Five days later in sub-freezing temperatures, he allowed just one hit and an unearned run, and held a 2–1 lead when his second matchup with Moore was called in the fourth inning because of darkness. Coming back the following day, he pitched better than in his first game but was undone by four errors and a general lack of offensive or defensive support. Cleveland coasted to an easy 6–1 victory as Bill Bernhard held the Reds to one hit—Ewing's ground single over second base in the eighth inning. This time Lajoie managed a single in three tries; counting the game that was halted short of completion, the "king of ballplayers"[110] had managed a sickly 1-for-8 showing against Ewing.

Ewing had played well enough to bolster the Reds' confidence in him. Certainly he showed better than most of his teammates in the series, as Cleveland won six of nine games. Financially, the venture was a disappointment; played over seven dates in four cities, the games attracted only 25,647 fans. The Cincinnati players, in addition to continuing to draw their regular salaries throughout the series, each received a $100 bonus.

With that, their obligations to the ballclub were discharged for the year. That freed the players to get together on their own—and play a little ball. For most players, an autumnal barnstorming tour was as much a part of the annual cycle of baseball as spring training. The ostensible purpose of these post-season excursions was to make a little extra money, but as often as not, barnstorming was mainly a lark—a sort of (hopefully) paid vacation that allowed teammates to just hang out together, free of training restrictions or managerial supervision, and play some games for fun. Facing mostly not-very-threatening opposition and out from under the pressure of league competition, the professional athletes could return briefly to small towns and rural ballfields that brought to mind the places most of them started out.

The Reds' post-season junkets were sometimes planned by business manager Frank Bancroft, who took care of scheduling, handled the money and got a chance to return to his own earlier days in baseball as a field manager. Other times, trips were organized by the players themselves on the "cooperative plan."[111] Participating players split the expenses and pooled the receipts, and whatever was left at the end of the tour they divided among themselves. In 1904 the Reds barnstormed clear into mid-November and it was reported that the players pocketed $220 apiece—less than two weeks' pay for many big leaguers, but still more cash than most American workers would take home in four months.[112] But many times the returns were meager. Uncertain fall weather, disappointing crowds or unexpected expenses could quickly wipe out any modest profits.

The players hardly seemed to care. The barnstorming troupe that discovered Bob Ewing in Sidney in 1901 spent a week on the road up and down Ohio's Miami Valley. By the time they got back to Cincinnati and parceled out the shares, each man came away $12 to the good.

"We didn't make much money," admitted outfielder Dick Harley, who acted as the team's manager, "but we traveled 500 miles and had a barrel of fun."[113]

Ewing, always happy to get back to Auglaize County, his shotgun and his chores around the farm, was never an especially enthusiastic barnstormer. But as long as he remained a bachelor, he always spent a few days touring with his mates after the season, sometimes pitching every other day, and he continued to make occasional post-season appearances as long as he remained with the Reds. Immediately after the Cleveland series ended in 1903, several Reds embarked on a 500-mile loop through Ohio, West Virginia and Kentucky, playing seven games in six days and winning five. Ewing pitched easy victories in Charleston, West Virginia, and Catlettsburg, Kentucky, and played left field the rest of the time. The tour wrapped up in Zanesville, Ohio, on October 18 and he headed for home.

Not long after, it was reported he had taken a face full of buckshot in a hunting accident. Ewing was quick to reassure the Reds that he was all right.

"Suppose you saw where I got shot," he wrote to Garry Herrmann. "Well it wasn't half as bad as the papers said."[114]

Contrary to the example of Harry "Bullets" Allemang, the tall right-hander never became Bob "Buckshot" Ewing. Cincinnati was getting comfortable with Old Wapak.

ENDNOTES

1   *Sporting Life,* Aug. 30, 1902.
2   At Ewing's intermediate stop, Kansas City, Mo., Jim Pendergast at the turn of the century was beginning to develop a Democratic machine that would eventually rival or surpass Cox's Republican organization in Cincinnati. Pendergast's personal influence reached its peak between 1900 and 1902, the same time Ewing was in Kansas City. But the machine would attain its fullest development only after 1910 under the direction of Jim's younger brother, Tom Pendergast, who would remain a power in state and local politics through the mid-1930s. See Lyle W. Dorsett, *The Pendergast Machine* (Lincoln, Neb.: University of Nebraska Press, 1968), pp. 30-41.
3   Randolph C. Downes, "The Boss," in Writers' Program of the Work Projects Administration, *Cincinnati: A Guide to the Queen City and its Neighbors* (Cincinnati: Wiesen-Hart Press, 1943), p. 116.
4   Clara Longworth de Chambrun, *Cincinnati: Story of the Queen City* (New York: Charles Scribner's Sons, 1939), pp. 293-94.
5   *The Sporting News,* Dec. 17, 1904.
6   *Cincinnati Times-Star,* quoted in *The Sporting News,* Dec. 24, 1904.
7   Lee Allen, *The Cincinnati Reds: An Informal History* (New York: G.P. Putnam's Sons, 1948), p. 73.
8   Zane L. Miller, *Boss Cox's Cincinnati: Urban Politics in the Progressive Era* (New York: Oxford University Press, 1968), p. 98. See also Hoyt Landon Warner, *Progressivism in Ohio, 1897-1917* (Columbus, Ohio: Ohio State University Press), p. 16.
9   As Herrmann's biographer points out, the story makes no sense in the Cincinnati context. Brush was eager to sell, and the machine's offer was more than generous. The story might actually have originated in New York, where a similar "negotiation" was described between Tammany Hall and John J. McGraw. See William A. Cook, *August "Garry" Herrmann: A Baseball Biography* (Jefferson, N.C.: McFarland and Co. Inc., 2008), pp. 28 and 38.
10 Joseph Lincoln Steffens, *The Struggle for Self-Government* (New York: McClure, Phillips and Co., 1906), pp. 199-200.
11 Joseph Benson Foraker, *Notes of a Busy Life,* Volume 2 (Cincinnati: Stewart and Kidd Co., 1917), p. 383.

12 *Cincinnati Enquirer,* April 26, 1931.

13 Downes, *op. cit.,* p.120.

14 Foraker, *op. cit.,* pp. 383-84.

15 *Cincinnati Enquirer,* April 27, 1931.

16 Alfred Segal, *Cincinnati Post,* April 25, 1931.

17 Steven A. Riess, *Touching Base: Professional Baseball and American Culture in the Progressive Era* (Westport, Conn.: Greenwood Press, 1980), p. 49.

18 *Ibid.,* pp. 29-30.

19 Baseball historian Lee Allen wrote that often, the spectators "included few besides the personal friends of the Fleischmanns." *The Sporting News,* April 19, 1950.

20 Alf Evers, *The Catskills: From Wilderness to Woodstock* (Woodstock, N.Y.: Overlook Press, 1982), p. 545.

21 *New York Sun,* reprinted in the *Cincinnati Enquirer,* July 13, 1900.

22 Clark Griffith, who later managed the Reds, was of the opinion that the Fleischmann brothers "never belonged in the business." Harold Seymour and Dorothy Seymour Mills, *Baseball: The Golden Age* (New York: Oxford University Press, 1971), p. 10.

23 *Sporting Life,* Feb. 28, 1903.

24 *The Sporting News,* Aug. 23, 1902.

25 *Ibid.,* Nov. 1, 1902.

26 *Ibid.,* Oct. 18, 1902.

27 *Sidney Daily News,* Sept. 29, 1902.

28 *Sporting Life,* Aug. 30, 1902.

29 Eugene C. Murdock, *Ban Johnson: Czar of Baseball* (Westport, Conn.: Greenwood Press, 1982), p. 48. Johnson's position on the reserve clause, not surprisingly, had been a major selling point for National Leaguers thinking about jumping to the American. In practice, Johnson's opposition to the system was tempered by practical considerations. In an October 1900 memo spelling out guidelines for recruiting players, Johnson said the AL would have a reserve clause, but – unlike in the NL, where the clause was renewable indefinitely – it "would be in effect for no more than three years." See Warren N. Wilbert, *The Arrival of the American League: Ban Johnson and the 1901 Challenge to the National League Monopoly* (Jefferson, N.C.: McFarland and Co. Inc., 2007), p. 28.

30 Topping the list of the commission's objectives was "perpetuation of baseball as the national pastime of America." *New York Times,* Aug. 30, 1903.

31 *The Sporting News,* Jan. 17, 1903.

32 *Ibid.,* Sept. 5, 1903.

33 *Cincinnati Commercial Tribune,* March 14, 1903.

34 *Sporting Life,* Oct. 18, 1902.

35 *Ibid.,* June 28, 1902.

36 *The Sporting News,* Sept. 20, 1902.

37 *Sporting Life,* Nov. 15, 1902.

38 *Ibid.,* March 14, 1903.

39 *The Sporting News,* May 30, 1903.

40 *Cincinnati Commercial Tribune,* March 16, 1903.

41 *Sporting Life,* Feb. 21, 1903.

42 Frederick G. Lieb, *The Baltimore Orioles: The History of a Colorful Team in Baltimore and St. Louis* (Carbondale, Ill.: Southern Illinois University Press, 2005 reprint of 1955 original), p. 68.

43 *The Sporting News,* Aug. 30, 1902.

44 *Ibid.,* Nov. 22, 1902.

45 *Ibid.*

46 *Ibid.,* Oct. 25, 1903.

47 *Sporting Life,* Aug. 30, 1902.

48 Henry Chadwick, ed., *Spalding's Official Baseball Guide, 1903* (New York: American Sports Publishing Co., 1903), p. 157.

49 Chadwick, ed., *Spalding's Official Baseball Guide, 1902* (New York: American Sports Publishing Co., 1902), p. 86.

50 *Cincinnati Commercial Tribune*, March 20, 1903. In fairness, Chadwick and Kelley's view wasn't as harebrained as it might sound. Major league pitchers completed 85 percent of their starts in 1903. Most analysts believe that, with the relatively remote danger of home runs, pitchers didn't work as hard during the dead ball era as they do today and didn't have to bear down on every pitch. With a two- or three-run lead, two out in the inning and no one on base, for example, even a batting-practice fastball down the middle of the strike zone was unlikely to result in anything worse than a relatively harmless single or double. Leonard Koppett estimated that in the dead ball era, a complete game typically required about half as many pitches as it would require 75 years later. See Koppett, *The New Thinking Fan's Guide to Baseball* (New York: Simon and Schuster, 1991), p. 43.

51 John J. Evers and Hugh S. Fullerton, *Touching Second: The Science of Baseball* (Chicago: Reilly and Britton Co., 1910), p. 225.

52 *Ibid.*, p. 234.

53 *The Sporting News*, April 11, 1903.

54 Christy Mathewson, *Pitching in a Pinch, or Baseball from the Inside* (New York: Stein and Day, 1977 reprint of 1912 original), p. 226.

55 *Cincinnati Enquirer*, March 17, 1903.

56 *Cincinnati Commercial Tribune*, March 17, 1903.

57 *Cincinnati Enquirer*, March 19, 1903.

58 *Ibid.*, March 26, 1903.

59 *The Sporting News*, May 9, 1903.

60 *Cincinnati Commercial Tribune*, April 10, 1903.

61 *Cincinnati Enquirer*, April 10, 1903.

62 Writers' Program of the Work Projects Administration, *Cincinnati: A Guide to the Queen City and its Neighbors* (Cincinnati: Wiesen-Hart Press, 1943), p. 105.

63 *Ibid.*, p. 104.

64 *Ibid.*, p. 112.

65 Lawrence S. Ritter, *The Glory of Their Times* (New York: Macmillan Co., 1966), p. 184.

66 From "a dispatch from Wapakoneta" printed in the *Lima Times-Democrat*, Oct. 21, 1901.

67 Bob Ewing, letter to Nelle Hunter, March 11, 1905.

68 *Sporting Life*, Aug. 11, 1906.

69 *Cincinnati Enquirer*, July 11, 1906.

70 *The Sporting News*, June 25, 1904; see also Greg Rhodes and John Snyder, *Redleg Journal: Year by Year and Day by Day with the Cincinnati Reds since 1866* (Cincinnati: Road West Publishing, 2000), p. 148.

71 Greg Rhodes and John Snyder, *Redleg Journal: Year by Year and Day by Day with the Cincinnati Reds since 1866* (Cincinnati: Road West Publishing, 2000), p. 148. The fan, a music teacher named Alfred Hartzell, apparently regarded a punch in the kisser as merely part of a day at the ballpark; Bowerman was released after Hartzell declined to press charges.

72 *Cincinnati Enquirer*, July 11, 1906.

73 *Sporting Life*, May 2, 1908.

74 *Ibid.*, Nov. 11, 1911.

75 *The Sporting News*, April 19, 1902.

76 Mathewson, *op. cit.*, p. 50. After managing the Reds for three years, Clark Griffith wrote, "Cincinnati was about the last city to get an idea that such a thing as

sportsmanship in baseball was possible. I know they were the last city to give up the practice of running players out of town. Indeed, I doubt they've given it up yet. ... The psychology of Cincinnati baseball crowds is a fearful and wonderful thing." Griffith blamed the problem on the city's "peculiar mixture of foreign blood." See Griffith, "25 Years of Big League Baseball, Part II" *Outing*, Vol. LXIV, No. 2 (May 1914), p. 167.

77   *The Sporting News*, Dec. 9, 1905.

78   Ewing was never ejected from a game and rarely if ever argued with an umpire. Once during a game against Philadelphia, it was observed that he "pursed his lips" as if about to protest a pitch call by umpire Charles Kennedy, but he thought better of it and said nothing; *Cincinnati Enquirer*, Aug. 22, 1904.

79   In his Baltimore days, Joe Kelley had been the Kingpin of the Orioles. The Giants' workhorse pitcher was Iron Man Joe McGinnity. When Frank Chance became a manager, he was the Cubs' Peerless Leader. Ewing's former minor league teammate Roger Bresnahan was known as the Duke of Tralee.

80   *Cincinnati Enquirer*, March 27, 1903.

81   *Sporting Life*, Dec. 5, 1903.

82   *Cincinnati Post*, June 3, 1903.

83   *Sporting Life*, Aug. 22, 1903.

84   *Atlantic City Daily Press*, Aug. 14, 1903.

85   *Ibid.*

86   *New York Journal*, Aug. 18, 1903.

87   *Cincinnati Enquirer*, Aug. 19, 1903.

88   *New York Herald*, Aug. 19, 1903.

89   *New York Tribune*, Aug. 19, 1903.

90   *New York World*, Aug. 18, 1903.

91   *Ibid.*

92   *New York Journal*, Aug. 18, 1903.

93   *Sporting Life*, Aug. 29, 1903.

94   *New York Times*, Aug. 19, 1903.

95   *Cincinnati Commercial Tribune*, Aug. 19, 1903.

96   *New York Sun*, Aug. 19, 1903.

97   *Sporting Life*, Aug. 29, 1903.

98   Ren Mulford, *Sporting Life*, Aug. 29, 1903; also *Cincinnati Enquirer*, Aug. 19, 1903.

99   *Cincinnati Post*, Aug. 19, 1903.

100   *Sporting Life*, Aug. 29, 1903.

101   *Cincinnati Enquirer*, Aug. 19, 1903.

102   *Lima Times-Democrat*, Aug. 19, 1903.

103   *Sporting Life*, Aug. 29, 1903.

104   *Cincinnati Post*, Aug. 19, 1903.

105   *Sporting Life*, Aug. 29, 1903.

106   *Cincinnati Enquirer*, Aug. 19, 1903.

107   This view was expressed by Nelle Ewing late in life in conversations with Jim Bowsher; Bowsher, interview with the author, July 23, 1999.

108   *Cleveland Leader*, Oct. 5, 1903.

109   *Sporting Life*, Oct. 10, 1903.

110   *Cleveland Leader*, Oct. 5, 1903.

111   *Cincinnati Enquirer*, Oct. 13, 1901.

112   Scott Derks, ed., *The Value of a Dollar: Prices and Incomes in the United States, 1860-1999* (Lakeville, Conn.: Grey House Publishing, 1999), p. 52.

113   *Cincinnati Enquirer*, Oct. 13, 1901.

114   Ewing, letter to August Herrmann, Nov. 3, 1903. The letter is on file in the A. Bartlett Giamatti Research Center at the National Baseball Hall of Fame.

"It may be...that the ballplayers are hustling in
order to *impress* Garry that their salaries
do not need cutting, but that won't do.
Salaries are bound to be cut and but few
of the Reds will escape."
—J. ED GRILLO[1]

CHAPTER 6

A New Beginning

JOE KELLEY HAD BIG PLANS for the Cincinnati Reds in 1904. After barely finishing in the first division two straight seasons, he went into the new campaign letting it be known that he planned to impose "strict rules" on the players.[2] Kelley had been nudged in this direction by the team's owners. They wanted no more incidents like the one last year when Cy Seymour showed up drunk on a Sunday afternoon and had to be jerked off the field after he stood rooted in center field and let a routine fly ball drop untouched while the batter circled the bases.[3]

Continuing to remake the team in his own image, Kelley had gotten rid of veteran first baseman Jake Beckley. Beckley was a perennial .300 hitter but, after 16 years in the major leagues, he was a throwback to the old school and, in the view of J. Ed Grillo, "not a player who has ever been able to take part in any sort of a scientific play."[4] In other words, he was one of those players Kelley disparaged "who can hit, but cannot play the game."[5] Gone also was Ed Poole, once regarded as the Reds' most promising young pitcher. His record had dipped to 7–13 in 1903 and he had fallen into further disfavor after repeatedly being caught reading novels on the bench when he wasn't in the game.[6]

With tighter discipline, more brains and deeper commitment, Kelley was convinced the Reds could be in the thick of a three-way pennant race with New York and Chicago. He headed to spring training promising to keep a tight rein on his players and to tolerate "no loafing on the trip this year." After last season's stumbling start, Kelley was particularly anxious to have his pitchers "in superb trim" by Opening Day.[7]

The players at the same time had worries of their own. Ever since the peace agreement ended competition between the National and American leagues for playing talent, it had been taken for granted that baseball's inflated "wartime" salaries would have to be pared. Reds president Garry Herrmann was regarded as a progressive thinker because he had promised not to renege on contracts already signed before the peace agreement. Even so, he acknowledged as far back as December 1902, "That eventually salaries will have to come down goes without saying."[8] Wartime contracts, in the view of *The Sporting News,* had put most players "on easy street."[9] Now those contracts were expiring and players were beginning to feel the squeeze. It was considered a mark of particular favor that Reds third baseman Harry Steinfeldt, after batting .312 in 1903, was not expected to take a pay cut.[10]

Ewing reported to spring training in Dallas after a 36-hour train trip and was soon "working with a vim that shows that the slabman who noses ahead of [him] will have to show something."[11] For once there was little griping about the food. The Reds were quartered at the Oriental Hotel, where the table was reported to be "more conducive to taking on weight than reducing avoirdupois."[12] But within days, things took a sharp turn for the worse in the Reds' camp. The entire party was fairly swamped by "an epidemic of Texas fever—chills, biliousness and other ills."[13] Ewing became seriously ill with symptoms of malaria, as did several teammates including Kelley, Seymour, Jack Sutthoff, pitcher Tom Walker and rookie outfielder Fred Odwell. Practically everyone in camp was affected to some degree. Elmer Fries of the *Cincinnati Post* was bedridden for a week and the *Enquirer*'s Ren Mulford, after sticking at his post through Opening Day, broke down and was off work for six weeks. As a result of this experience, a number of the Reds developed a permanent aversion for the Lone Star State. Ewing was among the most adamant. In future years when the club considered returning to the Dallas area for spring training, Ewing grumped that he would just as soon be handed his unconditional release as a train ticket to Texas.[14]

Back in Cincinnati as the season began, some changes were evident around the ballpark. Matty Schwab, who had pitched against Ewing in that pivotal 1901 exhibition in Sidney, had given up his aspirations as a ballplayer and come home to succeed his father as head groundskeeper. Throughout Ewing's remaining years in Cincinnati, Schwab would be an integral part of the Reds' organization. Besides caring for the playing field, he designed and built scoreboards, pitched batting practice and was occasionally pressed into service in exhibition games. When the club went on the road, he sometimes suited up and worked out with injured players who were left home for rehabilitation. Though Schwab would never throw a pitch in the major leagues, he would enjoy a far longer career with the Reds than Ewing or any of his other contemporaries.[15]

Notable additions to the ballclub itself included a brainy little second baseman who spent his off-seasons attending law school at the University of Cincinnati. Miller Huggins was a native Cincinnatian, son of an English immigrant grocer and graduate of the city's semipro ranks. Because his father frowned upon baseball as a profession, Huggins started out in the game under an assumed name: He first showed up in box scores as Proctor, a tag most likely borrowed from one of Cincinnati's prominent manufacturing concerns, the Procter & Gamble Co., maker of Ivory soap.[16] He had logged a season with Fleischmanns' Mountain Tourists and before that even played a summer in Wapakoneta—in 1898, when Ewing was with the Toledo Mud Hens. Most recently Huggins had spent three seasons in the minor leagues with St. Paul, helping the Saints to the American Association pennant in 1903.

Garry Herrmann had been angling for Huggins ever since he took over running the Reds. More than a year was required to close the sale. Herrmann's early overtures were brushed aside not only by the St. Paul club but by Huggins himself, demonstrating that even under the newly buttressed reserve system, a smart, educated player could still occasionally carve out some breathing room for himself. While baseball liked to showcase the college men—Bucknell's Christy Mathewson, Brown's Fred Tenney, the University of Pennsylvania's Roy Thomas and others[17]—who attested to the game's growing refinement and respectability, there was an uncomfortable sense within the establishment that this new breed might be more difficult to control than the rest of what Johnny Evers and Hugh

Fullerton called "the livestock, upon which the fortunes of the owners depended."[18] College men still had no more than limited control over their careers in baseball, but they had alternatives outside the game. For public consumption, an old-school type like Joe Kelley might dutifully acknowledge that Mathewson, Tenney and their sort were "a good influence on the general run of ballplayers," but he also suspected "the really ambitious collegians," as he called them, would bypass baseball in favor of more promising career options.[19]

Huggins wanted to play in the big leagues, and in his hometown if possible, but he made it clear he wasn't going anywhere until the deal was right. As late as the middle of 1903, the budding attorney told Herrmann, he had a contract with St. Paul that made it "impossible for any major league club to draft me unless I am willing."[20] The arrangement not only left Huggins free to work out his own contract with the Reds in advance of any sale, but also required St. Paul to pay him $1,000 of the purchase price.[21]

Of more immediate concern to Ewing, though, was that the Reds had a new catcher. Bill Bergen had been sold to Brooklyn and in his place Cincinnati had drafted 26-year-old George Schlei, who had batted .278 for Denver in the Western League the previous summer. Like Huggins, Schlei was a Cincinnati boy. Having attended St. Xavier High School and played for local semipro teams, he was acknowledged in the local papers as "the pride of the East End."[22] A stocky 5 feet, 8½ inches and 180 pounds, Schlei would soon acquire a reputation as a solid receiver, and also a distinctive nautical nickname inspired by a prominent naval officer of the Spanish-American War. In spring training Heinie Peitz, 33 years old and embarking on his 13th season in the National League, had been directed "to get his lungs in the best condition as soon as possible" in the expectation that he would be spending most of his time on the coaching lines[23] while "Admiral" Schlei handled the bulk of the catching.[24]

For Ewing, Schlei became a comfortable and compatible collaborator. Years later, when he was sent to New York to replace the fiery Roger Bresnahan, there were complaints that Schlei lacked the pepper-pot personality, the "dash and daring" that Giants fans were accustomed to in a catcher.[25] But he was always a conscientious, reliable, loyal partner. Over their years together, Schlei would catch Ewing more than 100 times. Schlei would be behind the plate for the lion's share of Ewing's major league victories and

Cincinnati native George "Admiral" Schlei was Bob Ewing's most frequent major league battery mate and caught the lion's share of his victories. Steady but unspectacular, he was known as "Old Faithful." *Photo: Chicago Historical Society, SDN-003079.*

shutouts, and for two Opening Day starts. Schlei would also help Ewing through the greatest turning point of his career.

Solidifying that relationship would take time. For now, there were adventures awaiting on and off the field. The National League schedule landed the Reds in St. Louis on April 30 for the opening of the Louisiana Purchase Exposition, popularly known as the St. Louis World's Fair. For a 50-cent admission charge, visitors could encounter such marvels as air conditioning, the dishwasher, a telephone answering device and a "wireless telegraph," a forerunner of radio. Along the Pike, the fair's mile-long midway, sightseers could take an excursion to the Tyrolean Alps, travel to the North Pole or cross Siberia on a simulated train ride. They could experience the Galveston flood of 1900 or take in a reenactment of the Boer War. Among the most popular exhibits on the 1,200-acre fairgrounds were aboriginal villages constructed and occupied by "primitive" peoples imported for the occasion from around the world.

The ice cream cone was invented at the fair and many Americans soon developed a taste for ground beef sandwiches like those cooked up along the Pike at Old Dave's Hamburger Stand. A breathtaking ride was George Washington Gale Ferris' giant observation wheel, more than 250 feet high. Designed for the Chicago World's Fair 11 years earlier, the original wheel was reassembled in St. Louis after being delivered in 175 freight cars. Among the Ferris wheel's millions of astonished riders was the celebrated Apache warrior Geronimo. Approximately 80 years old, he sold photographs and autographs along the Pike across from the hamburger stand, later boasting that he "often made as much as $2 a day."[26] Eighteen years after Geronimo's surrender to the U.S. Army, one of the functionaries assigned to keep an eye on him at the fair found him "an agreeable, amiable old man," usually "happy as a bird."[27]

More than 18 million people passed through the gates during the fair's seven-month run. Among the crowd on opening day were Joe Kelley, Mike Donlin, Miller Huggins "and some of the [other] boys."[28] Those who took in the fair after dark found it "like fairyland with its myriad of lights."[29]

In the final game of the St. Louis series, Ewing—pitching to Schlei for the first time in an official game—lost 4–3 on an error in the ninth inning. The result left Ewing winless after two starts. But for the most part, the 1904 season started out living up to Joe Kelley's high expectations. The

Reds weathered the loss of third baseman Harry Steinfeldt, almost asphyxiated when he accidentally pulled down a gas chandelier in his apartment; he was hospitalized nearly a month. Bolstered by good work from new pitchers Win Kellum and Tom Walker, Cincinnati held first place as late as May 26 and was still within two games of the lead in mid-June. The team's performance was "a big boon to [Cincinnati's] railroads, restaurants and hotels, ... as thousands of strangers flock[ed] to the city" to see the games, especially on Sundays.[30]

Throughout these high times, little was seen of Bob Ewing. Perhaps still suffering the debilitating effects of his pre-season illness, he remained behind when the team traveled, pitched little and was soon written off as "the disappointment of the [mound] corps."[31] Nearly three months into the season, he had won only one game.

While Ewing was in danger of becoming the forgotten man in Cincinnati, he wasn't forgotten elsewhere. John J. McGraw, seeing that the Reds weren't using Ewing and remembering his past performances against the Giants, asked the Reds to "put a price on the tall lad from Wapakoneta."[32] On the heels of McGraw's inquiry came a similar one from Hugh Duffy, manager of the Philadelphia Phillies. It was likely around this time that Garry Herrmann dictated the following undated communication to Reds secretary Max Fleischmann:

> Your telegram this morning received. I have already written to Potter in reference to Ewing. It is in our best interests to help Philadelphia, if we can do so in justice to ourselves. If we can get as much from Potter as we can from Brush or Dreyfuss, who also wants Ewing, I am in favor of letting Potter have him. In the meantime, you might, in a quiet way, without committing yourself to any deal, feel Brush out, and see what he would give for Ewing in the event we want to let him go. An offer from Brush would put us in a position to boost the price to the Philadelphia people. Please let me know what Brush says, if he says anything at all, as early as possible.[33]

The reason it was in the "best interests" of Herrmann and the Fleischmanns to help Philadelphia, if possible, rather than Barney Dreyfuss in Pittsburgh or John T. Brush in New York, was that the Cincinnati owners also held a substantial stake in the Phillies. When that club's longtime owners, John Rogers and sporting goods tycoon A.J. Reach, drained by the legal and competitive strains of the baseball war, decided to get out from under the economic burden of the franchise, Herrmann—along with Pittsburgh owner Barney Dreyfuss—helped to finance the purchase of the club by a local consortium headed by James Potter. When the deal was completed, Herrmann, Dreyfuss and the Fleischmann brothers reportedly owned $60,000 worth of Phillies stock, or nearly one-third of the ballclub.[34]

Though purists such as Henry Chadwick decried such interlocking or "syndicate" ownership as an "evil" that "aims a blow at the integrity of the professional [baseball] business at large,"[35] similar arrangements had long been tolerated, as when John T. Brush owned part of the New York Giants while running the Reds. Baseball required money and the operators were unlikely to reject a large infusion of cash from whatever source. Herrmann, at various times during his first several years as president of the Reds, owned stock in or loaned money to most of the teams in the National League.[36] Such practices raised clear and sometimes convoluted conflicts of interest, such as in 1906, when a dispute between Cincinnati and Philadelphia over the rights to pitcher Charles Roy threatened to land before the National Commission. At the time, Herrmann was not only president of the Reds and chairman of the commission but also, according to *The Sporting News,* "the largest stockholder in the Phillies."[37]

Potter, who took over as the Phillies' president in 1903, was a Philadelphia stockbroker and socialite, said to know "more about squash and indoor tennis than about baseball."[38] As for the team's other "fashionable stockholders," a Philadelphia sportswriter concluded, "Most of them prefer cricket or polo or tennis or golf—some gentlemanly game...in which a man can wear nice, white clothes with creases in the trousers."[39] Potter would relinquish the club presidency after less than two years, having demonstrated, according to *The Sporting News,* "only a superficial knowledge of the game."[40] Within months after he assumed the office, the Philadelphia correspondent for the same publication complained that, while Potter controlled sufficient stock to run the club on his own, he had "shown himself entirely willing to be influenced and controlled by Dreyfuss and Herrmann."[41]

No deal was consummated with regard to Ewing. For whatever reason, Herrmann decided it was not in Cincinnati's best interests to let the tall right-hander go.

Not that he was making any discernible contribution to the Reds. As of June 30, Ewing hadn't pitched in six weeks. Kelley contrived to get him some work in an exhibition game in Oil City, Pennsylvania, hometown of Reds pitcher Jack Harper. Kelley's notion was to have Harper pitch two innings against the local amateurs so the home folks could get a look at him, then pull him out so he would be fresh to start two days later in Pittsburgh, whose Pirates were dogging the Reds in the standings.

Everything went according to plan in Oil City. Harper dazzled the spectators with five strikeouts, then Ewing took over and completed a two-hit shutout as the Reds won handily, 3–0. But Kelley's strategy backfired in Pittsburgh. Harper had nothing on the ball and the entire team came out looking "slow and laggy."[42] After two innings the Pirates had a 12–0 lead and Ewing was called in to try to duplicate his Oil City performance.

The game was hopelessly out of hand—the final score was 14–2—but Ewing, looking more himself than at any time all season, "seemed to have a tonic effect on the whole team."[43] For the first time in months, Old Wapak was exhibiting "winning symptoms."[44] In Cincinnati a week later, he displayed "wonderful speed and good control"[45] in stifling the Phillies by a 7–1 count.

Ewing's revival was good news, and the Reds were in a mood for some. Though still in third place, they had slid a dozen games off the blistering pace set by the league-leading Giants. Noodles Hahn, after winning 106 games and pitching more than 1,600 innings in the previous five seasons, was increasingly looking like a pitcher who was "all in."[46] There was no movement on his fastball. There were rumblings that he was "going the way of all left-handers,"[47] which was to say he was "on the downgrade, mainly because his pitching arm is too near his heart."[48]

On top of that, the Reds' heaviest hitter was out of the lineup—for good, as it turned out. Kelley, whose leniency with fractious ballplayers had sometimes gotten him into embarrassing situations, was finding it necessary to crack down. A year earlier, when Kelley was forced to pull Cy Seymour off the field in the middle of a game, no disciplinary action followed. Now Mike Donlin's behavior had developed into a problem that couldn't be ignored. He had become "insulting and threatening," once trying to goad Kelley into a fight.[49] When Donlin went on a bender in St. Louis over the July 4 holiday, Kelley and Herrmann had had enough. Jettisoning the "diplomacy"[50] that characterized their handling of the Seymour case, they suspended Donlin—.356 batting average and all—for the second time, this time for 30 days. Herrmann, charging the player with "drunkenness and conduct that was reprehensible,"[51] practically vowed that Donlin would never play for the Reds again. Before his suspension ended, the wayward outfielder was dealt to New York as part of a three-sided trade in which Cincinnati received outfielder Jimmy Sebring from the Pirates. Sebring had "been in bad odor for some time" with his Pittsburgh teammates[52] after an altercation with star shortstop Honus Wagner.

Hopeful that Ewing was ready to resume a full workload, Kelley took the opportunity to sell off two other pitchers, Claude Elliott to New York and Jack Sutthoff to Philadelphia. Long Bob didn't immediately start racking up victories; he had been "up against it" all season and "his usual hard luck"[53] didn't turn around right away. August 21 found him locked in a grueling endurance contest with the Phillies and Sutthoff who, on his first Cincinnati appearance with his new team, "was presented with a handsome diamond-studded watch charm."[54]

In the seventh inning, with the score tied 2–2, Ewing lofted a fly ball to left-center field. Center fielder Hugh Duffy and left fielder John Titus, converging on the ball, "came together with a crash"[55] that sent both of them sprawling. Titus was knocked unconscious and the ball rolled up the terrace and all the way to the fence, more than 400 feet from home plate.[56] By the time Duffy recovered the ball, Ewing had rounded third base on the way to his first major league home run. He crossed the plate and "staggered with his tongue out" to the bench where Heinie Peitz, enacting one of baseball's ancient rituals, fanned the winded pitcher with a towel.[57]

It was an exhausting game all around. Ewing did his best to win it with his bat, belaboring Sutthoff with two doubles as well as the home run. But Philadelphia evened the score again in the eighth inning on two singles, a wild pitch and Duffy's long fly out. Ewing and Sutthoff toiled four more innings before the Reds won 4–3 in the 13th on a hit, a sacrifice and Peitz's line single to left. Still, the *Cincinnati Post* maintained, the Reds' support of Ewing had been markedly "saffron-hued at times." Even in victory, he remained "Hard Luck" Ewing.[58]

In ways that were difficult to pin down, things didn't seem to be going quite right. Despite maintaining a healthy winning percentage around .580, the Reds continued to slip farther behind the league leaders. Kelley was thrown out of half a dozen games for abusing umpires; a three-game suspension typically followed. When league president Harry Pulliam suspended both Kelley and Seymour, Ewing was pressed into service in the outfield. Newspapers grumbled about Kelley's frequent absences from the lineup and Barney Dreyfuss expressed the view that Cincinnati, despite having a strong team, had "kicked itself out of the fight."[59]

Nerves were a little on edge when a 22-year-old prospect arrived in town for a tryout. The candidate was an Ohio native, born 90 miles east of Cincinnati in Pike County, and a college man, educated at Ohio Wesleyan University. He had attracted attention while catching for Dallas in the Texas League. With the Reds, he played in exhibition games in Rushville, Indiana—where the local amateurs were "gorgeous as a flock of flamingoes" in their claret-colored uniforms[60]—and in Niles, Ohio. After shaking off some initial nerves, he acquitted himself respectably. His hitting was "nothing sensational,"[61] but he handled the deliveries of Win Kellum and Tom Walker "in fine style."[62]

It appeared Kelley had "picked a good one."[63] The Reds might well have signed the young man except that while they were pondering what to do, the Boston Beaneaters[64] came to town for a weekend series. The Beaneaters had three players who, for religious reasons, refused to play on Sunday—team captain Fred Tenney and pitchers Togie Pittinger and Irvin "Kaiser" Wilhelm. Such Sabbatarians were not uncommon in baseball. Several prominent players had clauses in their contracts or informal agreements with their clubs excusing them from Sunday games; the most famous was Christy Mathewson, star pitcher of the New York Giants. These arrangements were rarely troublesome for eastern clubs. Sunday ball was banned in Boston, as in most cities in the East. But Sunday baseball was a cultural fixture in the big league cities of the West, and an economic necessity to the Reds. Kelley was somewhat taken aback on Saturday afternoon when, at the conclusion of the first game in the series, he was informed that his aspiring backstop, in keeping with his devoutly Methodist upbringing, would not be at the ballpark the next day.

So the player didn't see what happened on Sunday. Boston, traveling with only a 13-man roster as a cost-saving measure, showed up with just 10 players in uniform. After the Reds assaulted starting pitcher Ed Mc-

Nichol for 11 hits and 11 runs in the first two innings, Tom Fisher, the only man on Boston's bench, was sent on in relief. He pitched into the fifth but hurt his hand and couldn't continue. With no other substitutes available, second baseman Jim Delahanty volunteered to pitch the rest of the game. Fisher had to go to the outfield and do the best he could in a reshuffled lineup. Cincinnati, pounding out 18 hits and benefiting from 10 walks, won 19–6. The Reds, who for much of the season had been bragging of "magnificent crowds, and from the best people,"[65] were not pleased that 6,447 home fans had been subjected to a sloppy farce. *The Sporting News* decried such an "imposition" on the patrons and berated players who "observe the Lord's day by abstaining from playing, but ... do not hesitate to draw salary for full time."[66]

The next day, Garry Herrmann sat his young catcher down for a talking-to. The situation was "made very plain":[67] There would be no Sabbatarians on the Cincinnati club. Herrmann gave the prospect a week to consider his position, and allowed him to remain with the team in the interim. The player agreed to think about what Herrmann had said, but a week later, as the squad returned from a road trip on a Sunday morning, he made his decision clear. According to C.J. Bocklet, Ed Grillo's successor as Cincinnati correspondent for *The Sporting News,* he refused to carry his catcher's mask from the train station "because he did not think it proper."[68]

That finished the youngster with the Reds. After they let him go, he was drafted by the Chicago White Sox and traded to the St. Louis Browns, with whom he made his major league debut in 1905. He never amounted to much as a player, batting .239 in 120 big league games. But he remained in the game as a manager and executive, eventually creating the first minor league farm system and making it possible for Jackie Robinson to break the color barrier in 1947.

Throughout 60 years in baseball, Branch Rickey made it a practice to stay away from the ballpark on Sunday.[69]

BY THE TIME RICKEY WAS TURNED LOOSE, the Reds had fallen into fourth place and were in the midst of losing five games out of six. Ewing, however, was beginning to find his footing. Amid the brouhaha surrounding the Sunday fiasco with Boston it got little notice, but Ewing pitched six very solid innings that day. After Cincinnati starter Win Kellum was roughly handled in the early going, Ewing came on and "did the best work of all the pitchers that were used in the game,"[70] scattering five hits and holding the Beaneaters scoreless for the last five innings.

In the days that followed, Ewing pitched creditably in losses to the Giants and Pirates, the latter by a 1–0 score. He then won two straight before losing another tough one, 3–2 to Carl Lundgren in Chicago.

So it came to pass that on September 23, 1904, Bob Ewing found himself in Boston preparing to take on the Beaneaters at the South End Grounds. The day before in New York, the Giants had beaten Cincinnati in the first game of a doubleheader to clinch the National League pennant. The Reds, having failed to live up to Joe Kelley's high hopes, were standing fourth, 23 games behind the leaders. Ewing, despite some encouraging developments of late, had won only seven games all summer, while losing 12. He had been in professional baseball for eight seasons and, at age 31, was well on toward middle age for one in his chosen field. In nearly three seasons with the Reds, he had been a .500 pitcher at best. All told, his major league balance sheet showed 26 victories against 31 defeats.

There was a decided chill in the air on that autumnal Friday afternoon in New England and if Ewing paused to take stock of his career to date, his situation might have seemed rather dismal. Outwardly, though, it appeared the season's setbacks had "not worried Bob in the least"; in the face of adversity, he kept "plugging away the same as ever."[71] Now, as he warmed up with Admiral Schlei before the game, Ewing had particular cause to be optimistic. He had been developing a new weapon for his ongoing battle with National League batters, and today was the day of its unveiling. Bob Ewing's baseball fortunes were about to change dramatically.

Undoubtedly he had been working on the spitball for weeks or even months. An attempt to master a tricky new breaking pitch might account for recurrent murmurings that Ewing's control had been "decidedly off-color"[72] for much of the season. It seems likely he would have tried out the new pitch in games, perhaps in the Oil City exhibition or while mopping up in those lopsided games with Pittsburgh and Boston. He might have thrown it a few times during his string of strong starts over the past three weeks. After all, Ewing in the past had occasionally incurred the displeasure of his manager by eschewing his good fastball and going instead with what Kelley described as "experimental shoots" of various kinds.[73] But his latest and greatest experiment had remained a fairly well-kept secret. Clearly he hadn't relied on the spitball; if he had employed it at all, it had attracted no notice. Certainly the writers covering the team had not tumbled to the fact that Old Wapak had something new in his bag of tricks.

They were about to have an awakening. Showcasing the spitball for the first time, leaning on it for his "out" pitch, Ewing was revealed as an entirely new pitcher. There was apparently nothing secretive or clandestine about what he was doing. Everybody in the press box and informed enthusiasts among the 1,282 spectators on the grounds recognized that he was feeding the Boston batters a steady diet of wet ones.

"Bob Ewing, the Cincinnati pitcher, undoubtedly has got perfect control of the spitball," one observer wrote in the *Boston Morning Journal*. "He worked it almost continually. ... It was particularly effective when [Boston's] chances for run-getting looked brightest."[74]

Soon after it became evident that Ewing was throwing the spitball, it became equally clear that the Beaneaters couldn't hit it. Ewing dominated the game, striking out 12 and not allowing a runner to second base until the sixth inning. Occasionally a pitch would get away from him: Schlei was charged with one passed ball and Ewing's wild pitch in the eighth inning contributed to Boston's only run. But he walked only one, and of Boston's seven hits, according to Charlie Zuber of the *Cincinnati Times-Star*, at least four were "the flukiest kind of flukes."[75] With the exception of Duff Cooley's clean single in the seventh, the *Enquirer* classified all of Boston's safeties as scratches, bloops, "and two ... that were pretty as hummingbirds."[76] The Reds, meanwhile, eked out an unearned run in the fourth and scored again in the seventh when Jimmy Sebring walked, was sacrificed to second and came home on Harry Steinfeldt's single. That was enough to beat Togie Pittinger 2–1. The entire affair took 93 minutes.

Ewing had announced himself as the National League's first master of the spitball, and the word spread quickly. The *New York Times*, which summarized the game in 45 words, informed the world that "Ewing

The Baseball Days of Long Bob Ewing

struck out 12 Boston players ... by employing the so-called 'spit ball.'"[77] Post-game reaction was swift and pointed.

"Unless that ball is cut out," Boston manager Al Buckenberger told anyone who would listen, "there will not be a .300 batter in either league next season."[78]

"Here we are pleading for more hitting," chimed James Billings, part-owner of the Boston club, "and the pitchers slip in a new wrinkle on us. There must be some legislation against it."[79]

As for Ewing, his course was set. The spitball would be his bread and butter for the rest of his time in baseball. He would be identified with the pitch to the point where writers would sometimes refer to him as "Spitter Bob" or "Spitball Robert."[80] The Boston game was also the final step in cementing the partnership between Ewing and Admiral Schlei. They had undoubtedly worked on the pitch together and on the day of the unveiling, Schlei—despite occasional difficulties with the elusive new addition to Ewing's repertoire—received plaudits for catching "a fine game."[81] Ironically, Heinie Peitz did not even see the performance that marked his pupil's graduation to full-fledged major league pitcher. A foul tip had "split his right hand" in New York and put Peitz out of action.[82] He had returned to Cincinnati the night before the game. Peitz, who had done more than anyone else to give Ewing his start in the majors, would never catch him again.

After Boston, Ewing stifled Philadelphia on five hits and stymied Brooklyn 5–1. In St. Louis on the next-to-last day of the season, he stopped the Cardinals 8–1 on four hits and went 3-for-4 himself as the Reds swept a four-game series and nudged ahead of Pittsburgh in the standings. Overall, in the final month of the season, Ewing posted a 6–2 record, winning more games than in the entire campaign prior to that time. Some observers credited Ewing and his spitball for beating Pittsburgh out of third place.[83]

"Ewing has been pitching great ball lately," C.J. Bocklet bubbled during the streak. "... Ever since he has been worked regularly he is pitching ball that no slab artist can beat. ... When the local club was willing to let one of their pitchers go early in the season, ... most all of the fans were willing to have the tin can degree attached to Ewing. ... I'll wager that not one of them would consent to part with the big fellow now."[84]

For the first time, Ewing had decisively stilled any nagging doubts that he deserved to "again [be] with the Reds when they start on their spring training trip next season."[85]

THE OFF-SEASON was full of its usual homely pleasures. Ewing had some fun on the annual barnstorming trip, teasing the overmatched competition when he "turned loose the spitball on a few of them."[86] He socialized at the Elks lodge, of which he was now a member.[87] Sportswriter Ren Mulford noted receiving "cheery messages" around the holidays from Ewing and several of the Reds' other "clever fellows."[88]

There was also one deep sadness. Just before Christmas Bob's father, Edward H. Ewing, passed away at age 62. Bob was at his bedside when he died, "after much suffering," in a Cincinnati hospital where he had gone for surgery to relieve lingering complications from his Civil War wound.[89]

A significant part of the winter was occupied with the delicate annual dance of contract negotiations, conducted mostly by mail between Ewing's farm in New Hampshire and Garry Herrmann's office in Cincinnati. December arrived with only Ewing and Tommy Corcoran still unsigned for 1905, leading Ren Mulford to speculate that "Old Wapakoneta is possibly looking for a dividend on his spitball."[90] Another explanation of the delay might be that Ewing was preoccupied with his father's declining health, but Mulford had hit on at least part of the truth.

For 1904, Ewing had been paid $3,000, nearly one-quarter of it in the form of a cash advance before the season.[91] His salary had climbed considerably from the $1,800 he had received as a rookie. He was fortunate to have signed for 1903 before the peace agreement was reached, when Herrmann was still handing out pay raises as insurance against further raids by the American League. Still, two years later, Ewing ranked only near the middle of the Reds' pay list, earning two-thirds as much as Noodles Hahn. Ewing was on a par with rookie Miller Huggins and pulling down only a few hundred dollars more than newcomers Tom Walker and Win Kellum.

For a couple years before 1903, players had the option of shopping their services to competing leagues and taking the best offer. With peace came both leagues' acceptance of the reserve clause, binding each player to the club that owned him, a situation that would remain unchallenged for the balance of Ewing's career. The owners, in agreeing to honor each other's contracts and reserve lists, had brought an end to costly competition among themselves and left the players with no say in where they would play. There were so-called "outlaw" leagues that weren't parties to the National Agreement, but these were usually fly-by-night operations that offered nothing in the way of job security, and merely stepping on the same field with outlaws would practically guarantee banishment from organized baseball. Outlaw ball held no appeal for anyone interested in a long-term career.

Ewing had no viable alternative to doing business with the Reds, and without an alternative, he had no leverage in contract talks. In the view of Johnny Evers and Hugh Fullerton, the typical ballplayer of the time was "a slave held in bondage,"[92] at the mercy of a system which was "contrary to civil law, in direct violation of the federal laws regulating combines and the blacklist, and in principle, directly in defiance of the Constitution and the Rights of Man."[93]

There had been efforts to organize the players for their mutual protection and benefit, but none had produced much in the way of lasting effects. In 1890 the Brotherhood of Professional Base Ball Players, under the leadership of the ballplaying lawyer John Montgomery Ward, had revolted against the established leagues and formed a circuit of its own. Despite attracting many of the game's top stars, the Players League folded after one year of financially ruinous competition. More recently, in June 1900, delegates from every National League team had formed the Protective Association of Professional Baseball Players, with an initiation fee of $5 and dues of $2 a month. The association never attracted more than halfhearted backing in the Cincinnati clubhouse. The organization was indifferently led and players were generally cautious in their support. By the time Ewing arrived on the scene, the association was on its last legs; it faded out of existence with the end of the 1902 season. The idea of unionizing, perhaps under the American Federation of Labor, surfaced occasionally during Ewing's years, but few in baseball took such talk very seriously.

"I don't see where we would gain anything by it," the Reds' Harry Steinfeldt said, "and we might be called on to quit playing whenever the teamsters or plumbers went out on strike."[94]

Two days after the 1904 season ended, Ewing opened contract negotiations with the first of a series of letters to Herrmann. Ewing pointed out that his winning percentage was almost as good as Noodles Hahn's, and suggested that both men should be paid the same. Even so, the proposal was more an entreaty than a negotiating position. "I am about a game behind him," Ewing wrote. "That won't knock me out of getting the same money as him, will it? I hope it won't."[95]

Ewing probably already suspected what the answer would be. Herrmann's side of the correspondence doesn't survive, but predictably he held a differing view. Three weeks later, Ewing betrayed a bit of petulance when he wrote:

> *You don't seem to think I am an old leaguer. You always*
> *compare me with Walker and Kellum. Why don't you put me*
> *with Harper and Hahn? Last year I was better than Harper*
> *and this year as good as Hahn and still you compare me*
> *with the young fellows just breaking in. ... I don't want to*
> *be stubborn, I think I am right in my price.*

As talks dragged on, Ewing was also becoming sensitive to comments in the press. "I see the *Commercial* has commenced to touch me up a little now," he wrote. "I am anxious to get it over and will pitch my arm off to please you. ... I am sure if I get the work like I did last fall I will do you lots of good."[96]

Despite those last conciliatory words, the tone now was decidedly cooler than in Ewing's first letter. That communication had ended with a cheery reference to the team's "grand finish" and was signed, "Your friend, Bob Ewing."[97] This one closed with a terse, "Send answer to New Hampshire, Ohio," and was signed with a perfunctory "truly."[98]

Six weeks later there was still no agreement. As Christmas approached, Ewing had lowered his sights somewhat. He had buried his father and was tired of arguing.

"If you will send me a contract for $3,600 I will sign it and return it at once and stop all this trouble," he wrote. At the same time, he asked if it might be possible to get some advance money when he signed.[99]

In the end, after nearly three months of intermittent haggling, Ewing probably got little or no increase over the $3,000 he received for 1904. The final letter in the sequence indicates that he would have to come down a bit more before Herrmann would be satisfied. There was still no agreement, but Ewing offered to call on Herrmann at his office, "and I am sure we will agree all right."[100]

Wringing a pay raise out of the Reds wouldn't get any easier in the years to come. Throughout baseball, ever since the peace agreement, management had been moving to cut costs. After the 1903 season, *The Sporting News* called for a one-third reduction in player salaries "to get the game on a paying plane."[101] In subsequent years the paper pushed for salary limits and a fixed wage scale for entry-level players. By 1905 pay cuts were common. While attendance throughout the major leagues (and in Cincinnati) more than doubled between 1901 and 1909, player salaries stagnated, averaging less than $2,500 for most of the decade.[102] "With few exceptions," *The Sporting News* reported, "[the] players yielded gracefully" to the owners' cost-cutting measures.[103]

Ewing fared better than many; by the end of his career, he was said to be "one of the highest-salaried flippers on the staff" in Philadelphia.[104] But even he accepted his circumstances with more resignation than grace.

The pattern of negotiations would hold true throughout Ewing's years in Cincinnati. After his best season, in 1905, his negotiations with Herrmann dragged on until the end of January. "I didn't think you would ask me to sign a contract for less than $4,000," Ewing wrote, sounding both surprised and hurt.[105] Herrmann undoubtedly responded with protestations of his own hurt feelings, and the suggestion that Ewing was ungrateful for the club's generosity. A week later, a chastened Ewing conceded that Herrmann had "always treated me all OK." Still the pitcher was frustrated.

"I am like everyone else. I want all I can get," he said candidly. "You can't blame me for that."

Having now been thoroughly backed down, Ewing could only try to salve his wounded pride. It "would help some," he said, if he could at least get $3,500. As usual, it was more a supplication than a demand. "How would that be, make it an even $3,500?" he wrote.[106] But the decision was out of his hands. He could argue and grumble, but he would ultimately have to take what the club was willing to give. After another week, he gave in.

"All right, I will leave it to you," he wrote to Herrmann. "I will sign my contract and send it in the first of the week."[107] After the best year of his career, Ewing apparently got no raise at all.[108]

As late as 1906, Ewing still wasn't making $3,600.[109] His communications with Herrmann usually remained cordial, sometimes bordering on deferential. As Ewing said, he "didn't like to be kicking all the time,"[110] but he increasingly rankled at having what he considered legitimate salary demands turned aside by Herrmann's avuncular assurances. Sometimes the ballplayer's feelings were assuaged by the prospect of a post-season bonus, but that bonus never seemed to materialize.

"Last spring …," Ewing reminded Herrmann in 1906, making a case for one such bonus, "you said for me to go ahead and sign … and leave it to you and you would make me satisfied after the season was over."[111] The bonus was never paid. One of the last surviving letters in which Ewing discusses money with Herrmann captures the player's sense of resignation. "You said leave it to you and if that's your answer, it's all right with me," Ewing wrote. "I will be satisfied."[112]

A similar sentiment had closed Ewing's first post-season letter in 1904. "Hope you will consider this and do the best you can by me," Ewing wrote at that time.[113] The nature of Ewing's relationship with the owners never changed. The only difference was that over time, Ewing's letters gradually lost their hopeful tone.

It's unlikely he was ever "satisfied." Toward the end of Ewing's career, there was talk of a ballplayers' Bill of Rights, with provisions for salary arbitration and the possibility of free agency after a predetermined number of years with one club.[114] But Ewing would not live to see such changes, much less have a chance to play under such a system. His only choice was to take what the club deigned to offer, or go home to the farm.

He wanted to play, so they had him.

1   *The Sporting News*, Sept. 19, 1903.
2   *Sporting Life*, Nov. 28, 1903.
3   Kelley said afterwards that he would have benched Seymour at the start of the game, but he wanted to avoid a loud and likely profane argument within earshot of the grandstand, "fearing that the large Sunday crowd of ladies would be shocked." *The Sporting News*, Aug. 8, 1903.
4   *The Sporting News*, Nov. 28, 1903.
5   *Ibid.*, Oct. 25, 1903.
6   *Ibid.*, May 7, 1904.
7   *Ibid.*, March 5, 1904.
8   *Ibid.*, Dec. 20, 1902.
9   *Ibid.*, July 25, 1903.
10   *Ibid.*, Sept. 19, 1903.
11   *Sporting Life*, March 26, 1904.
12   *Ibid.*
13   *Ibid.*, April 9, 1904.
14   *The Sporting News*, Jan. 12, 1907.
15   Matty Schwab (1879-1970) first worked at League Park in 1894, running errands and tending patrons' horses for tips. He succeeded his father as head groundskeeper in 1903 and remained with the Reds, in that capacity and later as ballpark superintendent, until his retirement in 1963. See *Cincinnati Post and Times-Star*, April 9, 1970; and *Cincinnati Enquirer*, April 2, 2001.
16   Around the time Huggins was beginning to attract notice on Cincinnati's sandlots, a history of the city described the 65-acre P&G complex in suburban Ivorydale as "the largest manufacturing plant ... in the world." See *History of Cincinnati and Hamilton County, Ohio: Their Past and Present* (Cincinnati: S.B. Nelson and Co., 1894), p. 323. Other sources suggest that teammates hung the name on the aspiring lawyer because he shared a gift for oratory with a well-known politician of the time. J. Proctor Knott (1830-1911) was a one-time member of Congress and later governor of Kentucky.
17   The press, ever eager to help burnish baseball's image, didn't usually give much scrutiny to the academic credentials of the game's so-called college men. While Mathewson, Tenney, Thomas and others did attend various institutions of higher learning, many ballplayers played for college teams without bothering to go to college. In an era when eligibility rules were lax or nonexistent, Eddie Plank pitched for Gettysburg College while taking high school courses in a college preparatory program, but he was never a student at the college itself. Hal Chase apparently registered at Santa Clara College, but he bragged that he never attended a single class. Harry Davis was occasionally identified as a product of higher education by virtue of having graduated from Girard College in Philadelphia, but Girard was in fact an elementary and high school for underprivileged boys. See Norman L. Macht, *Connie Mack and the Early Years of Baseball* (Lincoln, Neb.: University of Nebraska Press, 2007), p. 240; Martin Donell Kohout, *Hal Chase: The Defiant Life and Turbulent Times of Baseball's Biggest Crook* (Jefferson, N.C.: McFarland and Co. Inc., 2001), pp. 13-14; and Mike Grahek, "Harry H. Davis" in David Jones, ed., *Deadball Stars of the American League* (Dulles, Va.: Potomac Books, 2006), p. 579.
18   John J. Evers and Hugh S. Fullerton, *Touching Second: The Science of Baseball* (Chicago: Reilly and Britton Co., 1910), p. 29.
19   *The Sporting News*, Jan. 28, 1905.
20   Miller Huggins, letter to August Herrmann, Aug. 17, 1903. The letter is on file in the A. Bartlett Giamatti Research Center at the National Baseball Hall of Fame.

21 Another college man who found a way around the reserve system was Orval Overall. When he signed with Tacoma of the Pacific Coast League, he secured an agreement that he be unconditionally released at season's end. That left Overall free to negotiate his own deal with Cincinnati. Among his requirements was that the Reds pay him a signing bonus of $750, the amount of the draft fee they would otherwise have had to pay to Tacoma. *Cincinnati Times-Star*, reprinted in *The Sporting News*, Dec. 10, 1904.

22 *Cincinnati Post*, Sept. 12, 1906.

23 *Sporting Life*, April 2, 1904.

24 Rear Adm. Winfield Scott Schley (1839-1909) published his autobiography in 1904. Schlei was being called "Admiral" at least by July of that year. See *The Sporting News*, July 16, 1904.

25 *The Sporting News*, April 15, 1909.

26 S.M. Barrett, ed., *Geronimo's Story of His Life* (Alexander, N.C.: Alexander Books, 1999 reprint of 1906 original), p. 139.

27 Samuel M. McCowan, superintendent of the Indian school at Chilocco, Okla., quoted in Angie Debo, *Geronimo: The Man, His Time, His Place* (Norman, Okla.: University of Oklahoma Press, 1976), p. 412. Geronimo did not arrive at the fair until mid-May but he was in residence by the time the Reds returned to St. Louis over the Fourth of July.

28 *Cincinnati Enquirer*, May 1, 1904.

29 *Ibid.*, May 2, 1904.

30 *Cincinnati Commercial Tribune*, May 17, 1904.

31 *Sporting Life*, June 4, 1904.

32 *Cincinnati Commercial Tribune*, June 17, 1904.

33 August Herrmann to Max Fleischmann, undated memo in Bob Ewing's file in the A. Bartlett Giamatti Research Center at the National Baseball Hall of Fame.

34 *The Sporting News*, Dec. 5, 1903, and Oct. 22, 1904.

35 Henry Chadwick, ed., *Spalding's Official Baseball Guide* (New York: American Sports Publishing Co., 1902), p. 71.

36 Baseball historian Harold Seymour said that besides his Cincinnati and Philadelphia holdings, Herrmann "held shares in St. Louis, and made loans to both St. Louis and Brooklyn." Seymour and Dorothy Seymour Mills, *Baseball: The Golden Age* (New York: Oxford University Press, 1971), p. 32. Herrmann's biographer says he was a minority shareholder in the Chicago Cubs until 1905; William A. Cook, *August "Garry" Herrmann: A Baseball Biography* (Jefferson, N.C.: McFarland and Co. Inc., 2008), pp. 100-01. It was also reported that both Herrmann and Dreyfuss were part-owners of Boston's National League club; *The Sporting News*, Nov. 24, 1910.

37 *The Sporting News*, June 9, 1906. Herrmann, probably prudently, relinquished the Reds' claim to Roy, who made his debut with the Phillies on June 27. He never won a game in the big leagues.

38 Frederick G. Lieb and Stan Baumgartner, *The Philadelphia Phillies* (New York: G.P. Putnam's Sons, 1953), p. 67.

39 *Philadelphia North American*, reprinted in the *Cincinnati Enquirer*, Oct. 17, 1904.

40 *The Sporting News*, Dec. 10, 1904.

41 *Ibid.*, Dec. 5, 1903.

42 *Cincinnati Enquirer*, July 3, 1904.

43 *Ibid.*

44 *Ibid.*, July 1, 1904.

45 *The Sporting News*, July 16, 1904.

46 *Ibid.*

47 *Sporting Life,* July 23, 1904.

48 *Atlanta Journal,* reprinted in *The Sporting News,* July 30, 1904. The term might not have been current in Hahn's time, but sportswriters have sometimes referred to left-handed pitchers delivering the ball "from the heartside." See *The Lima News,* April 16, 1922.

49 *The Sporting News,* July 9, 1904.

50 *Ibid.,* Aug. 8, 1903.

51 *Cincinnati Enquirer,* July 8, 1904.

52 *The Sporting News,* Aug. 13, 1904.

53 *Cincinnati Post,* Aug. 22, 1904.

54 *The Sporting News.,* Aug. 27, 1904.

55 *Cincinnati Enquirer,* Aug. 22, 1904.

56 Dimensions of the playing field, as calculated from a 1904 Sanborn insurance map, were approximately 360 feet down the left-field line, 418 to left-center, 400 to center, 375 to right-center and 450 down the right-field line. Those distances would have remained unchanged throughout the Palace of the Fans years, which encompassed Ewing's entire time with the Reds. See Philip J. Lowry, *Green Cathedrals: The Ultimate Celebration of Major League and Negro League Ballparks* (New York: Walker and Co., 2006), p. 65; and Ronald M. Selter, *Ballparks of the Deadball Era: A Comprehensive Study of Their Dimensions, Configurations and Effects on Batting, 1901-19* (Jefferson, N.C.: McFarland and Co. Inc., 2008), p. 75.

57 *Cincinnati Enquirer,* Aug. 22, 1904.

58 *Cincinnati Post,* Aug. 22, 1904.

59 *Sporting Life,* Aug. 27, 1904.

60 *Cincinnati Enquirer,* Aug. 27, 1904.

61 *Ibid.,* Sept. 3, 1904.

62 *The Sporting News,* Sept. 3, 1904.

63 *Cincinnati Enquirer,* Sept. 3, 1904.

64 Team nicknames were much less formalized in Ewing's day than they are now. In the first years of the 20th century, Boston's NL club was often simply identified as the Nationals to differentiate it from the Boston Americans (later Red Sox) of the newer league. But sportswriters frequently adopted nicknames of their own liking, so the Boston Nationals were frequently called the Beaneaters early in Ewing's career and later the Doves when George Dovey was club president in 1907-09. Braves, the name that finally stuck, was chosen after James Gaffney took over, as a nod to Gaffney's connections to New York's Tammany Hall.

65 *Sporting Life,* July 9, 1904.

66 *The Sporting News,* Sept. 3, 1904.

67 *Ibid.*

68 *Ibid.,* Sept. 10, 1904.

69 Rickey's biographers, presumably relying on the version of the story Rickey told years later to his one-time assistant Arthur Mann, all recount this episode essentially the same way. They say Kelley was furious at the notion of one of his players refusing to play on Sunday and insisted that no such player be kept on the squad. Herrmann, on the other hand, is depicted as having Rickey in for a fatherly talk during which the club president "listened sympathetically" (Lowenfish) and his "calm and comforting manner" (Polner) proved a "pleasant surprise" (Mann) to the young catcher. All three report that when Rickey was let go, Herrmann wrote him a generous check (reported anywhere from $300 to more than $400) for salary and expenses during his time with the Reds. In any event, no matter how sympathetic Herrmann might have been or how impressed he was with

the genuineness of the young man's convictions, the hard-headed politician saw the impracticality of carrying and paying a player who would only be available six days a week. See Arthur Mann, *Branch Rickey: American in Action* (Boston: Houghton Mifflin Co., 1957), pp. 34-38; Murray Polner, *Branch Rickey: A Biography* (New York: Atheneum, 1982), pp. 36-39; and Lee Lowenfish, *Branch Rickey: Baseball's Ferocious Gentleman* (Lincoln, Neb.: University of Nebraska Press, 2007), pp. 25-28.

70   *Cincinnati Commercial Tribune,* Aug. 29, 1904.

71   C.J. Bocklet, *The Sporting News,* Oct. 1, 1904.

72   *Ibid.*

73   *Cincinnati Enquirer*, Oct. 4, 1903.

74   *Boston Morning Journal*, Sept. 24, 1904.

75   *Cincinnati Times-Star*, Sept. 24, 1904.

76   *Cincinnati Enquirer*, Sept. 24, 1904.

77   *New York Times*, Sept. 24, 1904.

78   *Cincinnati Enquirer,* Sept. 25, 1904; see also *Boston Morning Journal*, Sept. 24, 1904.

79   *Cincinnati Enquirer*, Sept. 25, 1904.

80   See for example the *Philadelphia Inquirer*, Jan. 21, 1910, and the *Cincinnati Commercial Tribune*, May 27, 1905.

81   *Boston Herald*, Sept. 24, 1904.

82   *Cincinnati Times-Star*, Sept. 23, 1904.

83   *Sporting Life*, April 8, 1905.

84   *The Sporting News*, Oct. 1, 1904.

85   *Ibid.*

86   *Cincinnati Enquirer*, Oct. 11, 1904.

87   Either because they were naturally gregarious or merely following the lead of their boss, numerous members of the Reds family joined the Elks. Besides Garry Herrmann and club officials Frank Bancroft and Max Fleischmann, the roll in Ewing's time included Tommy Corcoran, Joe Kelley, Jack Harper, Jimmy Sebring, Gabby Street, Hans Lobert and Dick Hoblitzell.

88   *Sporting Life*, Jan. 7, 1905.

89   *Cincinnati Enquirer*, Dec. 20, 1904: "The operation performed on Mr. Ewing was for the purpose of locating a bullet which lodged in his leg during the war."

90   *Sporting Life*, Dec. 10, 1904.

91   August Herrmann papers in the A. Bartlett Giamatti Research Center at the National Baseball Hall of Fame; see Greg Rhodes and John Snyder, *Redleg Journal: Year by Year and Day by Day with the Cincinnati Reds Since 1866* (Cincinnati: Road West Publishing, 2000), p. 147. Ewing's $3,000 salary in 1904 would have been equivalent to more than $78,000 in 2011.

92   Evers and Fullerton, *op. cit.*, p. 45.

93   *Ibid.*, p. 42.

94   *The Sporting News*, July 1, 1905.

95   Bob Ewing, letter to August Herrmann, Oct. 11, 1904. Ewing completed the 1904 season with a record of 11-13 (.458). Hahn finished 16-18 (.471). Ewing's letters to Herrmann are on file in the A. Bartlett Giamatti Research Center at the National Baseball Hall of Fame.

96   Ewing to Herrmann, Nov. 6, 1904.

97   Ewing to Herrmann, Oct. 11, 1904.

98   Ewing to Herrmann, Nov. 6, 1904.

99   Ewing to Herrmann, Dec. 23, 1904.

100 Ewing to Herrmann, Dec. 30, 1904.

101 *The Sporting News*, Dec. 26, 1903.

102 Robert F. Burk, *Never Just a Game: Players, Owners, and American Baseball to 1920* (Chapel H ill, N.C.: University of North Carolina Press, 1994), p. 243.

103 *The Sporting News*, May 20, 1905.

104 *Philadelphia North American*, Sept. 12, 1911.

105 Ewing to Herrmann, Jan. 13, 1906.

106 Ewing to Herrmann, Jan. 20, 1906.

107 Ewing to Herrmann, Jan. 27, 1906.

108 Ewing, with reference to the 1906 season, reminded Herrmann that he "received the same as I got last year," which is to say in 1905; Ewing to Herrmann, Jan. 3, 1907.

109 In a letter written after the 1906 season, Ewing described seeing one of teammate Bob Wicker's paychecks, in the amount of $300 – which, at two paychecks a month over the course of a six-month season, would amount to an annual salary of $3,600 – "and mine didn't come near that much." Ewing to Herrmann, Dec. 1, 1906.

110 Ewing to Herrmann, Dec. 1, 1906.

111 Ewing to Herrmann, Nov. 20, 1906.

112 Ewing to Herrmann, Dec. 12, 1906.

113 Ewing to Herrmann, Oct. 11, 1904.

114 *Chicago Tribune*, Sept. 15, 1910.

CHAPTER 7

Master of the Spitball

BUG HOLLIDAY, former Cincinnati outfielder and National League umpire, told the story of a scene he'd supposedly witnessed in a sporting goods store. It seems a youngster walked in and wanted to know how much it would cost to get one of those new spitballs, like the one Bob Ewing was throwing.[2]

The kid in Holliday's story went away disappointed, but his interest was understandable. The spitball had been the sensation of the 1904 season; soon it seemed almost every pitcher was looking to acquire one for his personal use. The pitch had caught on first in the American League, then spread to the National. The damp delivery's rise to prominence in the newer circuit prompted sportswriter Charlie Dryden to quip that the American League consisted of "Ban Johnson, the spitball and the Wabash Railroad."[3] Around the league, practically every club had somebody serving up wet ones: Harry Howell in St. Louis, George Mullin in Detroit, Case Patten in Washington, Bob Rhoads in Cleveland and Norwood Gibson, Ewing's former Kansas City teammate, in Boston. By far the most successful practitioner was Happy Jack Chesbro, who employed the pitch to win an astonishing 41 games for the New York Highlanders and manager Clark Griffith. The spitball's rapid emergence sent baseball writers scrambling for euphemisms, preferably alliterative: Soon the sports pages were full of expectoration balls, cuspidor curves, salivated slants, sputum spheres, slobber balls and saliva splatterers. In Atlanta, an up-and-coming young sportswriter named Grantland Rice was moved to contemplate the phenomenon in verse:

> Mr. Chesbro—thoughtful man—
> Devised a simple little plan—
> Where, by the use of vulgar "spit"—
> He makes each hitter throw a fit.
> No one can tell where it may curve—
> Or where the blooming thing may swerve—
> A damp tongue for each game he played—
> Was Mr. Chesbro's stock in trade.
>
> They ask no more about your "whip"—
> But "How's your tongue?" or "How's your lip?"
> They used to spring the "sore arm" cry—
> But now it's "H—l, my tongue is dry."
> Through his expectoration scheme
> Clark Griffith had a winning team.[4]

Some old-timers contended that pitchers had dabbled with the spitball for decades, at least since the 1880s; a few graybeards recalled Bobby Mathews throwing something that looked suspiciously like a spitter for the Lord Baltimores club clear back in 1868. But when the pitch came into vogue in the early 1900s, it was hailed as something new under the sun. The "invention" of this new pitch was widely attributed to a little right-hander who had crossed paths with Ewing in the minor leagues. Elmer Stricklett was a teammate of Ewing's at Toledo in 1900, but he didn't add the spitball to his repertoire until two years later, when he was pitching for Sacramento in the California League. Stricklett always disavowed credit for discovering the pitch. He said he learned it from outfielder George Hildebrand, later a longtime American League umpire. Stricklett had a sore arm at the time and was ready to try anything to avoid being released. With the spitball, he ran off 11 straight victories, saved his job and eventually earned a ticket to the big leagues.

Hildebrand's story—probably about as close to the truth as we're ever going to get—is that he had discovered the spitball by accident while playing for Providence in the Eastern League earlier in the 1902 season. Warming up one day with pitcher Frank Corridon, Hildebrand noticed that Corridon wet the tips of his fingers before throwing his changeup, a sort of spinless blooper pitch. When, as a joke, Hildebrand took the ball and "put a big daub of spit on it," his next throw took an eye-popping dip. Corridon immediately asked how he did that and Hildebrand demonstrated, releasing the ball with a forceful overhand motion. Using the pitch in an exhibition game a month later, Corridon struck out nine Pittsburgh Pirates in five innings. But he strained his arm and was thereafter leery of the spitball for a time.[5]

In 1904, after three straight 20-win seasons on the West Coast, Stricklett was invited to Texas for a tryout with the Chicago White Sox. That spring he showed the spitball to Jack Chesbro.[6] But Stricklett's star pupil was a big, strapping coal miner from eastern Pennsylvania. Ed Walsh, another rookie in the White Sox camp, studied Stricklett's technique closely. Stricklett again fell victim to arm trouble and was returned to the minors after appearing in only one game for the Sox; he never became more than a mediocre major leaguer, winning 35 games and losing 51 in four seasons.[7] Walsh, however, stuck in the big leagues and kept working on the spitball. At first he had difficulty controlling the pitch and for nearly two years "was practically worthless to the White Sox."[8] Then everything fell into place. Walsh became the premier spitballer of his day, and one of the premier pitchers, winning 40 games in 1908. Sam Crawford, who batted against Big Ed throughout his prime years, was convinced the ball disintegrated after leaving Walsh's hand and "when it went past the plate it was just the spit went by."[9]

Hitters throughout the era shared Crawford's frustration. Casey Stengel, whose 56-year career as player and manager began in 1910, years later described the spitball as "the pitch that almost drove me out of baseball when I was 25."[10]

There was little consensus at the time as to how or why the spitball worked, and the answers are not entirely certain today. Some hitters in Ewing's time suspected the ball was haunted. John Thorn and John B. Holway, in their book *The Pitcher,* maintained that the spit increases air resistance on the wet side of the ball, "making the ball, in its flight through the air, veer the other way—the path of least resistance, be it up, down or sideways."[11] Yale University's Robert Kemp Adair, who once served as the National League's official physicist, said the effect had more to do with the lubricant allowing the pitch to slide off the pitcher's fingers with little or no backspin; such a ball travels through the air with very little rotation, creating "asymmetric stitch configurations ... that lead to imbalances of forces and extraordinary excursions in trajectory."[12] Those explanations came decades later. Among Ewing's contemporaries, the thinking man's ballplayer, Christy Mathewson, viewed the spitter as "a style of delivery the science of which cannot be explained."[13]

Ewing, the Auglaize County farm boy, didn't tax his brain much about the science involved. "The mystery of the movement of the spitball is too deep a problem for me to solve," he confessed.[14]

Different pitchers employed different methods of moistening and throwing their spitballs, and there were widely varying descriptions or claims as to what the pitches could be expected to do. Chesbro said he released the spitball just like a curve. Harry Howell, on the other hand, cautioned against using a curveball motion, advising instead a straight overhand delivery "with a smart, short motion of the shoulder and a snap of the wrist."[15] Other specialists agreed with Spittin' Bill Doak, who appeared on the major league stage about the time Ewing was making his exit, that "a rigid wrist is absolutely essential."[16] Walsh favored "a high overhand delivery, releasing the ball at full speed." He shared the common view that the "one real essential" for a spitball pitcher was "speed and strength."[17] Johnny Evers and Hugh Fullerton agreed, saying an effective spitball pitcher required "immense power and speed."[18]

As the possessor of a good natural fastball, Ewing was a likely candidate. He described moistening the first two fingers of his pitching hand and gripping the ball lightly on the surface, not across the seams. Spitballers usually chewed gum, tobacco or most often slippery elm, from the bark of certain elm trees, to help generate sufficient saliva. Soon, imaginative pitchers were coating baseballs with all manner of lubricants in hopes to gaining the desired effect—Evers and Fullerton mention talcum powder, Vaseline and crude oil, in addition to slippery elm—but there is no indication that Ewing ever used anything but good, old-fashioned spit.[19] Delivered with the same motion as his fastball, Ewing's pitch slid off the wet fingers and reacted much like a knuckleball: It approached the plate at middling speed—midway between that of a fastball and a change of pace—with little or no rotation. Ewing said the pitch was "liable to take any kind of a shoot when it reaches the batsman"—down and in, down and out, or sometimes straight down.[20]

Many pitchers claimed to be able to determine or at least influence the break of the pitch by their grip or release. Chesbro asserted he could "make the spitball drop two inches or a foot and a half"[21] and that he could create an exaggerated version of a drop, outcurve or inshoot, depending on his release. Walsh said he could make the pitch break four different ways, depending on his grip. Burleigh Grimes, who threw the major leagues' last legal spitball in 1934, said his spitter would break downward when thrown overhand or outward when thrown sidearm, and "any [arm] angle between overhand or sidearm" would produce a corresponding break.[22] Stanley Coveleski, who broke into the major leagues around the end of Ewing's career, said he could make the pitch break down, out, or down and out, "and I always knew which way it would break."[23]

Ewing, at least early in his association with the pitch, made no such claim. His spitball sometimes dropped as much as 18 inches, he said, "making the batsman who struck at it seem extremely ridiculous."[24] But he was of the same school of thought as Harry Howell, who said the pitcher could not be certain whether the pitch would break in or out.[25] Ewing seems to have thrown the spitball much as a knuckleballer throws that pitch: Aim for the strike zone and hope for the best.

"All a pitcher can do is throw and take his chances of having it go in the right direction," he told a reporter near the end of the 1904 season.[26]

That's probably what most spitballers did. Control was the big problem. Throughout the 1904-05 off-season, there were panicky alarms that baseball would be taken over by this new pitch which, according to writer and old-time ballplayer Tim Murnane, made it "utterly impossible to hit the ball square."[27] Veteran catcher Chief Zimmer predicted darkly that the spitball "promises to become the sole reliance of a majority of twirlers in the business."[28]

It never happened. Though to some throwing a wet one appeared no more difficult than "pitching a medium-paced straight ball,"[29] only a relative handful of pitchers managed to harness the spitball as a reliable weapon. Branch Rickey, who taught the spitter as a college coach before becoming manager of the St. Louis Browns in 1913, claimed years later that sophomores at the University of Michigan "learned the spitball overnight" and that an observant professional "could learn to pitch the spitball while you are eating a club sandwich."[30] Experts disputed that contention. Burleigh Grimes granted that a boy might learn to throw the pitch in 15 minutes, but insisted controlling it was another matter. "You can't throw a spitball, you have to pitch it," Grimes said.[31]

The spitball didn't prove easy for Ewing's teammate Andy Coakley, who shelved the pitch after he tried it once in 1908 and absorbed a 10–1 beating. Some highly-touted spitballers—notably Marty O'Toole, purchased by Pittsburgh from St. Paul for the unheard-of sum of $22,500 in 1911—ultimately made little impression on major league hitters. Others who experimented with the pitch early on ultimately discarded it; Detroit's George Mullin, who eventually won 228 games in a 14-year career, built his record almost exclusively on a fastball and one of the game's best curves.

Christy Mathewson, never one for false modesty, believed he could control the spitball "as well as any other pitcher."[32] But Mathewson, who would soon develop a dazzling assortment of more than a half-dozen pitches—including one he called a "dry spitter," which sounds from various descriptions like a modern-day forkball or split-fingered fastball[33]—found the spitball unpredictable and therefore untrustworthy, and he rarely threw it.[34] Even Ed Walsh conceded that the pitch was largely "outside the pale of control."[35]

Ewing, blessed with the right physical tools for a spitballer, might coincidentally have possessed the ideal mental makeup: Patient and methodical, he was the type who would work on the pitch as long as it took to master it, while other pitchers grew exasperated and gave up. Pitching the spitball, Burleigh Grimes said, was an art that required long and systematic practice. As late as 1907, writer I.E. Sanborn observed that Ewing and Frank Corridon, then with the Philadelphia Phillies, were "about the only real spitball artists" in the National League.[36]

Even so, there were widespread complaints about the spitball. *The Sporting News* bemoaned the effects of the pitch that had contributed so much to the "dismay and demoralization of batsmen" in 1904.[37] *Sport-*

ing Life devoted an entire page to analyzing this "destroyer of batting skill" and stressing, as a headline proclaimed, "why it should be legislated against."[38] Even Ed Walsh's manager, Fielder Jones of the White Sox, declared himself "emphatically in favor of a measure to abolish it."[39] Some pitchers openly disdained the spitball.

"Anyone can master it," scoffed Cy Young, embarking on his 16th season in the major leagues, "and it will make a first-rater out of a man who has found it difficult to hold his own in fast company."[40] Jack Coombs, who came up with the Philadelphia Athletics in 1906, stated that any time he had to rely on the spitball to remain in the big leagues, he would give up baseball and go back to the farm.[41]

Others expressed misgivings on aesthetic or hygienic grounds. A *Sporting News* correspondent denounced the pitch as "filthy and unsportsmanlike."[42] In Newark, New Jersey, the president of the board of health declared the spitball a menace to public health and proposed that pitchers using it be fined under the city's anti-spitting ordinance.[43] The dramatic success of a few spitballers prompted numerous and sometimes extreme suggestions to counteract the pitch. Some observers called for extending the pitching distance. *The Sporting News* favored lopping off the bottom half of the strike zone.[44]

For the time being, little was actually done. Harry Pulliam, president of the National League, limited himself to ordering that pitchers "discontinue the disgusting practice...[of] moistening the ball with saliva in a way that the audience has full view of the proceedings."

"We are catering to a high class of people," Pulliam added, "and this sort of thing will not make them like the game any more."[45]

THE SPITBALL WASN'T THE ONLY THING new in Bob Ewing's life at the end of 1904. Exactly when Nelle May Hunter entered the picture isn't clear, but by now their romance had been going for some time. The 23-year-old daughter of a prominent Auglaize County physician, Nelle was described in a local newspaper as "one of Wapakoneta's most charming young women"[46] and elsewhere as "a handsome and clever society girl."[47] She was

Bob Ewing makes a fashion statement in 1905, when the Reds played at Chicago's West Side Grounds in both April and September. The double-breasted coat was just the thing for an early- or late-season visit to the Windy City. *Photo: Chicago Historical Society, SDN-002901.*

petite and lively and in 1903 had been chosen to reign as queen of a carnival parade in Wapakoneta.

She was also an avid baseball fan, an interest she shared with her father. Dr. Franklin Crittenden Hunter came from a family that produced at least five generations of medical men. Early in his career he was listed as an "eclectic physician" in the village of Freyburg,[48] just south of Wapakoneta. Shortly after Nelle's birth he relocated to the county seat, where he purchased a pharmacy that he operated in conjunction with his medical practice. Eventually he established a clinic in the Hunter Block, still a prominent building on West Auglaize Street in downtown Wapakoneta. As Ewing's career progressed, Dr. Hunter developed a system of reporting the day's baseball results, raising an American flag in front of his offices to announce a Reds victory or hanging out a small piece of black crape to acknowledge a defeat.

Hunter taught his youngest daughter about baseball and took her to games in Wapakoneta and Cincinnati. She was probably aware of Ewing's exploits on the diamond as far back as her mid-teens; she later recalled that they were first introduced at a ballgame.[49] Certainly she knew ballplayers, and she was fascinated by them as much as by the game. In many families, such an interest on the part of a daughter of marriageable age would have been cause for alarm. Protective parents often chased ballplayers away, and the players knew exactly where they stood socially.

"To the majority of cultured and refined people, the average professional baseball player is a personage of but little consideration," allowed Erwin "Zaza" Harvey, who gave up baseball in 1903 to become an entomologist and writer. "… They associate with him a life of dissipation and regard him as a man of few good qualities."[50] Even after he was well established in his chosen career, Ewing still had to contend with the attitudes of some in his hometown who didn't think playing a game was an appropriate way for a grown man to make a living.[51] Old-time pitcher Tony Mullane, observing the scene in 1904, ridiculed the notion that any girl from a well-to-do family would "hurl her heart and her coin at a pitcher with a dirty shirt, red where the flannel underwear has soaked through, and a quid of tobacco in each side of his face."[52]

Ewing surely had some concerns along those lines, if not about Nelle then certainly about her father. But the good doctor was more open-minded than many people of his day. An animated storyteller, Hunter was "one of those bluff but kindly gentlemen, who enjoy life to the full, and contributes his portion toward making the world happier."[53] If he had doubts about his daughter's tall, quiet suitor, they were soon enough put to rest. Before long the ballplayer and the physician were warily kidding back and forth, becoming accustomed to one another.

"He likes me a little, don't he?" Ewing wrote to Nelle in the spring of 1905. "He had better."[54]

At the same time he was striving to win over Nelle's parents, Ewing had to compete with other contenders for her attentions. Nelle had never suffered from a lack of admirers. The list had even included Miller Huggins, now Ewing's teammate in Cincinnati. Nelle and Huggins had dated in 1898, the summer he played semipro ball in Wapakoneta. Late in her long life, Nelle still delighted in recalling that youthful fling. A newspaper article when she was in her 80s noted discreetly that she had once enjoyed "more than a speaking acquaintance" with Huggins.[55] Even after it became clear that Ewing was the frontrunner for Nelle's affections, other hopefuls were reluctant to give up. One ardent swain continued to press his case well into the fall of 1904; while conceding that "Bob is a fine fellow," this persistent suitor wrote to Nelle:

> I still truly believe that your fondness for Bob is an infatuation. You can determine this for yourself, I believe, by asking yourself if he would have made an impression on you had he been shorn of his newspaper notoriety, or were he suddenly to lose it.[56]

In fact Ewing had more going for him than a superficial gloss of celebrity. He understood Nelle in a way other men did not. "I fear I tire you," Bob's rival wrote patronizingly. "My little girl, I don't want to worry you or perplex your brain." To the contrary, the fellow declared, "My dearest delight would be always to put my arms about you and laugh at your follies and smooth out your troubles."[57] While Bob's rival viewed Nelle as weak and dependent, and encouraged her to see herself that way, Ewing acknowledged her strengths and capabilities. He saw Nelle as the one who could "always fix things up."[58] His competitor expected her to play the flighty, helpless female, and took her at face value when she did: "You say you are foolish and changeable," he reminded her, offering to do the thinking for both of them.[59] Ewing, by contrast, recognized her for an intelligent and strong-willed woman who expected to be treated as an equal. Nelle's father acknowledged her intellect and capacity for independent thought, and she would accept no less from a husband.

According to Nelle, the reticent ballplayer never did actually propose, he just came to take it for granted that they would marry. She finally had to tell him it was time to ask her father for her hand.[60] By early 1905, she had made her decision. She and Bob probably became engaged before he left for spring training.

"A week ago tonight you had a beau and I had a girl, but now it's different," he wrote from the Aragon Hotel in Jacksonville, Florida. "Gee but I wish I was there or you were here."[61]

ARRIVING IN JACKSONVILLE for spring training, Ewing was confronted by a significant alteration in his baseball world. For the first time in the major leagues, he faced the prospect of a season without Heinie Peitz. After more than 1,100 games, Peitz's arm was about shot; he was throwing the ball to second base "like a rainbow."[62] At age 34, after nine years with the Reds and 13 in the league, the German Baron had been traded to Pittsburgh for another catcher, 26-year-old Ed Phelps.

The big noise in the Reds' camp in 1905, however, was Orval Overall. Twenty-four years old and former captain of the football team at the University of California, the big right-hander had won 32 games in the Pacific Coast League in 1904, leading Tacoma to the pennant. Raised in the shadow of the Sierra Nevada Mountains, Overall appeared to the eastern writers like some Wild West character out of a tall tale. Having never before ventured east of the Rockies, he traveled four days by train to reach Cincinnati. He arrived with a ready-made reputation as "the Mathewson of the West."[63] He was "the best-advertised minor league player that has stepped into fast company in many years."[64] Before the season even started, Garry Herrmann ordered the printing of large posters with Overall's picture, intending to promote his appearances around the National League "the same as the Cleveland club is doing with Lajoie"[65] in the American.

That spring some of the Reds' hitters got their first introduction to the spitball. Owing to the relatively small number of spitballers in the National League, the Reds had rarely if ever faced the pitch. In a pair of exhibitions against Boston's American League champions, the Cincinnatians were completely befuddled by the dampened deliveries of Norwood Gibson and George Winter, the latter holding the Reds hitless through seven innings. Cincinnati's sluggers repeatedly swung and missed at pitches that nearly bounced on home plate.

"It was a crying shame to see men like Kelley, Seymour and Corcoran hit six inches above balls," *The Sporting News*' Boston correspondent reported, dry-eyed.[66]

Ewing got a measure of revenge when the two clubs met again in Cincinnati two days before the start of the season. With Gibson and Winter dividing the pitching for Boston, Ewing scattered six hits and beat the team "heralded as the world's greatest"[67] by a 5–2 score.

The Reds lost their league opener 9–4, the Pittsburgh Pirates erupting for a six-run sixth inning against Jack Harper as Heinie Peitz, "beside himself with joy" coaching the bases for the visitors, "jigged on the lines, laughed gleefully and shot stabs of sarcasm at Manager Kelley."[68] Ewing evened the slate the next day, striking out 10 and allowing only four singles en route to a 7–0 shutout. He also popped up a bunt with runners on second and third, triggering the first of six triple plays the Reds would figure in during the 1905 season. For most of the 2,300 who turned out in chilly 45-degree temperatures, the game provided "their first good look at the spitball in action," and they were appropriately appreciative. The same couldn't be said for Ed Phelps, attempting to corral Ewing's "freak delivery" behind the plate.

"Phelps had as much trouble trying to hold the ball as the batters did trying to hit it," the *Cincinnati Commercial Tribune* reported. "Neither one succeeded."[69]

The spitball era was no fun for catchers. The same qualities that made the pitch difficult to hit also made it a chore to catch. With little or no rotation, the pitch came in, in the words of spitball pitcher Harry Howell, "with the dull, dead, penetrating heaviness of lead."[70] Even if the batter made contact, the ball just died off the bat. Meanwhile, catching the heavy pitch left receivers bruised, sore and often with broken or dislocated fingers. Bucky Crouse, who caught Red Faber in the 1920s, said his spitball was "dead weight," the kind of pitch that "just beats your hand all up."

"My hand would swell up that high every time I caught him," Crouse told Eugene Murdock. "I could hardly shut my hand."[71]

The prospect of having their catchers chronically banged up, if not outright maimed, contributed to some managers' dislike for the pitch. The spitball's exaggerated and often unpredictable breaks only exacerbated the catcher's problems. Paddy Livingston, who caught for the Reds in 1906, said he often ended up stopping the ball with his bare hand; other times, "I'd throw my whole body in front of the pitch to block it."[72]

Spitball pitchers paid a price for the effectiveness of the pitch. For a variety of reasons, spitballers were more likely to be victimized by stolen bases and unearned runs. Wet baseballs were harder to handle in general. They contributed to an increase in passed balls and also errors, catchers and infielders sometimes losing their grip on slippery baseballs or unleashing their own inadvertent spitballs while trying to throw to bases.

Professional courtesy toward battery mates who relied on the spitball usually kept catchers from complaining in public. Most did their job doggedly, if not always cheerfully. Ed Phelps clearly didn't enjoy teaming with Ewing. "When Bob Ewing pitches," one reporter observed, "Ed Phelps acts as if he'd do better if he had a bath towel tucked in his belt."[73] Paddy Livingston, on the other hand, developed a reputation as a specialist in handling spitballers. After leaving Cincinnati, he enjoyed his best seasons with the Philadelphia Athletics as the favorite receiver of spitball pitcher Cy Morgan. Whenever Ewing had an outstanding game, his usual battery mate, Admiral Schlei, always received plaudits not so much for the brilliance of his play as for his uncomplaining diligence in the midst of trying circumstances.

In any event, the spitball made for interesting baseball. Opponents dreaded facing the pitch and took extraordinary steps to discourage it. Ewing soon ran into such obstructionist tactics. The season was barely three weeks old when the Reds and the Pirates found themselves locked in a contentious Sunday afternoon struggle before more than 14,000 fans at League Park. Each team eked out runs one at a time, neither side able to forge more than a one-run lead. Both Ewing and Pittsburgh's Chick Robitaille were pushed to the limit, each throwing nearly 150 pitches.

The crowd was in a frenzy by the time the Reds tied the score 3–3 with two out in the bottom of the ninth. The inning featured a jarring collision at second base that touched off a boisterous argument, the Pirates surrounding umpire Bob Emslie and demanding an interference call against Ewing. Attempting to break up a double play, Long Bob "ran into [second baseman Claude] Ritchey's outstretched arm with such force that the ball was knocked into left field."[74] Emslie called Ewing out but Miller Huggins, safe at first on the fielder's choice, scored minutes later on third baseman George McBride's throwing error, sending the game into extra innings.

All day the Pirates had engaged in various surreptitious practices designed to make life difficult for Ewing. Huggins spied McBride spitting licorice on the ball; in combination with Ewing's saliva, the *Commercial Tribune* contended, McBride's contribution "would have made a delightful gum that would have glued [Ewing's] fingers to the seams." Another time Pittsburgh shortstop Honus Wagner was caught doctoring the ball with "Tabasco sauce, nitric acid or some such lively chemical."[75] Most likely Wagner was testing the effects of liniment, capsicum salve or some other concoction from the trainer's medical kit, anything that might be likely to make Ewing sick if he repeatedly went to his mouth after getting the substance on his fingertips. In both instances the ball was thrown out of play.

Throughout the game, Ewing was wild and constantly behind in the count. He walked four batters and hit one; Admiral Schlei "was unable to do more than grapple with the wild shoots and slants that the wet ball took."[76] Ewing retired the first two batters in the 10th inning, but then he walked Ritchey and McBride. With runners on first and second, Ewing unloosed two disastrous wild pitches, his third and fourth of the game. On the final errant delivery, Ritchey scampered home with what proved to be the winning run.

Ewing was sharply criticized for his part in the game's "sad and pitiful ending."[77] He was second-guessed for not pitching "hard, straight ball" in critical situations[78] and for letting "two mediocre batters" like Ritchey and McBride walk on breaking pitches when fastballs might have gotten them out.[79] Schlei loyally stuck up for his pitcher, contending Ewing should not be held responsible for the deliveries that got away in the 10th inning.

"They were passed balls, all my fault," Schlei told the *Cincinnati Enquirer*'s Jack Ryder. "... I don't know why I didn't get them, but I certainly should have had them."[80]

The writers didn't buy it. Ryder and C.J. Bocklet, in *The Sporting News*, placed the blame squarely on Ewing. The *Commercial Tribune* made the game the centerpiece of a lecture on "the Lesson of the Spitball":

> *It is not the safe and sane pitching policy to put the freak delivery at work with one run needed to win and a man on third. ... You don't always have to hit the spitball. Just duck and keep it from killing you and there is a pretty fair chance of getting around.*[81]

The reaction to this single painful defeat reflected the love-hate relationship fans and writers had with the spitball. They loved seeing opposing batsmen flail impotently at the unpredictable pitch, but they were quick to condemn on those occasions when it backfired. The most famous example had already occurred: Jack Chesbro had accounted for nearly 45 percent of the New York Highlanders' victories in 1904, but he became the whipping boy when his wild pitch cost them the American League pennant on the final day of the season.

Ewing's spitball worked more often than not. A month after the 10th-inning loss to Pittsburgh, he smothered Brooklyn on three hits to push the Reds over .500. Starting July 2, he won four straight games, striking out 23 batters and walking only one in 34 innings. Clinging to a 4–3 lead with runners at the corners and none out in the ninth inning at Boston on July 14, Ewing secured the final victory in the streak when Ed Abbaticchio grounded into a game-ending triple play. Ewing's win string ended four days later in Philadelphia when Bill Duggleby outlasted him 5–4 in a 14-inning marathon.

WHEN THE REDS REACHED NEW YORK on their eastern swings, they customarily eschewed the lodgings of Manhattan and stayed instead at Long Island's Bath Beach, some players bringing their wives for a sort of working vacation at the seaside. In July 1905 the players could beat the record-setting heat with a morning swim in the surf. After the afternoon game, for those who still had the energy, Coney Island was only 10 minutes from the team's hotel—and open 24 hours a day.

Coney Island's first amusement park had opened in 1897. The first year the Reds stopped at Bath Beach, 1903, was marked by the opening of a second, the fantastical Luna Park, where at night 1.2 million electric bulbs transformed the landscape into a scene of "glowing towers and spinning wheels of pure light."[82] A year later Luna Park faced further competition from Dreamland, with its re-creations of Venetian canals and Swiss mountains, and immense tableaux reenacting real-life catastrophes such as the 1889 Johnstown flood. During a later 1905 trip, however, the Reds had to switch to the Hotel Marlborough on Manhattan's Herald Square in order to get away from an outbreak of typhoid fever at Bath Beach.

Intestinal disease wasn't the only form of unpleasantness Ewing and company encountered in New York that summer. In the final week of July the Reds made their second visit of the season to the Polo Grounds. They had a respectable 46-40 record but were in fifth place, 14½ games behind the front-running Giants, who were winning at better than a .700 clip. Through a quirk in the schedule, the two teams were about to play each other eight times in nine days, four in New York and then four in Cincinnati with a travel day in between. Viewed optimistically, it was an opportunity for the Reds to climb into the pennant race, or at least into the first division.

Instead, it was a disaster. John McGraw and his "chesty gentlemen," as another National League manager described them,[83] beat the Reds eight straight. Ewing was the goat in the third game, walking eight batters and committing two costly throwing errors in a 6–5 loss. The next day Frank "Noodles" Hahn, the once-great left-hander, was pummeled to a 9–3 defeat in his final appearance in a Cincinnati uniform. Though Hahn would attempt a comeback the following season with the New York Highlanders, the Reds' former mainstay was effectively washed up at age 26.

The Reds were humiliated. They were also finished as a factor in the 1905 race. By the time the Giants left Cincinnati on August 1, the Reds were 22½ games out of first place. New York, eventually extending its winning streak to 13 games, would soon hold an insurmountable lead over second-place Pittsburgh and would cruise to its second consecutive National League championship. By the time the Cincinnatians dragged themselves out of his town for the last time in 1905, the *New York Sun's* Joe Vila—who doubled as New York correspondent for *The Sporting News*—was convinced it was time to put them out of their misery.

"Will somebody please chloroform the Cincinnati Reds?" Vila pleaded. "If they could play all season with McGraw's men and every game should take place at the Polo Grounds, the game in this city would be killed as far as the National League is concerned."[84]

The Reds eventually got back on the positive side of .500, but they never got out of fifth place. For the season, they beat the Giants only five times in 23 tries. In one stretch of 16 meetings, Cincinnati's best result was a tie. Ewing made a better showing than most of his mates. He gained two of his team's five victories, beating the Giants twice in as many days early in the season—the first time in extra innings, in relief of Jack Harper, and the next day bettering Joe McGinnity on a three-hit complete game. But overall, when matched against the league's best team, Ren Mulford wrote, Cincinnati was consistently "outplayed, outfooted, outfielded and outgeneraled."[85]

The season wasn't half over before there began to be rumblings that Joe Kelley, field boss of the Reds since 1902, was on his way out. Garry Herrmann, in his public pronouncements, initially stood behind his manager, but the expressions of confidence became less and less convincing. By the final week of the season, when confronted with a point-blank question as to whether Kelley would manage the club in 1906, the best reply Herrmann could muster was, "We will have Kelley here next season. That is all I care to say at present."[86]

Amid the season's disappointments and uncertainties, Ewing stood out as the team's most consistent winner. On August 2 he beat Brooklyn 8–7 with a run-scoring single in the bottom of the 13th inning. Four days later he beat the same team 2-0 on a two-hitter, no runner reaching third base. With three weeks left in the season he had amassed a career-high 17 victories against 10 defeats. In his next two starts, he shut out Pittsburgh and Boston.

The Giants secured the pennant October 1 by shading Ewing 5–4 in the first game of a doubleheader. The Reds still had games to play, but the race was over and the pressure was off. Before wrapping up the season, they spent a day putting on an exhibition just for fun, and for the entertainment of a "select assemblage" of Garry Herrmann's intimates[87] at his private club. The Laughery Club was on the Indiana side of the Ohio River about 20 miles downstream from Cincinnati. The club was founded in 1900 by Herrmann and Boss Cox. Its luxurious 32-room clubhouse and surrounding cottages provided a retreat for their friends and associates from Cincinnati and Covington, Kentucky, becoming famous in its rural neighborhood for lavish parties which "occasionally some local people were invited to attend."[88] Transportation from Cincinnati for such events was often provided by chartered riverboat.

As one of its founders—and the man who annually made up its operating deficit out of his own pocket—Herrmann inevitably put the stamp of his congenial personality on the club. Sportswriter Frank Graham, who traveled with the New York Giants before World War I, remembered the club vividly, and the convivial feasts Herrmann hosted there late into the night:

> There would be dinner in the clubhouse and, later, beer at
> an outdoor bar in a grove at the edge of the Ohio River. And
> along about midnight there would be a charcoal fire burning
> in a grill, and waiters would serve broiled sausages and Lim-
> burger cheese and rye bread, and everybody would be singing
> or telling stories.[89]

Out-of-town writers were sometimes invited to these affairs, and even the loyal opposition. John J. McGraw, "although he was not much of a singer," occasionally joined in Herrmann's midnight sing-alongs, "raising his voice loudly, but slurring over the words because he didn't know them."[90]

The Reds enjoyed Herrmann's hospitality for 24 hours. Then, "immediately after a bounteous repast served in the lavish Laughery Club style, on the beautiful lawn in front of the clubhouse,"[91] as 150 members and guests settled into lawn chairs set out for the occasion, the players divided up for an intrasquad game between the Colts and the Vets. Ewing, playing first base for Tommy Corcoran's veterans, drove a pitch beyond the wire fence in left field but was thrown out trying for a home run when Fred Odwell vaulted over the barrier to retrieve the ball. Another highlight of the contest was a pinch-hitting appearance by Herrmann himself; he managed one belated swing at right-hander Rip Vowinkel, on a pitch that nearly grazed his belt buckle, before relinquishing the rest of his at-bat to Matty Schwab.

The Reds returned to serious business two days later. On the last day of the season, before a Sunday afternoon crowd of more than 10,000 in Cincinnati, the Reds beat Pittsburgh 3–1 in the first game of a doubleheader as another triple play rescued Orval Overall from a none-out, bases-loaded predicament in the seventh inning. Ewing drew the start in the final game of the year, taking the mound with a 19–11 record. He nailed down the victory with relative ease, scattering six hits and contributing a run-scoring single to hold a 4–1 lead when the game was called in the eighth inning because of darkness.

Ewing's 20th victory passed without notice in the press. One reason was that 17 pitchers won 20 or more games in the major leagues in 1905, and victory totals of 30 or more were not rare among the workhorse pitchers of the time; New York's Christy Mathewson, on the way to his third straight 30-win campaign, had notched his 20th victory clear back in mid-August. Of more interest to fans and writers was the afternoon's confrontation between Cy Seymour and Honus Wagner, with the National League batting championship at stake.

With the pennant decided and both Pittsburgh's and Cincinnati's places in the standings "as firmly fixed as the stars in the Milky Way,"[92] there was "absolutely nothing of moment depending upon the result of the games" except individual batting honors.[93] Wagner came to town with a season's average of .364. Seymour, at the culmination of the most remarkable year of his life, began the day at .375. Before the first game, the rival sluggers met on the field and shook hands, drawing cheers from the crowd. Each hefted the other's bat, then "each took a chew of tobacco (from different plugs) and the game was on."[94]

The day belonged to Seymour. Wagner, facing a steep uphill climb, went hitless in his first four at-bats before managing two singles off Ewing in the second game; The Dutchman finished the season batting .363. Seymour rapped two hits in each game, elevating his average to .377. The day capped a season few hitters could ever imagine. In the process of winning the batting title, Seymour also led the league in hits (219), doubles (40), triples (21), total bases (325) and slugging average (.559). He fell one short of sharing the home run crown, won by teammate Fred Odwell with nine.[95]

AS USUAL, the post-season barnstorming tour started the day after the season ended. Ewing, in fine form, couldn't resist the chance to pitch a couple more times before settling in for the winter. He struck out 16 in an exhibition in Dayton, pitching a two-hit shutout and dominating a team of minor leaguers so thoroughly that the *Cincinnati Enquirer* had to coin a new verb: The newspaper reported that Ewing "Mathewsoned" the opposition.[96]

Ewing also made another appearance in Wapakoneta. The big attraction was the matchup between Long Bob and a local phenom named Ed Van Anda. Van Anda was the scion of a prominent local family, the son of a former county prosecutor and half-brother of Carr Van Anda, managing editor of the *New York Times*. Pitching for local teams since his teens, the younger Van Anda had received a buildup the likes of which Ewing never saw. When the youngster played for the Wapakoneta Reds, the club placed advertisements in out-of-town newspapers, urging fans from surrounding communities to come and see "Van Anda, the wonder boy."[97]

Ewing and the Reds had seen Van Anda before. He pitched against them in Wapakoneta in 1903, attracting "the largest crowd ever on the grounds,"[98] and again in Dayton in 1904. The second time he gave them a run for their money before losing 4–3. Even then he was described as "a well-developed young giant" walking around with his chest stuck out like the breast of a pouter pigeon. In the early going, when his team was leading the Reds, a reporter worried that Van Anda might burst the buttons off the sweater he donned to keep warm between innings.[99]

By 1905, 24 years old and in his second year of professional baseball, he was a 20-game winner in the Central League, drafted by the Reds for a tryout the following spring.

"If self-confidence is of any material benefit to a man, Van Anda will hold on," Ren Mulford predicted, "for he is chock full of it."[100]

Eighteen hundred excited fans gathered at the Wapakoneta ballpark to see how the new local favorite would acquit himself against Ewing and the other big leaguers. The two teams were ready to take the field when suddenly Wapakoneta's pitcher staged a one-man sit-down strike. Van Anda, a local newspaper reported, "refused to pitch until a purse had been raised for him."[101]

One can only imagine the consternation of the Wapakoneta management, not to mention the reaction of such hard-boiled veterans as Seymour, Corcoran and Harry Steinfeldt. Ewing and his mates cooled their heels while the hat was passed and Van Anda pocketed the proceeds. Then they went out and scored four runs in the first inning.

The game went downhill from there. The Reds pounded Van Anda for 14 hits while Wapakoneta kicked, fumbled and threw away the ball for eight errors. Ewing, pitching "as if he had it in for his old friends and fellow townsmen,"[102] struck out eight and permitted only three singles. After five innings, the barnstormers had built a 12–0 lead and were content to take it easy the rest of the way.

A few weeks later, an inconspicuous item appeared in the National League notes column of *Sporting Life*:

"The Cincinnati club has decided not to experiment further with pitcher Van Anda."[103]

AGAIN THE REDS barnstormed well into November, but the road held little allure for the 32-year-old Ewing. Within days after his performance in Wapakoneta, he was home in New Hampshire, looking forward to the hunting season and writing to see whether Garry Herrmann would like him to send along "a nice mess of quail."[104]

By now, though, there was more to Ewing's life than hunting, or even baseball. On November 15, 1905, with little or no advance notice to friends and family, in a quiet ceremony in the parsonage of the English Lutheran Church in Wapakoneta, Bob Ewing and Nelle Hunter were married.

Bob and Nelle Ewing married in 1905 and remained together for the rest of his life. Her passion for baseball matched his own. *Photo: Charlotte Ewing-Preville.*

1   *Sporting Life*, April 8, 1905.

2   *The Sporting News*, Oct. 29, 1904.

3   John J. Evers and Hugh S. Fullerton, *Touching Second: The Science of Baseball* (Chicago: Reilly and Britton Co., 1910), p. 114.

4   *Atlanta Journal*, reprinted in *The Sporting News*, April 8, 1905.

5   *The Sporting News*, March 23, 1955. See also Martin Quigley, *The Crooked Pitch: The Curveball in American Baseball History* (Chapel Hill, N.C.: Algonquin Books, 1984), pp. 153-54; and John Thorn and John B. Holway, *The Pitcher* (New York: Prentice Hall Press, 1987), pp. 164-65. Though Stricklett's name remained widely associated with the discovery for decades, the Corridon-Hildebrand version was published at least by 1913. The writer said he had refrained from revealing "the real inventor" sooner out of concern that the disclosure might undermine Stricklett's chances of remaining in the big leagues. See P.A. Meaney, "Who Invented the Spit Ball," *Baseball Magazine*, Vol. 6, No. 7 (May 1913), pp. 59-60.

6   Chesbro described their encounter in *The Sporting News,* Jan. 28, 1905, and his manager, Clark Griffith, recalled it in *The Sporting News*, April 6, 1955; see also John Thorn and John B. Holway, *The Pitcher* (New York: Prentice Hall Press, 1987), p. 165. David L. Fleitz found evidence that Chesbro might have experimented with a spitball as early as 1896, three years before his major league debut. But Fleitz also quotes Chesbro saying that he "became a spitball pitcher" only in 1904, after Stricklett showed him how to control it. See Fleitz, *Ghosts in the Gallery at Cooperstown: 16 Little-Known Members of the Hall of Fame* (Jefferson, N.C.: McFarland and Co. Inc., 2004), pp. 50-53.

7   Stricklett, who spent most of his big league career with Brooklyn, is sometimes credited as the first man to throw the spitball in the National League. But he never pitched in the league until 1905, the year after Ewing unveiled his spitball.

8   *The Sporting News*, Oct. 8, 1908.

9   Lawrence S. Ritter, *The Glory of Their Times: The Story of the Early Days of Baseball Told by the Men who Played It* (New York: Macmillan Co., 1966), p. 56.

10 William Curran, *Big Sticks: The Batting Revolution of the '20s* (New York: William Morrow and Co. Inc., 1990), p. 132.

11 John Thorn and John B. Holway, *The Pitcher* (New York: Prentice Hall Press, 1987), p. 160.

12 Robert Kemp Adair, *The Physics of Baseball* (New York: Harper and Row, 1990), p. 29. This is actually Adair's explanation of a knuckleball, but he says elsewhere that use of a lubricant allows a spitballer "to emulate what a skilled knuckleball pitcher can accomplish legally." Adair, *op. cit.,* pp. 37-38.

13 *New York American*, Aug. 27, 1908, quoted in G.H. Fleming, *The Unforgettable Season* (New York: Holt, Rinehart and Winston, 1981), p. 189.

14 Unidentified newspaper clipping, 1905.

15 *The Sporting News*, Dec. 3, 1908.

16 *New York Times*, Nov. 11, 1961.

17 Edward Walsh, "Strength and Endurance Needed by a Pitcher," in John B. Foster, ed., *How to Pitch* (New York: American Sports Publishing Co., 1912), p. 51.

18 Evers and Fullerton, *op. cit.,* p. 111.

19 Ewing also shunned the spitball's various poor relations, which proliferated later in the era. He was never reported to throw an emery ball, scuff ball or shine ball, which required nicking, scuffing or otherwise defacing the baseball.

20 *Sporting Life*, Oct. 15, 1904.

21 *The Sporting News*, Jan. 28, 1905.

22 Martin Quigley, *The Crooked Pitch: The Curveball in American Baseball History*

(Chapel Hill, N.C.: Algonquin Books, 1984), p. 157; see also *The Sporting News,* March 30, 1955.

23   Ritter, *op. cit.,* p. 115.

24   *Sporting Life,* Oct. 15, 1904.

25   *The Sporting News,* Oct. 29, 1904.

26   *Sporting Life,* Oct. 15, 1904.

27   *Ibid.*

28   *Ibid.*

29   Tim Murnane, *Sporting Life,* Oct. 15, 1904.

30   *The Sporting News,* Nov. 23, 1949.

31   *Ibid.,* March 30, 1955.

32   *Sporting Life,* April 8, 1905.

33   See for example Ray Robinson, *Matty: An American Hero* (New York: Oxford University Press, 1993), p. 86; and Roger Kahn, *The Head Game: Baseball Seen from the Pitcher's Mound* (New York: Harcourt Inc., 2000), p. 91.

34   Mathewson might have had a slightly higher regard for the spitter than he let on. Several years after both of them were retired, Honus Wagner made this interesting observation: "I never saw [Mathewson] use the spitball often. But he had it when he wanted to turn it loose. That boy never overlooked anything." William R. Cobb, ed., *Honus Wagner on His Life and Baseball* (Ann Arbor, Mich.: Sports Media Group, 2006), p. 123.

35   Walsh, *op. cit.,* p. 51.

36   *Sporting Life,* April 20, 1907.

37   *The Sporting News,* Oct. 15, 1904.

38   *Sporting Life,* Oct. 15, 1904.

39   *The Lima Daily News,* April 28, 1905. Jones' view didn't change appreciably even after Walsh helped him win the 1906 World Series. Jones continued to argue that the spitball was "not natural …, not cleanly" and was "doing a great injury to the game." *Sporting Life,* May 11, 1907. Across town, Cubs manager Frank Chance also was no fan of the wet one. When a reporter asked Mordecai Brown about the spitter, the pitcher replied that he didn't throw it because Chance wouldn't allow him to. *Denver Express,* Sept. 17, 1909, quoted in Cindy Thomson and Scott Brown, *Three Finger: The Mordecai Brown Story* (Lincoln, Neb.: University of Nebraska Press, 2006), p. 87.

40   *Sporting Life,* April 22, 1905.

41   *Ibid.,* April 20, 1907.

42   Timothy Sharp, *The Sporting News,* May 6, 1905.

43   *Sporting Life,* June 17, 1905.

44   *The Sporting News,* Oct. 15, 1904.

45   *Cincinnati Times-Star,* reprinted in *The Sporting News,* May 13, 1905.

46   Unidentified Auglaize County newspaper, November 1905.

47   Unidentified newspaper clipping, 1907.

48   H.G. Howland, *Atlas of Auglaize County, Ohio, from Records and Original Surveys* (Philadelphia: Robert Sutton, 1880), p. 44.

49   *Wapakoneta Daily News,* undated clipping, *c.* 1965.

50   *Sporting Life,* Oct. 19, 1907.

51   Jim Bowsher, interview with the author, July 23, 1999. Such attitudes were not universal, however. Carey Orr (1890-1967), who grew up in Auglaize County and became a Pulitzer Prize-winning editorial cartoonist for the *Chicago Tribune,* recalled Ewing as a boyhood hero. Orr aspired to be a pitcher himself and eventually paid his way through art school with money earned playing semipro ball. See William J. McMurray, ed., *History of Auglaize County,* Volume II (Indianapolis: Historical Publishing Co., 1923), pp. 660-61.

52 *The Sporting News,* Feb. 6, 1904.
53 John B. Walsh, *Atlas of Auglaize County, with Historical and Biographical Sketches* (Wapakoneta, Ohio: Atlas Publishing Co., 1898), p. 30.
54 Bob Ewing, letter to Nelle Hunter, March 11, 1905.
55 *Dayton Daily News,* undated clipping, April 1962.
56 Undated letter to Nelle Hunter, September/October 1904. The identity of the writer is not known.
57 *Ibid.*
58 Ewing to Hunter, *op. cit.*
59 Undated letter, *op. cit.*
60 *Wapakoneta Daily News, op. cit.*
61 Ewing to Hunter, *op. cit.*
62 The observation is from catcher George Gibson, a teammate of Peitz's in Pittsburgh. Ritter, *The Glory of Their Times,* enlarged edition (New York: HarperCollins Publishers Inc., 2002 reprint), p. 71.
63 *Sporting Life,* Feb. 18, 1905. Months earlier, the *Cincinnati Enquirer* (Sept. 3, 1904) had referred to Overall as "the Mathewson of the Pacific Coast."
64 *The Sporting News,* Feb. 4, 1905.
65 *Ibid.,* April 8, 1905.
66 Frederic P. O'Connell, *The Sporting News,* April 8, 1905.
67 *Sporting Life,* April 22, 1905.
68 *Ibid.,* April 29, 1905.
69 *Cincinnati Commercial Tribune,* April 16, 1905.
70 *The Sporting News,* Dec. 3, 1908.
71 Eugene C. Murdock, *Baseball Players and Their Times: Oral Histories of the Game, 1920-40* (Westport, Conn.: Meckler Publishing, 1991), p. 84.
72 *Ibid.,* p. 6. Livingston was speaking with specific reference to catching spitballer Cy Morgan.
73 *Sporting Life,* May 27, 1905.
74 *Cincinnati Commercial Tribune,* May 8, 1905.
75 *Ibid.* Christy Mathewson wrote that early on, Wagner developed a particular aversion to the spitball, though in time it proved "as near being Wagner's 'groove' as any curve that has found its way into the big leagues." See Mathewson, *Pitching in a Pinch, or Baseball from the Inside* (New York: Stein and Day, 1977 reprint of 1912 original), pp. 37-38.
76 *Cincinnati Commercial Tribune,* May 8, 1905.
77 *Cincinnati Enquirer,* May 8, 1905.
78 *Cincinnati Commercial Tribune,* May 8, 1905.
79 *Cincinnati Enquirer,* May 8, 1905.
80 *Ibid.,* May 9, 1905.
81 *Cincinnati Commercial Tribune,* May 8, 1905.
82 Kevin Baker, "The Original Fantasy Island: A World of Ups and Downs," in Michael W. Robbins, ed., *Brooklyn: A State of Mind* (New York: Workman Publishing, 2001), p. 50.
83 Ned Hanlon, *The Sporting News,* Aug. 25, 1906.
84 *The Sporting News,* Sept. 2, 1905.
85 *Sporting Life,* Sept. 2, 1905.
86 *Ibid.,* Oct. 7, 1905.
87 *Cincinnati Enquirer,* Oct. 6, 1905.
88 Dillon R. Dorrell, *Mostly About Ohio County Folks* (Rising Sun, Ind.: Ohio County Historical Society, 1989), p. 131.
89 Frank Graham, *McGraw of the Giants: An Informal Biography* (New York: G.P. Putnam's Sons, 1944), p. 163.

90 *Ibid.*

91 *Cincinnati Enquirer*, Oct. 6, 1905.

92 *Sporting Life*, Oct. 21, 1905.

93 *Cincinnati Commercial Tribune*, Oct. 9, 1905.

94 *Ibid.*

95 Modern sources also credit Seymour with the league leadership in runs batted in (121), a statistic not officially tabulated until 1920. Seymour led both major leagues in hits, triples, total bases, batting average and slugging average (plus runs batted in). He tied for second in the major leagues in home runs (behind Odwell, tied with American League leader Harry Davis).

96 *Cincinnati Enquirer*, Oct. 16, 1905.

97 *Lima Times-Democrat*, July 4, 1903.

98 *Auglaize County Democrat*, Aug. 6, 1903.

99 *Cincinnati Enquirer*, Oct. 17, 1904.

100 *Sporting Life*, Sept. 9, 1905.

101 *Auglaize County Democrat*, Oct. 19, 1905.

102 *Cincinnati Enquirer*, Oct. 14, 1905.

103 *Sporting Life*, Dec. 30, 1905.

104 Ewing, letter to August Herrmann, Nov. 1, 1905. The letter is on file in the A. Bartlett Giamatti Research Center at the National Baseball Hall of Fame.

"The acquisition of Hanlon has transported
the local club into the full glare of the winter
spotlight which burns fiercely and sheds
varicolored rays.... It is pleasing to have
among us...a real celebrity."
—DONALD DUNBAR[1]

CHAPTER 8

The Coming of Foxy Ned

THE AX FELL on Joe Kelley in December 1905. Throughout his three-plus seasons as manager, the Reds had always been at least marginally respectable—always above .500, finishing in the first division three campaigns out of four. But they never finished within 16 games of first place. In fact they were never within 15 games in September and never truly in the race after the first couple months of the season. After a disappointing 79–74 record and a fifth-place finish in 1905, the Cincinnati owners decided it was time for a change.

The move came as no great surprise. Rumors of Kelley's impending demise had been swirling for months. There had been reports as far back as spring that Garry Herrmann was casting about for Kelley's successor. Herrmann at first emphatically denied such suggestions, but his denials became fainter and feebler as the season progressed. Herrmann was still issuing qualified denials at season's end; as late as the end of October, Kelley was still assuring reporters that he was signed, sealed and delivered to manage the Reds again in 1906. But somehow, Ren Mulford wrote just days before the official beheading, the impression had leaked out "like water from a battered tub" that Kelley's days were numbered.[2] Cincinnati was making no discernible progress toward its first National League pennant—a prize so long desired, a hope so often denied—and the simmering discontentment was impossible to ignore. *Sporting Life*, in its season review, presumably written by editor Francis C. Richter, concluded:

> *The Cincinnati team once again ran true to form, and therefore, as usual, proved to be the great disappointment of the season.... This team of hard hitters...was never in the hunt for the pennant...and after June remained continually among the also-rans in the second division.... The failure of the team was due largely to Manager Kelley's laxity of discipline, and his demoralizing rows with the umpires.*[3]

The sad fact was, Mulford acknowledged, "Kelley had not proved a leader of men."[4]

But if Kelley couldn't bring a pennant to Cincinnati, perhaps Kelley's mentor could. In making a change, the Reds again reached back to the celebrated Baltimore Orioles of the 1890s, this time for their manager, Ned Hanlon. Kelley wasn't necessarily saddened to give up the reins. His first experience as a major league manager had taken a toll. He had aged visibly in the past four years. Now, at 34, he stepped aside gracefully and agreed to stay on as a player under his old boss. "I will work as hard for the Reds next season as any man on Mr. Herrmann's payroll," Kelley promised. "I know that Hanlon will get results."[5]

The move, when announced, was precisely the one both Herrmann and Hanlon had been denying for months. There was a feeling that the owners had finally gotten what they wanted all along. In hiring Kelley in 1902, the Reds had gotten a great player with a track record as a winner. In Hanlon, they got something more: an experienced manager, the architect of a whole string of championship teams, a man acknowledged, in the words of *Sporting News* correspondent Donald Dunbar, as "one of the few geniuses of the game."[6]

Hanlon was a native New Englander who had played for local teams from his mid-teens and began his professional career in Providence, Rhode Island, in 1876. Noted mainly for his speed and defensive skills, he played 13 years in the major leagues as an outfielder. A left-handed batter who struggled mightily against left-handed pitchers, he recognized early on the advantages of pitting right-handed hitters against left-handed pitchers and vice versa. He gained acclaim as a manager, winning three straight National League pennants for Baltimore in 1894-96 and two more after moving to

Brooklyn in 1899. Meticulous and systematic, Hanlon built his successful clubs on speed, aggressiveness and fundamentals. In Baltimore he worked his teams endlessly, perfecting cutoff plays and pickoff moves, drilling his pitchers on covering first base. Admirers credited the Orioles with a long list of inventions including "the hit-and-run play, sacrifice hits, bunts, base stealing and place hitting," making Baltimore "the birthplace of modern baseball"[7] and Hanlon "the father of modern baseball."[8]

Hanlon's reputation as an innovator isn't undeserved, but it is probably overstated. The Boston Beaneaters were working the hit-and-run before Hanlon won his first pennant and the sacrifice was an established tactic by 1890. Johnny Evers and Hugh Fullerton claimed that much of what came to be known as "inside baseball" was pioneered by the Chicago White Stockings in the early 1880s, and Dickey Pearce was honing his mastery of bunting and place hitting as far back as the 1860s. Still, Foxy Ned's ceaseless attention to the fine points enabled his teams to refine and develop an array of offensive and defensive skills that could be used, as one writer put it, "like burglar's tools" to steal a ballgame.[9]

At 48, Hanlon could look back on a long and lucrative career. Magnates aside, he was believed to be the wealthiest man in baseball, his net worth estimated in 1906 at $150,000 and a few years later at $500,000.[10] He owned a minor league team in Baltimore and had invested profitably in real estate there and elsewhere. He had been well paid and also enjoyed considerable status in Brooklyn, where the team was commonly referred to as Hanlon's Superbas—a name borrowed from a popular vaudeville troupe. But in recent years his situation had taken a sharp turn for the worse. After nearly a decade of unbroken success, Hanlon had suffered three straight second-division finishes, finally landing in last place in 1905. At the same time, he found himself an increasingly disgruntled minority stockholder in the Brooklyn regime of club president Charlie Ebbets. The relationship between owner and manager hit bottom when Ebbets unilaterally slashed Hanlon's extravagant five-figure salary almost in half.[11] While managing the Reds, Hanlon filed a series of lawsuits against his former employer before reaching an agreement to sell his Brooklyn stock in 1907.

Hanlon's arrival in Cincinnati was greeted with something approaching euphoria. Ren Mulford, while acknowledging that the past three years had knocked some of the luster off Hanlon's reputation, pronounced his hiring "the best possible [move] Garry Herrmann could have made on the checkerboard of diamond action."[12] Other Cincinnati scribes were even more effusive. "I think it can be truthfully said that not in the last 15 years has the outlook for the Cincinnati team been as promising as it is at present," Jim C. Hamilton wrote in *The Sporting News* before the season started. "Had President Herrmann failed to sign a single additional player, ... the solitary addition of Ned Hanlon as manager would undoubtedly have put [the team] in the running."[13] Similar endorsements came from precincts where Hanlon had previously operated. In New York, Joe Vila predicted that Hanlon's presence "would make the game boom in Redville as it has never been boomed before."[14] Hanlon's friend Joe Cummings in Baltimore went even further. "From what I know about Mr. Hanlon," Cummings proclaimed, "I unhesitatingly say that a pennant will float in Cincinnati ... by the work of the 1907 team at the very latest."[15]

A few dissenters in the press, such as Boston's Tim Murnane, who had the temerity to suggest that Herrmann might have bought a "gold brick" when he signed Hanlon, were shouted down and drowned out.

Hanlon expressed relief at being out of Brooklyn and out from under Charlie Ebbets' control. Hanlon boosters, such as Joe Vila, looked forward to seeing what Hanlon could do "with Garry's open purse at his command."[16]

"For years, I have been up against the tough proposition of trying to make the best of a club which had no money to back it up," Hanlon said. "In Cincinnati I will have unlimited capital to make a pennant-winning team."

"It will be up to me if I fail," he added.[17]

The Reds were already embarking on a makeover by the time Hanlon's appointment became official. Among the first to go was Harry Steinfeldt. At 28, he had been a fixture in the infield since 1898, but had fallen into disfavor after getting into a drunken brawl with Tommy Corcoran after the previous October's outing at the Laughery Club.[18] Less than three weeks later, Steinfeldt was sent to Chicago for left-hander Jake Weimer, Bob Ewing's former Kansas City teammate. Weimer, 32 years old and winner of 58 games in three seasons with the Cubs, was viewed as a replacement for Noodles Hahn. Some believed the Reds had landed "the premier southpaw of the National League"[19] but in Chicago, Hugh Fullerton opined that Weimer would merely "add to the streak of yellow in the Cincinnati club."[20]

After his finest season in 1905, Ewing was one of the few Reds whose job was secure. Besides Steinfeldt, those jettisoned by the first few weeks of the new season included pitchers Tom Walker, now deemed never to have been worth the $2,500 the Reds paid for him, and Jack Harper, whose record had slid from 23–9 in 1904 to 9–13 in 1905. Al Bridwell, a promising infielder who had been personally scouted by Herrmann in the minor leagues, got entangled in a contract squabble and was abruptly shipped to Boston after only one year in Cincinnati. Outfielder Jimmy Sebring, who had been absent from the club for several weeks in 1905 caring for his ailing wife in Pennsylvania, refused to report when assigned to Chicago in the Steinfeldt-Weimer trade. Subsequently blacklisted for playing outlaw ball in his hometown, Sebring spent years trying to get reinstated. His case wasn't helped by a dispute with Herrmann over repayment of cash advances he had received from the Reds. Sebring finally got back to the major leagues in 1909, only to die of Bright's disease[21] later the same year, at age 27.

New faces included pitcher Chick Fraser, a 35-year-old veteran of 10 seasons with four major league teams, who began the season playing semipro ball while holding out from the miserly Boston Beaneaters. Also on board was Jim Delahanty, who had played semipro ball against Ewing in 1897. Competing with Delahanty for Steinfeldt's old job at third base was stocky, bowlegged John Bernard Lobert, a 25-year-old speedster who was called "Hans" because he was thought to look like a scaled-down version of Pittsburgh's great Honus Wagner.

Hanlon went south promising that if he couldn't put "baseball brains" into the players' heads, he would at least make sure they made use of what gray matter they had.[22] The team returned to Texas, this time to Marlin Springs, 25 miles southeast of Waco. Because of its hot mineral spring, discovered in 1892, Marlin was emerging as a health resort; in years to come, it would become a favorite spring training venue of John J. McGraw and the New York Giants. Marlin around this time had fewer people than Wapakoneta, Ohio, and training facilities that could only be categorized as primitive. One of McGraw's biographers describes a ballfield with a "falling-down fence and ramshackle little bleachers."[23] That would have been Emerson Field, built by the Giants in 1908 a mile south of town along the railroad tracks as a presumed improvement on the east side fairgrounds site used by the Reds.[24] And the central Texas climate, in the words of another authority, "made it very difficult to maintain a suitable playing field."[25] Aside from the supposed curative powers of the waters, McGraw liked Marlin Springs because it offered few opportunities for players to get into mischief. "My idea of no setting for a pleasure party is Marlin Springs, Texas," grumbled Giants pitcher Christy Mathewson.[26]

In any event, Marlin didn't prove a very healthy locale for Ned Hanlon. Shortly after the team reached Texas, he came down with symptoms of something like malaria. Hanlon promptly headed north again in search of a more congenial climate. He ended up missing most of spring training, leaving the lame duck Kelley in charge of preparations for the season. Still, optimism about the Reds wasn't dimmed, nor was the readiness to give credit to Hanlon, regardless of whether he deserved it.

"I have been south with many teams," business manager Frank Bancroft proclaimed a few days before the opener, "but the Cincinnati bunch is the best that I have ever had anything to do with. … I believe that it was the teaching that [Hanlon] administered to the boys in the South that brought forth these results."[27]

Ewing managed to avoid a recurrence of the "Texas fever" that had laid him low in 1904, but by the time the team returned to Cincinnati he was nursing a sore arm. He didn't pitch for nearly two weeks as the Reds limped to a 4–9 start. Even after his debut—toiling through 7⅔ innings of an 8–5 victory over St. Louis on April 25—Ewing was sent home to rest his ailing extremity. While the Reds were engaged with Pittsburgh at League Park on April 29, Ewing was in Wapakoneta taking in an exhibition game between the local amateurs and a minor league team from Lima. The game was one-sided, but the afternoon was not uneventful. A brewery wagon delivering beer to the ballpark overturned, leaving 200 disappointed fans with "not even an odor of the foaming beverage." In the middle of the game the gas tank in the popcorn wagon under the grandstand exploded and the blazing vehicle had to be wheeled out into the open to prevent the whole park from burning down. The popcorn man was out of business, but a collection was taken up for him and he came out ahead in the end.[28]

While Ewing was out of action, Orval Overall was getting all the work he could handle, and then some. The big Californian had carried a heavy load throughout his rookie year, starting 39 games (to Ewing's 34) and relieving in three others, pitching a total of 318 innings. At season's end, the

Mathewson of the West had won 18 games and lost 23. Hanlon, who announced during spring training that he planned to carry only five pitchers,[29] immediately took up where Kelley left off, leaning on Overall as the staff's workhorse. He started three games in the first week of the season and by April 23, when he dropped a 7–5 decision to St. Louis, the first ripple of uncertainty ran through the Cincinnati press. "But one real fault has been found in Hanlon's management," Jim C. Hamilton wrote. "That has been pitching Overall as often as he has. Overall has been worked in four games and he has succeeded in losing just as many."[30]

On May 12, Ewing scattered five hits over 11 innings and beat the Giants 3–2. But he still wasn't right. One view was that his arm was "harboring several recalcitrant nerves."[31] Another was that he was "troubled with occasional visits of the rheumatism."[32] Or, as later reported, he "had caught cold in his arm."[33] Whatever the reason, he was "having his annual misery with that uncertain wing of his,"[34] and this year's miseries were serious. They would dog him for most of the season.

By June 1 the Reds were in sixth place. With Ewing "by no means in his best condition" and Jake Weimer gripped by a streak of "unparalleled" hard luck,[35] "the pitching staff was never in such wretched condition."[36] By far the biggest disappointment was Overall. The fans were riding him and, even though he had won four of his last five decisions, it was said the team "was never confident as long as he was in the box."[37]

"Orval Overall today is not as good a pitcher as he was when he came out of the West," Ren Mulford declared.[38] The *Enquirer*'s Jack Ryder summed up Overall's performance in two words: "rankly ineffective."[39]

Seven weeks into his second season in the major leagues, the Reds gave up on the brightest prospect they had signed in years. They traded him to Chicago for right-hander Bob Wicker. Wicker, four years older than Overall, had won 50 games in three seasons with the Cubs, but his victories and his innings had declined annually from his 20-win peak in 1903. Moreover, there were ominous suspicions about his constitution; the Reds, Hanlon later admitted, "knew that Wicker had weak lungs and was not physically strong."[40]

But the Reds were determined that Overall had to go. Even when the Cubs refused to consider a deal involving any of their top pitchers—Mordecai Brown, Carl Lundgren or Ed Reulbach—Cincinnati pushed ahead.

"Big Jeff [Overall] has been doing nothing for us, while in Wicker we get a pitcher who was one of the best in the league last season," Hanlon said.[41]

To seal the deal, the Reds threw in $2,000 cash. Herrmann worked out the details with Charles Webb Murphy. A few years earlier, Murphy had been an ink-stained wretch in the employ of the *Cincinnati Enquirer* and later the *Times-Star,* sometimes traveling with the Reds. After John T. Brush transferred his operations to New York, he hired Murphy as the Giants' press agent. In 1905, hearing that the Chicago club was for sale, Murphy convinced his former boss—Charles P. Taft, owner and editor of the *Times-Star*—to loan him $100,000.[42] With that the former sportswriter, not yet 40 years old, became president of a National League club and found himself negotiating as an equal with Garry Herrmann. In finalizing the cash in the Overall trade, Herrmann tried to draw the line at $1,500 but Murphy held out for $2,000. They finally agreed to settle the matter with a coin flip. Herrmann lost.[43]

Murphy's manager, Frank Chance, had long coveted Overall. They were born within 50 miles of each other in California and had been friends for years. Chance was convinced Overall's problems in Cincinnati were the result of overwork,[44] a situation that could be easily remedied.

In Cincinnati, the trade got mixed reviews. While one paper entertained the fond hope that the transaction had "every appearance of being the best one that has gone through this season,"[45] another observed sourly that the acquisition of Wicker "does not look to be the best move in the world."[46] Even such skeptics accepted that some kind of a trade, even a bad one, was probably necessary. "Any pitcher was better than Overall in this city," Jim C. Hamilton wrote.[47]

Overall-for-Wicker marked the beginning of the end for Ned Hanlon. In time the fallout from the trade produced considerable finger-pointing between Hanlon and Herrmann. Hanlon was still defending his role in the episode after he was gone from the major leagues. Sure, he allowed, he had agreed to swap Overall for Wicker even up but, he insisted, "I was opposed to handing over one red cent."[48]

The trade proved to be "the joke of the season."[49] Wicker won six more games before disappearing from the major leagues. Overall quickly became one of the best pitchers in the National League; he went 12–3 for the balance of 1906 and, along with Harry Steinfeldt, represented Chicago in four

World Series over the next five years. Overall never again started more than 32 games in a season.[50]

In Cincinnati, meanwhile, the *Commercial Tribune* reported, "The fans are trusting in Hanlon and hoping for the best."[51] A week later, *The Sporting News* surveyed the season to date and concluded, "Cincinnati has a 'dead rabbit' team and Hanlon is as helpless as he has been for several seasons."[52]

EWING AND HIS TEAMMATES weren't sure what to expect when they arrived in Brooklyn two weeks later for a scheduled Sunday game. Sunday baseball had been a touchy issue for years, and rarely more so than in 1906. Even in Cincinnati, where Sunday ball had been permitted for decades, new political breezes were stirring up a potential threat to what one sportswriter called "the pure cream of the Reds' schedule."[53] In November 1905, with Julius Fleischmann not standing for re-election, the voters of Cincinnati had handed Boss Cox's Republican Party machine a rare setback. The selection of Edward J. Dempsey as mayor, coupled with the choice of another Democrat as the new governor of Ohio, created shock waves that registered even on the sports pages. Within days of the election, Ren Mulford told his *Sporting Life* readers that the Queen City was "in the throes of a political upheaval."[54] He foresaw a "political revolution" which threatened to "upset many old customs in Cincinnati."[55] Shortly after the new administration took office, *Sporting News* correspondent Donald Dunbar penned a dispatch from a city under siege:

> *Friday evening the lid was put down on this city.... The saloons were closed at midnight. It has been officially announced that the Sunday theatrical performances are the next to go. And then—the Sunday baseball. It is only a surmise that this latter catastrophe will befall, but the surmise is based on the words and doings of the powers that be.*[56]

Whatever actual impetus there was to shut down Sunday baseball in Cincinnati, such a move was seen as having solid backing from the state capital. The new governor, John M. Pattison, was "a staunch Methodist [and] well known ... temperance man"[57] and was said to be bent on

Bob Ewing was sometimes called "Old Wapak," but even in his 30s he still had an almost boyish face. This photograph, taken when he was 31, was used on Fan Craze and Ramly Cigarettes baseball cards issued in 1906 and 1909. *Photo: National Baseball Hall of Fame Library, Cooperstown, New York.*

enforcing a statewide ban on professional games on the Sabbath. Garry Herrmann was sufficiently alarmed to go looking for a site where the Reds could play Sunday games across the Ohio River in Kentucky.

Herrmann's fears were never realized. After considerable fretting and hand-wringing by club officials and the press, Sunday ball continued in Cincinnati without hindrance.[58] Brooklyn, however, was not Cincinnati. Nowhere was the long battle over Sunday baseball livelier than in the self-proclaimed City of Churches, where blue laws prohibited the Superbas[59] from playing home games—or at least from charging admission—on Sunday. Owner Charlie Ebbets, recognizing the potential windfall represented by big Sunday crowds, tried all sorts of tactics to get around the law. He would advertise a band concert, collect admission and then, after a few musical numbers, treat the concertgoers to a "free" baseball game. Or he would schedule a ballgame and admit the spectators free—then charge them several times the going rate for scorecards, on a sliding scale based on the location of their seats. Eventually Ebbets settled on simply opening the gates and placing boxes at the entrances for "donations."

The law was sufficiently ambiguous, and local authorities sufficiently ambivalent, to keep the matter kicking around the courts unresolved for more than two years. By 1906, Ebbets and the police had worked out a delicate minuet which they danced around the issue while waiting for the courts to come down on one side or the other.

That's where the situation stood on Sunday afternoon, June 17, 1906, when Ned Hanlon called the Reds together before their scheduled game at Brooklyn's Washington Park. Having spent the previous seven seasons in Brooklyn, Hanlon knew what to expect. He needed someone—preferably a pitcher who was not slated to work that day—to take one for the team. Hanlon initially offered the honor to Charlie Chech, but Chech begged off. When Hanlon offered a $25 bonus as an inducement to volunteers, he immediately had more than he could use. Ultimately Chick Fraser was selected and penciled in as the Reds' leadoff hitter.

As game time approached, fans filed into the park. "The contribution box system" was in effect, the *New York Times* reported.[60] Then the Superbas took their positions in the field and umpire Bill Klem bawled, "Play ball!" Fraser stepped into the batter's box and took two pitches from Brooklyn's Mal Eason. At that point, as expected, two plainclothes officers walked out onto the field and took Eason and Fraser into custody. Ebbets was also arrested, along with opposing managers Hanlon and Patsy Donovan.

Once that business was out of the way, the game began again in earnest. Ewing took the mound for Cincinnati against Brooklyn's Doc Scanlan. As the stands rocked with more than 10,000 fans, Ewing spun a three-hit shutout, winning the game 3–0. Meanwhile at the police station, Fraser, Hanlon and the rest of the miscreants were released after posting $200 bond. All charges were later dropped.

For his part, Chick Fraser took his brush with the law in stride. "I've never been arrested," he said, "although I often thought that I deserved to be."[61]

It would be 10 years before Brooklyn played another home game on a Sunday.[62]

BY MID-SEASON the sportswriters had virtually given up hope that the Reds could rise above the second division. The team, second in the league in runs scored a year earlier, had tumbled into a seemingly bottomless slump. Even in the context of a sharp drop in scoring throughout the National League, the Reds' problems were shocking. While run production fell more than 13 percent league-wide, the drop-off in Cincinnati was twice that. Old standbys such as Tommy Corcoran and Joe Kelley were showing their age in their batting averages. The Reds' season was becoming littered with failed experiments. Charlie Carr, Hanlon's Opening Day choice at first base, was back in the minor leagues by mid-May. Thirty-one-year-old Jimmy Barrett, who had played for Cincinnati in 1899 and 1900, was reclaimed after being discarded by the Detroit Tigers; he was gone again after going hitless in five games. Hanlon continued to tinker with the roster in an effort to find a winning combination. He acquired pitcher Charley "Sea Lion" Hall, who had managed an 8–13 record with the second-best team in the Pacific Coast League, and signed John Wesley "Snake" Deal, a 27-year-old first baseman who had been playing outlaw ball in his hometown of Lancaster, Pennsylvania.[63] Injury-plagued Fred Odwell, the National League's 1905 home run leader, was sent to Toledo along with Charlie Chech—another of the numerous "pitching finds of the season"[64] who came and went during Ewing's years in Cincinnati—in exchange for outfielder Frank Jude. An Ojibwe from the White Earth Reservation in Minnesota, Jude had played football as well as baseball at the Carlisle Indian School in Pennsylvania. The Cincinnati writers promptly dubbed him the Little Chief.

Hall won four games for Cincinnati over the balance of the season and lost eight. Both Jude and Deal proceeded to hit .208. The pitchers bore the brunt of Cincinnati's offensive malaise, and none more than Ewing. Starting June 30, he lost two 2–1 decisions in five days. Five days after that, and still complaining of a sore arm, he "was hit much harder than usual"[65] but again lasted the complete game in a 5–3 loss to New York.

Right about now, in the midst of a season of on-field frustrations, the Reds encountered a major off-field embarrassment. Garry Herrmann was forced to publicly repudiate a bet on the outcome of the National League pennant race. As a sporting man, Herrmann was deeply chagrined at having to back out of a wager. But as chairman of the National Commission—effectively the chief justice of what was often called baseball's supreme court—he found it even more uncomfortable to be foolishly entangled in a conflict of interest serious enough to be labeled "the Phelps scandal."[66]

Betting was endemic in baseball in the early 20th century. The situation inspired much cluck-clucking and periodic pushes to "clean up" the game. Such efforts met with little success. Weeks before the Herrmann brouhaha blew up, *The Sporting News* reported a "small riot" when police attempted to arrest gamblers in the stands in Boston.[67] For the most part players and especially owners felt free to maintain a "sporting interest" in the game. Much of the wagering was done in fun and was relatively harmless. The year after the Herrmann incident, Cincinnati second baseman Miller Huggins bet Pittsburgh owner Barney Dreyfuss a new hat on the outcome of the first game pitched by the Pirates' Howie Camnitz.[68] Other propositions were deadly serious, with large sums of money at stake. In 1902, the Pittsburgh Pirates heard that Frank de Hass Robison, president of the St. Louis Cardinals, was prepared to bet $10,000 that Pittsburgh wouldn't win the pennant. The Pirates pooled $10,000 of their own and wired Robison that his challenge was accepted.[69]

Herrmann maintained that the wager that got him into trouble grew out of nothing more than some good-natured kidding among friends. But when the news got out, the size and timing of the bet suggested the possibility of something considerably less innocent. Herrmann had offered 3-to-1 odds that Pittsburgh wouldn't win the 1906 pennant. He claimed he expected the stakes to be set at a relatively nominal sum, perhaps $100, and was shocked when the other party in the transaction—identified in the press as "Leo Mayer, the New York bookmaker"[70]—put up $2,000. This placed Herrmann in the position of either risking $6,000 or backing off. He ultimately posted the $6,000, as *The Sporting News* put it, "rather than be twitted at backing down."[71]

This all transpired around the same time the National Commission was weighing a dispute between Pittsburgh and the Boston Americans over the rights to catcher Ed Phelps, who had been put up for sale by Cincinnati. The decision initially went in favor of Boston, but after Herrmann's wager came to light, he was forced to do some hasty backtracking. Hoping to head off the anticipated uproar, Herrmann repurchased Phelps from Boston "and gave him unconditionally to Pittsburgh." It was said that American League president Ban Johnson, widely regarded as the true power on the commission, prevailed on Boston to relinquish the player, facilitating the transaction "as a personal favor to Mr. Herrmann."[72]

Herrmann released the text of his correspondence asking Mayer to annul the wager. News of the bet, he acknowledged, had "created a great deal of comment, on account of the position that I occupy in baseball." He admitted making "a serious mistake" that would "subject me ... to very severe, and, I may add, deserved criticism." Herrmann stressed that he "did not solicit the wager [which] ... was brought about after a good deal of jesting." Even so, he told Mayer, he presumed to ask out of the bet only "on account of our long friendship."[73] The *Cincinnati Enquirer* also printed Mayer's reply, graciously agreeing to call the whole thing off.

For a time, the episode raised baseball's consciousness of the dangers of gambling. *The Sporting News*, deploring widespread coverage of betting on the World Series a few months later, spoke of "a menace to [baseball's] integrity."[74] But there was no generalized outrage over Herrmann's actions or his choice of friends. Even *The Sporting News* expressed "unimpaired confidence in his personal and official integrity."[75] Whether newspapers should include betting odds with their baseball coverage continued to be warmly debated for years in Cincinnati. Ren Mulford likened the practice to a cancer, but the *Enquirer*'s Jack Ryder defended the legitimate news value of baseball as "an attractive betting proposition,"[76] and sometimes even held the stakes for readers looking for a little action.[77]

A chastened Herrmann issued a public promise never to bet on baseball again. It was not an easy promise to keep. The pledge might have made Herrmann more circumspect about associating with bookmakers and it might have limited his subsequent wagering. But the following year, he was reported wearing a new $200 overcoat, provided by Chicago White Sox owner Charles Comiskey in payment of a World Series bet.[78] Herrmann's papers at the National Baseball Hall of Fame document baseball bets he continued to make with other major league executives until at least 1916.[79]

1906 WASN'T TURNING OUT to be Herrmann's favorite year, and he wasn't alone. With the team more than a dozen games below .500, Hanlon's honeymoon with the press was coming to an end. Reporters tired of finding Hanlon less than forthcoming and when, for lack of information, they filled their columns with speculation, he became annoyed in turn. Finally Hanlon turned on the writers with a broadside about "outsiders … butting in" with unwanted advice on how to run his club, and in the process "sow[ing] discord among the players."[80]

But discord had already taken root. Veteran players were beginning to look askance at their famous manager. Shad Barry had batted .324 for Cincinnati after coming over from Chicago the previous season and established himself with teammates and fans as "one of the most popular players that ever wore a red-legged uniform."[81] By mid-1906 he was under suspension by the club and "clearly not on good terms with manager Hanlon."[82] Cy Seymour was equally disenchanted, and his state of mind was reflected in his performance. After a month-long slide, the defending National League batting champion was hitting a lackluster .257. One reported source of Seymour's unhappiness was Hanlon's insistence that he alter his unorthodox batting style.[83] It was widely believed and openly asserted that Seymour had simply decided to lie down on the job until the Reds were forced to trade him. He made no secret of his ambition to play for the Giants. He had played for John McGraw in Baltimore and it was McGraw who had converted him from a pitcher to an outfielder. Tensions in Cincinnati were not eased by McGraw's public acknowledgement that he would love to have Seymour in New York.

On July 14, with the Reds languishing in fifth place and the second-place Giants straining to gain ground on Chicago's league-leading Cubs, the inevitable deal was consummated. Cincinnati sold its recalcitrant slugger to McGraw for the stunning sum of $12,000—enough to pay three or four front-line players for a year. The Reds reinstated Shad Barry so he could fill Seymour's position for a few days, until a deal was worked out sending Barry to St. Louis for outfielder Homer Smoot. If the acquisition of Smoot generated little excitement, the departure of Seymour prompted few tears. "There was hardly a fan in town but what had soured to more or less extent on Cy," Jim C. Hamilton wrote. "… When he was sold there was more rejoicing than regret."[84]

Once free of Cincinnati and Hanlon, Seymour quickly recovered his batting eye. He swung at a .320 clip for the balance of the season and remained with the Giants until 1910. Homer Smoot hit .259 after coming to Cincinnati and vanished from the major leagues after the 1906 season. Yet when one Cincinnati newspaper urged fans to greet Seymour with a shower of lemons and a chorus of "groans, hisses, hoots and catcalls"[85] when he returned to League Park as a Giant, the campaign fell flat. Seymour appeared on the field wearing "a lovely crop of false whiskers" and a wave of laughter drowned out the boos and hisses.[86]

The day after Seymour's departure, the Reds suffered one of their strangest defeats of Ewing's career. The sportswriters believed that Ewing cost himself a victory by hitting a home run—and Ewing agreed.

Locked in a tight pitchers' duel with Brooklyn's Doc Scanlan before a Sunday afternoon overflow crowd at League Park, Ewing had allowed only five hits and was clinging to a 1–0 lead when he came to bat with two out in the seventh inning. He lined one through the gap to the fence in left-center field, "a legitimate triple at least," in the view of Jack Ryder, and when left fielder Lew Ritter and shortstop Phil Lewis were a little careless in relaying the ball back to the infield, Ewing "labored all the way around the circuit" for a home run,[87] the second of his career.

Miller Huggins made the final out of the inning moments later and Ewing "scarcely had time to get his breath" before he had to go back to work on the mound.[88] He got the first two outs in the eighth inning, but surrendered singles to Harry Lumley and Whitey Alperman. Then John Hummel lashed a hot shot through the box. Ewing knocked it down but couldn't make a play as Lumley scored from third. When Hans Lobert fumbled Lewis' routine grounder, Alperman crossed the plate with the tying run.

It was a hot day and suddenly Ewing was spent. "I had plenty of speed and good command of the spitball up till that time," he said later. "But the hard run took my wind. ... I seemed to lose my speed after that."[89]

Hanlon sent Bob Wicker out to pitch the ninth inning. Brooklyn touched him up for three hits and two runs and won the game 4–2.

Though there is no specific record of Nelle Ewing being at the ballpark that day, it might have been this game that inaugurated what she remembered as "the jinx." The newspapers did note that in addition to trying to win the game, in legging out the home run Bob was attempting to win for her the box of chocolates that was among the prizes customarily awarded for such a feat;[90] and he might have been doubly driven to make the costly extra effort if he knew his "pretty black-eyed bride"[91] was watching. What is certain is that sometime in 1906 Nelle became convinced that she was a jinx and determined never to go to the park when Bob was expected to pitch. Traveling with the team late that season, she talked with a reporter about her quandary.

"She believes that her presence hoodoos him, so she stays away to help him win ... though she loves baseball," he wrote. "... She has never seen Bob win."[92] Years later, Nelle said that after she watched Bob lose two straight games, he asked her to stay away.[93] It's more likely the idea originated with her. A story at the time reported that Bob "has all along refused to believe that his wife's presence ... was a hoodoo."[94] She, on the other hand, was a lifelong bundle of superstitions. Grandchildren remember that she refused to walk under a ladder and wouldn't tolerate an open umbrella in the house, and the lucky rabbit's foot she carried was always prominently displayed when she attended Opening Day games in Cincinnati.

Nelle's self-imposed exile lasted more than a year. The Cincinnati papers officially declared the jinx broken as of August 11, 1907, after another game in which Bob hit a home run against Brooklyn. In later years, Nelle sometimes said she showed up for that game under the mistaken impression that someone else was scheduled to pitch. In fact she might have gone to

Bob's game intentionally, having resolved to test the power of the hoodoo and see whether it could be undone. This scenario conforms to a story she told Jim Bowsher and also to a newspaper article at the time that says she decided to risk seeing Bob pitch after "a friend persuaded her that hoodoos don't last forever" and this one might have run its course. "She was nervous all through the game till that great seventh-inning batting rally which her husband so gloriously topped off with a home run," the article said. Then she settled back and enjoyed the remainder of the game.[95]

What if Bob had lost again after she consciously challenged the jinx, Bowsher asked her 60 years later.

"I never would've told him I was at the game," Nelle said.[96]

IN MID-1906, any upturn in Ewing's fortunes, or the Reds', was a long time in the future. Ewing pitched better, but the improvement wasn't reflected in his won-lost record. Two weeks after his ill-fated home run, Ewing was on the losing end of a 2–1 decision to the Giants, who got both runs in the first inning after Tommy Corcoran was called for interference on a rundown play between third base and home plate. Ewing was "absolutely invincible" over the last eight innings,[97] allowing only two hits, but Cincinnati managed only a solitary single off Red Ames all afternoon.

Baseball was at the height—or in the depths—of the dead ball era. In a year when 23 percent of all National League games resulted in shutouts for one side or the other, Ewing's season was typified by what *Sporting Life* applauded as "the longest and greatest game ever seen in Pittsburgh."[98] The date was September 11, 1906. Ewing put on a performance in many ways superior to his near no-hitter of 1903, and still couldn't gain a victory. He dueled two Pittsburgh hurlers for two hours and 51 minutes. When the game was called because of darkness after 15 innings, not a single runner for either team had dented the plate.

Ewing's game was a monument to dogged determination. Six of Pittsburgh's eight hits came leading off innings. The Pirates got runners to third base in the second, third, seventh and 10th innings, but Ewing always turned them back. He was at his best in the game's numerous crises, and seemed to grow stronger as the afternoon shadows grew longer. He allowed only three hits in the last seven innings.

He struck out four and walked four while dispatching the lion's share of Pittsburgh batters on routine ground balls. When darkness fell, the Pirates had left 10 men on base, the Reds 14.

Ewing's magnificent work was matched by the performance of his battery mate. "The Admiral caught an admirable game," Jack Ryder wrote, "and he had a busy afternoon for Ewing had the spitball dodging around in every direction."[99] Catching all 15 innings, Schlei threw out two base runners and tagged out another at the plate when Tommy Sheehan missed a spitball on an attempted suicide squeeze.

Pittsburgh manager Fred Clarke made a bid to end the game in the 10th inning when, with two runners on base, he sent up a pinch-hitter for pitcher Deacon Phillippe. But Ewing retired Ginger Beaumont and the marathon continued, with Ewing now matched against Vic Willis. Honus Wagner, hobbled by a charley horse, hadn't started the game for Pittsburgh, but in the 12th, Clarke sent his gimpy star in for Sheehan at third base. Wagner looked "perfectly helpless" in two at-bats against Ewing.[100]

The Reds had their best chance to score in the 13th, when Miller Huggins led off with a double and Joe Kelley walked. When Wagner bobbled Frank Jude's sacrifice bunt, the bases were loaded with none out. But Homer Smoot and Hans Lobert grounded weakly to the drawn-in infield, resulting in two force outs at home, and Schlei flied to center to end the inning.

That was the last serious threat by either side. Ewing received "a great round of applause" from the Pittsburgh fans when he came to bat in the 14th, and he responded with a clean single to right, but nothing came of it. When the epic contest was over, two Cincinnati papers observed that Ewing looked as if he could have gone on indefinitely. Ryder offered this assessment:

> While every man on each team did something at some time or other during the three hours of play...the shining light of the afternoon fell directly on the long, lank form of Mr. Robert Ewing, the tall sycamore of old Wapakoneta.... He was the personification of coolness and courage.[101]

Back in July, Ewing had characterized that 4–2 loss to Brooklyn that featured his ill-omened home run as "a difficult game to pitch" in which he "did not dare rest a minute."[102] He was describing his entire season. The final three weeks offered no respite. He held Brooklyn to four hits but lost 1–0 to Elmer Stricklett. He toiled through 11 scoreless innings before beating Boston 2–1 in the 12th on a two-run homer by Schlei. In his final start—against Big Jeff Pfeffer before a Tuesday-afternoon crowd of 911, again in Boston—Ewing struck out nine, walked one and scattered seven hits. The only runs he allowed, according to *Sporting Life*, "resulted from poor playing" by his teammates.[103] The game was called after 12 innings, ending in a 2–2 tie.

Coming off the best year of his career in 1905, Ewing had tumbled to a disappointing 13–14 record. The Reds, a winning team a year earlier, had fallen even further. They finished sixth, 51½ games out of first place. Ned Hanlon, in his first year as manager, had gone through 35 players. One of the few to prosper was Jake Weimer, who shook off the early doldrums to post a 20–14 record. Of the rest, 12 would not find a place on any major league roster in 1907 and four others would see their big league careers end by mid-season. On the whole, Ren Mulford concluded, Hanlon's first Cincinnati club was "the most expensive team of demoralized and dismal failures in all balldom."[104]

Some observers tried to look on the bright side. *Sporting News* correspondent Jim C. Hamilton shrugged off the slighting opinions of "the eastern critics" and argued that Hanlon had offered "at least proof that he is trying."[105] Still, Hamilton admitted, that much sought-after Cincinnati pennant was "hardly a possibility" in 1907.[106]

1   *The Sporting News,* Jan. 6, 1906.

2   *Sporting Life,* Dec. 9, 1905.

3   *Ibid.,* Oct. 14, 1905.

4   *Ibid.,* Dec. 9, 1905.

5   *The Sporting News,* Jan. 6, 1906.

6   *Ibid.*

7   Francis F. Beirne, *The Amiable Baltimoreans* (New York: E.P. Dutton and Co., 1951), pp. 261-62.

8   Harry Grayson, *They Played the Game: The Story of Baseball Greats* (New York: A.S. Barnes and Co., 1945), p. 70.

9   Joseph Durso, *The Days of Mr. McGraw* (Englewood Cliffs, N.J.: Prentice-Hall Inc., 1969), p. 24.

10   *The Sporting News*, April 14, 1906; Alfred H. Spink, *The National Game* (Southern Illinois University Press, 2000 reprint of 1911 original), p. 284.

11   Exact figures are disputed. Different sources place Hanlon's salary between $11,500 and $12,500 before the cut and between $6,000 and $7,500 afterward, with cuts amounting to anywhere from 35 percent to 52 percent.

12   *Sporting Life*, Dec. 30, 1905.

13   *The Sporting News*, March 3, 1906.

14   *Ibid.,* Dec. 9, 1905.

15   *Ibid.,* Dec. 30, 1905.

16   *Ibid.,* Dec. 9, 1905.

17   *Ibid.,* Dec. 23, 1905.

18   William A. Cook, *August "Garry" Herrmann: A Baseball Biography* (Jefferson, N.C.: McFarland and Co. Inc., 2008), pp. 65 and 81.

19   *Cincinnati Times-Star,* reprinted in *The Sporting News*, Oct. 7, 1905.

20   *Chicago Tribune,* Oct. 29, 1905, reprinted in Arch Ward, ed., *The Greatest Sport Stories from the Chicago Tribune* (New York: A.S. Barnes and Co., 1953), p. 64. In baseball parlance, "yellow" did not exactly connote cowardice, but the term was applied to any critical failure of nerve by a team or player, and to sloppy or thoughtless play in general. See Paul Dickson, *The Dickson Baseball Dictionary* (New York: Facts on File, 1989), p. 428.

21   Bill Lee, *The Baseball Necrology: The Post-Baseball Lives and Deaths of Over 7,600 Major League Players and Others* (Jefferson, N.C.: McFarland and Co. Inc, 2003), p. 357. Some sources at the time reported the cause as pneumonia; *Sporting Life*, Jan. 1, 1910.

22   *The Sporting News*, March 31, 1906.

23   Charles C. Alexander, *John McGraw* (New York: Viking Penguin Inc., 1988), p. 130.

24   Monte Cely, *Marlin Democrat*, Feb. 5, 2008.

25   Peter Morris, *Level Playing Fields: How the Groundskeeping Murphy Brothers Shaped Baseball* (Lincoln, Neb.: University of Nebraska Press, 2007), p. 102.

26   Christy Mathewson, *Pitching in a Pinch, or Baseball from the Inside* (New York: Stein and Day, 1977 reprint of 1912 original), p. 213.

27   *The Sporting News*, April 14, 1906.

28   *Lima Daily News*, April 30, 1906.

29   *Sporting Life*, March 17, 1906.

30   *The Sporting News*, April 28, 1906.

31   *Sporting Life*, June 9, 1906.

32   *Cincinnati Commercial Tribune*, June 2, 1906.

33   *Cincinnati Enquirer,* July 10, 1906.

34   *Sporting Life,* June 9, 1906.
35   *Cincinnati Commercial Tribune,* June 2, 1906.
36   *Ibid.,* June 3, 1906.
37   *Ibid.,* June 2, 1906.
38   *Sporting Life,* June 9, 1906.
39   *Cincinnati Enquirer,* June 3, 1906.
40   Hanlon made this confession after it was clear the trade was a bust; *Sporting Life,* Feb. 22, 1908.
41   *Cincinnati Enquirer,* June 2, 1906.
42   Murphy's foray into the business of baseball brought still more Cincinnati Republican money into the National League. Charles P. Taft was a former Republican congressman and half-brother of future president William Howard Taft. Murphy eventually antagonized powerful people in baseball, notably Ban Johnson, and was pressured to sell out to Taft in 1914.
43   Several modern sources show the Reds receiving the $2,000 along with Wicker, but contemporary newspaper accounts are unanimous in spelling out that the Cubs received the cash as well as Overall. See for example *Sporting Life* columns by W.A. Phelon, June 16, 1906; Ren Mulford, June 23, 1906, and May 15, 1909; Charles H. Zuber, Dec. 14, 1907; and J.M. Cummings, Feb. 22, 1908. See also the *Cincinnati Commercial Tribune,* June 3, 1906, and John J. Evers and Hugh S. Fullerton, *Touching Second: The Science of Baseball* (Chicago: Reilly and Britton Co., 1910), p. 72.
44   John J. Evers and Hugh S. Fullerton, *Touching Second: The Science of Baseball* (Chicago: Reilly and Britton Co., 1910), p. 72.
45   *Cincinnati Commercial Tribune,* June 2, 1906.
46   *The Sporting News,* June 16, 1906.
47   *Ibid.*
48   *Sporting Life,* Feb. 22, 1908.
49   Evers and Fullerton, *op. cit.*
50   Despite strictly limited work, Overall became a 20-game winner twice. He won two-thirds of his decisions in his years with the Cubs and went 3-1 in World Series play.
51   *Cincinnati Commercial Tribune,* June 3, 1906.
52   *The Sporting News,* June 9, 1906.
53   *Ibid.,* Nov. 18, 1905.
54   *Sporting Life,* Nov. 18, 1905.
55   *Ibid.,* Nov. 25, 1905.
56   *The Sporting News,* Jan. 13, 1906.
57   Zane L. Miller, *Boss Cox's Cincinnati: Urban Politics in the Progressive Era* (New York: Oxford University Press, 1968), p. 183.
58   One factor in the Reds' favor in their heavily Catholic city was the endorsement of Sunday baseball by the Right Rev. Henry Moeller, archbishop of Cincinnati; see *Sporting Life,* Dec. 9, 1905. In general, according to Norman L. Macht, Protestant clergy were more vehement in their opposition to Sunday ball, for the practical reason that their services started later and lasted longer; Macht, "Sunday Baseball" (2003), article written for the annual convention of the Society for American Baseball Research, p. 3. Another reason Cincinnati avoided a confrontation on the issue might have been that Pattison served as governor for only a few months before dying in office on June 18, 1906.
59   Oddly, the name "Superbas" remained at least informally attached to the Brooklyn club for five years after Ned Hanlon's departure before being supplanted by "Dodgers" around 1910.

60   *New York Times*, June 18, 1906.

61   Greg Rhodes and John Snyder, *Redleg Journal: Year by Year and Day by Day with the Cincinnati Reds since 1866* (Cincinnati: Road West Publishing, 2000), p. 154.

62   For a good account of the long-running battle over Sunday baseball in Brooklyn, see Charlie Bevis, *Sunday Baseball: The Major Leagues' Struggle to Play Baseball on the Lord's Day, 1876-1934* (Jefferson, N.C.: McFarland and Co. Inc., 2003), pp. 152-63. See also Steven A. Riess, *Touching Base: Professional Baseball and American Culture in the Progressive Era* (Westport, Conn.: Greenwood Press, 1980), pp. 128-31.

63   The Reds were allowed to sign Deal because, although he had previously played in the minor leagues, he was not currently on the reserve list of any team in organized ball and was therefore, as a correspondent for *The Sporting News* carefully explained, "not a [contract] jumper." *The Sporting News*, July 14, 1906.

64   *Sporting Life*, July 1, 1905.

65   *Cincinnati Enquirer*, July 10, 1906.

66   *The Sporting News*, July 14, 1906.

67   *Ibid.*, June 30, 1906. Open gambling in the stands was by no means unique to Boston. On one of Ewing's first appearances at the Polo Grounds, a New York paper devoted four paragraphs to the activities of a couple hundred boisterous "western men" who were waving their money around and taking bets "on any feature of the game." Though the Giants were in first place and the Reds in sixth, the Cincinnati fans were confidently taking even money on the outcome of the game, and it turned out to be a good bet: Ewing beat the Giants (and Christy Mathewson), 4-1. *New York World*, May 12, 1903.

68   *Cincinnati Enquirer*, April 8, 1907.

69   *Sporting Life*, May 3, 1902.

70   *Cincinnati Enquirer*, July 5, 1906.

71   *The Sporting News*, July 7, 1906.

72   *Ibid.*, Dec. 29, 1906.

73   *Cincinnati Enquirer*, July 5, 1906. Herrmann's biographer interprets the reference to "jesting" to mean that the wager was made "during a serious drinking episode"; Cook, *op. cit.*, p. 78. In the end, Chicago won the pennant by 20 games over New York, with Pittsburgh a distant third.

74   *The Sporting News*, Oct. 20, 1906.

75   *Ibid.*, July 14, 1906.

76   Jack Ryder, quoted in *Sporting Life*, Aug. 13, 1910.

77   In 1909 the following item appeared on the sports page of Ryder's paper: "A Zanesville man wants to wager $180 against $100 that Pittsburgh will beat out the Cubs in the National League race. He will leave his money up for one week in the hands of the sporting editor of the *Enquirer*." *Cincinnati Enquirer*, June 19, 1909.

78   *Sporting Life*, Dec. 21, 1907.

79   See Charles H. Ebbets, letters to August Herrmann, Oct. 16 and 23, 1916, on file in the A. Bartlett Giamatti Research Center at the National Baseball Hall of Fame. See also Kevin Grace, "Sporting Man: Garry Herrmann and the 1909 Cincinnati *Turnfest*," Cincinnati Occasional Papers in German-American Studies, University of Cincinnati, No. 3 (2004), p. 29, note 37; and Grace, "Cincinnati's King of Diamonds – Garry Herrmann," in Mark Stang and Dick Miller, eds., *Baseball in the Buckeye State* (Cleveland: Society for American Baseball Research, 2004), p. 28.

80   *Sporting Life*, Aug. 11, 1906.

81 *The Sporting News*, July 21, 1906.

82 *Ibid.*, July 14, 1906.

83 *Sporting Life*, July 28, 1906. Bill James has concluded that Seymour might have exhibited the strangest batting stance of the decade, "with his weight very far forward, and his bat stuck over his shoulder, parallel to the ground." James, *The Bill James Historical Baseball Abstract* (New York: Villard Books, 1986), p. 62.

84 *The Sporting News*, Dec. 8, 1906.

85 *Cincinnati Post*, quoted in *Sporting Life*, Sept. 15, 1906.

86 *Sporting Life*, Sept. 15, 1906.

87 *Cincinnati Enquirer*, July 16, 1906.

88 *Ibid.*

89 *Ibid.*

90 Unidentified newspaper clipping, July 1906.

91 Unidentified newspaper clipping, August 1907.

92 Unidentified newspaper clipping, October 1906.

93 Jim Bowsher, interview with the author, July 23, 1999.

94 Unidentified newspaper clipping, August 1907.

95 *Ibid.*

96 Bowsher, *op. cit.*

97 *Cincinnati Enquirer*, July 27, 1906.

98 *Sporting Life*, Sept. 22, 1906.

99 *Cincinnati Enquirer*, Sept. 12, 1906.

100 *Ibid.*

101 *Ibid.*

102 *Ibid.*, July 16, 1906.

103 *Sporting Life*, Oct. 13, 1906.

104 *Ibid.*, Feb. 2, 1907.

105 *The Sporting News*, Sept. 22, 1906.

106 *Ibid.*, Oct. 6, 1906.

"Old Wapakoneta has again fooled the Red
Headsman and I for one *hope* the Gentleman
from Hampshire will ... make as good as a
broiled lobster served at Sherry's."
—REN MULFORD[1]

CHAPTER 9

An Opening and a Closing

IF BOB EWING'S 1906 SEASON HADN'T EXACTLY CRACKLED with excitement, the deficiency was somewhat made up by the eventful off-season that followed. Finding themselves with almost nowhere to go but up, the Reds cleaned house. They jettisoned aging, high-salaried players and plunged wholeheartedly into a youth movement. Garry Herrmann promised to give his manager "a string of players who are not too old to learn."[2] In the midst of this upheaval, Long Bob—who would turn 34 years old early in the coming season—went from untouchable to undesirable and back again within a matter of weeks.

Given the club's performance in its first year under Ned Hanlon, wholesale changes were not unforeseen. Since at least the previous August, it had been predicted that by spring, the last of the players Herrmann had inherited from the Brush regime would be gone. Even so, Ewing initially seemed to have some degree of job security for now.

"There are seven men on the team for whom no proposition whatever will be considered," Herrmann announced around the beginning of December. "... These men are stars in their respective lines—so high that they could not be duplicated, and for that reason we have placed them on a sort of immune list."[3] Ewing was among the select seven.

Six weeks later, Ewing's status had changed entirely. In mid-January, Herrmann stated unequivocally, "The only thing certain about Ewing … is that [he] will not be with the Reds this year."[4]

While Ewing's stock rose and fell wildly, the entire Cincinnati roster was in flux. Bob Wicker, Snake Deal and Frank Jude were shipped back to the minor leagues, never to return. Outfielder Homer Smoot was demoted to Toledo and outfielder Fred Odwell recalled from the same club. Jim Delahanty, another player who had suffered the slings and arrows of the boisterous fans along Rooters Row, was waived out of the National League and sold to the St. Louis Browns. Thirty-five-year-old Joe Kelley, dumped by the Reds, landed in the Eastern League as player-manager of the Toronto Maple Leafs. Tommy Corcoran, 38, and Chick Fraser, 36, were also "put on the bargain counter,"[5] where they were picked up cheap by the Giants and Cubs, respectively.

One of the few veterans added to the roster was first baseman John Ganzel. Soon to be 33 years old, Ganzel had been in organized ball more than a decade. In and out of the major leagues since 1898, he had been tried and found wanting by both clubs in New York, where the newspapers disparagingly nicknamed him "Pop-Up John."[6] Ganzel eventually paid $3,000 out of his own pocket to buy his release from the New York Highlanders and took a flier at being a magnate—as player/manager/owner of a minor league club in Grand Rapids, Michigan. It was from that genteel obscurity that the Reds plucked him. Hanlon needed an experienced field captain to fill the void left by Corcoran and Kelley. While the writers scratched their heads trying to remember another instance of a player being promoted directly from the minor leagues to the captaincy of a big league club, one of them conceded that Ganzel was likely as good a field leader as the Reds could expect to obtain "at this stage of the game."[7]

As fans and writers watched all these comings and goings, behind the scenes Ewing and Herrmann carried on their usual long-distance dickering over a contract for the coming campaign. Ewing grumbled more than usual but by mid-December he accepted the inevitable and agreed to Herrmann's less-than-satisfactory offer. But even with the contract signed, his future was suddenly more uncertain than ever. Whenever his name appeared in print, the matter under discussion was his imminent departure from Cincinnati.

"There is one Red whose release has been a certainty for some time, though his destination is not settled," the *Cincinnati Post* reported. "... He is Bob Ewing."[8] Ren Mulford pronounced Ewing's exit "probable," adding by way of an obituary to his career the opinion that the pitcher "never quite fulfilled the promises that were made for him."

"In nearly every season of his Red career he pitched a streak of as brilliant ball as a Mathewson might have done," Mulford wrote, "but just when greater things were expected came the disillusion."[9]

Barely a month earlier, Ewing had been among the players Herrmann classed as irreplaceable. Reasons for his fall from grace aren't difficult to guess. Obviously his advancing age and lackluster 1906 record suggested he might belong to the Reds' past more than their future. Perhaps Herrmann was annoyed by the unusually prickly tone of Ewing's correspondence during their contract negotiations. One thing that's clear is that Ewing, like many of the team's other veterans, had developed a marked dislike for Ned Hanlon. Friction probably began early in the 1906 season, possibly when Ewing—laboring with a painfully sore arm—asked to be removed after four innings of a home game with Brooklyn. To Hanlon, whose managerial philosophy was forged on the baseball battlefields of the 1890s, the request would have smacked of a lack of competitive zeal. He might have deemed it downright unmanly.

Ewing, setting ego aside, took a more pragmatic view. "Hope is a fine thing in baseball, " he told the *Cincinnati Times-Star* after the contest, "but common sense will win more games."[10] (In this instance, Ewing's approach prevailed. With Orval Overall taking over on the mound, the Reds won, 6–4.)

Now, as the new season approached, Ewing's feelings bubbled to the surface in a letter he wrote to Herrmann on January 3, 1907.

Responding to comments by Hanlon—either aired in the press or passed along by Herrmann—Ewing scoffed, "I see he refers to a couple of games in Philadelphia that I weakened."

"He should [have] told you how they were lost," Ewing continued, adding that he "could tell you of a dozen close games that were lost for me" by the failings of teammates "if I wanted to be a kicker."

As for Hanlon, Ewing was uncharacteristically blunt: "I don't consider him much of a man to talk like that."[11]

In that atmosphere, only one outcome seemed likely. "Bob Ewing will hear the cuckoo call before the days of spring arrive," Ren Mulford prophesied.[12] There was speculation that the disgruntled pitcher would wind up with one of the Boston clubs or in Pittsburgh. Then suddenly the wind shifted again. The Reds had asked waivers on Ewing, but when the Boston Nationals put in a claim, Herrmann halted the proceedings by announcing that he wouldn't let Long Bob go for less than $7,500.

What had happened? It's possible that other teams' interest in Ewing caused the Reds to reevaluate his prospects. Perhaps, out of the view of prying reporters, Ewing had been the object of a tug-of-war between Hanlon and Herrmann. Cincinnati papers later claimed that while Hanlon was bound and determined to unload Ewing, Herrmann insisted on setting the price so high that no one would touch him.[13] If so, Mulford claimed, it wouldn't have been the first time a deal for Ewing "was called off by presidential edict."[14] Another possibility is that at a crucial moment, another veteran baseball man in the organization got Herrmann's ear: Business manager Frank Bancroft was said to be a fan of Ewing.

Most likely the ultimate decision to keep Ewing was merely a matter of logic, or the absence of a reasonable alternative. In all their off-season personnel shuffling, the only seasoned pitcher the Reds had obtained was 24-year-old Andy Coakley. A college boy who broke into the major leagues under an assumed name while still attending Holy Cross, Coakley had won 18 games for the Philadelphia Athletics in 1905. But, dogged by ill health, he had fallen to 7–8 the following year, making him something of an unknown quantity when he arrived in Cincinnati. Further exacerbating the pitching situation, the Reds were at an impasse in contract talks with 20-game-winner Jake Weimer. Herrmann, indignant at the pitcher's stubbornness, told reporters, "Weimer has been offered as much money as any pitcher in either of the big leagues will get this year, with the possible exception of Christy Mathewson,"[15] but Tornado Jake was holding out for more.

As for new pitching prospects, one optimist in the press corps declared that Hanlon had secured "the cream of the minor leagues."[16] A more sober assessment came from Ren Mulford. As the team prepared to return to Marlin Springs for spring training, he considered the mound staff and concluded it looked "like a bunch of Louisiana lottery tickets."[17]

Given that state of affairs, the Reds had little choice but to try to mollify steady, predictable old Bob Ewing. The decision to keep him, when it came, was cause for a minor celebration. A month earlier Mulford was expounding on Ewing's shortcomings and bidding him an affectionate but emphatic farewell. Now, on February 10, 1907, Mulford wrote in his weekly column for *Sporting Life*:

> Bob Ewing's good angel has once again turned aside the
> stroke of the snickersnee and the blade has been given
> an edge like a circular saw.... Just why the program was
> changed nobody knows, but to a man in Norwood the ac-
> tion has a Solomonesque look.[18]

When the team returned from Texas, Ewing was the senior member of the club in terms of service. Aside from the reclamation project Coakley and the still-unsigned Weimer, the rest of the pitching staff owned a grand total of six lifetime victories in the major leagues. The entire team was "an experiment," according to Jim C. Hamilton.[19] Ganzel, the new captain—the leader counted on to "instill an unlimited amount of ginger into the men under him"[20]—was dishearteningly candid about what he saw. As he was leaving for spring training, Ganzel had told a reporter, "I am not highly elated over our prospects."[21]

A month later, there was no reason to alter that assessment, or this earlier one from Hamilton: "They may make good and then again they may not, but one thing is sure. Ned Hanlon has a team to handle after his own heart."[22] At least publicly, that was Hanlon's view as well. "Mr. Herrmann has backed me up to the limit," he said.[23]

Yet even before the season began, all was not bliss in Redland. Less than a week before the opening game, Garry Herrmann hosted a grand banquet in honor of his friend Charles Comiskey, whose Chicago White Sox were the defending World Series champions. The ballroom on the top floor of Cincinnati's Sinton Hotel was redecorated to suggest a ballpark, complete with a ticket window, turnstiles, an outfield fence and "a huge banquet table ... in the shape of a perfect baseball diamond with a monster bouquet of American beauty roses in the pitcher's box and the entire diamond covered with green grass."[24] National League president Harry Pulliam, unable to attend, sent along a gracious toast titled "Here's to the American League." The American League's Ban Johnson responded with

"Three Cheers for the National League." But the evening ended on something of a sour note after George B. "Boss" Cox, who was not scheduled to speak, insisted on adding himself to the previously announced "batting order" of after-dinner orators.

Cox, the most prominent of the Reds' quartet of principal owners, was normally a man of few words, and he had never taken much interest in the operation of the ballclub. But, perhaps after one drink too many, he stood up before a roomful of sportswriters and prominent baseball men and unburdened himself of a lecture in which he "declared that any man who manages a Cincinnati team in the future must make good or give way to someone who can." Cox said his comments were not intended as a slap at Hanlon, but he delivered them looking straight at the manager.

Hanlon, taken aback, replied awkwardly to the effect that he hoped to put together the best team Cincinnati had ever seen, or at least a team that would "satisfy Herrmann, Cox and his other employers."[25] Herrmann stepped in and tried to smooth things over with conciliatory words, but the hard feelings hung in the air. Days later, the same newspapers that trumpeted the start of the season reported that Cox had sold his one-third interest in the ballclub and retired from the baseball business. The new co-owner was Thomas J. Logan, identified as a "fashionable tailor"[26] and a close friend of Herrmann's.

AS THE PUTATIVE ACE of Cincinnati's revamped pitching staff—a title he inherited almost by default—Ewing was the logical choice to start the opening game on April 11 against Pittsburgh. Starting the opener in Cincinnati was a particular honor for a pitcher. Ewing's name had come up for consideration in other years, but somehow the distinction had always been bestowed elsewhere.

By 1907, Opening Day was one of the grand sporting and social events of the year in Cincinnati. It was a festival of music and parades, a day of noisy fun and high fashion, an occasion to skip school or knock off business for the afternoon and go to the ballpark, where the cream of Cincinnati society and the elite of local politics were sure to be conspicuously mingling. Nothing—not even the disaffection of Boss Cox or the almost undisputed expectation that the team was facing another season near the bottom of the standings—could cast a pall over Opening Day.

The man most responsible for this uniquely Cincinnati celebration of the national pastime was Frank Bancroft, the Reds' longtime business manager. Sixty years old and a veteran of the Civil War, Bancroft had at various times trained in the circus business, managed minstrel troupes, run an opera house, owned a hotel and a roller-skating rink. He had been involved in baseball, in the words of one contemporary, "ever since it was worth talking about."[27] He organized his first baseball club in 1877 and managed the Providence Grays to a National League pennant in 1884. Bancroft took the first team of American barnstormers to Cuba in 1879 and was credited with staging baseball's first home plate wedding at Cincinnati's League Park in 1893.[28]

He also effectively invented Opening Day. Bancroft organized, promoted and encouraged all sorts of festivities that gave the day a flavor all its own. The pattern had been set by the mid-1890s with the introduction of the trolley parade through downtown and the pre-game band concert at the ballpark; both were established traditions by 1907. Some of the most avid rooters formed "tallyho parties," arriving at the park in large open-air carriages. The *Commercial Tribune* doubted that any city had ever before seen such a gathering of tallyhos for a baseball game. The largest were drawn by as many as six horses and could carry up to 40 people. Many tallyhos were decorated with large banners and their occupants decked out as if for Halloween, "in all sorts of absurd costumes."[29] Garry Herrmann typically turned out in all his sartorial splendor. Charles Dryden, the Chicago sportswriter, encountered Herrmann on another Opening Day in this period "arrayed in a suit of modest check, fashioned after the latest design in kitchen linoleum, including the color scheme."[30]

After all the winter's trafficking in human flesh, the side the Reds sent out to inaugurate the new season was made up mostly of newcomers. Aside from Ewing, the only returning regulars in the lineup were Miller Huggins at second base and Admiral Schlei behind the plate. Center fielder Alphonzo "Lefty" Davis, like John Ganzel, was on the elderly side of 30 and returning to the big show after an extended exile in the minor leagues. Of the rest, three were youngsters making their major league debuts. Outfielders Mike Mitchell and Art Kruger, and Johnny Kane—starting at third base in place of Hans Lobert, who was out with a sprained ankle—were all recruits from the Pacific Coast League. Twenty-two-year-old Mike Mowrey, who had spent most of 1906 on loan to Ned Hanlon's Baltimore club, was the youngest of the lot. He was playing his 29th game in the major leagues, but only his second at shortstop.

Pittsburgh, by contrast, had one of the most experienced and formidable teams in baseball, led by player-manager Fred Clarke, third baseman Tommy Leach and the magnificent Honus Wagner, widely regarded as the greatest player in the National League and perhaps in all of baseball. Counting pitcher Deacon Phillippe, nearly half of the Pirates' starters had been together since 1901. They had won three pennants, never finished out of the first division, and averaged 93 victories a season.

The Reds had won only one opener in five tries since Ewing's arrival. Among the defeats was a 7–1 embarrassment in 1903, when Phillippe pitched a two-hitter. Having never pitched an opener, Ewing was understandably anxious to show up well in this one. The omens were not promising for him. He hadn't worked a complete game in spring training and there was some question whether he was ready to go nine innings. Known as a hot-weather pitcher, Ewing was rarely at his best amid the April showers and intermittent cold snaps of springtime in Ohio.

The weather mattered to Ewing. More than other ballplayers, spitball pitchers were weather-watchers. Ewing's experience might have been similar to that of latter-day spitballer Preacher Roe, who said his wet one worked best in warm weather; it seemed to "dry up quicker" when it was cool.[31] Stanley Coveleski said the first thing he did upon arriving at the ballpark was check the wind direction. He found that his spitball broke more sharply when pitched into the wind.[32] Bill Doak told an illuminating story about pitching in the rain. One time when he was with the St. Louis Cardinals, a light rain began to fall as he went out to pitch the fifth inning. Doak alerted manager Branch Rickey that it would be a good idea to warm up a relief pitcher. Rickey thought Doak seemed OK and ignored the suggestion. Doak quickly blew a two-run lead and the Cardinals lost the game. Asked afterward if he had had a premonition of disaster, Doak assured his manager that premonitions had nothing to do with it.

"Mr. Rickey," the pitcher explained, "when it rains and that ball is wet all over, a spitball pitcher just doesn't have any spitball."[33]

The day did not dawn auspiciously. A scheduled exhibition with the Chicago White Sox had been canceled the day before for fear the players would catch pneumonia. Early-morning temperatures on Opening Day were barely above freezing—a bad day, observers agreed, for Ewing and for baseball. Herrmann and Bancroft had hoped for a turnout approaching 20,000, but had to settle for half that. Gamblers were offering odds of 3-to-1 and even 4-to-1 against the home team. The Reds gave away one run on Schlei's throwing error in the second inning and another when Ewing issued a bases-loaded walk in the third. Phillippe, meanwhile, escaped a couple of ticklish situations and held the Reds scoreless through five.

The temperature had risen into the mid-40s by game time and the bundled-up crowd made up in enthusiasm what it lacked in numbers. A band played between innings and the rooters kept up a racket with bells, whistles, bugles and "every conceivable instrument to make noise."[34] The decibel level reached new heights in the sixth, when Cincinnati tied the score on Kane's double, Wagner's error and Mitchell's long triple to right field. Ewing, working deliberately as always and leaning on the spitball in critical moments, was wild all afternoon. He got into trouble again with two walks in the eighth, but extricated himself by foiling pinch hitters Otis Clymer and Alan Storke with the bases loaded. The Reds failed to score in their half of the inning despite a walk, a single and a double.

Pittsburgh gained a 3–2 lead in the top of the ninth inning on a walk, a sacrifice and Clarke's slow roller, which trickled into right field for a single after Huggins, in the deepening gloom of what had been throughout a cold and dark afternoon, misread the ball off the bat and broke the wrong way. By this time, the *Commercial Tribune* noted, both teams "had apparently thrown the game away … several times."[35]

After nine innings, Ewing had walked eight men. But he had struck out six and limited the Pirates to six singles, one of them Clarke's dribbler and another on a misjudged pop fly, and had stranded 10 base runners. Through many trying moments, Jack Ryder wrote, "He never lost his courage for an instant."[36]

Ewing was scheduled to lead off the bottom of the ninth for Cincinnati, but he had put in a day's work and the managerial wheels were turning at full speed. Hanlon called Ewing back and sent Larry McLean out to hit. McLean was another West Coast import, a big catcher whose free-swinging style had early in his career earned him the nickname "Slashaway."[37] McLean slashed at the first offering from Al "Lefty" Leifield, on in relief of Phillippe. The pitch was over the outside corner of the plate; McLean swatted it down the right-field line and slid head-first into second base with a hustling double. Hanlon sent in Fred Odwell to run for McLean, and Huggins bunted him to third.[38]

Now Lefty Davis was due up. Hanlon went to his bench again and sent up Eddie Tiemeyer, as the *Enquirer* explained, "in order to put a right-hand batter against Lefty Leifield."[39] Tiemeyer walked. The persistent murmur and rumble of the crowd rose to a cacophonous din. From the parking area under the grandstand, "unearthly shrieks" issued from a whistle on an automobile, timed and calculated to wreak maximum havoc on Leifield's fraying nerves.[40] Leifield walked Kane as well, loading the bases with one out.

That placed matters squarely in the hands of John Ganzel. In his official debut as the Reds' captain, Ganzel had stung the ball all day but had no hits to show for it. This time he lofted a little blooper just over the infield and out of the reach of second baseman Ed Abbattichio. As he crossed first base, Ganzel looked back to make sure Odwell and Tiemeyer had touched the plate, then sprinted for the clubhouse ahead of the jubilant fans, who spilled onto the field intent on joyously manhandling any Cincinnati players they could catch.

The underdog Reds had come from behind to win the opener 4–3. The *Enquirer*'s Jack Ryder exulted over "as grand and game a finish as was ever pulled off on a ballfield."[41] The *Times-Star*'s Charlie Zuber pronounced the contest "undoubtedly ... the most exciting opening game ever captured on these or any other grounds." A headline in the same paper assured readers that the Reds' "alleged yellow streak is a thing of the past."[42] The managerial maneuverings of the final inning—three substitutions, a sacrifice bunt, a lefty-righty switch, a crucial run scored by a pinch runner for a pinch hitter—were recounted in breathless detail and held up as the supreme demonstration of Foxy Ned Hanlon's baseball acumen. "Every move was made that could be thought of to give the team the slightest advantage," Ryder wrote, "and the players did the rest."[43]

There were heroes enough to fill a pantheon. Johnny Kane and Mike Mowrey, each with a single and a double, drew applause for their work in the field and at the bat. More lavish praise was heaped upon Mike Mitchell as the former Coast League batting champion introduced himself to the big time with two singles and a triple, driving in two runs. Larry McLean won plaudits for his "hard and nervy" hitting in the clutch.[44] Highest honors were reserved for Hanlon, whose "shrewd managerial trick" made headlines,[45] and for Ganzel, whose "inspiring leadership … was in evidence at all stages of the contest."[46] Ewing wasn't entirely overlooked, but after the game's dramatic finish he was somewhat pushed into the background. A celebratory "Casey at the Bat" parody in the *Cincinnati Post* mentioned him only as being pulled for a pinch hitter. The *Times-Star*'s "Headliners of the Game" column went on for nine paragraphs without mentioning him at all.

Hanlon, while pleased that his youngsters had "behaved splendidly under fire," also made a point to praise the old-timer Ewing. Perhaps mindful of the past winter's bruised feelings, Hanlon found an opportunity to say that the pitcher "did not show signs of weakening at any stage of the game."[47]

The Opening Day victory over Pittsburgh ranked with the near no-hitter against New York in 1903 as one of the proudest moments of Ewing's career.[48] But in a city where the opening of the baseball season was always page-one news, Ewing's dramatic victory got pushed off the front pages of some of the local newspapers. While the *Commercial Tribune* splashed the Reds' "whirlwind ninth-inning finish" across an eight-column headline at the top of page one,[49] the *Post* and the *Times-Star* were preoccupied with a different kind of drama that had transfixed the nation.

The story had all the elements to captivate and titillate the popular imagination—glamour, celebrity, money, jealousy, scandal, sex and murder. The lurid tale first burst upon the public consciousness the previous summer when Stanford White, New York's most prominent architect and a major arbiter of taste for the city's social elite, was shot to death in front of dozens of witnesses in the open-air theater atop Madison Square Garden, one of White's most famous creations. The killer was Harry K. Thaw, the unpredictable and obsessive son of a Pennsylvania coal and railroad baron, known as the Mad Millionaire of Pittsburgh. The point of contention between them was Thaw's 21-year-old wife, showgirl and artist's model Evelyn Nesbit, one of the great beauties of the era. Two years after their marriage, Thaw still seethed at the thought that Nesbit had been seduced and "ruined" in a teenage affair with White. On June 25, 1906, near the end of the opening performance of a musical called *Mamzelle Champagne*, shortly after a tenor onstage finished singing "I Could Love a Thousand Girls," Thaw stepped up to White's table and shot him three times at point-blank range.

What followed was the young century's first "trial of the century." The defense argued temporary insanity and, continuing a campaign launched by a press agent hired by Thaw's mother, painted the defendant as the chivalrous defender of a wronged wife. Thaw's attorneys attacked White's character, revealing him as a middle-aged voluptuary with an insatiable appetite for young girls. Testimony took the jurors inside White's private penthouse in the 320-foot Italianate tower above Madison Square Garden, topped with a 13-foot statue of a nude Diana, Roman goddess of the hunt. There, Nesbit—described by Irvin S. Cobb, who covered the trial for the *New York World*, as "the most exquisitely lovely human being I ever looked at"[50]—was the Girl in the Red Velvet Swing, cavorting naked for White's entertainment.

The newspapers couldn't get enough. Cobb sometimes cranked out 12,000 words a day. Additional telegraph cables were run into the courthouse through the central skylight, enabling papers across the country to fill columns and pages with the sensational details of love and death among what the *New York Times* termed "the fast set."[51]

The trial lasted 11 weeks. By the time Ewing and the Reds polished off the Pirates on April 11, the case was in the hands of the jury and thousands of people had gathered outside the courthouse to await the verdict. But the story that pushed Ewing off the front pages turned out to be an anticlimax: After 47 hours of deliberation, the trial ended in a hung jury. It would take a second trial, and 25 more hours of deliberation by another jury, before Thaw was declared not guilty by reason of insanity. Committed to an asylum for the criminally insane, he would remain institutionalized—except for an extended interlude of freedom after an escape that generated more sensational headlines—until 1924.

BEFORE THE OPENER, Ewing's concerns went beyond the cold weather and Pittsburgh's potent bats. By now, his history of arm trouble was a source of recurring worry. After months of chronic pain in 1906, it was anybody's guess whether his arm would last another season. But for once, Long Bob started off like a well-oiled machine. Near the end of training camp, Admiral Schlei had assured a reporter, "Ewing's arm is working better this spring than it ever did."[52] A few days into the season, Jim C. Hamilton surveyed the Reds' pitchers and pronounced Ewing "in the best condition of the bunch."[53]

Fans soon saw for themselves. Ewing won four of his first five games, his only loss coming by a 1–0 score to Mordecai Brown and the Chicago Cubs; the game was scoreless until the ninth inning, when Jimmy Slagle tripled and scored on an error. With Ewing "pitching the greatest ball of his career," Hamilton was now convinced that "the luckiest thing that happened to the Redland squad this season was [its] inability to sell Ewing."[54]

Ewing's performance was one of the few bright spots for the team. Despite a 3–1 start, by May 25 the Reds had fallen to a 10–21 record and were already 15½ games out of first place. With Weimer still absent and the other hurlers struggling, Hanlon stated publicly that he had the worst pitching staff in the National League.[55]

"Ewing has been the wet nurse of hope in the Cincinnati family," Ren Mulford wrote. "He has kept alive the one spark of enthusiasm that has glowed in the pitching department."[56]

Under such circumstances, it wouldn't take much to stir up any latent feelings of discontent on a ballclub, and an issue soon arose. For years the Reds had routinely spent their off days in exhibitions against minor leaguers or tank-town amateurs. Of late, on top of the frustrations of being buried in the second division, the Reds had encountered fresh annoyances on their excursions off the beaten path. There was grumbling about unsatisfactory arrangements in Yonkers, New York, where the Reds were faced with an unruly crowd and a minor league field "deep in mud."[57] The aggravation was heightened by the misfortune of rookie pitcher Ed "Cotton" Minahan, who injured his right (pitching) shoulder in a base-path collision against a team of local amateurs in Elizabeth, New Jersey; it was reported that Minahan would be back in action in a few days, but within a week, the club asked waivers on him. He never played in the major leagues again.

Against this backdrop, several players now rose up and suggested that unless the club agreed to cut them in on the receipts, they would henceforth refuse to participate in any more unofficial contests during the season. Exactly how this topic was broached isn't clear. The front page of *Sporting Life* headlined the (unidentified) players' "demands," but the accompanying article referred mildly to a "request" that had been put before Garry Herrmann.[58] In either case, any possibility of a player revolt was quickly extinguished. Herrmann curtly reminded his employees that they were under contract from the beginning of the season until its end, and if they hoped to remain in organized baseball, they would play where and when management directed them to play. Faced with the implied threat of suspension or banishment, the players meekly folded.

As usual in any such dispute, most of the press lined up squarely behind the owners. The newspapers often made note of the financial benefits of in-season exhibitions. Mulford, undoubtedly relying on information from the Reds' owners, had previously reported that only the $10,000 taken in on exhibitions had saved the organization from losing money in 1906.[59] A single stop in a Pennsylvania mining town had netted more than $600, according to the *Cincinnati Enquirer*—enough, the paper said, to pay half the team's board bill for an entire eastern road trip.[60] When the players balked at playing additional games without additional pay, *Sporting Life* responded with a headline stressing their already "liberal treatment ... by [the] princely Herrmann."[61] Mulford insisted the players had no "moral or legal right" to share in the gate receipts from exhibitions. On the contrary, he wrote, the typical big league ballplayer "is in clover and it is most unseemly for him to howl about living up to the terms of the contract he signs."[62]

The employees of the princely Herrmann got no additional money, no additional days off and no relief from risking their limbs and their careers on rough, rocky playing fields where, as Jim C. Hamilton acknowledged, "players lay themselves decidedly open to injury."[63] Mostly they got broadsides like the one in which Mulford chastised them for awakening "the specter of selfishness" and attempting "to poison the fan mind against the team."[64]

Though quickly stifled, the threatened strike wasn't the end of player unrest on the team. Days later, pitcher Del Mason confronted Hanlon in the clubhouse. The Reds had bought Mason from Hanlon's minor league club in Baltimore, and Mason had decided he was entitled to a percentage of the sale price. When Hanlon laughed in his face, Mason walked out of the clubhouse and off the team.[65]

By this time, the wayward Jake Weimer had agreed to a contract and returned to the fold, but his arrival eased Hanlon's pitching woes only somewhat. Weimer showed up 20 pounds overweight and, though he pitched well enough to lose 1–0 to St. Louis on June 8, it would be weeks before he began to show the form that had made him the team's big winner in 1906. By season's end, he was 11–14 and full of contrition.

"I learned a lesson and will be on deck when the pitchers start for Florida," he promised. "… Next spring I'll be there as soon as any of the Reds' pitchers."[66] He was better than his word, heading south in 1908 in advance of the rest of the staff, but events would soon show that Tornado Jake had pretty well blown himself out.

With Weimer fading and among the new pitchers only Andy Coakley standing up to major league competition, Ewing shouldered a heavier load than ever before for the Reds and pitched some of the best ball of his life. Still, victories didn't come easily. He lost 1–0 to St. Louis on June 2. Four days later he pitched 15 innings for a 4–4 tie with Brooklyn. He secured a win on June 16 by shutting out Philadelphia 2–0.

Two days later, Admiral Schlei drew some catcalls when he trundled out and took his place behind the plate in the ninth inning of a 4–3 loss to the New York Giants at League Park. He was modeling the latest in protective gear for catchers. Shin guards had become a topic of discussion around baseball since Opening Day, when the Giants' Roger Bresnahan took the field in a pair of modified cricket pads. Bresnahan was widely credited with a new invention, but in fact backstops across the country had been experimenting with shin guards for years.[67] Bresnahan was mainly responsible for making them acceptable. Before this time, catchers had strived for protection that wouldn't attract attention. Red Dooin of the Philadelphia Phillies used shin guards, first of rattan and later papier-mâché, designed to be worn inconspicuously under his stockings.[68] Bresnahan, as a star player on a top major league team and a certifiable tough guy, didn't bother to hide his pads. Nobody was going to call him a sissy.

Schlei, neither star nor tough guy, faced rougher sledding in introducing shin guards to Cincinnati. The *Enquirer*'s Jack Ryder dismissed the pads as "silly" and said they should be done away with because they limited the catcher's mobility.[69] Such curmudgeonly views notwithstanding, shin guards caught on quickly once they received Bresnahan's endorsement. *The Sporting News* predicted that within a few years, shin guards would be as commonplace as the catcher's mask and chest pad. In Cincinnati, Jim C. Hamilton declared shin guards "the best thing that have been put upon the baseball market since the advent of the big mitt and the mask," and forecast that by the time another season rolled around, "over half the catchers in the National League will have adopted Roger Bresnahan's innovation."[70] Within a few weeks the Reds' other catcher, Larry McLean, was also wearing shin guards.[71]

While the shin guards saved Schlei and McLean a few bruises, the team continued to take its lumps. By mid-July, Cincinnati had fallen to seventh place, more than 25 games off the lead. Blame for the club's poor performance fell squarely on Hanlon. He was criticized for his frequent absences from the team, sometimes on supposed scouting trips that never seemed to produce anything, and accused of trying to manage the team by telephone. Hamilton went so far as to suggest that the team played better when Hanlon wasn't around.[72] It was no secret that the Reds weren't a happy family. The young players weren't committed to Hanlon's approach to the game and some of the veterans were openly antagonistic. Ren Mulford sampled the attitudes of fans and quoted a barber named Oscar Harenberg, who said bluntly, "Half the team doesn't like Hanlon"[73]—a view Mulford likely shared but didn't dare express on his own. It was becoming clear, as Hamilton would eventually write in a sad epitaph for Foxy Ned's time in Cincinnati, that "a large number of the boys absolutely refused to put their best efforts in the game for Hanlon."[74]

On July 30, with no indication that the situation was likely to get better, Hanlon announced that he planned to quit the major leagues at season's end. He would settle down in Baltimore, where he could better watch over his other various enterprises. He had come to the realization, he said, that in spending seven months a year with the Reds, "I am doing myself an injustice by neglecting my home and my other business affairs."[75] In any event, Hanlon told Hamilton, he saw no reason to remain in Cincinnati and be a target for abuse when, after all, "he does not have to depend on baseball for an income."[76]

Herrmann claimed he tried to get Hanlon to reconsider. If so, the effort was probably halfhearted. Overall, the prospect of Hanlon's retirement occasioned little sorrow. A few years earlier he had been acclaimed a baseball genius. After two disastrous years in Cincinnati, a *Sporting News* editorial stated, he would leave the game "utterly discredited," his reputation in ruins.

"Hanlon, when hustling to build up a fortune, was a great manager," the writer continued. "Since he acquired wealth, he has been unsuccessful as a leader." The ultimate impression, the piece concluded, was that the lure of money had kept Hanlon in the game several seasons after his results failed to justify his large salary.[77]

THERE WAS NOTHING for Ewing and his teammates to do except slog onward. On August 6, Ewing's spitball almost cost the Reds one of their infrequent victories. Cincinnati was holding a 3–1 lead in the eighth inning and Boston had Fred Tenney on second base when Ginger Beaumont slapped one of Ewing's wet ones into left field for a single. Fred Odwell charged, fielded the ball cleanly and came up throwing. But the saliva-slicked ball slipped out of Odwell's hand and sailed far over the head of Admiral Schlei, coming to rest within reach of the avid field-level fans along Rooters Row. As Tenney crossed the plate, one overeager supporter grabbed the live ball and flipped it back to Schlei. The umpire immediately called a "blocked ball," requiring the pitcher to hold the ball on the rubber before attempting to secure another out. Ewing, who had come in to cover home plate, had to hustle back to the mound, by which time Beaumont had circled the bases with the tying run.

The *Cincinnati Times-Star* held up the incident as an example of "how much damage the spitball can do" when handled by fielders.[78] But for once there was a happy ending: The potential goats of the piece pulled out a 4–3

Bob Ewing wasn't an exceptional hitter but in his day, everybody swung a big bat. The club he's hefting in this 1908 photo probably weighed at least 40 ounces. At his best, Long Bob batted .262 in 1905; his career average was .195. *Photo: Chicago Historical Society, SDN 054496.*

victory in the ninth inning when Odwell tripled and scored on Ewing's long fly out.

Ewing secured another dramatic decision five days later. He was battling Brooklyn's Harry McIntire at League Park and the score was tied 1–1 in the seventh inning until another Odwell triple, this one with two men on, gave Cincinnati a 3–1 advantage. Ewing followed with a line drive that bounded past Al Burch in right field, enabling Old Wapak, "under a full head of steam," to round the bases for an inside-the-park home run.[79]

The two-run shot gave the Reds a seemingly safe 5–1 lead, but the circumstances were uncomfortably similar to those a year earlier when another home run sprint had sapped Ewing's energy and cost him a victory against this same Brooklyn team. Ewing hadn't forgotten, and neither had his teammates. This time, instead of sending him right back to the mound, the Reds stalled for several minutes, buying time every way they could to allow Ewing to catch his breath. Miller Huggins fouled off several pitches before grounding out to end the inning. The Reds then ambled slowly to their positions in the field.

When at last Ewing made his unhurried way out to the mound, he was cheered loudly by the home crowd. He gave up leadoff hits—Brooklyn's fifth and sixth of the afternoon—in each of the final two innings, but completed the game without facing another serious threat.[80]

More tough losses followed in the final weeks of the season. Ewing allowed only five hits but lost 2–1 to the Cubs and Orval Overall. He allowed six hits and lost 3–2 to Overall's teammate Ed Reulbach. Ewing gained his final victory of the year October 1, shutting out Brooklyn 3–0 with another five-hitter. He closed out his campaign on the next-to-last day of the season, losing 1–0 to Pittsburgh's Howie Camnitz. Ewing permitted only two hits, both singles; the Pirates' Tommy Leach scored the game's lone run in the seventh inning with the help of two infield errors.

Ewing finished a laborious season with 17 victories against 19 defeats, a losing record that was still 41 percentage points better than his team's. He had made more appearances (41) than any other Cincinnati pitcher and ranked second in the National League in complete games (32), innings pitched (332⅔) and strikeouts (147). He had limited his opponents to 7.6 hits every nine innings.[81] "Without Ewing," concluded one post-season post mortem, "the Reds would have made a very sorry showing in the race."[82]

They made a sorry showing anyway. Though they managed two more wins than in Hanlon's first season, the Reds again finished in sixth place, 41½ games out of first. Of the team's 87 losses, 39 were by one run. In two years under Hanlon, the club had won less than 43 percent of its games. *Sporting Life* once again pronounced the Reds a major disappointment, and predicted that fans had nothing to look forward to except "further costly and trying experimenting."[83]

As the long season meandered to its unsatisfactory conclusion, Ned Hanlon had a change of heart about retiring. Hoping for one last chance to go out a winner, he offered to return to Cincinnati in 1908. He was willing to accept a fan's proposal that he be compensated on a sliding scale pegged to the team's performance: If he won the pennant, he would be paid $15,000; if he finished last, he would receive no pay at all.

"That's a fair proposition," Hanlon said. In any case, he added, "Money won't figure in any other attempt at [baseball] success, if I make one."[84]

Garry Herrmann politely declined the offer.

ENDNOTES

1   *Sporting Life,* Feb. 16, 1907.
2   *The Sporting News,* Jan. 19, 1907.
3   *Ibid.,* Dec. 8, 1906.
4   *Ibid.,* Jan. 26, 1907.
5   *Ibid.,* Dec. 15, 1906.
6   See *Sporting Life,* May 30, 1908, and *New York Press,* reprinted in *The Sporting News,* Aug. 16, 1908.
7   *The Sporting News,* Nov. 10, 1906.
8   *Cincinnati Post,* reprinted in *The Sporting News,* Jan. 12, 1907.
9   *Sporting Life,* Jan. 12, 1907.
10 *Cincinnati Times-Star,* May 22, 1906.
11 Bob Ewing, letter to August Herrmann, Jan. 3, 1907. The letter is on file in the A. Bartlett Giamatti Research Center at the National Baseball Hall of Fame.
12 *Sporting Life,* Feb. 2, 1907.
13 *Cincinnati Times-Star,* reprinted in *The Sporting News,* Feb. 27, 1908.
14 *Sporting Life,* Jan. 12, 1907.
15 *The Sporting News,* Feb. 23, 1907.
16 *Ibid.,* Dec. 15, 1906.
17 *Sporting Life,* Feb. 2, 1907.
18 *Ibid.,* Feb. 16, 1907. "A man in Norwood" was Mulford's way of referring to himself: He lived in that Cincinnati suburb and served for a time as its mayor.
19 *The Sporting News,* Jan. 19, 1907.
20 *Ibid.,* Nov. 10, 1906.
21 *Ibid.,* March 2, 1907.
22 *Ibid.,* Jan. 19, 1907.
23 *Ibid.,* March 9, 1907.

24 *Ibid.*, April 13, 1907.

25 *Ibid.*

26 *Sporting Life*, April 20, 1907. When Logan inquired about his chances of buying Cox's piece of the ballclub, Cox replied that he would sell any property he owned for the right price. The Boss ended up getting a good deal: The sale price was not confirmed, but a figure of $75,000 was suggested – half the amount Cox and company paid for the entire Reds operation in 1902. Logan did not retain the entire one-third share, immediately selling one-quarter of his stock to another investor who had expressed an interest in buying Cox's shares.

27 Alfred H. Spink, *The National Game*, second edition (Carbondale, Ill.: Southern Illinois University Press, 2000 reprint of 1911 original), p. 279.

28 The happy couple were Louis Rapp, a groundskeeper at the park, and his fiancée, Rosie Smith. The ceremony featured booming cannon and a band playing the wedding march. The Reds' management presented the Rapps with a parlor set and two tickets to the Chicago World's Fair, and fans chipped in with an ice chest. Lee Allen, *The Hot Stove League: Raking the Embers of Baseball's Golden Age* (New York: A.S. Barnes and Co., 2000 reprint of 1955 original), p. 163.

29 *Cincinnati Enquirer*, April 12, 1907.

30 *Chicago Tribune*, April 15, 1908.

31 Dick Young, "'The Outlawed Spitball was My Money Pitch,'" *Sports Illustrated*, Vol. 3, No. 1 (July 4, 1955), p. 60.

32 Eugene C. Murdock, *Baseball Players and Their Times: Oral Histories of the Game, 1920-40* (Westport, Conn.: Meckler Publishing, 1991), p. 14.

33 *New York Times*, Nov. 11, 1961.

34 *Cincinnati Commercial Tribune*, April 12, 1907.

35 *Ibid.*

36 *Cincinnati Enquirer*, April 12, 1907.

37 *Baltimore American*, April 27, 1901.

38 Though most newspaper stories noted Odwell's participation in the game, box scores almost without exception omitted his name and credited his run scored to McLean.

39 *Cincinnati Enquirer*, April 12, 1907.

40 *Cincinnati Commercial Tribune*, April 12, 1907.

41 *Cincinnati Enquirer*, April 12, 1907.

42 *Cincinnati Times-Star*, April 12, 1907.

43 *Cincinnati Enquirer,* April 12, 1907.

44 *Ibid.*

45 *Cincinnati Times-Star*, April 12, 1907.

46 *Cincinnati Enquirer*, April 12, 1907.

47 *Cincinnati Times-Star*, April 12, 1907.

48 When Ewing died in 1947, the obituaries – drawing on information supplied by Nelle – mentioned one game in particular: "One of the highlights of his pitching career was a victory over Pittsburgh in the opening game for the Reds." *The Lima News*, June 22, 1947.

49 *Cincinnati Commercial Tribune*, April 12, 1907.

50 Michael Macdonald Mooney, *Evelyn Nesbit and Stanford White: Love and Death in the Gilded Age* (New York: William Morrow and Co. Inc., 1976), p. 256.

51 *New York Times*, quoted in Mooney, *op. cit.*, p. 247.

52 *The Sporting News*, April 6, 1907.

53 *Ibid.*, April 22, 1907.

54 *Ibid.*, May 11, 1907.

55 *Sporting Life*, May 25, 1907.

56 *Ibid.*

57 *Cincinnati Enquirer*, May 13, 1907. Jack Ryder reported that after local management doubled the usual grandstand admission to 50 cents, irate fans "broke through the gates and swarmed over the field." John Ganzel helped to defuse the situation by proposing that those who had gotten in without paying should instead buy scorecards for 25 cents, thus demonstrating that they were "honorable and fair-minded citizen[s]," not thugs. Still, Ryder estimated that out of a crowd of 2,000, probably 500 or more paid nothing at all.

58 *Sporting Life*, May 25, 1907.

59 *Ibid.*, March 16, 1907.

60 *Cincinnati Enquirer*, July 27, 1906.

61 *Sporting Life*, May 25, 1907.

62 *Ibid.*, June 1, 1907.

63 *The Sporting News*, May 25, 1907.

64 *Sporting Life*, June 1, 1907.

65 With nowhere else to go in organized ball, Mason soon returned to the fold, but his days were numbered. In August, the club secured waivers and sold him to the New York Highlanders. He didn't stick in New York and never pitched in the major leagues again.

66 *The Sporting News*, Dec. 5, 1907.

67 Chuck Rosciam found that catchers were wrapping their shins in leather or newspaper as early as 1890; Rosciam, "The Evolution of Catcher's Equipment," *The Baseball Research Journal*, Vol. 39, No. 1 (summer 2010), p. 108. Bill James says a black catcher, George "Chappie" Johnson, wore shin guards with the Chicago Union Giants in 1902 and Jay "Nig" Clarke wore them briefly in the American League in 1905; James, *The Politics of Glory: How Baseball's Hall of Fame Really Works* (New York: Macmillan Publishing Co., 1994), pp. 41-42. In 1904, A.R. Cratty reported on Tom Needham of the Boston Nationals trying metal shin guards; *Sporting Life*, Oct. 15, 1904, quoted in Peter Morris, *A Game of Inches: The Game on the Field* (Chicago: Ivan R. Dee, 2006), p. 440.

68 Norman Macht, "Charles Sebastian 'Red' Dooin," in Tom Simon, ed., *Deadball Stars of the National League* (Washington, D.C.: Brassey's Inc., 2004), p. 189.

69 *Cincinnati Enquirer*, quoted in Greg Rhodes and John Snyder, *Redleg Journal: Year by Year and Day by Day with the Cincinnati Reds* (Cincinnati: Road West Publishing, 2000), p. 156.

70 *The Sporting News*, June 22, 1907.

71 Ironically, another incident the day Schlei unveiled his shin guards would lead Bresnahan to look into another piece of innovative equipment. Bresnahan was hit in the head and knocked unconscious by a pitch from Cincinnati's Andy Coakley; a priest was called to administer last rites as the fallen player lay motionless near home plate. Bresnahan recovered, but was hospitalized for several days. For a time after he returned to action, Bresnahan availed himself of the Reach Pneumatic Head Protector, a leather protective headgear patented by the sporting goods manufacturer in 1905. Unlike shin guards – and despite the death of Cleveland shortstop Ray Chapman after being hit by a pitch in 1920 – the batting helmet did not become standard equipment in baseball until the 1950s. See *The Sporting News*, July 25, 1907.

72 *The Sporting News*, July 18, 1907.

73 *Sporting Life*, July 20, 1907.

74 *The Sporting News*, Jan. 30, 1908.

75 *Sporting Life*, Aug. 3, 1907.
76 *The Sporting News*, Aug. 1, 1907.
77 *Ibid.*
78 *Cincinnati Times-Star*, reprinted in *The Sporting News*, Aug. 15, 1907.
79 *Cincinnati Enquirer*, Aug. 12, 1907.
80 The home run was Ewing's third and last in the major leagues. This game also marked the first time in more than a year that Nelle Ewing had seen her husband win a game, bringing an end to her so-called jinx (see Chapter 8).
81 Earned run averages were not yet in use in 1907, but Ewing's has since been calculated at 1.73, the best of his career and more than two-thirds of a run better than the league as a whole.
82 *Cincinnati Times-Star*, reprinted in *The Sporting News*, Feb. 27, 1908.
83 *Sporting Life*, Oct. 12, 1907.
84 *Ibid.*, Oct. 5, 1907.

"Spitball pitchers are scarce in the National League. Consequently when one does appear, he is a *troublemaker*." —SAM CRANE[1]

"In Bob Ewing, we have the *best* spitball pitcher in the National League." —JOHN GANZEL[2]

CHAPTER 10

Year of the Stopgap

GARRY HERRMANN spent most of the winter trying to find a manager. His brightest idea and fondest hope was to swing a deal with Pittsburgh for Tommy Leach and install him as the new leader of the Reds. Leach was a veteran, a winner and could plug a hole at third base or in the outfield. He also had Ohio connections, having grown up in Cleveland playing sandlot ball with the Delahanty brothers. But when Herrmann attempted to initiate negotiations, Fred Clarke started throwing out names like Miller Huggins and Mike Mitchell, preferably as part of a two- or three-player package that might also include Admiral Schlei, Hans Lobert and/or Larry McLean.

The trade talks went nowhere. Soon it was mid-January. Spring training was six weeks away and the Reds still didn't have a manager. Herrmann bowed to necessity and offered the position to John Ganzel.

Ganzel's best qualifications were that he was available and he wanted the job. When Ned Hanlon disclosed his intention to step down, Ganzel's was the first and most obvious name to come up as a potential successor. But a month after the season ended, Herrmann was reported to be shopping for a replacement for Ganzel at first base, having concluded he was "too slow for fast company."[3] Herrmann inquired about the availability of either Fred Tenney or Roger Bresnahan, now both with the Giants, but those feelers were rebuffed. By the time the managerial appointment was announced, other alternatives having been exhausted, Ganzel was said to be the near unanimous—if not necessarily enthusiastic—choice of the Cincinnati press.

Ganzel's managerial experience was limited to two years in the middling minors as leader of the Grand Rapids Furniture Makers[4] of the Class B Central League, where he won a pennant in 1906. Ganzel was his own best player on that team, leading the league in both home runs and batting average. He wasn't likely to be able to give himself that advantage in the National League. His hiring was greeted in some quarters with derision. "The engagement of John Ganzel as manager of the Reds is regarded as one huge joke by baseball men in this part of the country," one New York newspaper commented.[5]

Moreover, Ganzel came to his new job with some awkward baggage. As the Reds' captain in 1907, he had sometimes found himself in a sort of no-man's land between the players and the manager. The players regarded him as Hanlon's spy; Hanlon suspected him of angling for his job. Sometime in the uncertain weeks between Hanlon's departure and Ganzel's promotion, Ren Mulford tossed out an instructive story:

> During one of Hanlon's periodical spells of absenteeism
> three Reds wandered off on a toot. ... Captain Ganzel
> remonstrated with them, and made an official report of the
> breaches of discipline to Hanlon. Did Hanlon visit any pun-
> ishment upon the offenders? The yarn told in Redland is that
> he tipped Ganzel off as the "informer" to the trio, who at
> once joined the Society of Hammer Throwers.[6]

Further complicating his situation, Ganzel was regarded in some Cincinnati circles as something of an oddity: a German who didn't drink beer.

Even more than most managers, John Ganzel was hired to be fired. Herrmann never saw him as anything more than a stopgap. Before the season was much more than half over, unbeknownst to Ganzel, his replacement would already be on the Reds' payroll, looking over his shoulder.

Under the circumstances, the club made no big plans for 1908. Two weeks before heading for spring training, Ganzel—doubtless on instructions from Herrmann—stated that he expected to stand pat with the roster he had been given. For the most part, the Reds would stick to that program. Throughout the season, most of the load would be carried by players who had been on the Opening Day roster in 1907. Most of the few notable "new" players—pitchers Bob Spade and Billy Campbell, and outfielder Dode Paskert—had joined the club before the end of the 1907 campaign.

Spring training was in St. Augustine, Florida, selected because it would be full of northern tourists in March and Frank Bancroft guessed the Reds would be able to draw good crowds for exhibition games. Bob Ewing left for Florida around March 1, with Nelle but without a signed contract. He was trying—probably without success—to talk Garry Herrmann out of an additional $500. If the disagreement made Ewing irritable, he didn't let it interfere with the business of getting into shape. While some players found the Florida heat enervating, Ewing again returned to Cincinnati in top condition. He signed a contract upon his return, tossed off a string of scoreless innings in a 1–0 exhibition victory over the Chicago White Sox and on April 9, five days before the season opener, beat the Washington Senators 3–2 in another pre-season game at League Park, batting in the winning run himself with a single in the ninth inning.

Ewing was nearly 35 years old and entering the twilight of his career. Still, he was one of the main supports on which his new manager expected to lean. "Ewing will be the same old boy," Ganzel said, "and Bob always has been ranked as a good, strong pitcher."[7]

Ewing was also still learning and growing as a pitcher. He let slip that this year he would rely less on the spitball,[8] though it is difficult to know exactly what to make of the comment. For one thing, it's difficult to ascertain how frequently he used the pitch in the first place. As late as 1907, three years after mastering the spitball, he was described as relying mainly on "great speed and a puzzling drop curve," going to the spitter "only at critical moments, when a strikeout is necessary."[9] There were games when "Ewing used nothing but the spitball,"[10] but there were others like one in 1907 when Jack Ryder insisted that "Ewing used the spitball only once"—to secure an inning-ending strikeout with two runners in scoring position.[11] In all likelihood, Ewing's reliance on the spitter varied considerably from one game to the next, depending on atmospheric conditions, the specific weaknesses of opposing batters, and how well Long Bob's other pitches were working.

Still, regardless how often he actually used it, Ewing referred to the wet one as "my best pitching asset."[12] In 1908, the spitball remained highly controversial. Some observers asserted that the only people in baseball who opposed outlawing the spitball were the spitball pitchers themselves.[13] Among the pitch's influential critics was National League president Harry Pulliam, who said "there should be no place in [baseball] for a freak delivery" that undermined the efforts of batters and fielders alike. Pulliam predicted that both leagues would reach an agreement, possibly before next season, to "do away with this offensive style of pitching."[14] That prospect constantly haunted all spitball artists. Ewing may have been formulating a survival plan against the day his bread-and-butter pitch would be declared illegal. On the other hand, he may just have been engaging in an attempt to mislead opposing batters: Like most spitballers, Ewing regularly went through the motions of loading up even when he had no intention of throwing a wet one. The pitch was as much a psychological weapon as a physical one.

Once again, Ewing was tapped to start the opening game, on April 14 against the Chicago Cubs. He became the first pitcher to start consecutive openers for the Reds since Tacky Tom Parrott in 1894 and '95.[15] Opening Day was its usual festive self in Cincinnati, but amid the traditional forms and trappings of gaiety there were also signs of change. The newspapers commented on the unprecedented number of automobiles carrying fans to the ballpark. Herrmann arrived by automobile, and so did Max and Julius Fleischmann. The first horseless carriage had appeared on the streets of Cincinnati in 1891. By 1905 automobiles were sufficiently numerous that the city had seen the need to establish speed limits—7 mph downtown, 15 mph in outlying areas.[16] Now, six months before the appearance of the first Model T Ford, the sheds at League Park, originally built for the horse-drawn carriages of wealthy patrons, "were crowded with machines of various sizes and power."[17]

Less affluent fans also made their way to the park in large numbers, lured by all the usual Opening Day attractions and further encouraged by a more than usually promising spring day. All streetcars heading to the park were jammed to overflowing for three hours before the game. Some rooters gave up trying to squeeze into the cars and walked all the way from Fountain Square. The crowd began gathering at 11 a.m. and by the time the gates opened at 12:30 p.m., "the lines around the ticket offices had doubled up and were reaching the entire length of the ballpark."[18] All reserved seats had been sold in advance, but still there was such a crush of game-day walk-up traffic that Frank Bancroft ordered the ticket windows closed nearly an hour before the 3 p.m. start time. Even so, fans were still making their way into the park in the second inning. The throng overflowed the stands and spilled into "the remote suburbs of the outfield, where human beings stood packed on end, like stogies in a paper box."[19] Official paid attendance was announced at 19,257,[20] topping by more than 1,500 the previous record crowd for a baseball game in Cincinnati.

The *Chicago Tribune*'s Charles Dryden marveled at the spectacle that was Opening Day in the Queen City. He savored a concession stand menu that included ice cream, pigs' knuckles and hot sausages with "real horse-less horseradish" on the side at no additional charge, and described "an army of gentlemanly suds salesmen" moving efficiently through the crowd "in red helmets and a high state of perspiration."

"Half a million paper megaphones in all colors of the rainbow ... were handed out free of cost," Dryden added, "... so that even the most conservative of fans could squawk at opportune moments."[21]

In addition to all the usual delights, Opening Day 1908 offered fans a chance to inaugurate the season with a look at the greatest baseball team on the planet. As Ewing warmed up, his mind was turning over how he would deal with the Chicago lineup that had marched through the National League schedule with 107 victories in 1907, then humbled Ty Cobb's Detroit Tigers in the World Series.

Among the stars of the Cubs' World Series sweep were Ewing's former teammates Orval Overall, who allowed just two earned runs in 18 innings, and Harry Steinfeldt, who batted .471. Both would be aligned against Ewing today. Chicago's batting order also included four players who had faced Ewing in his ill-starred major league debut back in 1902: center fielder Jimmy Slagle, shortstop Joe Tinker, catcher Johnny Kling[22] and manager Frank Chance, at first base. In the interim, the Cubs had also strengthened their hand with two outstanding outfielders, fleet-footed Jimmy Sheckard and hard-hitting Frank Schulte. At second base was Johnny Evers, who came on board late in 1902, completing the double-play combination that would be immortalized in verse by Franklin Pierce Adams—Tinker to Evers to Chance.[23]

The game started well for Cincinnati. Five hits and three uncharacteristic Chicago errors gave the Reds a 5–0 lead before anyone was out in their half of the first inning. The Cubs got two runs back on four consecutive crisp singles in the second. Ewing still held a 5–3 lead when the Reds came to bat in the bottom of the fourth, but he was not sharp. Though temperatures were in the mid-70s and "the air was almost summer-like in its softness,"[24] a slight drizzle had fallen during the first two innings, dampening the grass and possibly compounding whatever other problems Long Bob was having.

"The wet ball prevented him from using his famous spitter, his control was not of the best and he was unable to put enough on the ball to fool the tail end of the Cub batting order," Jack Ryder summarized. So when Ewing drew a walk with one out in the fourth, Ganzel lifted him in favor of a pinch runner—"wisely," in Ryder's opinion—and entrusted the remainder of the afternoon's pitching chores to Billy Campbell.[25]

By then the tide was turning. The Cubs continued to battle back and Cincinnati aided the Chicago cause with a series of costly blunders. Campbell's balk led to a Cubs run in the fifth inning and Steinfeldt scored the game-tying tally in the sixth after belting a ground-rule triple among the spectators in left field. The Reds killed their last two scoring opportunities when Admiral Schlei was picked off second base in the eighth and pinch hitter Larry McLean, hoping to duplicate his Opening Day heroics of a year ago, was thrown out attempting to stretch a single into a double in the ninth. The Cubs scored last, on Heinie Zimmerman's pinch single in the ninth, and won the game 6–5.

Chicago swept the season-opening series, three games straight, but the Reds quickly recovered. They swept a three-game series with Pittsburgh and began to climb in the standings. Starting May 10, Ewing tossed back-to-back shutouts against St. Louis and Boston, allowing just four hits in each game. On May 27 he beat Brooklyn 8–2 and Cincinnati moved into second place. Except for a few days, the Reds would hold that lofty perch until mid-June, while Ewing continued to pitch inspired baseball. When he beat Boston with a three-hitter on June 9, his record stood at 7–2.

The city was ecstatic. "The notorious Ganzel gang"[26] was the surprise of the National League and John Ganzel was a hero. For once, the Reds were "shining in good society," Ren Mulford wrote, and it was "an exhilarating experience."[27]

The dream of being a genuine contender was too good to last. The Reds were beginning to slip by June 13, when Ewing held the New York Giants scoreless through eight innings before losing 3–2 in the 10th in front of 17,000 people at the Polo Grounds. The Reds appeared to have the game won until Dode Paskert's throwing error and Miller Huggins' muffed pop fly allowed the Giants to tie the score in the bottom of the ninth.

"Cincinnati erred last, and therefore erred worst," observed W.W. Aulick in the *New York Times*.

"What I have to say to Messrs. Paskert and Huggins will be spoken in German," Ganzel told reporters. "… No other tongue so admirably meets the requirements of the occasion."[28]

The team was still in third place on June 18, when Ewing beat George McQuillan 1–0, the first of Cincinnati's three straight shutout victories over Philadelphia. But the gang was starting to feel the heat. Three days later, the Pirates beat the Reds 5–1 in a steam bath at League Park. Pittsburgh first baseman Harry Swacina was overcome by the heat and had to leave the game after legging out a triple in the fifth inning. Ewing toiled through eight innings, then collapsed after leaving for a pinch hitter. For more than two weeks afterward, he suffered recurring bouts of weakness and dizziness and had to stay out of the sun as much as possible. At times he could hardly stand.

By July 6, the team had dropped to fourth place and the pitching staff was pushed almost to the limit. Ganzel looked to the skies and prayed for rain, which threatened in the early afternoon. When the rain didn't come, he turned to Ewing and asked if he could pitch. A Claude Shafer cartoon in the *Cincinnati Enquirer* showed Long Bob climbing out of a sickbed to take the mound against Christy Mathewson and the New York Giants.

Ewing still didn't feel well, but he limited the visitors to six hits. He allowed only two bases on balls, but both came around to score. The game was tied 1–1 with two out in the fifth inning when Larry Doyle broke from first base on a delayed steal and Admiral Schlei's wild throw permitted Fred Tenney to score from third. That gave the Giants a 2–1 lead, and that's how it stayed. "With perfectly clean play," Jack Ryder pointed out, the Reds would have won the game 1–0.

"Also," he added, "if the dog had not stopped to bark at a rat hole, he would have captured the rabbit."[29]

Still, the newspapers were optimistic, expressing the hope that Ewing was ready to resume a full workload. In his next start, four days later, he beat Boston 5–4, but he was hit hard and "the hot sun was quite a handicap to him."[30] Though Ewing remained the workhorse of the Cincinnati staff and would again pitch nearly 300 innings, he would not fully recover his health for the balance of the season. As Ren Mulford put it, "Bob Ewing's spirit was willing, but his legs were weak."[31]

Ewing's delicate health further complicated the Reds' increasingly tenuous pitching situation. Billy Campbell and Bob Spade, both in their 30s and experiencing their first full season in the big leagues, did creditable and in Spade's case often exceptional work. Andy Coakley pitched well enough most of the time but couldn't beat anybody; his record slumped to 8–18 before he was finally sold to the Cubs in September. Jake Weimer, trying to regain the form that made him a 20-game winner in 1906, was good for only half a season's work. Sold to the New York Giants for the $1,500 waiver price, he would pitch only one more time in the major leagues. By the end of July, when left-hander Jack Doscher quit the team to go home to his other job as a court clerk, the Reds were left with only five functional pitchers.

The team was in the middle of a three-week road trip and there was no rest for weary arms. In early August, the Reds played seven games in five days and Ewing worked four times. He pitched eight solid innings against the Giants only to see the Reds lose 4–3 in 12. The next day, asked to hold a one-run lead for Billy Campbell, Ewing gave up the tying run in the ninth inning, just before the game was called because of rain. He got a break as Bob Spade pitched a 5–0 shutout against New York, then came back the following afternoon with his own complete-game victory over Brooklyn. On the final day of the marathon, Ewing had a couple shaky moments but managed to nail down the final five outs and preserve an 8–6 win for Campbell. When Sunday finally came to Brooklyn and the Reds got a day off, they had broken even: three wins, three losses and a tie in five days.

The club's modest talent was getting stretched thin. At the same time, Ganzel's limitations as a manager were beginning to show. Ren Mulford detected "a marked timidity" in Uncle John's handling of pitchers.[32] Moreover, the man once hailed as the bringer of a new era of "temperate living"[33] after the relaxed regimes of Joe Kelley and Ned Hanlon had proven a failure as a disciplinarian. Larry McLean, a notorious rounder, had first fallen from grace during spring training. In mid-July, following "repeated breaches of discipline,"[34] he was hit with a 10-day suspension, and more of the same was to follow. When all was said and done, the *Cincinnati Post*'s Frank Rostock maintained, several players "did not give their best services to the club," in large part because of "Ganzel's failure to sit down on them good and hard."[35]

Against the odds, the team continued to hang around the fringes of respectability. This in spite of some costly injuries incurred in management's continuing pursuit of a stray buck any time there was a break in the schedule. Mike Mitchell was out of action for a month after turning an ankle against a team of railway workers in Piqua, Ohio. On September 14 Billy Campbell was carried off the field in Clarksburg, West Virginia, with a wrenched knee—lost, for all practical purposes, for the balance of the season.[36]

Yet for one of the few times in Ewing's career, the Reds—undermanned, injury-plagued and fading in the standings—found themselves with a role to play in determining who would fly the National League pennant. As the season approached its climax, the perennial contenders New York, Chicago and Pittsburgh were battling tooth and nail for first place. On September 23 at the Polo Grounds, the Giants were deprived of a crucial victory over the Cubs when, with the scored tied 1–1 and two out in the bottom of the ninth inning, base runner Fred Merkle neglected to touch second base on an apparent game-winning single by ex-Red Al Bridwell. As euphoric fans spilled onto the field, a wild melee ensued. The Cubs eventually recovered the ball and Johnny Evers stood on second base holding it over his head, claiming an inning-ending force out on Merkle, thus nullifying the Giants' go-ahead run. By this time so many people were swarming over the diamond that it was impossible to resume play. Amid mounting chaos, umpire Hank O'Day declared the game a tie. Merkle, 19 years old and in the lineup only because of nagging injuries to the veteran Fred Tenney, went into the annals of baseball as the perpetrator of the most infamous blunder of all time, known forever afterwards as "Merkle's boner."

Two days later the fifth-place Reds were in New York for the first of back-to-back doubleheaders. The Giants, hanging onto a tenuous lead over the Cubs, were wound tight, seething over league president Harry Pulliam's decision to uphold O'Day's call, and once again counting on Fred Tenney, 36 years old and racked with physical miseries, to play first base in place of the disgraced Merkle. "A one-legged man with a noodle is better than a bonehead," one New York writer observed.[37]

In this supercharged atmosphere, Giants manager John McGraw chose the first game of the series for the unveiling of his latest acquisition. Twenty-one-year-old Rube Marquard was a lanky left-hander the Giants had purchased from Indianapolis for the stunning sum of $11,000. Even in ordinary circumstances, in the words of Damon Runyon, the Polo Grounds of this era was apt at any moment to be transformed into "a bowl of howling humanity,"[38] and these were not ordinary circumstances. Making his major league debut in a critical game before a home crowd in New York, young Marquard had "speed to spill"[39] and a terrific case of stage fright. The Reds chased him after five innings and won the game 7–1, with Bob Spade doing the pitching. Then they took the second contest as well, winning 5–2 behind rookie Jean Dubuc, barely 20 years old and only a few months out of the University of Notre Dame.

The double defeat left the Giants in first place by a single percentage point. McGraw's men regained some of their dignity the next day. Before a Saturday afternoon standing-room crowd of 30,000—more people than Ohio native Rube Marquard "had ever seen collectively in the course of his natural life," one writer speculated[40]—New York beat Cincinnati 6–2 and 3–1. Christy Mathewson trounced Ewing in the opener and Red Ames won the nightcap despite another excellent performance by Dubuc, pitching his second complete game in as many days. But the twin triumphs gained the Giants no ground in the pennant race. While they were taking two from Cincinnati, a few miles away the Cubs were shutting out Brooklyn in both ends of another doubleheader. Ed Reulbach did all the pitching for Chicago, allowing just five hits in the first game and just three in the second.

The following week, Philadelphia's Harry Coveleski, a big rookie from the Pennsylvania coal-mining country, beat the Giants three times in five days. New York finished its schedule in a first-place tie with Chicago. The Cubs clinched the pennant the next day as Mordecai "Three-Finger" Brown outlasted Mathewson 4–2 in a replay of the Merkle game.

Merkle eventually played 10 years for the Giants, helping them win three consecutive pennants. McGraw never blamed him for losing the 1908 pennant. Instead he pointed to the inability to beat Coveleski even once in three tries, and to the doubleheader loss to the Reds.

CINCINNATI WAS NOT A FACTOR in the final days of the drama. But as the season wound down, it was clear that John Ganzel had made about as much as anyone could have expected out of the nondescript 1908 Reds. Though they hadn't managed to climb out of the second division, they had won more games than in either of the two previous seasons. They had remained at or above .500 until the final week of August and in contention for fourth place into late September. Ganzel, never one to harbor grandiose expectations, had said before the season that he would "make it his business to finish no lower than a good fifth,"[41] and he had made good on that promise.

There was almost a pleading quality to Ganzel's statements that he hoped to manage the club again in 1909, but everyone seemed to know he wouldn't. For one thing, his services were no longer required in the infield. Late in the season the Reds had acquired a promising new first baseman, 19-year-old Dick Hoblitzell, whom they had wrested from the St. Louis Cardinals after arguing their claim before the National Commission. If there was any question about Ganzel's future as manager, the final nail was driven into his coffin on the next-to-last day of the season, when Larry McLean had to be benched after committing three passed balls in the first inning of a home game against Chicago. The Cubs piled up a 14–0 lead by the third inning and went on to win the game by the humiliating score of 16–2. Ganzel swore he was certain McLean hadn't been drinking, but when Ganzel's head rolled a few weeks later, Ren Mulford attributed Honest John's fall to "misguided kindness toward disloyal roisterers."[42]

The final game of the season was preceded by a baseball "field day" with the players competing in such events as fungo hitting and long-distance throwing. Hans Lobert was credited with "a new record"[43] when he circled the bases in 14 seconds. Ewing then took the mound and defeated St. Louis 5–1 on a four-hitter.

NEITHER GANZEL NOR EWING participated in the team's most interesting road trip of 1908. Forming a sort of epilogue to the season, the excursion was a six-week barnstorming tour to Cuba, the first of its kind by a big league team. The trip was organized by Frank Bancroft, an old Cuba hand. Ewing, no lover of tropical climates and a lukewarm barnstormer under the best circumstances, passed on the opportunity to visit the Caribbean and went home to the farm.

For players who went along, the trip was an eye-opener. American ballplayers had been visiting Cuba for 30 years, developing an enthusiastic following for baseball on the island and sowing seeds that would produce generations of great home-grown players. Still playing host to U.S. troops following the Spanish-American War, Cuba made for an exotic winter vacation destination. It offered big crowds and a chance for touring big leaguers to make some serious money. They could also test themselves against outstanding players who would never break into the stateside leagues of organized baseball. And therein lay the rub. John J. McGraw, who loved Cuba and visited the island several times both with and without ball teams, summed up the major leagues' attitude during a barnstorming trip in 1911. After a galling defeat that suggested some of his league-champion Giants weren't taking the games as seriously as McGraw expected, he slapped a fine on outfielder Josh Devore and snarled, "I didn't come down here to let a lot of coffee-colored Cubans show me up."[44]

The 1908 Reds, a long way from a championship club, did all right in the early stages of the tour. With a roster that included Miller Huggins, Hans Lobert, Johnny Kane, Dick Hoblitzell, Mike Mitchell, Larry McLean and pitchers Bob Spade, Jean Dubuc and Billy Campbell, they played their way south through Florida with few untoward incidents. But when they arrived in Cuba the big leaguers found they had their hands full. In seven encounters with the Almendares club, described by a *yanqui* correspondent for *The Sporting News* as "native Cubans and as black as your hat,"[45] the Reds gained only one win and a tie. They also received a 9–1 drubbing at the hands of the Brooklyn Royal Giants, a team of black players who were also visiting from the states.[46]

In one meeting with Almendares, the Reds came within an eyelash of having a no-hitter thrown at them. The disaster was averted only by Huggins' infield single in the ninth inning. The author of this pitching masterpiece was José Méndez, the legendary "Black Diamond" of Cuban baseball. Only 21 years old, Méndez was a 5-foot-9, 150-pound right-hander with impressive speed, uncanny control, a snapping curve and a tantalizing change of pace. He was also, according to Cuban baseball historian Roberto González Echevarría, "an unmixed black with unmistakable African features."[47] Overall, Méndez faced the Reds three times. They did not score against him in 25 innings.

The New York Giants, who saw Méndez on their Cuban tour three years later, christened him "the black Matty."[48] McGraw described him as "sort of Walter Johnson and Grover Alexander rolled into one."[49]

"Méndez is a corker," Frank Bancroft declared upon his return to Cincinnati. "If he'd been the right color, I'd [have] put handcuffs on him and brought him back to Redland. ... He'd have made a big National League [drawing] card if there was only some way of bleaching him."[50]

Three years later, Cincinnati imported its first two Cuban players, both of whom had played against the Reds on their Cuban tour. Infielder Rafael Almeida and outfielder Armando Marsans, who both played minor league ball in the United States starting in 1908, became the first Cuban-born major leaguers since the 1870s.

Before putting them on the field, Garry Herrmann attempted to head off any potential protests by assuring his fellow owners that the players' ancestry had been thoroughly researched and he was "ready to prove that Almeida and Marsans ... are not Negroes" but rather descendants of Spaniards of pure Castilian blood.[51] The "research" apparently consisted mainly of eliciting a testimonial from the Cuban sportswriter Victor Muñoz, who promised Herrmann that he knew both players' parents and that "their claim to [be] members of the white race is as good as yours or mine."[52]

1   *New York Evening Journal,* April 1908, quoted in G.H. Fleming, *The Unforgettable Season* (New York: Holt, Rinehart and Winston, 1981), p. 51.

2   *The Sporting News*, April 2, 1908.

3   *Sporting Life*, Nov. 16, 1907.

4   *The Sporting News* applied this nickname to the Grand Rapids team on Nov. 11, 1905, around the time Ganzel was taking over. The team was also known during his tenure as the Orphans or the Wolverines. See Benjamin Barrett Sumner, *Minor League Baseball Standings: All North American Leagues, through 1999* (Jefferson, N.C.: McFarland and Co. Inc., 2000), p. 247.

5   *New York Globe,* reprinted in *The Sporting News*, Feb. 8, 1908.

6   *Sporting Life*, Dec. 21, 1907.

7   *The Sporting News*, Feb. 13, 1908.

8   *Sporting Life*, Jan. 18, 1908.

9   Unidentified newspaper clipping, 1907.

10 *Chicago American*, April 20, 1905.

11 *Cincinnati Enquirer*, May 27, 1907. This particular spitball, served up to Chicago's Harry Steinfeldt, must have been a dandy. "The third strike broke down so fast that it hit the ground before it got to Schlei's hands," Ryder reported, "but the Admiral blocked it and threw Steiny out at first."

12 Unidentified newspaper clipping, 1905.

13 *Sporting Life.*, Aug. 8, 1908.

14 *Ibid.*, Sept. 19, 1908.

15 Ewing was the only Cincinnati pitcher to achieve this distinction in a span of more than 20 years. After Ewing in 1907-08, the next Reds pitcher to start two consecutive openers was Pete Schneider in 1917-18.

16 Writers' Program of the Work Projects Administration, *Cincinnati: A Guide to the Queen City and Its Neighbors* (Cincinnati: Wiesen-Hart Press, 1943), p. 92.

17 *Cincinnati Enquirer*, April 15, 1908. In April 1908, the alternatives available to an aspiring autoist varied widely by region. Forerunners of the Model T were available from Ford, and other established or emerging brand names included Maxwell, Stearns, Oldsmobile and Locomobile. The *New York Times* (April 5, 1908) carried an advertisement for a Hotchkiss automobile, "built like a gun by gunmakers." But the automobile was still mainly a creature of the cities. Though a dealership on the Public Square in Lima advertised the Thomas Flyer, the electric-powered Pope-Waverly and most prominently Buick, "the New York and Chicago sensation" (*Lima Daily News*, April 10, 1908), an automobile would have been practically useless to Bob Ewing living 15 miles away on the farm near New Hampshire. According to Pete Davis, "In the rural United States as late as 1907, there was not a single mile of paved road." Davis, *American Road: The Story of an Epic Transcontinental Journey at the Dawn of the Motor Age* (New York: Henry Holt and Co., 2002), p. 11.

18 *Cincinnati Commercial Tribune*, April 15, 1908.

19 *Chicago Tribune*, April 15, 1908.

20 This was the figure used by most newspapers. The *Cincinnati Post*, for some reason, said 19,256.

21 *Chicago Tribune*, April 15, 1908.

22 Kling did not start the 1902 game, but came in as a substitute after Frank Chance was ejected by umpire Bob Emslie.

23 Adams' famous poem was first published in the *New York Evening Mail* on July 12, 1910.

24 *Cincinnati Enquirer*, April 15, 1908.

25   *Ibid.*

26   *New York Times*, June 14, 1908.

27   *Sporting Life*, June 6, 1908.

28   *New York Times*, June 14, 1908.

29   *Cincinnati Enquirer*, July 7, 1908.

30   *Ibid.*, July 11, 1908.

31   *Sporting Life*, July 11, 1908. As if heat stroke weren't enough, Ewing was later reported to be "laid up with an attack of tonsillitis." See *Sporting Life*, Aug. 22, 1908.

32   *Ibid.*, Sept. 26, 1908.

33   *Ibid.*, Feb. 22, 1908.

34   *Ibid.*, July 25, 1908.

35   *Cincinnati Post*, quoted in *Sporting Life*, Nov. 21, 1908.

36   Campbell would appear in only one more league game in 1908 – an ineffectual relief appearance on the next-to-last day of the season.

37   James E. "Gym" Bagley, *New York Evening Mail*, quoted in G.H. Fleming, *The Unforgettable Season* (New York: Holt, Rinehart and Winston, 1981), p. 255.

38   *New York American*, April 1911, reprinted in Damon Runyon, edited by Jim Reisler, *Guys, Dolls, and Curveballs: Damon Runyon on Baseball* (New York: Carroll and Graf Publishers, 2005), p. 114.

39   *New York Times*, Sept. 26, 1908.

40   *Ibid.*, Sept. 27, 1908.

41   *Sporting Life*, March 21, 1908.

42   *Ibid.*, Nov. 28, 1908.

43   *Ibid.*, Oct. 10, 1908.

44   Charles C. Alexander, *John McGraw* (New York: Viking Penguin Inc., 1988), p. 159.

45   *The Sporting News*, Dec. 17, 1908.

46   Piecing together accounts from different sources, the Reds seem to have compiled a record of 5-7-1 during nearly a month in Havana. See Roberto González Echevarría, *The Pride of Havana: A History of Cuban Baseball* (New York: Oxford University Press, 1999), pp. 132-33; and *Sporting Life*, Nov. 28 through Dec. 19, 1908.

47   Roberto González Echevarría, *The Pride of Havana: A History of Cuban Baseball* (New York: Oxford University, 1999), p. 130.

48   *The Sporting News*, Jan. 25, 1912.

49   James A. Riley, *The Biographical Encyclopedia of the Negro Baseball Leagues* (New York: Carroll and Graf Publishers Inc., 1994), p. 546.

50   *Sporting Life*, Dec. 26, 1908.

51   *Ibid.*, July 15, 1911; see also Lonnie Wheeler and John Baskin, *The Cincinnati Game* (Wilmington, Ohio: Orange Frazer Press, 1988), pp. 174-75.

52   Peter T. Toot, *Armando Marsans: A Cuban Pioneer in the Major Leagues* (Jefferson, N.C.: McFarland and Co. Inc., 2004), pp. 38-39.

CHAPTER 11

Meet the New (Old) Fox

AS LATE AS SEPTEMBER 1908 Garry Herrmann had been telling reporters there was "no possible chance" that Clark Griffith would manage the Cincinnati Reds in 1909.[2] In fact, the decision to hand him the job had already been made.

Herrmann, who always regarded John Ganzel as merely a temporary expedient, had never stopped looking for a man of more substantial reputation to step into the shoes formerly worn by Joe Kelley and Ned Hanlon. Griffith, an outstanding major league pitcher for 15 years and pennant-winning manager of the Chicago White Sox in the American League's first major league season, became the focus of Herrmann's attention as soon as he became available. But Griffith was a staunch American League loyalist, a friend of Ban Johnson who had been instrumental in recruiting players for the new circuit when it announced itself as a rival to the National League in 1901.[3] Even after abruptly resigning as manager of the New York Highlanders in June 1908, according to baseball historian Lee Allen, Griffith found the idea of returning to the National League "repugnant."[4]

Still, a job is a job. With no suitable American League position on the horizon, Griffith consented to be placed on the Reds' payroll as a scout. Throughout the second half of the 1908 season, Griffith paid his way into games in Cincinnati and monitored the proceedings unobtrusively from the bleachers. He then reported his observations directly to Herrmann. Ganzel, who hadn't been fond of Griffith when they were together in New York, was kept in the dark. From the moment Griffith first took up his "scouting" duties for the Reds, there seems to have been little doubt who would manage the team in 1909. Counting Frank Bancroft's three-week interregnum in 1902, Griffith was Bob Ewing's sixth manager in eight years in Cincinnati. The *Cincinnati Enquirer* lauded Griffith as "a hard worker, a hard loser, and a man who has the nerve to accept the responsibility of running the team."[5] At a time when increased media interest forced managers to devote more and more time to dealing with reporters, Griffith also sometimes created problems for himself with what *The Sporting News* characterized as his "press-be-damned" attitude.[6] A Cincinnati writer would later chide Griffith for having "skin as thin as tissue paper."[7]

As a player, Griffith had pitched in the major leagues since 1891. Only 5 feet, 6½ inches tall and weighing no more than 160 pounds, with a fastball that contemporaries insisted "would not have cracked a sheet of spun sugar at 20 feet,"[8] he amassed 237 victories, seven times winning more than 20 games in a season. A wily competitor and careful student of hitters, Griffith relied on an assortment of off-speed pitches and every trick the rules permitted or the umpires let him get away with. His approach to the game eventually earned him a nickname that followed him through most of his six-plus decades in baseball: the Old Fox.[9]

As a manager, Griffith was among the first to make systematic use of relief pitchers; in New York he regularly used himself in that role. Unlike his Cincinnati predecessors, Griffith announced plans to look at as many as 19 pitchers and to keep "as many … as show that they are of National League caliber."[10] He was aided in expanding the pitching staff by an increased roster limit. For several years major league teams had been limited for most of the season to 16 active players. But enforcement seems to have been inconsistent and by 1909, the leagues were moving toward formalizing the modern roster limit of 25. Around the time Griffith took the reins in Cincinnati, a comment in *The Sporting News* said, "At present a major league club can carry as many men as it cares to … [with] no limit except the pocketbook of the club owner."[11]

When the Reds reported to Atlanta for spring training, Griffith also brought along the club's first full-time trainer. Mike Martin had worked with boxers, bicycle racers and assorted college athletes before linking up with Griffith in New York; during their long association, Martin would demonstrate considerable talent for curing sore arms.[12]

Before his teammates even got off the train in Atlanta, Bob Ewing was well into a spring training routine of his own in Hot Springs, Arkansas. Situated in the foothills of the Ouachita Mountains, Hot Springs was a city of 14,000 known for the dozens of naturally heated springs that bubbled up out of the ground. The growth of the nation's rail system in the late 19th century had turned the town into a popular health resort. Ballplayers had been coming to Hot Springs since 1886, when Cap Anson's Chicago White Stockings conducted pre-season workouts there.

By Ewing's time Hot Springs was a mecca for players, who came in February and March to hike in the hills, drink the thermal waters, soak in the mineral baths and generally "boil out" the kinks and stiffness of the long winter. Promoters touted Hot Springs as the "ideal city for training purposes."[13] The Pittsburgh Pirates, Boston Red Sox and other teams made "the City of Vapors" their training base, and numerous individual players went to Arkansas on their own to get a head start on the season. Schedules had to be worked out so that everyone could get time on the limited number of ball diamonds. In 1909 Ewing asked the Reds to pay his way to Hot Springs for some preliminary conditioning work. When the club refused, he paid for the trip himself.

Getting on in years and anticipating a lively competition for roster spots, Ewing was eager to get off on the right foot with his new manager. As for Griffith, shortly after taking office he made an astonishing discovery: Cincinnati was paying higher salaries for a second-division club, he claimed, than the American League generally paid for a pennant contender. He declared that no pay raises would be forthcoming in 1909.[14] Ewing, winner of 17 games for a fifth-place team in 1908, got the message. He was one of the first players to sign a new contract, at the same salary as the year before.

Ewing reached Atlanta in mid-March, after three weeks in Hot Springs. The Reds' camp reflected the personality of the new manager—disciplined, businesslike and cerebral. Griffith let it be known that he expected his men to be serious about getting into shape. "I can't stand a fat ballplayer," he declared.[15] Beyond that, the routine would consist mainly of morning and afternoon games, with less time devoted to running and hitting fungoes and more to what he called "the real features of baseball."[16] Griffith strongly discouraged cigarette smoking and put the kibosh on late-night poker games, enforcing an "early to bed, early to rise" policy that suited Ewing fine. Griffith's training schedule also typically included semi-weekly "black-board talks" at the hotel in the evening, with the team sequestered behind locked doors and a couple of bellboys stationed outside to shoo away eavesdroppers.

As he knew he would, Ewing found the team undergoing changes. Griffith's first move, within days of taking over, was to dispatch Ewing's longtime battery mate, Admiral Schlei, to New York as part of a three-cornered deal that sent Roger Bresnahan to St. Louis, where he would take over as manager of the Cardinals. The Reds acquired pitchers Ed Karger and Art Fromme, and Griffith made it clear that he wasn't afraid to make a bold move. In disposing of Schlei, Griffith committed himself to John Ganzel's nemesis, Larry McLean, as the Reds' No. 1 catcher.

For good or ill, Larry McLean was everything Admiral Schlei was not. Where Schlei was short and stocky, McLean was one of the biggest men in baseball, 6-feet-5 and nearly 230 pounds. Where Schlei was a singles hitter who batted as high as .250 only once in his major league career, McLean had the reputation of a slugger. Where Schlei was a quiet, unobtrusive personality, McLean had an "ingrained weakness for the merry-go-round of life"[17] and a propensity for attracting attention, wanted or not, both on the field and off.

As a player, Schlei was conceded to be "a hard-working and conscientious fellow," but little more.[18] McLean, despite an uneven record that kept him bouncing between the majors and the minors for six years before he stuck with the Reds, was universally acknowledged to have the makings of a star. Schlei was known in Cincinnati as "Old Faithful."[19] McLean had muffed earlier opportunities in his career because he "did not lead an athletic life and made a bluff at playing ball."[20]

John Bannerman McLean was born in Fredericton, New Brunswick. His family called him Jack, but he became known in baseball as Larry after someone detected a facial resemblance to Cleveland's Napoleon "Larry" Lajoie. McLean grew up in Cambridge, Massachusetts, where, he liked to tell reporters, he went through Harvard University—"in 10 seconds flat one morning when the janitor wasn't looking."[21] John McGraw listed McLean among the five most picturesque characters he had encountered in baseball.[22] He was a snappy dresser with a vocabulary, it was said, that would make a pirate blush. As a minor leaguer, he survived the San Francisco earthquake of 1906, when he was in the city with his Portland teammates for a series against the hometown Seals. McLean fancied himself a prizefighter and sometimes served as a sparring partner for the Canadian heavyweight Sandy Ferguson, a trial horse for such top battlers as Joe Jeannette, Sam Langford and Jack Johnson. After Johnson cemented his claim to the heavyweight championship by demolishing Jim Jeffries in 1910, McLean announced himself ready to take on Johnson and, as the writer telling the story put it, "bring the championship title back to the white race."[23]

No one, including McLean, seems to have taken the challenge seriously. It was probably issued merely to help a reporter fill space on a slow day. That's the kind of guy McLean was. A Cincinnati writer described him as "a witty, companionable sort of a fellow and a general favorite," at least when sober.[24] Though he drove managers to distraction, McLean delighted writers and fans wherever he went.

On the field, he was ponderously slow afoot but had a terrific arm. He was a dangerous bad-ball hitter described as being "of the Hans Wagner type."[25] From his earliest days in the big leagues, McLean was recognized as "a deucedly clever mitt artist."[26] Given a chance to play regularly in Cincinnati, he exhibited, at least sporadically, the potential to be "the greatest catcher in the business."[27]

But McLean's career was punctuated by repeated suspensions, occasional brawls and periodic scrapes with the law. McLean's problem was alcohol, and it was a problem he never overcame. Sobriety clauses were appended to his contracts even in the minor leagues; in 1906 his employers withheld $200 of McLean's pay until season's end, extracting a promise that he remain "sober and temperate and otherwise conduct [himself] in a gentlemanly manner, as not to bring the Portland Baseball Club, its members or management into ill repute." Manager Walt McCredie was appointed "the exclusive judge" of whether McLean lived up to his end of the bargain.[28]

McLean tried to control his demons. He preached, apparently sincerely, against the evils of alcohol and implored younger players not to drink.[29] He issued almost annual off-season assurances that he was "leading the simple life,"[30] and once pledged $1,000 against his promise to remain alcohol-free for one full year.[31] Even so, his own teammates once kicked him off a post-season barnstorming tour "because of his failure to keep the fairly straight and occasionally narrow path."[32]

Despite all of that, Damon Runyon was convinced that "drunk or sober, McLean was the superior of most of the backstops in the league."[33] Griffith gambled that McLean would respond to a regimen of hard work and responsibility. Even after McLean pulled a disappearing act on an early-season visit to New York, Griffith tapped him to take over as team captain when Hans Lobert requested some time off because of illness. McLean reacted enthusiastically and ran around "issuing his instructions to the boys not to stay out too late and to be sure to be early at morning practice."[34] When Griffith was down for a few days with a case of food poisoning, he chose McLean to serve as acting manager.

McLean had taken on an increasing share of the Reds' catching duties during the previous two seasons, but throughout 1908 Schlei remained Ewing's regular partner. Perhaps this was because Schlei was more familiar with the challenges of corralling the spitball, or perhaps he was considered a steadier presence generally behind the plate—a practical consideration, given the aggravations that often came with catching the unpredictable pitch. Or maybe it was just a matter of not wanting to break up an established and successful team. In any case, Schlei's departure probably did not affect Ewing as much as had earlier changes of battery mates. The record indicates no marked decline in Ewing's effectiveness when working with McLean as opposed to Schlei. By this time, Ewing was his own man and his own pitcher.

His own spitball pitcher, to be precise. And the spitball was still an issue in baseball. While there had as yet been no formal move to get rid of the spitter, there was continual "agitation" in the press[35] against the pitch that Chicago writer W.A. Phelon described as "sloppy, dirty and disgusting."[36] For its 1909 edition, *Spalding's Guide* surveyed sportswriters on the spitball, and most respondents came out in favor of a ban. Ren Mulford, who had followed Ewing's career from his earliest days in Cincinnati, said he found the pitch "creepy and 'slimy,'" and he went on record calling the spitball "a life preserver" which allowed its users "to remain in fast company longer than they could possibly have done" without it.[37]

Certainly Ewing's new manager was no fan of the spitball. There was some irony in this, given all the victories Clark Griffith had enjoyed in New York thanks to Jack Chesbro's wet one. The irony was compounded by the fact that in his own playing days, Griffith had been a master of all manner of dubious or outright illegal deliveries. He doctored balls with mud and scuffed them on his belt buckle. One of his favorite tricks was to scrape the ball against his spikes on the pretense of knocking the dirt out of them. Perhaps Griffith became disenchanted with the spitball as a result of Chesbro's heartbreaking wild pitch on the last day of the 1904 season. Or perhaps Griffith simply didn't like the spitball because he could never throw a good one. "You know, only pitchers who had natural speed could throw the spitball," Griffith told the *Washington Post*'s Shirley Povich many years later. "… I couldn't throw it because I wasn't a fastball pitcher."[38]

After leaving Cincinnati, Griffith would actively campaign for the abolition of the spitball. For now, as the new boss of the Reds, he set about making spitballers feel as unwelcome as possible. He dumped Marty O'Toole, who had pitched respectably in a brief trial with the Reds in 1908. Two years after O'Toole was released by Cincinnati, Pittsburgh's Barney Dreyfuss would shell out $22,500 for the spitballer, calling him "the most likely-looking twirler of the season."[39] Griffith's "no raises" policy antagonized spitballer Bob Spade, a 17-game winner as a rookie in 1908, prompting a holdout that lasted until mid-season. A year later, Griffith showed no interest in Larry Cheney, who would move on to Chicago and use his wet one to become a three-time 20-game winner for the Cubs.

"I don't like spit-pitchers," Griffith told Garry Herrmann. "The only use they are to a club is to use in pinches for relief duty."[40]

WHATEVER GRIFFITH THOUGHT of Ewing's pitching repertoire, one thing he didn't hold against him was his age. Any manager would have approved of Ewing's sober habits and quiet lifestyle. As he approached his 36th birthday, Long Bob was collecting dividends on a lifetime of temperance and moderation. In an era when few pitchers lasted much past the age of 30 and a pitcher of 35 was regarded as ancient, Ewing was forging into territory relatively few had explored before him. Ewing was the oldest player on the Reds' roster and before the season was much advanced, he would be the oldest full-time starting pitcher in the National League.[41]

Griffith knew that older players could be of value. "Take care of the old player," he advised. "Don't shove him back. An old head sometimes is needed to steady down the brilliant but youthful players."[42]

There would be a lot of "steadying down" to be done. The 1909 Reds would definitely be a youthful team, if not always a brilliant one.

The few prospects inherited from the Ganzel administration included some good ones. Dick Hoblitzell and Bob Bescher, who both debuted on the same day in September 1908, would be Reds regulars for several years; Bescher, a fleet-footed 200-pound outfielder, would lead the National League in stolen bases four consecutive years, inspiring flattering if over-enthusiastic comparisons with the American League's Ty Cobb. And now, after mostly marking time for a year under Ganzel, the Reds launched a full-scale talent search. Before the season was over, Griffith would try 45 players, 18 of them making their first appearances in the major leagues. Most of the time, the everyday lineup wouldn't include any player over 29. In one of Griffith's less successful moves, second baseman Miller Huggins, barely 30, would be benched in favor of 24-year-old Dick Egan. Egan's most memorable moment would occur May 8, when he came off second-best in a vicious post-game fistfight with Chicago's Joe Tinker.

On Opening Day, Pittsburgh's Howie Camnitz shut out the Reds 3-0. In retrospect, the most noteworthy feature of the afternoon was Cincinnati's pre-game concert which, for the first time, included a new song that was gaining popularity among baseball enthusiasts. With lyrics by vaudeville performer Jack Norworth and a tune by Tin Pan Alley composer Albert von Tilzer, "Take Me Out to the Ball Game" soon became a staple at ball-parks everywhere.[43]

The next day, Ewing evened the Reds' record by beating Vic Willis 7-2. A week later, when Ewing beat the Pirates again in their home opener[44]—pulling off an unassisted double play in the process—Cincinnati found itself in first place with a 6–2 record.

On May 11, Ewing beat the Boston Doves for the 100th victory of his major league career. The milestone passed without comment, and the game was otherwise unremarkable except as one of the least stylish wins Ewing ever claimed. The two teams combined for 10 errors in an exhibition the *Boston Herald* deemed "hardly worthy of major league talent."[45] Ewing was chased from the mound in the seventh inning, when the Doves scored five times, but Billy Campbell managed to put out the fire and Cincinnati held on for a 10–8 decision.

Other days were better, and some were worse. A good day was May 25, when Ewing held the Phillies without a hit until the seventh inning. He won the contest by the narrowest of margins, the only score coming on Dick Hoblitzell's solo home run off Tully Sparks. Ewing's next start, on May 30, was the worst of his career. He pitched to six St. Louis batters and didn't retire any of them. Griffith pulled him with the score 4–0, but the Cardinals scored seven more times before Ed Karger, the Reds' third pitcher, finally got out of the first inning. St. Louis laughed all the way to a 12–2 victory.

The next day Griffith tapped Ewing and Harry Gaspar, who couldn't get three outs between them against St. Louis, to try again before 10,000 home fans in a Memorial Day doubleheader against Chicago. This time both acquitted themselves well. Gaspar won the morning game and in the afternoon, Ewing allowed just five hits and two unearned runs in eight innings before being removed for a pinch hitter. The Cubs, behind the pitching of Ed Reulbach, won 3–2 in 11 innings. The victory was the first of 14 straight for Reulbach, who did not lose again for 2½ months.

Everywhere Ewing looked, there were imposing adversaries. He met the most imposing of them all on June 12 in Cincinnati. Christy Mathewson, seven years younger than Ewing, had broken into the National League two years sooner. The pitching mainstay and acknowledged golden boy of John McGraw's New York Giants, "Big Six" was the league's dominant hurler throughout Ewing's career. During the 11 years Ewing was in the league, Mathewson won 278 games, an average of more than 25 a season. No other pitcher in the major leagues won as many as 200 over the same span. Besides being one of the great pitchers of all time, Mathewson was a sort of real-life Frank Merriwell, often described as the first all-American boy. A dazzling combination of looks, grace and extraordinary talent, Matty also possessed a degree of refinement seldom encountered in baseball in the first decade of the 20th century. Journalist and historian Lloyd Lewis, who was a 20-year-old college student when he first saw Mathewson in 1911, described the pitcher as "all bone and muscle and princely poise," and he noticed something else as well—the "slow, lordly contempt" with which Mathewson regarded his opponents as they warmed up before the game.[46]

The game of June 12, 1909, would mark Ewing's last meeting with the legendary Matty. Ewing had won their first duel in 1903, ultimately prevailing by a 4–1 score on a day when the then 22-year-old Mathewson struck out 13 and held the Reds hitless through seven innings. Since then, despite some outstanding performances, Ewing's efforts had met with nothing but frustration. Mathewson had vanquished him five times in a row.

On the day of their final meeting, Ewing was a graybeard entering his twilight years in baseball. Mathewson, not yet 30, was in his prime. As usual, Mathewson was backed by the superior team. Ewing was facing much the same squad that had finished 25 games ahead of Cincinnati in 1908, including Fred Tenney, Art Devlin, Larry Doyle, Buck Herzog and ex-Red Al Bridwell. The lineup also included an impressive rookie catcher, Jack "Chief" Meyers, and a new cleanup hitter, outfielder Red Murray, obtained in the same trade that sent Admiral Schlei to New York and Roger Bresnahan to St. Louis.

Ewing rose to the occasion. Before a Saturday afternoon crowd of 10,000, he limited the Giants to six hits. He matched Mathewson almost pitch for pitch until the fifth inning. Then, with one out, New York loaded the bases with two hits and a walk, and Mathewson punched a single into center field to give himself a 1–0 lead.

That was enough. Matty "simply toyed with the boys from Redland," holding them to "four measly hits, scattered through as many innings."[47] When Cincinnati shortstop Tom Downey led off an inning with a double, Mathewson stifled the threat by methodically striking out Ewing, Bescher and Egan in succession. Ewing battled valiantly through eight innings before being lifted for a pinch hitter; the Giants nicked relief pitcher Jack Rowan for another run in the ninth and won the game 2–0.

The Cincinnati correspondent for *The Sporting News* credited Mathewson with "as pretty an exhibition of twirling as has been shown here ever."

"Ewing's work," the writer added, "… was pretty close to the Mathewson standard—and that's praise, indeed."[48]

On June 18, when Ewing handed the Philadelphia Phillies a convincing 4–1 defeat, the Reds were still holding onto third place in the standings. But unusual as it was to still be in the fight in mid-season, that was nothing to the spectacle that unfolded at League Park after the sun went down. It was another ballgame, and certainly as curious a one as Bob Ewing ever witnessed.

By this point in Ewing's career, the notion of playing baseball at night was neither entirely new nor particularly startling. The first experimental night game was played in Hull, Massachusetts, on September 2, 1880, less than a year after Thomas A. Edison first demonstrated his incandescent light. Major league operators soon recognized the potential goldmine that would open up if games could be played after dinner rather than on weekday afternoons, when most fans were at work. But overcoming the obstacles to make night baseball a reality was another matter. In the early years of the 20th century, the major leagues largely remained at a distance while nocturnal experiments were conducted by minor league clubs and touring teams with portable lighting systems.

Garry Herrmann was one of the first major league executives to seriously explore the possibilities of night baseball. In 1908 he hooked up with George F. Cahill, an inventor from Holyoke, Massachusetts, who thought he had a system that would work. Herrmann convinced some business acquaintances to form the Night Baseball Development Co., and invested $4,000 of his own money.[49] Three light towers were erected at the ballpark. One hundred feet tall and each supporting 14 arc lights, the structures were likened to giant oil derricks; Dode Paskert's life was suddenly complicated by having to run around the center-field tower in pursuit of long drives by opposing batters.

Plans for an October demonstration game were pushed back when it was determined that two more towers were needed. Herrmann did test the system on November 2, 1908, engaging "two scrub teams" to play a few innings under the lights in an otherwise empty ballpark. Even so, the unannounced switching on of the 42 big bell-shaped lamps created quite a commotion, and inquisitive denizens of the west side neighborhood got a considerable eyeful through knotholes in the fence.[50]

By June 1909, everything was in place for a full-scale trial. Herrmann initially planned to test the effectiveness of Cahill's system by having the Reds play an all-star collection of local amateurs under the lights. But at the last minute he got cold feet and decided not to risk his high-priced

"Bob Ewing is every inch a pitcher," sportswriter Ren Mulford observed, "and there are a good many inches of him." The dark blue uniform is what the Reds wore on the road in 1909. *Photo: National Baseball Hall of Fame Library, Cooperstown, New York.*

talent in a potentially dangerous experiment. Instead he used his fraternal connections to arrange a contest between two Elks lodges from Cincinnati and Newport, Kentucky.

A crowd reported at anywhere from 3,000 to 4,500 turned out for something they had never seen before. All the Reds were there, and most of the Phillies. When the lights came on, "an outburst of delighted surprise" rose from the spectators. There were five light towers "scattered about the field and above the grandstand so as to fill the airspace over the park with a strong light."[51] Cahill's breakthrough was the creation of a projector that would diffuse the illumination so he could light a large field without blinding players and spectators. The carbon filaments in the projectors were the size of baseball bats, and workers were stationed by the lamps to reload filaments as the carbon burned off. The system was powered by a huge 250-horsepower dynamo that Cahill had installed under the grandstand.[52] "The atmosphere was very smoky and thick," Ren Mulford reported, "so much so, indeed, that the light struck on it like a wall."[53]

The Cincinnati Elks won the game 8–5. Witnesses said there was adequate light on the infield, but anything hit to the outfield—either above the lights or on the ground—was an adventure. One ball was lost when the lights went out in left field. The 18 errors in the game might say more about the skill level of the participants than about the playing conditions, but the 24 strikeouts suggest that, contrary to comments from Larry McLean and others, visibility around home plate may have been less than ideal. "The game was a novelty and at times took on all the elements of diamond comedy," Mulford wrote.[54]

The star of the show was Emil Haberer, catcher for the Cincinnati team. The big, strapping son of a prosperous local carriage maker, Haberer was a perennial standout in the city's Saturday afternoon amateur league. He had shunned numerous contract offers from the Reds and other professional clubs, but for 10 years he had a standing agreement to help out the home team in emergencies—provided, that is, that the National League pennant race didn't impinge too severely on his business responsibilities.

"I've too good a business proposition to think of playing [baseball] professionally," Haberer told Ren Mulford while on an eastern trip with the Reds in 1903. "It was fortunate that I was able to break away for a few weeks during the dull season, but I couldn't entertain a thought of joining the regulars."[55] When the club returned to Cincinnati, the following note appeared in the *Commercial Tribune*:

> *Emil Haberer did not go to Chicago with the team. His vacation ended yesterday and he was forced to return to work at his father's carriage factory.*[56]

Between 1901 and 1909, Haberer appeared in 16 league games and was on the Reds' bench for several others. But he always returned to the family business of building carriages and later Cino automobiles, named for their hometown of Cincinnati, Ohio.

Under the lights, Haberer stroked a single, a triple and a home run. The latter resulted when all three outfielders lost sight of the drive, leaving only the second baseman hopelessly chasing the ball into the vast, gloomy recesses of right field. Despite such moments, the demonstration was at least a qualified success. The *Chicago Tribune* said that for the most part, the amateur players "seemed to perform as well as if it had been broad daylight."[57] The big leaguers in attendance indicated they could at least imagine the possibility of someday playing serious baseball under the lights. Herrmann, in a fit of enthusiasm, declared, "Night baseball has come to stay."[58]

In a more realistic next breath, Herrmann conceded that Cahill's system needed "some little further development."[59] That further development would require another 25 years. But the major leagues' first night game would be played on the same site on May 24, 1935, before a fairly dazzled crowd of 25,000. The contestants were the Cincinnati Reds and the Philadelphia Phillies, the same two teams that watched the 1909 exhibition, and among the spectators, by this time well into his 90s, was George F. Cahill, who lived just long enough to see his vision become a reality.

CAHILL'S GLOWING INNOVATION NOTWITHSTANDING, the Reds couldn't come up with enough bright ideas to keep themselves in the pennant race. Two days after the venture into nighttime baseball, they slipped into fourth place. The team continued to perform respectably, but the gap between Cincinnati and the serious contenders gradually widened into a yawning gulf. By July 30, when Ewing labored through "13 hard, nerve-racking innings"[60] to a 2–2 tie with Brooklyn, the Reds were 20 games out of first place.

Around this time, Brownie Burke showed up. Garry Herrmann had "discovered" him at a convention where Burke was serving as assistant drum major of a marching band from Helena, Montana, where he had sold newspapers on the street and worked as a page in the state Senate. Burke was 16 years old and according to contemporary descriptions stood 3 feet, 8 inches tall when he was "picked up and used as a watch charm" by Herrmann.[61] In Cincinnati, Burke filled a role that was common with many ballclubs of the time, that of official mascot. Mascots were sometimes pets but just as often humans, sometimes dwarfs or hunchbacks. The Reds' mascots in recent years, according to Ren Mulford, had ranged "from monkeys and bulldogs to cross-eyed pickaninnies."[62]

Outfitted in a uniform, Burke took on the duties of batboy, cheerleader and good-luck talisman. He remained with the club for six seasons and proved to be a clever and handy fellow, sometimes entrusted with missions in the line of espionage or diplomacy. He was said to have once helped the Reds gain a victory—and infuriated John J. McGraw—by taking one of the Giants' mascots to lunch and wheedling some of New York's signals out of him. Burke's talents proved useful again when Charles "Victory" Faust, the eccentric Kansas farmer whose stint as the Giants' mascot had fed his delusion that he was a major league pitcher, turned up in Cincinnati hoping to enlist Herrmann's aid in securing back pay. Burke was assigned the job of entertaining Faust and keeping him away from the chairman of the National Commission until he could be shunted out of town.[63]

Burke became a local celebrity. His connection with the Reds enabled him to meet three presidents and he eventually went on the stage in Cincinnati and elsewhere.[64] When the Orpheum Players stock company mounted a Cincinnati production of a play that had been a Broadway hit for Lillian Russell a couple years earlier, they drafted the Reds' mascot for the scene-stealing role of the slang-talking stable boy. Newspaper ads proclaimed, "*Wildfire*, with Brownie Burke as 'Bud.'"[65] According to the sportswriters, at least, he brought down the house every night.[66]

Initially, though, Burke didn't bring the Reds much luck. Shortly after his arrival, the team lost four straight to Philadelphia, dropping its record below .500. Days later, Larry McLean fractured his left kneecap in a home plate collision with Boston's Roy Thomas and was lost for the season. Soon, with the team facing a stretch of 12 games in eight days, another call went out for the emergency catcher, Emil Haberer.

Meanwhile, Ewing was having his own troubles. On August 18, matched against Chicago's formidable Ed Reulbach, Ewing held the Cubs to three hits—or, as they were classified in the *Chicago Tribune*, "two hits and a technicality"[67]—but he lost the game 1–0. The only run scored with two out in the bottom of the ninth inning on a wild pitch—a spitball in the dirt.

By mid-September, both Ewing and the Reds were in a struggle to finish the season above .500. As of September 23, when he committed three of the team's eight errors in a 12–2 drubbing by the Phillies, Ewing had lost three straight and his record had fallen to 10–12. Still, the *Cincinnati Enquirer* allowed, "Bob Ewing has done pretty well this year, losing a number of hard-luck contests. He is not through by any means."[68]

The day after that assessment appeared, Ewing beat Brooklyn 4–3, striking out nine and walking one. His performance was witnessed by only 600 thoroughly chilled home fans and was rather lightly passed over in the press accounts of a game that had other features of interest. One was a rare triple steal, pulled off by Brooklyn in the third inning. Another was the appearance of Lee Meyer, making his major league debut at shortstop for the Superbas. Meyer was a former member of Matty Schwab's grounds crew at League Park.

Schwab and his subordinates watched the game with divided loyalties, cheering Meyer as he rapped three singles. The Reds fell behind 2–0 in the early going but tied the score in the fifth inning and went ahead on Bob Bescher's sacrifice fly in the seventh. Ewing "improved as he went along and finished at a great clip,"[69] not allowing a runner to third base after the fourth inning. The three hits off Ewing were the only ones Meyer ever got in the big leagues. He went hitless in six subsequent games and never played in the majors again.

The Reds swept a doubleheader that day. A week later, on October 3, when they took the first half of another twin bill against St. Louis, they were assured of both a winning record (their first since 1905) and a first-division finish (their first since 1904). Clark Griffith celebrated by giving all his regulars the rest of the day off.

Griffith had been looking for an opportunity to conduct a little experiment and now, with no more goals to shoot for and only one more playing date on the schedule, he did it. For the second game of the St. Louis doubleheader, he drew up a lineup composed almost entirely of rookies. Of the eight position players, two were making their first major league appearances. Four others had been in the majors less than a month. The "veteran" of the group was second baseman Chappy Charles, a second-year big leaguer who had come to Cincinnati barely a month earlier in a trade for Mike Mowrey. Aside from Charles, the entire group had logged fewer than two dozen games in the big leagues.

Looking over this assortment of prospects and suspects, Griffith did a noble thing: Rather than subject one of his veteran hurlers to the ordeal that was likely to ensue, he penciled himself in to pitch. Six weeks shy of his 40th birthday, Griffith had been playing baseball since before some of his fresh-faced fielders were born, but he hadn't taken the mound in a major league game in two years and hadn't pitched with any regularity since 1906.

The results of Griffith's experiment were not surprising. They also were not pretty. According to Charlie Zuber, the rookies muffed fly balls, made wild throws and "allowed base hits to scoot past them without so much as saying 'howdy.'"[70] The Cardinals piled up 11 hits, stole five bases and took advantage of as many errors. When the game was mercifully halted because of darkness after only six innings, the Reds trailed 8–1.

Two of Griffith's youngsters survived this sink-or-swim baptism and went on to what would qualify as successful careers. The teenage third baseman, Al "Cozy" Dolan,[71] played seven years in the majors and was later a coach for McGraw's Giants. First baseman Wheeler "Doc" Johnston lasted until 1922 in the big leagues, playing more than 1,000 games. The rest disappeared quickly and in most cases permanently. Of the seven rookies, only center fielder Arthur "Swat" McCabe played even (barely) a dozen games for Cincinnati.[72]

EWING PROBABLY DIDN'T SEE Griffith's gamble with the kids. Once his plans were set for the final days, Griffith allowed some of his veterans to go home early. Long Bob didn't pitch in the last week of the season.

The 1909 season wasn't yet over, but already Griffith was focused on 1910 and beyond. When Ewing boarded the train for Wapakoneta at the end of his eighth season with the Reds, he surely expected to be part of whatever future Clark Griffith was mapping out. Though his record for 1909 was lackluster, Ewing had tied for second on the staff in games started and third in victories; for the seventh straight year, he had withstood the strain of National League competition for more than 200 innings. With an athlete's typical self-confidence, he undoubtedly agreed with the *Enquirer*'s expectation that he "should be a valuable man next year."[73] He probably paid little attention to the rumblings of change that began making their way into print in December. Over the years, trade rumors had linked Ewing with every team in the league, but the rumors never came to anything. Cincinnati was Long Bob's baseball home, and by now he probably thought the association was likely to continue as long as he remained in the game.

Clark Griffith's thinking, however, was moving in a different direction. He was convinced that if the Reds could upgrade their pitching, they could be pennant contenders. Just before Christmas, Griffith tossed a line into the water to see if anybody would bite. He asked waivers on Ewing. But when the only offers received were for cash, not pitchers, Ewing's name was withdrawn from the waiver list. By mid-January, it appeared the trade winds would again peter out and Ewing would remain in Cincinnati.

But Griffith kept tacking into the wind and on January 21, 1910, headlines in two cities heralded a major shift in Bob Ewing's well-ordered life. The Reds had packaged him up with a young pitching prospect, Ad Brennan, and shipped them both to Philadelphia in exchange for Frank "Fiddler" Corridon, another spitballer, and the erstwhile Giant-killer, Harry Coveleski.

As he passed his 37th birthday and embarked on his 14th year in baseball, Ewing would face the challenges of finding his place in a new organization, proving himself to new teammates and acquainting himself with a new city.

1   *The Sporting News,* March 30, 1907.
2   *Sporting Life,* Oct. 3, 1908.
3   Griffith's biographer credits him with signing 39 National Leaguers for the AL. Another student of this chapter in baseball history pegs the number at "upwards of 50." See Ted Leavengood, *Clark Griffith: The Old Fox of Washington Baseball* (Jefferson, N.C.: McFarland and Co. Inc., 2011), p. 40; and Warren N. Wilbert, *The Arrival of the American League: Ban Johnson and the 1901 Challenge to the National League Monopoly* (Jefferson, N.C.: McFarland and Co. Inc., 2007), p. 28.
4   Lee Allen, *The Cincinnati Reds: An Informal History* (New York: G.P. Putnam's Sons, 1948), pp. 90-91.
5   *Cincinnati Enquirer,* reprinted in *The Sporting News,* Nov. 12, 1908.
6   *The Sporting News,* July 2, 1908.
7   Ren Mulford, *Sporting Life,* Sept. 16, 1911.
8   William Curran, *Strikeout: A Celebration of the Art of Pitching* (New York: Crown Publishers Inc., 1995), p. 93.
9   Some secondary sources date this nickname to as early as 1894, when Griffith was 24 years old, but it seems likely to have been acquired considerably later than that. It was not used in newspapers during Griffith's first year in Cincinnati, when he was 39 and prematurely gray.
10 *Sporting Life,* March 27, 1909.
11 *The Sporting News,* Feb. 4, 1909.
12 Henry W. Thomas, *Walter Johnson: Baseball's Big Train* (Washington, D.C.: Phenom Press, 1995), pp. 92-93; see also pp. 169 and 201.
13 Tim Murnane, quoted in *Sporting Life,* Dec. 9, 1911.
14 *The Sporting News,* Jan. 21, 1909.
15 *Ibid.,* March 4, 1909.
16 *Ibid.*
17 Damon Runyon, *Boston American,* undated clipping, March 1921.
18 *Sporting Life,* June 23, 1906.
19 *Ibid.,* June 12, 1909.
20 *The Sporting News,* Sept. 12, 1907.
21 Walter Trumbull, unidentified newspaper clipping, August 1913.
22 The other four were Rube Waddell, Bugs Raymond, Ossee Schreckengost and McGraw's old Baltimore teammate Steve Brodie, who was known to recite Shakespeare in the outfield. John J. McGraw, *My 30 Years in Baseball* (New York: Arno Press, 1974 reprint of 1923 original), p. 25.
23 Unidentified newspaper clipping, 1910.
24 *Cincinnati Commercial Tribune,* reprinted in *The Sporting News,* April 7, 1910.
25 *Cincinnati Enquirer,* reprinted in *The Sporting News,* Feb. 6, 1908.
26 *Sporting Life,* July 9, 1904.
27 *Cincinnati Enquirer,* Dec. 10, 1911.
28 *The Sporting News,* March 10, 1906.
29 Runyon, *op. cit.*
30 *The Sporting News,* Dec. 19, 1907.
31 *Ibid.,* Nov. 19, 1908.
32 *Ibid.,* Nov. 9, 1911.
33 Runyon, *op. cit.*
34 *Cincinnati Enquirer,* June 19, 1909.
35 *The Sporting News,* Oct. 15, 1908.
36 John B. Foster, ed., *Spalding's Baseball Guide, 1909* (New York: American Sports Publishing Co., 1909), p. 47.

37   *Ibid.*, p. 45. Charlie Zuber, another Cincinnati writer who had followed Ewing's career, made the same point.

38   *The Sporting News*, April 6, 1955.

39   *Sporting Life*, Aug. 5, 1911.

40   Clark Griffith, letter to August Herrmann, March 25, 1910. The letter is on file in the A. Bartlett Giamatti Research Center at the National Baseball Hall of Fame.

41   The long-running Pittsburgh tandem of Sam Leever and Deacon Phillippe were both older than Ewing, but after 1908, neither ever started more than 13 games in a season in the big leagues. In the American League, Cy Young, still a force to be reckoned with at 42, was in a class by himself.

42   *The Sporting News*, March 30, 1907.

43   John Erardi and Greg Rhodes, *Opening Day: Celebrating Cincinnati's Baseball Holiday* (Cincinnati: Road West Publishing, 2004), p. 198.

44   This was the Pirates' last opener at Exposition Park, where baseball had been played at least since 1878. Pittsburgh's magnificent new concrete and steel baseball stadium with the double-decked grandstand, Forbes Field, would open on June 30. Three Rivers Stadium was later erected on the site of Exposition Park. See Philip J. Lowry, *Green Cathedrals* (Cooperstown, N.Y.: Society for American Baseball Research, 1986), pp. 71-72.

45   *Boston Herald*, May 12, 1909.

46   Lloyd Lewis, "Christy Mathewson," in John P. Carmichael, *et al.*, *My Greatest Day in Baseball: 47 Dramatic Stories by 47 Stars* (New York: A.S. Barnes and Co., 1945), p. 210.

47   *New York Times*, June 13, 1909.

48   *The Sporting News*, June 17, 1909. Despite a 1-6 record in their starts against each other, Ewing generally pitched well against Mathewson. Long Bob completed six of seven starts, struck out twice as many as he walked and compiled a 2.40 earned run average – better than the figure for his career. Mathewson, typically, was even better. He struck out 48, walked only seven, allowed an average of just 5.6 hits every nine innings and posted an ERA of 1.62. After his initial defeat, he was overwhelming, 6-0 with a 1.21 ERA. Ewing need not have felt embarrassed by his inability to beat Mathewson. As of June 12, 1909, Matty had beaten Cincinnati nine times in a row in a run that started June 17, 1908. His winning streak against the Reds would extend over three years and reach 22 straight before it was finally broken on Aug. 19, 1911. Over his career, Mathewson beat the Reds more times than any other team he faced. See Ronald A. Mayer, *Christy Mathewson: A Game-by-Game Profile of a Legendary Pitcher* (Jefferson, N.C.: McFarland and Co. Inc., 1993), pp. 340 and 342.

49   David Pietrusza, *Lights On! The Wild Century-Long Saga of Night Baseball* (Lanham, Md.: Scarecrow Press Inc., 1997), pp. 28-29.

50   *Sporting Life*, Nov. 14, 1908.

51   *Ibid.*, June 26, 1909.

52   Pietrusza, *op. cit.*, p. 31; see also *The Sporting News*, Oct. 24, 1935.

53   *Sporting Life*, June 26, 1909.

54   *Ibid.*

55   *Ibid.*, Aug. 22, 1903.

56   *Cincinnati Commercial Tribune*, Aug. 29, 1903.

57   *Chicago Tribune*, June 19, 1909.

58   *Sporting Life*, June 26, 1909.

59   *Ibid.*

60   *Cincinnati Post*, July 31, 1909.

61   *Sporting Life*, Dec. 23, 1911.

62 *Ibid.*, Aug. 21, 1909.

63 Gabriel Schechter, *Victory Faust: The Rube Who Saved McGraw's Giants* (Los Gatos, Calif.: Charles April Publications, 2000), pp. 136, 232-33.

64 Frank J. "Brownie" Burke made his vaudeville debut in Cincinnati. The high point of his theatrical career was touring with Maude Adams in *Quality Street* in 1915. Perhaps the most remarkable chapter in his brief but busy life came during World War I, when he talked his way into the Army (despite being at least six inches shy of the minimum height requirement) and served 12 months doing clerical work in Europe. On his return, Burke was widely hailed as the smallest man sent overseas with the American Expeditionary Forces. He died in California in 1931, at age 38. See *Bakersfield Californian*, Nov. 10, 1931; *Montana Standard*, Nov. 14, 1931.

65 *Cincinnati Enquirer*, Dec. 3, 1911.

66 See for instance Ren Mulford's rave review in *Sporting Life*, Dec. 23, 1911. At least one Cincinnati sportswriter was actually qualified to assess Burke's performance. For much of his time at the *Times-Star*, Charlie Zuber served as the baseball writer in the summer and the theatrical critic in the winter.

67 *Chicago Tribune*, Aug. 19, 1909; one of Chicago's hits was awarded to Solly Hofman when his ground ball struck a base runner. This game also marked Reulbach's first start after the end of his 14-game winning streak, which had been snapped by the Giants on Aug. 14. During the streak, Reulbach pitched five shutouts and permitted only 14 runs.

68 *Cincinnati Enquirer*, Sept. 26, 1909.

69 *Ibid.*, Sept. 28, 1909.

70 *The Sporting News*, Oct. 7, 1909.

71 Not to be confused with outfielder Patrick Henry "Harry" Dolan, also known as "Cozy," who played for Cincinnati from 1903 to 1905.

72 Among the others, shortstop Roy "Slippery" Ellam had another brief trial with Pittsburgh nine years later, when he was 32 years old, and right fielder Del Young, after playing two games for Cincinnati in 1909, got back to the majors for 92 more in the Federal League in 1914-15. Left fielder Claire Patterson, who attracted the Reds' attention by winning the Western Association batting title in 1909, was on the verge of a second shot at the big leagues with the St. Louis Browns four years later when he died of tuberculosis at age 25; see *Los Angeles Times*, Jan. 20 and March 29, 1913.

73 *Cincinnati Enquirer*, Sept. 26, 1909.

"He looked strange in the gray uniform of the Phillies but the fans did not forget his long service here and gave him a *very* glad hand when he came to bat for the first time."

—JACK RYDER[1]

CHAPTER 12

Two Years in Another Town

THE DEAL WAS WIDELY HAILED as "one of the biggest baseball trades of the winter,"[2] and Bob Ewing was by far the most solidly established player involved. Frank Corridon, 29, in the big leagues since 1904, had reached his peak with an 18–14 record for Philadelphia in 1907 but his win totals had declined annually since then. Ad Brennan was a 22-year-old left-hander whose pitching career to date consisted of less than two full seasons in the minor leagues, mostly with teams in his native Kansas. Ewing, after eight seasons, owned half again as many major league victories as the other three pitchers combined. But most of the publicity about the trade centered on Harry Coveleski, the young lefty whose late-season heroics in 1908 had played such a large part in denying the Giants a pennant.

Since then, the fates had not been kind to Coveleski. The celebrity from his Giant-killing exploits still trailed after him, but had become more of an encumbrance than a mark of distinction. Going into 1909 with sky-high expectations that he would be both a major pitching star and a moneymaking fan attraction, he soon developed shoulder problems from overwork and stumbled to a meager 6–10 record for the fifth-place Phillies. Just like that, at the tender age of 23, Coveleski had worn out his welcome in the City of Brotherly Love. In bidding him farewell, the *Philadelphia Record* dismissed Coveleski as "a big disappointment"[3] and the *Inquirer*, while allowing that the young man might still bounce back, didn't seem distressed to see him go: "Coveleski was not the howling success last summer that he was in the fall of 1908"[4]—or, the writer hardly needed to add, that had been expected in 1909. The *Evening Bulletin* concluded that the Phillies had received two potentially valuable hurlers "for one known quantity and a pitcher who had outlived his usefulness."[5]

For his part, Coveleski was glad to go. He told a reporter he was pleased with the trade and added that "he had a couple of enemies on the Philadelphia team … [who] were responsible for him not making a better showing."[6]

The Cincinnati papers expressed delight at the acquisition of "the huge Hun"[7] (though at 6 feet tall and 180 pounds, Coveleski was not as tall as Ewing, and only a few pounds heavier). "Griff Uncorks a Great Trade," blared a headline in the *Commercial Tribune*.[8] Charlie Zuber, *The Sporting News'* man in Cincinnati, reported "much joy … spread over the local baseball colony." Doping out the exchange, Zuber judged Corridon-for-Ewing about even, leaving Coveleski-for-Brennan "all to the peaches for the locals."[9]

Clark Griffith's take on the deal was that Corridon was an improvement on Ewing, and as for the Reds' other newcomer, Griffith said, with a reasonable workload and some refinement of his control, "I think that he will deliver the goods."[10] A recollection from trainer Mike Martin suggested the manager had higher ambitions for Coveleski. Martin said that when Griffith first looked over Coveleski in 1908, he remarked, "I'd like to take hold of that fellow. I believe I could make a great pitcher out of him."[11]

Around Cincinnati, there were many kind words for Ewing but no profound dismay at his departure. Throughout the years, Ewing had been, in the approving words of one writer, "as tractable a ballplayer as there is in the business."[12] At the end of his Cincinnati run, he was more respected for his personal qualities than idolized for his pitching triumphs. The *Commercial Tribune* pronounced him "one of the most popular twirlers that ever wore a Red uniform."[13] Ren Mulford called him "one of the best pitchers Cincinnati ever had,"[14] but lauded him more vigorously as a player who "has … always taken 100 percent good care of himself … and has husbanded his resources"—the implication being that they were limited—"by living the kind of life that really pays best."[15] Jack Ryder, while praising Ewing as "a hard and willing worker," added that he had "been very unlucky … for some time, pitching a lot of close games, which he lost by small scores."[16]

Fans surveyed about the trade acknowledged some regret at Ewing's passing. "A grand fellow and a good pitcher," one called him. But most went along with the prevalent view in the press that after eight years in Cincinnati, Ewing might "show new life" in new surroundings—and that, in Coveleski, the team had obtained a man who might well develop into a star.[17]

"Faithful followers of the Reds will be sorry to see Long Bob Ewing go," Ryder concluded, "in spite of the fact that he has not been a big winner for a number of years."[18]

What Ewing thought about being bartered away is difficult to discern. He doesn't seem to have spoken to a reporter at the time. Having no say in the matter, and regardless how he might have felt privately, he apparently took the diplomatic course of telling his new employers that he was happy to be coming to Philadelphia.[19] Some Philadelphia papers reported that he had become "dissatisfied" in Cincinnati and requested to be traded.[20] But Jack Ryder, who was closer to the situation, wrote later that Ewing had hoped to finish his career close to home and was "pretty sore" when informed of the transaction.[21]

A somewhat uncertain welcome awaited Ewing in Philadelphia. Red Dooin, the recently-appointed manager of the Phillies, learned of the trade while completing a vaudeville engagement in Boston. A reporter who tracked him down there got the impression that the deal had been consummated without Dooin's knowledge. The manager "was a bit surprised" and all he would say for publication was that his club "got none the worse of the deal."[22]

Though Dooin later denied that the swap was made behind his back, such a move would not have been out of character for the Phillies' new president, Horace Fogel. A former sportswriter who had bounced around several Philadelphia papers, Fogel had once had a brief, chaotic tenure as manager of the pre-McGraw New York Giants. Contemporaries described Fogel as a man with "a chronic dry whistle"[23] and a tendency to talk "just a trifle too much."[24] Fellow scribe Fred Lieb said that, like most newspapermen of the day, Fogel "lived from one payday to the next."[25] So it came as a shock after the Phillies were sold in November 1909—for the third time in seven years—to learn that the new man in charge was none other than Horace Fogel.

No one believed Fogel could come up with $350,000 to buy a ballclub on his own. Rumors immediately surfaced that he was merely a front for out-of-town money. Reporters soon sniffed out a connection to Chicago. They asserted that the Cubs' Charles Webb Murphy, seeking a reliable ally in league politics, had persuaded his own sponsor, Charles P. Taft, to set up Fogel with the Philadelphia franchise.[26] That is precisely what had happened. But for the moment, Fogel was busily striving to demonstrate that he was the one and only power behind the Phillies. One of his first moves, two weeks before the Ewing trade, was to fire manager Billy Murray and replace him with Dooin, the Phillies' veteran catcher.

"Billy Murray is a nice fellow," Fogel said. "I like him, but he didn't put enough fight into the club."[27]

Fogel was full of ideas to breathe new life into his team. He had a newsman's nose for publicity and quickly set out to secure the goodwill of his former confreres. To make their work easier, he sometimes wrote up his own press releases. He also installed a switchboard in the press box and telephones in the clubhouse and on the Phillies' bench. He tried to persuade the writers to drop the club's longstanding nicknames and to refer to the team instead as the Live Wires. That name sneaked into print occasionally, but when scribes reached for an alternative to "Phillies" or "Quakers," they more often settled on "Dooin's Daisies." Fogel, once accused of approaching the game in "Barnum & Bailey fashion,"[28] even bought an elephant from a bankrupt circus, thinking it could be trained to cover the infield with a tarpaulin when it rained. According to W.A. Phelon, the pachyderm proved a willing enough worker, but the first time it was tried out, the two-ton beast's huge feet sank into the soggy turf with every step and nearly ruined the playing field.[29]

Fogel's reign ultimately came to a bad end. In a moment of indiscretion (likely fueled by alcohol), he accused National League umpires of favoring the New York Giants and ex-Giant Roger Bresnahan, then manager of the St. Louis Cardinals, of lying down against his former mates. Fogel was tried by a court made up of the other National League owners, with Cincinnati's Julius Fleischmann serving as presiding judge. After 12 hours of testimony over two days, Fogel was found guilty of "making charges against the integrity and intentions" of the umpires and league president Thomas J. Lynch, and kicked out of the league.[30]

But when Ewing joined the Phillies, Fogel was running the show. Regardless what Dooin might have thought of the trade, or of his boss, the manager did his best to put a good face on the situation.

"As a catcher I think I ought to know when a pitcher is good," Dooin told Francis C. Richter, "and I certainly think Ewing is going to win some games for us."[31]

Charles Sebastian "Red" Dooin was another of the numerous Cincinnatians in baseball. The son of a cabinetmaker, he had attended the same high school as Admiral Schlei and played one summer for Fleischmanns' Mountain Tourists. Dooin also possessed a fine Irish tenor, which earned him the nickname the Scarlet Thrush; he was regarded as one of the few ballplayers who could have made a full-time living in vaudeville without any assistance from his parallel celebrity as an athlete. On the field, he was described as a man who could talk, smile and fight all at the same time.[32] At 30, the 165-pound Dooin had been the Phillies' regular catcher for eight years. He had been familiar with Ewing longer than that, having first played against him in the Western League in 1901.

Arriving in Southern Pines, North Carolina, for spring training, Long Bob had hardly unpacked his suitcase before he was denying rumors of a sore arm.[33] Such talk was nothing new for Ewing. Two weeks later he had a scare of an entirely different and completely unexpected kind. The Phillies were in bed shortly after 2 a.m. one morning when lightning hit their hotel, snapping the flagstaff off the cupola, ripping a hole in the roof and striking a gas pipe directly over the bed occupied by pitcher Jim Moroney. Almost miraculously, no one was injured, but rookie pitcher Louis Schettler, one of Moroney's roommates, was so badly shaken that he didn't speak for two hours.

Asleep in the next room, Ewing was showered with plaster from the ceiling. Startled ballplayers spilled into the hallway, wondering what had happened. Moroney, however, was unfazed. Sounding every bit the left-hander he was, he spelled out the lesson of the night's events: "Even the lightning can't hit me," he said.[34]

That was the extent of the drama for Ewing during spring training. By the end of March, when the team made its last stop on the northward journey back to Philadelphia, he hadn't pitched in three weeks. Dooin announced that "if weather conditions are favorable," he would let Ewing test his wing in an exhibition game against the Washington Senators.[35]

But first, while in the nation's capital, the Phillies arranged a visit to the White House. Its occupant at the time was a big baseball fan, in more ways than one. Cincinnati native William Howard Taft, half-brother of the Phillies' behind-the-scenes backer Charles P. Taft, had promoted the game in the Philippines while serving as governor general there after the Spanish-American War. Growing up in the Cincinnati suburb of Mount Auburn in the 1870s, Taft had been an enthusiastic amateur player.[36] During his presidential years, it was not unusual to see Taft's 300-pound bulk settled in the box seats in Washington or, when he traveled, at other major league parks. A reporter who observed the first fan at a Chicago Cubs game during the first months of his presidency wrote that Taft was "attentive and appreciative and exhibited enthusiasm over plays out of the ordinary."[37] Two weeks after meeting the Phillies, Taft took part in a presidential "first" that firmly solidified the connection between national politics and the national pastime. On April 14, 1910, as a movie camera whirred and news photographers clicked their shutters, Taft removed his overcoat, kid gloves and silk top hat and threw out the first ball for the Opening Day game between the Senators and the Philadelphia Athletics.

According to one sports-page account, the Phillies' audience with the president took place on "one of his particularly busy days, and some important callers had to be sidetracked" so Taft could squeeze in a few minutes with the ballplayers.[38] There were 20 team members in the party; Horace Fogel and a few others were accompanied by their wives. The president shook hands with the players as they were introduced. As a Cincinnatian, Taft most likely recognized Ewing and was familiar with his career. After "an exchange of pleasantries conducted in the language of the fan," Taft offered "a few words … to the ladies."[39] As the players prepared to leave, he "complimented manager Dooin on the splendid condition of his team."[40]

That afternoon, Ewing tossed the first five innings of a 4–1 victory over the Senators. He allowed only two hits and the Philadelphia writers were of the opinion only one of those—a third-inning double by Clyde Milan—was "clean." Also while in Washington, Ewing renewed acquaintances with former Cincinnati sportswriter J. Ed Grillo, now with the *Washington Post*. During their conversation, Ewing dropped a bombshell: He informed Grillo that he had abandoned the spitball.

"I don't think that I will ever use a spitball again unless they drive me to it," Ewing said. "… I am through with it unless these batters force me to go back to it."

"While I was using that delivery, I had a lot of trouble with my curveball," he added, "and now that I am not using it my curveball is breaking fine and I am not having any trouble with my arm."[41]

Critics of the spitball had claimed for years that the pitch was responsible for ruining many pitchers' arms. Ewing had heard that song from, among others, his previous manager, Clark Griffith. Three months before trading Ewing to Philadelphia, Griffith asserted, "All pitchers, five years ago, were 'spitball crazy,' especially the youngsters. … Many promising cubs ignored curves and speedy straight balls altogether. A few succeeded, but hundreds ruined their arms and sunk into oblivion."[42] In Philadelphia, Red Dooin sang a similar tune. "Very few pitchers have any sort of control over the thing," Dooin said. Presumably speaking from painful experience, he added that the spitter was "really harder on the catcher than on the batter."[43]

After relying heavily on the pitch for more than five years, Ewing seemed to have bought into the various arguments against it. "The trouble with the spitball," he told Grillo, "is that when you deliver the ball, it slides off your fingers and there is no resistance, hence it is very wearing on your arm."[44]

Regardless of such concerns, Ewing's spitball didn't remain on hiatus for long. The batters may have "driven him back to it" within a week after the Washington exhibition. Philadelphia fans got their first look at Ewing in his new uniform on April 6, during the pre-season series between the Phillies and Connie Mack's Athletics. Dooin, having decided to "use the spring series to experiment" rather than worry about winning,[45] left Ewing in the box for an entire game while the A's enjoyed eight innings of batting practice. Ewing served up 11 hits, issued five walks and absorbed a 6–1 beating. Frank Baker, leading off the third inning for the Mackmen, "measured one of Ewing's fast ones just right" and hit it over the right-field wall. It sailed clear out of Shibe Park and "broke up a party of roller skaters in 20th Street."[46] Evidently Ewing's "fast ones" alone weren't enough to tame major league hitters, and his curveball provided only limited help, if that. Few spitballers possessed outstanding curveballs, and any pitcher who could throw a good curve without undue strain on his arm had little reason to bother developing a spitter. By mid-season, a closely observed caricature by the famous writer and cartoonist Edgar Wolfe—whose work appeared in the sporting pages of the *Philadelphia Inquirer* under the appropriately athletic *nom de plume* "Jim Nasium"—depicted Ewing with two large globules of saliva dripping from the first two fingers of his pitching hand.[47]

Because extensive renovations to the Phillies' park were not yet completed, the entire pre-season series was played on the Athletics' grounds. When Ewing got his first look at his freshly remodeled new home, he couldn't have been pleased. The Phillies' Huntingdon Street Grounds (to be renamed the Baker Bowl a few years later, after still another change of ownership) still had the distinctive main entrance surmounted by battlements like those of a medieval castle. But inside, the playing field had been substantially altered, and not in a way to give any comfort to pitchers. In the process of expanding existing bleachers and adding new ones, increasing the park's seating capacity to 18,800, the left-field line had been chopped from 390 feet to 335. The distance to the right-field corner, never more than a pop fly from home plate, remained just over 270 feet.[48] Compared to the wide open spaces of Cincinnati's League Park, the place was positively claustrophobic.

Of all the men who were regulars in the National League when Ewing debuted in 1902, no more than two dozen were still front-line players in the major leagues in 1910. Like many aging veterans, Ewing seemed to be a distinct afterthought in his manager's plans. The Phillies got off to a flying 7–1 start, filling the sports columns with paeans of praise for pitchers George McQuillan, Lew Moren and Earl "Crossfire" Moore. The season was nearly two weeks old before Long Bob made his first appearance, surviving a shaky start for a come-from-behind 5–4 victory over Boston. His best review came from the *Public Ledger*, which termed his performance "fair."[49]

The worm began to turn in early May, when Dooin sent McQuillan and Moore home from Cincinnati for breaking training. In McQuillan's case, it was the first of a series of disciplinary actions that would ultimately sideline him for much of the season. Ewing, meanwhile, had won his second start, holding the Giants hitless until the seventh inning and lifting the Phillies into a tie for first place. He soon followed with a three-hit shutout over Pittsburgh, banging out four straight singles himself and knocking in two of Philadelphia's four runs. He was impressive again on Memorial Day, matching New York's Red Ames for 16 innings only to lose 4–3.

By that time, Ewing had experienced his first brush with his former teammates, inaugurating perhaps the most trying series of games in his career. On May 10, matched against Jack Rowan on a Tuesday afternoon in Cincinnati, Ewing found himself saddled with two runs by the time he got his first out. The first batter he faced, Bob Bescher, smacked Ewing's 3–2 pitch to the distant right-field corner for an inside-the-park home run. Dode Paskert followed with a walk, went to third on Dick Hoblitzell's single and scored on Mike Mitchell's sacrifice fly.

Ewing settled down after that and didn't allow another run, and the Phillies tied the score in the fifth inning. When they mounted a rally in the top of the sixth, Dooin called on Joe Ward to bat for Ewing. Ward delivered a two-run double and subsequently scored, keying an outburst that gave Philadelphia a comfortable 6–2 lead. But the Reds climbed all over relief pitcher Earl Moore and came back for an 8–6 victory.

"Bob Ewing pitched grand ball after the first inning," Jack Ryder told readers of the *Cincinnati Enquirer*, adding, "If Ewing had been left in the game, the Quakers would have had a much better chance to win."[50]

The game, with its heightened tensions and manifold frustrations, typified much of what followed in Ewing's battles with Cincinnati. Before the season ended, he made six starts against his former team, and if we can believe half of what we are told by the sportswriters on the scene—Jack Ryder in particular—the contests contained enough drama to fill an opera.

The visits to Cincinnati were particularly stressful. The fans were responsive; on Ewing's first appearance against the Reds, Cincinnati admirers gave him "a fine traveling bag and a handsome umbrella,"[51] and the next time he pitched at League Park, friends from Auglaize County presented him with "a large and valuable diamond pin."[52] Such gestures of appreciation seemed only to add to Ewing's discomfiture. On the latter occasion, Ryder wrote, "He was embarrassed ... by the presence of large numbers of rooters from his hometown" and the rays from the diamond "dazzled him so that he could not locate the plate."[53]

"Perhaps ... he was the victim of a presentation speech," the *Commercial Tribune*'s Myron Townsend observed on the same day. "Such affairs are hoodoos to the stoutest-hearted athlete."[54]

Ewing pulled out all the stops against the Reds. More than once he employed a "quick return" to slip over a sneaky strike on an inattentive batsman. The success of this tactic never failed to annoy Jack Ryder, who railed against batters who spent too much time "arguing with the umpire or admiring the scenery in the grandstand" rather than tending to business.[55] Another time Ewing was caught attempting to mutilate the ball by grinding it under his spikes.

The former Red badly wanted to beat Cincinnati and when he couldn't, it galled him. He "retired somewhat crestfallen"[56] from one failed effort and, according to Ryder, left the field with tears in his eyes on another afternoon when he was removed from the game in the middle of an inning.[57]

At best, Ewing had an up and down campaign against his former mates. The high point came June 16 in Philadelphia, when the "renowned plowman and stock breeder"[58] dominated the Reds, permitting just six singles and allowing no runner past first base in a 10–0 rout. "Long Bob Gives Old Pals Handsome Coat of Purest Whitewash," exclaimed a headline in the *Cincinnati Post*.[59] Even so, the *Times-Star* dismissed Ewing's performance as "a surprise of the most bewildering order."[60] By the time he had faced the Reds three times, Myron Townsend was satisfied that Clark Griffith "made no mistake in letting Long Bob go."[61]

THE USUAL EXCITEMENT of the baseball season was eclipsed for a few weeks in the early summer of 1910 by something novel and, to many, terrifying. Tradition held that the approach of Halley's Comet was always "preceded or accompanied … by war, bloodshed, pestilence and calamity."[62] Even in the enlightened 20th century, and despite the calm and reasoned assurances of responsible scholars that there was "not the remotest possibility of danger,"[63] anticipation of the celestial visitor rose to something like hysteria. In a magazine article titled "The Menace in the Skies," a Pennsylvania college professor resurrected the prediction of an earlier astronomer that if the Earth should pass through the tail of the comet, the result would be "a tremendous explosion, followed instantly by a deluge of water, … leaving the burnt and drenched Earth no other atmosphere than the nitrogen now present in the air, together with a relatively small quantity of deleterious vapors."[64] There were stories of terror-stricken individuals going mad or committing suicide. While some sought refuge in religion at all-night revival meetings, the rich and socially prominent threw themselves into desperate merrymaking, quaffing champagne at nightly "comet parties" on the rooftops of New York's poshest hotels. In Cincinnati, the *Enquirer* reported, "many families have packed their belongings and are calmly awaiting their end."[65]

But the comet came and went, and the worst catastrophe that befell the Philadelphia Phillies was a precipitous losing streak that dropped them from first place on May 14 to sixth place 10 days later. And even in the midst of such disarray, it was becoming clear that the Phillies had indeed gotten the better of their trade with Cincinnati. Far from blossoming into the star Clark Griffith envisioned, Harry Coveleski was a quick and thoroughgoing failure in the Queen City. After walking 10 in a mortifying relief appearance in St. Louis on May 4, he was demoted to Birmingham in the Southern Association, with a farewell from Charlie Zuber to the effect that unless he developed a better sense of direction, he could "stick in the minors until doomsday, so far as the [Cincinnati] club is concerned."[66]

Nothing went right for Cincinnati in the aftermath of the Ewing-Coveleski trade. Two weeks after that deal was made, Griffith got rid of his new spitballer, sending Frank Corridon to St. Louis along with Miller Huggins and outfielder Rebel Oakes for right-hander Fred Beebe and utility infielder Alan Storke. Corridon proved no great loss but Huggins and Oakes became every-day players for the Cardinals for several seasons. Beebe made a brilliant debut with the Reds, out-dueling Orval Overall over 10 innings for a 1–0 victory on Opening Day. But after that he

After he halted the Phillies' 10-game losing streak on June 4, 1910, Bob Ewing was the subject of a caricature by the *Philadelphia Inquirer's* Edgar Wolfe, signed with his famous "Jim Nasium" pseudonym. Note the droplets of spit flying off Long Bob's right hand. *Photo:* Philadelphia Inquirer.

didn't win again for two months. Storke never donned a Cincinnati uniform. Twenty-five years old and a Harvard law student between seasons, he developed complications from influenza and died following surgery in Massachusetts while the Reds were in spring training.

Meanwhile, notwithstanding whatever troubles he had with his former teammates, Ewing demonstrated admirable durability and pitched consistently well against the rest of the league. Ad Brennan, though he started only five games, remained with the Phillies all season and was generally effective when called upon. "If St. Louis only had Fred Beebe back … and Bob Ewing was in Redland," Ren Mulford calculated in mid-June, "Cincinnati would be leading the National League parade."[67] That was speculation, but the balance sheet clearly showed that Griffith had given up four useful players—Brennan, Oakes, Huggins and Ewing—and all he had to show in return was Beebe. "And he has a sore arm," one unkind critic noted.[68]

Still, not everything was coming up roses for Dooin's Daisies. As of June 3, they had wilted all the way to seventh place, losing 14 of their last 15 games including the last 10 in a row. Ewing broke the string with a 4–1 verdict over St. Louis and started the team on a dramatic turnaround. Rookie Eddie "Smoke" Stack, leaping directly from a Chicago semipro league to the majors, burst on the scene with a three-hit shutout over the Cubs, and added three more complete-game victories in barely two weeks. The day after Stack's fourth triumph, Ewing beat Boston 4–0, allowing just three singles; spinning his second straight shutout, he faced more than three batters in an inning only once. A month after the end of the long losing streak, the Phillies were back at .500 and again rising in the standings.

For a short time, the pitching staff functioned "in grand style."[69] But Stack faded as suddenly as he had bloomed and Tully Sparks, a mainstay for the Phillies since 1903, finally gave out and was let go at age 35. George McQuillan was unable to mend his ways and was suspended for the final six weeks of the season. The staff's ace, Earl Moore, continued to take his regular turn, plus the occasional relief assignment, despite a very sore arm. Dooin hoped his charges could claw their way into the first division, but he worried publicly about whether they could stay there.

At the end of August, Ewing had won 11 and lost 11 and was experiencing some arm troubles of his own. But he started September with an impressive 3–2 victory over Hooks Wiltse[70] and the Giants. Three days later he beat Boston 6–3 as Philadelphia swept a doubleheader and moved into fourth place. By September 14, Ewing had won three straight and the surprisingly resilient Phillies were four games over .500 as they prepared to host Chicago in another twin bill.

Frank Chance's Cubs were on the way to their fourth pennant in five years. They were among the perennial front-runners in a league that had a clear line of demarcation between the "haves" and the "have nots." Between 1902 and 1910, the first-place team in the National League won an average of 104 games annually. The last-place team lost an average of 100, and the standings usually underwent only a minor shakeup from one season to the next. Chicago, Pittsburgh and New York won all the pennants and (after John J. McGraw's arrival in Gotham) were always contenders. St. Louis, Boston and Brooklyn were typically near the bottom of the heap, leaving Cincinnati and Philadelphia in the middle of the pack, fighting it out for fourth place and the last shreds of first-division respectability.

Ewing's record largely reflected the realities of an era with no notion of competitive parity. Over the years, he routinely feasted on Boston and Brooklyn, and won consistently against other second-division clubs. He elevated himself above the common run of pitchers with a string of notable conquests over good Pittsburgh teams and, though victories over New York were often hard to come by, he had a deserved reputation for giving the Giants a hard time. One reason the Phillies wanted Ewing, according to *Sporting News* correspondent William G. Weart, was that he had demonstrated "that he could beat the Giants and the Pirates."[71]

Chicago, however, was another matter. The Cubs were the one team that always seemed to have Ewing's number. Some of his managers even adjusted their pitching plans so he could avoid them. Ewing himself joked that there seemed to be something about the cooking in Chicago that kept him from generating the right kind of spit.[72] For whatever reason, in the words of one Windy City sportswriter, Chicago teams usually "exhibited little respect for Bob Ewing and his inelegant spitball."[73]

Before September 14, Ewing had started against the Cubs only once all season; roughly handled on that occasion, he "had not conquered them in many moons."[74] This time Ewing started off matching goose eggs with Chicago's Ed Reulbach. Through five innings, the Cubs managed only two hits and got only one runner past first base.

They threatened to score with two out in the sixth when Solly Hofman singled and stole second. Jimmy Archer followed with another base hit, but Hofman was cut down at the plate on a perfect throw from center fielder Johnny Bates. The game was still scoreless when Philadelphia came to bat in the bottom of the inning, but Otto Knabe walked, Bates singled and Sherry Magee ripped a double to left, scoring both runners. By the end of the inning, the Phillies had a 5–0 lead and Reulbach was on his way to the showers.

Chicago mounted another threat with two out in the ninth when Archer doubled and Harry Steinfeldt walked, but Ewing got Frank "Wildfire" Schulte[75] on an infield pop-up to end the game. For the day, Ewing had struck out four, walked three and permitted just five hits. More significantly, he had fashioned his 19th career shutout and his first against the Cubs. Coupled with his earlier whitewashing of Cincinnati, the victory gave him at least one shutout against every team in the National League.[76]

Three days later, the Reds thumped Ewing in their final meeting, leaving him with a 2–3 record in six starts against his former club. But Long Bob got the last laugh. By winning five and losing only two in September, he helped Philadelphia secure the final berth in the first division—a finish that landed them one notch ahead of Cincinnati and reversed the teams' positions from a year earlier.

Ewing scored his final victory on September 29, in the Phillies' last home game of the season. He gave up only two hits and an unearned run, beating St. Louis 6–1. He finished the season 16–14. At age 37, he led the team in complete games and was second in innings and wins. He matched his career high in shutouts (four) and pitched five complete games in which he allowed three hits or fewer. *Sporting Life*'s Francis C. Richter, in his post-season review, ran down a long list of Philadelphia's pitching disappointments and then added, "It was fortunate that the veteran Ewing … rose nobly to the emergency and pitched the best ball of his career."[77]

HOT SPRINGS, ARKANSAS, in February and March 1911 was teeming with ballplayers. The Cincinnati Reds, Brooklyn Dodgers, Pittsburgh

Pirates and St. Louis Browns were training there, along with numerous members of other clubs. A local newspaper counted "almost 200 men of national note in the game" on the city's two fields.[78] Soon an additional "diamond of regulation size" was laid out on the grounds of the Park Hotel, where workouts by players staying there "were eagerly watched by the [other] guests …, who lined the veranda."[79] Games of "picked stars" pitted the American League against the National.[80] Ewing's arrival in Hot Springs was noted on February 27 along with those of Cleveland's Cy Young and Brooklyn's Zack Wheat.

After another year of recurring arm trouble, Ewing had returned to Arkansas to get an early start on working out the kinks. The Phillies even agreed to pay his train fare, though all other expenses were the player's responsibility. But the celebrated waters did him little good. When he joined the Phillies two weeks later in Birmingham, Alabama, he was barely able to throw. "The tall veteran looks physically fit," the *Philadelphia Inquirer* reported, "but his arm is not strong."[81]

It was a disheartening start to Ewing's season, especially as it came amid much optimism in Philadelphia. The Athletics were defending world champions and the Phillies, though underdogs in the battle for the hearts, minds and dollars of the city's fans, were expected "to make a big bid for leading honors in the National League."[82]

A whopper of an off-season trade had reunited Ewing with some former Cincinnati teammates, bringing Hans Lobert, Dode Paskert and Jack Rowan to Philadelphia along with Fred Beebe. In exchange, the Reds received infielder Eddie Grant, outfielder Johnny Bates and two pitchers, Lew Moren and the incorrigible George McQuillan. Starting out for the first time with a roster entirely of his own choosing, Red Dooin went so far as to tell a reporter, "I honestly expect to see the Phillies win the National League pennant this season, unless things break very bad for us."[83]

Ewing became the first bad break. For the second year in a row, he got little work in the South, then took a severe beating in the pre-season city series. Playing this time at the Huntingdon Street Grounds, he served up another home run to Frank Baker, this one traveling "a mile or two over the right-field fence into Broad Street," and generally "didn't appear to have anything on the ball … but the cover."[84] When the Phillies went to New York to open the season, Ewing probably didn't even make the trip.[85]

In that case, he missed one of the dramatic events of the 1911 season, and one that would have been particularly poignant for him. Shortly after midnight on April 14, hours after Philadelphia completed the second of back-to-back victories over the formidable Giants, fire swept through the stands at the Polo Grounds. The blaze, possibly ignited by a dropped cigar or cigarette under the right-field bleachers, lit up the night sky over upper Manhattan, the Bronx and eastern Queens. Within an hour the conflagration, driven by a brisk wind, turned the ballpark into "one huge bonfire, the flames leaping nearly 100 feet in the air."[86] Throughout the night and into the following morning, thousands flocked to the bluffs overlooking the scene to view the spectacular blaze and then to contemplate the sorry aftermath, the double-decked grandstand reduced to "only a blackened crescent, with here and there a gaunt girder standing upright."

"Then the rain came and soaked the dismal pile of ashes," Damon Runyon added, "and drove the curious to cover."[87]

Several Giants and some of the Phillies were among those who looked on, stunned, as the flames consumed the grandstand and most of the bleachers. The loss was estimated at $250,000 and the Giants were temporarily homeless, forced to accept the hospitality of the American League Highlanders at Hilltop Park until the Polo Grounds could be rebuilt. Had Ewing been in the crowd, he undoubtedly would have thought back to August 18, 1903, and wondered if he was seeing the last moments of the scene of one of his greatest triumphs.

The fire robbed Philadelphia of a chance to begin the season with a three-game sweep of the Giants. Nonetheless, the Phillies roared out to an 8–1 start. On April 24, they were riding a six-game winning streak and holding down first place in the standings. Meanwhile their cross-town rivals, the Athletics, had stumbled out of the gate with a 2–6 record. "For the time being," William G. Weart observed in *The Sporting News*, "the Phillies are nearly the whole thing in this city."[88] Ewing hadn't been seen since that dreary pre-season performance against the A's, but he was still counted among the five pitchers expected to be Dooin's regular starters.

Dooin's plans were about to change, and the chief agent of that change was a tall, gangling Nebraska farm boy the Phillies had latched onto after he won 29 games for Syracuse in the New York State League. He had a terrific sinking fastball and a hard, late-breaking curve, both delivered with an easy sidearm motion and pinpoint control. Watching him work, Ewing must have suddenly felt old. The rookie was named after the man who had occupied the White House the year Long Bob entered professional baseball. Grover Cleveland Alexander gained his first major league victory on April 19.

In many ways, Alex was just a big, good-natured kid. He enjoyed rough horseplay with his teammates, including underwater wrestling matches with Mickey Doolan in the large swimming pool in the Phillies' clubhouse. But before the season was a month old, the Philadelphia writers had christened him Alexander the Great. Before the summer was over, Horace Fogel was trumpeting his intentions to lock Alexander into a long-term contract that would make him "the highest-priced pitcher in captivity."[89] On his way to a 28–13 record with seven shutouts, the big rookie was singularly unimpressed with so-called "fast company."

"There isn't much difference between the majors and the bushes," he told a reporter.[90]

Sunday ball was still taboo in Philadelphia, so when the club got a day off on May 21, Ewing traveled 25 miles to test his arm against a team of amateurs in Phoenixville, Pennsylvania. The game attracted 4,000 spectators from up and down the Schuylkill Valley. Backed mainly by second-stringers and spare parts from the Phillies, and using the new cork-centered ball the writers were crediting for an early-season flurry of home runs, Ewing was battered for 15 hits but staggered to a 10–7 victory.[91] After that, Ewing largely disappeared. He didn't pitch in an official game until June 13, when he was pulled after four innings in St. Louis, trailing 8–2. He wasn't much better two weeks later against Brooklyn, taking his lumps for seven innings in a game the Phillies eventually won 8–7.

Later, during a final forlorn bid to hang on in the major leagues, Ewing would insist "there was nothing really wrong with him [in 1911] … except that Dooin would not give him a chance to work."[92] Clearly that wasn't the case. As late as August 1910, Alfred H. Spink remarked on Ewing's "tremendous speed,"[93] but a year later, his velocity had evaporated. Long Bob had been dogged by arm trouble most of his career; now it had become chronic.

He was searching for a solution when he considered giving up the spitball in 1910, but in all likelihood he was unable to face up to the true problem. It's improbable that the spitball, thrown with the same direct and natural motion as his fastball, was the cause of Ewing's miseries. More likely, after averaging more than 260 innings a year for 13 years, Ewing's arm was simply wearing out. He was probably over-throwing in an effort to compensate—and thereby further aggravating what was by now a constantly sore arm.

One of the painful ironies of Ewing's career is that after enduring heavy use to a ripe old age, his arm ultimately failed just when he finally found himself in the middle of a legitimate pennant race. The Phillies were in first place for most of the first half of the 1911 season, battling on even terms with New York and Chicago. Ewing could hardly help indulging in daydreams of the World Series and his own moment of glory on baseball's biggest stage. Almost annually he had seen former teammates emerge from the fall classic with new and glittering laurels. The list of October standouts included Roger Bresnahan, Mike Donlin, Orval Overall, Harry Steinfeldt, Jim Delahanty and even George Rohe, the former Wapakoneta semipro who became an unlikely hero for the White Sox when their "Hitless Wonders" upset the mighty Cubs in 1906.

Now that Ewing's World Series dream seemed within reach, he was reduced to a spectator. Yet while other pitchers were traded or demoted, Ewing remained in Philadelphia. In his current condition he had no trade value, and a provision in his contract barred the team from sending him to the minors. If the Phillies wanted to be rid of him, they would have to release him outright.

Ewing hung around and made himself useful. He threw batting practice. He offered spitball instruction to teammates.[94] He spent many afternoons coaching the bases and, despite his circumstances, managed to enjoy himself when he was on the field.

"Bob Ewing makes a noise on the coach lines like a farmer calling home his cows," Jimmy Isaminger reported in the *North American*. "His voice carries as far as Tioga."[95] The description presents an unusual image of a man usually identified as one of the more reserved figures in baseball, but if Isaminger had known more about Ewing's farming operation, he would have realized Long Bob was calling hogs, not cows.

The Phillies won their first five games in July, but back-to-back doubleheaders in nearly 100-degree heat sapped the players' strength and they proceeded to lose three straight to lightly-regarded St. Louis. In the third inning of the last of those contests, after being called out on strikes on what Francis C. Richter saw as "a palpably high ball,"[96] Sherry Magee flipped his bat in the air and was promptly ejected from the game by rookie umpire Bill Finneran. Magee rushed at Finneran and laid him out with a single punch.

League president Thomas J. Lynch, a former umpire, suspended the Phillies' most potent hitter for the balance of the season.

Philadelphia was still in first place when the Chicago Cubs came to town on July 20. In 10 years in the big leagues, it was by far the latest in the campaign that Ewing had ever enjoyed such a lofty vantage point. But each day seemed to bring with it new difficulties. On this afternoon, Dooin's immediate headache was a case of chills and fever that had felled his scheduled starting pitcher, Sleepy Bill Burns. Casting around for a last-minute replacement, Dooin watched as Ewing pitched batting practice.

Maybe Dooin was desperate. Or maybe the old man truly did appear to have something on the ball. For whatever reason, Dooin told Ewing to go into the clubhouse and get a rubdown, then come back out and warm up. As game time approached, Ewing and Eddie Stack limbered up their arms side by side as the manager looked on. Then he handed the ball to Ewing.

What followed, according to William G. Weart, was "quite a ballgame."[97] From a Chicago perspective, I.E. Sanborn called it "the most bitterly fought combat of the present trip, ... a stiff uphill game the Cubs had to play against the most determined and brilliant kind of defense."[98]

Ewing hadn't tried his arm in a game in three weeks. Matched against his frequent nemesis Ed Reulbach, Long Bob poured all he had into one gallant last stand. Summoning up everything that was left in his 38-year-old arm and everything he had stored over the years in his 38-year-old head, he scratched and scuffled for every out.

Working carefully to the Cubs' dangerous sluggers, he got through the lineup the first time without allowing a base runner. Ewing pulled his old "quick return" trick on Heinie Zimmerman, slipping over a second strike while the hitter argued about the first one; when Ewing tried to do it again, Zimmerman barely managed to get the bat on the ball and slapped a docile grounder to third base.

Though "the visitors batted Ewing's curves viciously at times,"[99] he held them in check—with one exception. After the Phillies took an early 2–0 lead, Frank "Wildfire" Schulte got Chicago on the board with a run-scoring double in the fourth inning. In the sixth he tripled to drive in another run, then came home on Solly Hofman's single to tie the score at 3–3.

The game was still deadlocked when the Cubs came to bat in the eighth, but Ewing was wearing down. Shortstop Mickey Doolan made a one-handed stab on Reulbach's hot smash and fired to first for one out, and Ewing legged it over to cover the bag and nip Jimmy Sheckard on a grounder to the right side. That brought Schulte up again, and when Ewing got a pitch out over the plate, he pulled it high and deep. Right fielder Fred Beck could only watch as the ball cleared the fence by 10 feet.

Schulte's home run—the 10th of his league-leading 21 in 1911—gave the Cubs all they needed for a 4–3 victory. Still, when it was over, some optimists dared to hope that Dooin had found himself a much-needed additional pitcher. One Philadelphia scribe wrote hopefully of Ewing's "return to form," terming it "pleasant news to the Philly team."

"It was apparent that Old Bob had everything," Chandler Richter told readers of the *Evening Times*. Aside from Schulte, he added, "None of the other heavy-hitting Cubs could do anything with Ewing's shoots."[100]

The realists in the press box saw an entirely different game. To them it was clear that for most of the afternoon, various Phillies had kept Ewing in the game by running all over the lot making circus catches. Doolan and center fielder Dode Paskert came in for fulsome praise, and Red Dooin got in on the act when he scuttled down to third base and tagged out Joe Tinker trying for an extra base after a throw from the outfield was mishandled. Left fielder Jimmy "Runt" Walsh made the biggest grab of the day, racing toward the foul line and picking a drive out of the air before crashing into the concrete barrier in front of the bleachers, robbing Jimmy Doyle of a potential home run.

There would be no comeback for Ewing, and no pennant for Philadelphia. Two days later the Phillies were out of first place and before the week was out, Dooin broke his leg in a home plate collision with the Cardinals' Rebel Oakes. Dooin was lost for the season. Even after Thomas J. Lynch relented and lifted Magee's suspension after five weeks, the club never got back to the top of the standings.

The pitching situation became increasingly dire. Most of the load fell on the rookie Alexander and 34-year-old Earl Moore. Between starts, Moore slipped over to Youngstown, Ohio, to be worked on by the celebrated John

D. "Bonesetter" Reese, the dead ball era's foremost specialist in the restoration of dead arms.[101] The fight to remain in contention becoming ever more desperate, Alexander eventually volunteered to pitch every other day if necessary. By season's end, he and Moore had started nearly half of the team's games and combined for 675 innings while only one other Philadelphia pitcher—the Scottish-born rookie George Chalmers—pitched as many as 125. The excitement of the race pushed the Phillies' home attendance to a near-record 416,000—a 40 percent increase over 1910—but the best finish they could manage was fourth, the same as the previous year.

If there had been any chance Ewing could help, he surely would have gotten the opportunity. But he pitched only once more for Philadelphia—a humiliating mop-up assignment in a 13–0 trouncing at Pittsburgh on August 8. He languished for another month before, on September 12, the Philadelphia papers reported that he had been given the required 10 days' notice of his unconditional release.

For the first time in his 15 years in baseball, Bob Ewing was unemployed.

ENDNOTES

1   *Cincinnati Enquirer*, May 11, 1910.
2   *Washington Post*, Jan. 21, 1910.
3   *Philadelphia Record*, Jan. 21, 1910.
4   *Philadelphia Inquirer*, Jan. 21, 1910.
5   *Philadelphia Evening Bulletin*, Jan. 22, 1910.
6   *Philadelphia Record*, Jan. 22, 1910.
7   The phrase graced the pages of both the *Cincinnati Enquirer* and the *Cincinnati Post* on Jan. 21, 1910. Coveleski was referred to elsewhere as "the hurling Hun" and the "Red Hun."
8   *Cincinnati Commercial Tribune*, Jan. 21, 1910.
9   *The Sporting News*, Jan. 27, 1910.
10   *Cincinnati Enquirer*, Jan. 21, 1910.
11   *Cincinnati Times-Star*, Jan. 22, 1910.
12   *Cincinnati Times-Star*, reprinted in *The Sporting News*, Feb. 27, 1908.
13   *Cincinnati Commercial Tribune*, Jan. 21, 1910.
14   *Cincinnati Times-Star*, Jan. 22, 1910.
15   *Sporting Life*, Feb. 5, 1910.
16   *Cincinnati Enquirer*, Jan. 21, 1910.
17   *Cincinnati Times-Star*, Jan. 22, 1910.
18   *Cincinnati Enquirer*, Jan. 21, 1910.
19   *Philadelphia Bulletin*, Jan. 22, 1910.
20   *Ibid.*, Jan. 21, 1910; see also *Philadelphia Record*, Jan. 21, 1910.
21   *Cincinnati Enquirer*, July 25, 1910.
22   *Washington Post*, Jan. 23, 1910.
23   Frederick G. Lieb and Stan Baumgartner, *The Philadelphia Phillies* (New York: G.P. Putnam's Sons, 1953), p. 84.

24 *Cincinnati Times-Star*, quoted in *The Sporting News*, June 14, 1902.

25 Lieb and Baumgartner, *op. cit.*

26 Taft, who had taken his first big plunge into baseball when he enabled Murphy to take control of the Cubs, was later said to also have financial interests in the Cincinnati Reds and Boston Braves, as well as the minor league club in Louisville, Ky. In 1912, he was described as "the largest single financial power behind American baseball" with an "investment [that] reaches into the millions." Edward Mott Woolley, "The Business of Baseball," *McClure's Magazine*, Vol. XXXIX, No. 3 (July 1912), p. 246.

27 Lieb and Baumgartner, *op. cit.*, p. 87.

28 H.W. Lanigan, *The Sporting News*, March 28, 1912.

29 *Sporting Life*, June 11, 1910; see also *Washington Post*, Feb. 18, 1910.

30 *The Sporting News*, Dec. 5, 1912.

31 *Sporting Life*, Jan. 29, 1910.

32 John J. Evers and Hugh S. Fullerton, *Touching Second: The Science of Baseball* (Chicago: Reilly and Britton Co., 1910), p. 98.

33 *The Sporting News*, March 3, 1910.

34 Unidentified newspaper clipping, March 1910.

35 *Washington Post*, March 30, 1910.

36 Lee Allen, *The Cincinnati Reds: An Informal History* (New York: G.P. Putnam's Sons, 1948), p. 3; see also William B. Mead and Paul Dickson, *Baseball: The President's Game* (Washington, D.C.: Farragut Publishing Co., 1993), pp. 23-26. Mead and Dickson dispute the persistent myth that young Taft was an outstanding player. The most reliable scouting reports, they say, indicate that he was a heavy hitter but no terror on the base paths.

37 *The Sporting News*, Sept. 23, 1909.

38 *Sporting Life*, April 9, 1910.

39 *Ibid.*

40 *Washington Post*, April 1, 1910.

41 *Ibid.*

42 *Cincinnati Times-Star*, reprinted in *Sporting Life*, Oct. 23, 1909.

43 *Winchester* (Ky.) *News*, Oct. 17, 1908, quoted in Peter Morris, *Catcher: How the Man Behind the Plate Became an American Folk Hero* (Chicago: Ivan R. Dee, 2009), pp. 239-40.

44 *Washington Post*, April 1, 1910. Seventy-five years later the same argument was still being made against the spitball. In 1987, Oakland Athletics coach Joe Rudi told Roger Angell that the spitball was the most dangerous delivery a pitcher could use. "When that part of the ball is wet," Rudi said, "the ball suddenly comes flying out of there, and there's ... no resistance at all. Your arm accelerates exactly at the point when it's begun to decelerate, and that's a great way to blow it out for good." See Angell, *Once More Around the Park: A Baseball Reader* (New York: Ballantine Books, 1991), p. 291.

45 *The Sporting News*, March 24, 1910.

46 *Washington Post*, April 7, 1910.

47 *Philadelphia Inquirer*, June 5, 1910.

48 Left-field dimensions from Ronald M. Selter, *Ballparks of the Deadball Era: A Comprehensive Study of Their Dimensions, Configurations and Effects on Batting, 1901-19* (Jefferson, N.C.: McFarland and Co. Inc., 2008), p. 129; Selter also says the distance to straight-away left-center was reduced from 418 feet to 379. See also Rich Westcott, *Philadelphia's Old Ballparks* (Philadelphia: Temple University Press, 1996), p. 50. Westcott says the left-field line was 415 feet before alterations, and that the right-field line was extended from 272 feet to 273. Selter shows right field unchanged at 272.

49 *Philadelphia Public Ledger*, April 27, 1910.

50 *Cincinnati Enquirer*, May 11, 1910.

51 *Ibid.*

52 *Ibid.*, July 25, 1910.

53 *Ibid.*

54 *Cincinnati Commercial Tribune*, July 25, 1910.

55 *Cincinnati Enquirer*, Aug. 29, 1910; see also Aug. 17, 1910. Under today's rules, a pitcher attempting to quick-pitch the batter would be penalized with a called ball (with bases empty) or a balk (with runners on base), but such tactics were tolerated in the National League throughout Ewing's career. Peter Morris says American League umpires were instructed to crack down on the practice in 1913 and it was effectively eliminated from both major leagues by the late 1920s. But the prohibition and penalties may not have been spelled out in the official rules until as late as 1950. See Morris, *A Game of Inches: The Game on the Field* (Chicago: Ivan R. Dee, 2006), p. 498; and Thomas R. Heitz, "Rules and Scoring: Chronology of Rule Changes, 1877-1988," in John Thorn and Pete Palmer, eds., *Total Baseball*, first edition (New York: Warner Books, 1989), p. 2,234.

56 *Ibid.*, Sept. 18, 1910.

57 *Ibid.*, Aug. 29, 1910, with reference to the game of July 24.

58 *Cincinnati Post*, June 17, 1910.

59 *Ibid.*

60 *Cincinnati Times-Star*, June 17, 1910.

61 *Cincinnati Commercial Tribune*, July 25, 1910.

62 *New York Times*, May 14, 1910.

63 *Cincinnati Enquirer*, May 18, 1910.

64 D.J. McAdam, "The Menace in the Skies, Part I: The Case for the Comet," *Harper's Weekly*, Vol. LIV, No. 2786 (May 14, 1910), p. 12.

65 *Cincinnati Enquirer*, May 18, 1910.

66 *The Sporting News*, May 19, 1910. Recalled late in the season, Coveleski gained his one and only Cincinnati victory in September, but two more abysmal performances followed. In his final start for the Reds, on Sept. 28, Coveleski was left to suffer through the entire game, a 16-4 pounding in New York. According to Christy Mathewson, when Coveleski looked toward the bench for help, Clark Griffith yelled out to him, "Stay in there and get it." See Mathewson, *Pitching in a Pinch, or Baseball from the Inside* (New York: Stein and Day, 1977 reprint of 1912 original), p. 81. Again exiled to the minor leagues, Coveleski eventually reemerged as a three-time 20-game winner with the Detroit Tigers from 1914 through 1916. He ultimately pitched nine seasons in the major leagues, winning 81 games and losing 55.

67 *Sporting Life*, June 25, 1910.

68 *The Sporting News*, May 19, 1910. Beebe redeemed himself in the second half of the season, rebounding from a 1-9 start to finish 12-14, but his record still fell considerably short of Ewing's.

69 *Ibid.*, June 23, 1910.

70 George "Hooks" Wiltse was the younger brother of Ewing's former Toledo teammate Lew "Snake" Wiltse.

71 *The Sporting News*, May 12, 1910.

72 *Chicago American*, April 20, 1905.

73 *Chicago Tribune*, April 20, 1905.

74 *Ibid.*, Sept. 15, 1910.

75 Schulte owed his distinctive nickname to the play of the same name starring Lillian Russell (see Chapter 11). The actress toured in the show, about a young

widow with a racing stable, starting in 1907 and eventually took the production to Broadway. Schulte and some teammates saw the play in Vicksburg, Miss., during spring training and met Russell after the performance. Schulte, who raced trotters on the ice in the winter, subsequently named one of his horses after the horse in the play. When Chicago sportswriters learned the story, they hung the name on him and it stuck. The nickname was fitting for Schulte, a daring base runner who stole home 22 times during his major league career. See Scott Turner, "Frank M. 'Wildfire' Schulte," in Tom Simon, ed., *Deadball Stars of the National League* (Washington, D.C.: Brassey's Inc., 2004), pp. 107-08.

76   Ewing pitched five shutouts against Boston, four against Pittsburgh, three each against Brooklyn and Philadelphia, and one each against New York, Chicago, Cincinnati and St. Louis.

77   *Sporting Life*, Oct. 22, 1910.

78   *Arkansas Gazette*, March 4, 1911.

79   *Ibid.*, March 5, 1911.

80   *The Sporting News*, Feb. 23, 1911.

81   *Philadelphia Inquirer*, March 14, 1911.

82   *The Sporting News*, March 9, 1911.

83   *Ibid.*, Feb. 2, 1911.

84   *Philadelphia Inquirer*, April 8, 1911.

85   Ewing wasn't listed on the Phillies' Opening Day roster published April 13, 1911, in *The Sporting News*. However, he was on the roster published April 15, 1911, in *Sporting Life*. In any event, the club likely would have left him at home if he wasn't expected to pitch in the New York series.

86   *New York Times*, April 14, 1911.

87   *New York American*, April 1911, reprinted in Damon Runyon, edited by Jim Reisler, *Guys, Dolls, and Curveballs: Damon Runyon on Baseball* (New York: Carroll and Graf Publishers, 2005), pp. 111-12.

88   *The Sporting News*, April 27, 1911.

89   *Ibid.*, Aug. 17, 1911. There were some reports that Alexander had already signed a new three-year contract, but that must have just been talk from Fogel. According to Alexander's most recent biographer, the pitcher did not sign the new contract until January 1912, after holding out for some months for more money. See John C. Skipper, *Wicked Curve: The Life and Troubled Times of Grover Cleveland Alexander* (Jefferson, N.C.: McFarland and Co. Inc., 2006), pp. 30-31.

90   *Sporting Life*, July 29, 1911.

91   The cork-centered ball had been slipped into some major league games in 1910 before coming into regular use in 1911. Experts disagree about the actual effect of the cork center on the ball's liveliness, but runs increased 16 percent in the major leagues from 1910 to 1911, and home runs jumped 42 percent. Makers of the baseballs were more than willing to take credit. The A.J. Reach Co., which produced official balls for the American League, promised its cork-centered ball "will absolutely keep its shape and will go off the bat with the *snappy crack* which all fans like to hear" (*The Sporting News*, Oct. 6, 1910). Another advertisement drew attention to the large number of extra-base hits early in 1911 and touted the cork-centered ball as "the big improvement in baseball" (*The Sporting News*, May 18, 1911). A.G. Spalding made a similar ball for the National League.

92   *The Sporting News*, March 12, 1912.

93   Alfred H. Spink, *The National Game*, second edition (Carbondale, Ill.: Southern Illinois University Press, 2000 reprint of 1911 original), p. 130.

94   One Phillie reported to be "practicing" with the spitball was Jack Rowan. Ewing had time on his hands and, as the team's only established spitballer, surely he took a hand in Rowan's instruction. The pitch didn't do Rowan much good; traded to Chicago in August, he won only one more game in the major leagues. See *Sporting Life*, Aug. 5, 1911.

95   *North American*, June 29, 1911.

96   *Sporting Life*, July 15, 1911.

97   *Philadelphia Evening Telegraph*, July 21, 1911.

98   *Chicago Tribune*, July 21, 1911.

99   *Philadelphia Evening Telegraph*, July 21, 1911.

100 *Philadelphia Evening Times*, July 21, 1911. Chandler Richter was the son of Francis C. Richter, editor of *Sporting Life*.

101 Reese (1855-1931) was a Welsh-born osteopath with only a smattering of formal medical training, but his long list of patients included a veritable who's who of baseball. Among Ewing's contemporaries, they included pitchers Cy Young, Chief Bender, Addie Joss, Jack Coombs, Orval Overall, Ed Reulbach, Rube Marquard, Ed Walsh, Grover Cleveland Alexander, Walter Johnson and Christy Mathewson, not to mention such position players as Harry Steinfeldt, Roger Bresnahan, Frank Chance, Ty Cobb, Nap Lajoie and Honus Wagner. Considering all the arm trouble Ewing encountered during his career, it's surprising that there doesn't seem to be any record of his ever paying a call on the Bonesetter. See David W. Anderson, "Bonesetter Reese, Baseball's Unofficial Team Physician" in Brad Sullivan, ed., *Batting Four Thousand: Baseball in the Western Reserve* (Cleveland: Society for American Baseball Research, 2008), pp. 99-103.

"Now and then, Ewing and Steinfeldt stand back and look at the youngsters with interest. No doubt the veterans are thinking of when they were able to race about the field with little *thought* of becoming crippled and sore."

—*ST. LOUIS GLOBE-DEMOCRAT*[1]

CHAPTER 13

St. Louis to Buffalo to Parts Unknown

AMONG THOSE WHO KNEW HIM, there was genuine sadness at the thought of Bob Ewing passing from the sporting scene. "It's really a pity that a man like Ewing, who has always been a credit to the game from every point of view, should be shunted aside," Charlie Zuber wrote in *The Sporting News*. "The Ewings are not so numerous in baseball that they can be recklessly spared."[2] More than one sportswriter paid Ewing the highest compliment they could imagine for a veteran player at the end of the line—that he would make an excellent minor league manager.

Ewing never showed much interest in that possibility. So the writers seemed relieved that they could soften the news of his release with assurances that, in baseball or out, Ewing should face no financial hardship with the end of his playing career. Every city in the major leagues had old ballplayers who could be seen hanging around the lobbies of the hotels where visiting teams stayed, looking for handouts. Ewing had been pegged early in his career as a man who "spends his coin judiciously" and could expect, when his playing days were through, to "go back to the farm with enough money under the old pickle barrel to keep him the rest of his life."[3] When he was released by Philadelphia, a paper in Ohio reported that he had "invested his baseball earnings wisely and ... has a Dun & Bradstreet rating that would cause many a financier to turn green with envy."[4] Referring to Ewing's prosperous hog farm near New Hampshire, Zuber wrote, "So long as people eat ham or bacon and eggs, he's not worrying."[5] In fact, Zuber said, Ewing expected that breeding "blue-blooded piggies" would soon "be much more profitable than flinging a spitball."[6]

Ewing claimed he didn't much care whether he got another offer to play, but his actions tell a different story. Passing through Cincinnati on business during the off-season, he inquired about prospects for the fledgling United States League, an ambitious new circuit planning to start up with franchises in Cincinnati and several other big league cities. Anxious to avoid the damning label of "outlaws," organizers promised not to tamper with players on anyone's reserve list and to sign only collegians and free agents. Still, they were operating outside the National Agreement and were viewed by the baseball establishment as interlopers and unwanted competition.

Most likely Long Bob was just making small talk when he asked about the U.S. League. A shaky new circuit wasn't the type of undertaking Ewing would eagerly throw in with, and in this case his natural caution served him well. The league managed to attract a few former major leaguers, but most were castoffs who, having little chance of getting back to the top clubs, were willing to risk official displeasure for a few more paychecks before hanging up their spikes for good. The United States League began play May 1 and folded five weeks later with heavy financial losses.

Ewing opened a more promising line of inquiry when he contacted one of his oldest acquaintances in baseball, St. Louis Cardinals manager Roger Bresnahan. They would have been unlikely friends, the combative, hot-tempered Bresnahan and the slow and steady, six-years-older Ewing. But they went back a long way together, practically to the start of their careers. They had pitched against one another as semipros back in 1897, had been minor league teammates briefly in Toledo and competed against each other for a decade in the National League.

One somewhat starry-eyed view from the press box was that Bresnahan offered Ewing a tryout "out of the goodness of his heart."[7] Realistically, neither goodness nor friendship nor sentiment of any kind probably had much to do with bringing Ewing to St. Louis. Like any manager of an also-ran club, Bresnahan was looking for help anywhere he could find it. He had come from New York in 1909 to take over a team that, as Bill James pointed out, had lost 105 games the season before and then traded its two best players, outfielder Red Murray and pitcher Bugs Raymond, to get him.[8] Since then, Bresnahan had laboriously squeezed out a few more victories each year, finally achieving a 75–74 record in 1911—the club's first winning season in a decade. He had transformed the Cardinals into "a plucky fighting aggregation that is one of the biggest attractions in the circuit."[9] Still, he had gotten only as high as fifth place in the standings. As the 1912 season approached, the Duke of Tralee figured his team was still two pitchers away from breaking into the first division. Closing in on his 39th birthday, Ewing had two points to recommend giving him a look: First, he had once been an effective major league pitcher. Second, he was available.

If the usual cares of a second-division manager weren't enough to keep Bresnahan's stomach churning, he had another complication to deal with that was uniquely his own. He was working for a woman.

Helene Hathaway Robison Britton was the daughter of former Cardinals president Frank de Hass Robison and the niece of M. Stanley Robison, who continued to run the ballclub after his brother's death in 1908. When her uncle died suddenly at age 54 shortly before the start of the 1911 season, Mrs. Britton inherited 75 percent of the club, with the other 25 percent going to her mother.

The idea of a female owner in the major leagues was not only unprecedented, it was almost unimaginable. The other National League owners assumed Mrs. Britton would quickly sell the franchise and leave baseball as it had always been, a male-only enterprise. But Lady Bee, as she was called, shocked them all. Not only did she decide not to sell, she moved from Cleveland to St. Louis and let it be known that she intended to take an active hand in the operation of her new business.

When Bob Ewing joined the Cardinals, Helene Britton was 33 years old, the attractive—some went so far as to say beautiful—mother of two young children, and an outspoken proponent of woman suffrage. She had played sandlot ball as a girl and claimed to have as good a throwing arm as any boy in the neighborhood. At Cardinals' home games, she could usually be found sitting high in the grandstand, keeping score. As owner, she strove to attract more women to the ballpark and spoke of women as a "refining influence" on the game.[10] She declared every Thursday ladies' day at Robison Field, admitting women with male escorts free, and moved the Cardinals' downtown ticket agency out of a barroom and into a candy and drug store.

She also became a regular at the league's annual meeting, obliging her fellow magnates to curtail their cigar smoking and curb their language. It was reported that American League moguls, viewing these developments with dismay verging on alarm, instituted an unwritten agreement "that no woman shall ever be left in control of a club in that league."[11] Under the Britton administration, the Cardinals were sometimes disparagingly referred to as the Suffragettes.

Bresnahan and Lady Bee were an even more unlikely couple than Bresnahan and Ewing. Bresnahan was a take-charge guy who didn't like taking orders from anybody, much less a woman. After the death of Stanley Robison, Bresnahan made repeated offers to buy the club, but his overtures were rebuffed.

For a time, though, Bresnahan and the lady owner got along famously. Mrs. Britton was so delighted with the Cardinals' showing in 1911 that she rewarded her manager with an extraordinary new five-year contract calling for an annual salary of $10,000, plus 10 percent of the team's profits. The honeymoon would come to an abrupt end within a matter of months. While St. Louis stalled out in its push for the first division, Bresnahan rankled under front-office criticism, real or imagined. The blowup would come in August, with the Cardinals in sixth place. After yet another loss, Mrs. Britton had the effrontery to offer a suggestion with regard to managerial strategy. A noisy—and, on Bresnahan's side, profane—confrontation ensued. He stormed out of her office and the two reportedly never spoke again.[12] Mrs. Britton determined to fire Bresnahan and replace him with second baseman Miller Huggins—which she did at season's end, even though it cost her $20,000 to settle Bresnahan's contract.

Though Mrs. Britton initially contented herself with the title of vice president, there was no doubt who controlled the club's purse strings, and in 1912 she gave strict orders that the Cardinals should indulge in "no extensive or expensive spring trip."[13] So instead of going south, they went east. They left St. Louis on March 1. Bresnahan's plan was to spend 10 days at the Indiana resort of West Baden Springs, then return home for a few exhibition games against minor league clubs in preparation for the pre-season series with the American League St. Louis Browns. Instead, the Cardinals embarked on one of the strangest road trips ever endured by a major league club.

They found West Baden inundated with heavy rains and flooding. But Bresnahan was not easily deterred. On their first day in camp, he rousted the players out at 5 a.m. and led them on a strenuous hike over the southern Indiana hills. He insisted on another hike in the afternoon, despite the fact that snow was falling and his morning exertions had left him barely able to walk. The weather didn't improve and the next day "few of the players ... even went so far as to venture out of doors."[14] They whiled away the time bowling, shooting billiards or playing cards. Most of the exercise Bresnahan's athletes got over the next few days, a reporter observed, was at the dinner table.[15]

Even amid the lavish surroundings of the West Baden Springs Hotel,[16] the ballplayers grew restive. Bresnahan worked the telegraph wires and long-distance telephone lines in search of an available training site with more inviting weather. After more than a week of enforced inactivity in Indiana, he determined to move the team south.

On March 10, passing back through St. Louis, the team caught a late train for Jackson, Tennessee. Once there, a reporter calculated, the team would still need "a couple of days' seasoning ... before anything like ballplaying can be attempted."[17] Leaving St. Louis, the train ran head-on into a hailstorm, which kept the players awake much of the night in their Pullman berths.

It was raining hard when the Cardinals reached Jackson, Tennessee, but they hardly stayed long enough to get wet. It quickly became clear that the town didn't have a hotel capable of accommodating the entire party, though the manager of one hostelry suggested he might be able to squeeze them all in if the players wouldn't mind sleeping two to a bed. From the luxurious surroundings of West Baden Springs, Ewing and his teammates found themselves transported to a "Godforsaken mud hole ... where there wasn't even room for the athletes to sleep, much less exercise."[18] Bresnahan found a telephone and, after a long conversation with the mayor of Jackson, Mississippi, he herded his charges back onto the train and continued southward. If the Mississippi capital didn't meet his requirements, he said, the team would continue on to Gulfport.

"The truth of the matter," the *St. Louis Globe-Democrat* told the readers back home, "is that there is no telling just where the Cardinals are liable to land within the next few days."[19]

More than 12 hours later, at 5 a.m. on March 12, they again disembarked. They had traveled all night through another storm, and rain was still falling when they stepped off the train. But the players, after two weeks of doing their training in hotels and Pullman cars, were eager to get out and stretch their limbs. Bresnahan called a practice for that afternoon. Under the manager's careful scrutiny, the players started out exercising gingerly. But after about 30 minutes, several of the veterans sneaked off and commenced batting practice. "The players, once turned loose in baseball uniforms and spiked shoes," the *Globe-Democrat*'s man reported, "were just like a lot of schoolboys."[20]

Over the next week, the Cardinals got their first real workouts of the spring. Ewing got in a couple of innings in an intrasquad game. Bresnahan also took a look at 34-year-old Harry Steinfeldt. A veteran of 14 years in the league and four World Series with the Cubs, Steinfeldt had spent 1911 with the Boston Braves, but played only a handful of games before suffering what was characterized as "a nervous collapse."[21] With the Cards' regular third baseman, Mike Mowrey, a holdout, Bresnahan made a point to tell the newspapers that Steinfeldt appeared to have "a lot of good baseball left in him."[22] The papers described Steinfeldt and Ewing methodically going about their business in practice, "seldom heard to utter a sound … [and never] seen to cut loose with a hurried or swiftly-thrown ball."[23] While the press was ready enough to believe Steinfeldt would solve the third base problem should Mowrey fail to come to heel, Ewing was another matter. "Ewing not so long ago was considered one of the high-class twirlers of the National," the *Globe-Democrat* remarked a few days after he came into camp, "but apparently he has shot his bolt."[24]

At this point he was seen, at best, as someone who could pitch relief, allowing Bresnahan to "hold his other pitchers for their regular turn instead of using them up finishing out games."[25]

With the city series against the Browns scheduled to open March 23, the Cardinals headed back to St. Louis. Another long train ride left Bresnahan's vagabonds "grouchy and out of sorts," and despite a few good days in Mississippi, the squad was "full of lame arms, charley horses, kinky legs and other ailments."[26] They arrived home to find Robison Field frozen over; when the sun came out in the afternoon, the ice melted and the diamond turned to a greasy muck. The start of the city series was pushed back a week.

With their home field unplayable and the team little closer to playing shape than when it arrived in West Baden Springs three weeks earlier, Bresnahan dispatched a group of pitchers and catchers to Hot Springs, Arkansas. Veterans Jack Bliss and Slim Sallee headed the detachment. Ewing went along, lumped in with five youngsters who, like him, were fighting for spots on the roster. While Ewing and his companions boarded yet another train, Bresnahan and the rest of the squad moved into a St. Louis armory, where they put in their time playing basketball and indoor baseball.[27]

After three days, however, they were forced to move again. On March 28, the armory was booked for a speech by former President Theodore Roosevelt. After leaving the White House in 1909, Roosevelt had spent a year hunting big game in Africa. He returned by way of Europe, where he hobnobbed with Kaiser Wilhelm II, stopped off in Norway to belatedly pick up the Nobel Peace Prize he had been awarded in 1906 for mediating an end to the Russo-Japanese War, and arrived in London just in time to represent the United States at the funeral of England's King Edward VII.

Back on U.S. soil, Roosevelt had broken with his handpicked successor, William Howard Taft, and launched a bid for an unprecedented third term as president. Before a standing-room crowd in St. Louis, Roosevelt inveighed against "the aristocracy of naked and brutal wealth" and declared that the country was engaged "in a great struggle for social and industrial justice."[28] Three months later, having failed to wrest the Republican nomination from Taft, Roosevelt would desert the GOP and accept the endorsement of the upstart Progressive Party. When a voice from the crowd along the campaign trail inquired how he felt, the 53-year-old Roosevelt responded heartily, "Like a bull moose."[29] From then on, he was the standard-bearer of what was popularly known as the Bull Moose Party.

Running on a platform that called for woman suffrage, old-age insurance, limitations on campaign spending, the eight-hour workday and the right of labor to organize, Roosevelt ultimately garnered 4.1 million votes in the November election. All he succeeded in doing was splitting the Republican vote, thereby ensuring an easy victory for Democrat Woodrow Wilson.

Bresnahan, evicted from his training base in favor of the Bull Moose, considered organizing a practice under the grandstand at Robison Field, but gave up the idea because of wet conditions and a leaky roof. Instead, he told his players to take the afternoon off and "to attend the most amusing show they could find … in the hope of getting them to smile again."[30] By now, the team's springtime odyssey had qualified as "the most costly training trip that the Cardinals have ever taken."[31] By the time Ewing returned to St. Louis, he and some of his teammates had traveled 2,000 miles over more than half a dozen states. Bresnahan, meanwhile, hadn't seen enough of his new men to determine whether any of them were going to be of any use.

"If it so happens that the Cards make a good showing," *The Sporting News* commented, "it will be a splendid argument against training a ball team at all in the springtime."[32]

DESPITE THEIR HAPHAZARD PRE-SEASON, the Cardinals looked surprisingly sharp when they finally faced some competition, beating the Browns five games to two in the city series. Mike Mowrey rejoined the team and Harry Steinfeldt was quickly forgotten; his only action during the city series involved getting into a fistfight with the Browns' Jimmy Austin. Bresnahan still had no idea whether Ewing could still pitch, but he hadn't been bowled over by any of his other new pitchers, either. As Opening Day approached, the Duke made his decisions: He let Steinfeldt go and signed Ewing to a contract, "believing he will be of use as a stopgap."[33]

Though the prognosticators didn't think much of St. Louis' prospects, the team won its first three league games. Then reality set in. Over the next 18 contests, the pitching staff got pounded for 130 runs. By May 9, the Cardinals had lost 15 of their last 16 and were in last place. "The fans of St. Louis are not enthusiastic about Bresnahan's team," a writer for an out-of-town paper noted.[34]

For three weeks, Bresnahan relied exclusively on three starting pitchers—Bob Harmon, Bill Steele and Slim Sallee—and Ewing didn't pitch at all for the first month of the season. But inevitably the time came when Bresnahan had to find out whether Long Bob was worth keeping. The test came on May 13. It was a Monday afternoon at Robison Field and the eighth-place Cardinals were playing host to the fifth-place Boston Braves. None of the papers bothered to report the attendance.

Ewing's day didn't start well and it didn't last long. Boston's leadoff hitter, Bill Sweeney, cracked a drive off Ewing's shin. The ball rebounded away from the defense and Sweeney ended up on second base. Ewing managed to retire the next three hitters, and St. Louis took a 1–0 lead in the bottom of the inning. But in the second, Boston's Art Devlin doubled to deep left and went to third on a long fly out. When Ed McDonald walked, Bresnahan had seen enough. He lifted Ewing and called in Bill Steele.

The game lasted nearly three hours. St. Louis ultimately came from behind to win 4–3 in 11 innings. Amid that drama, the papers wasted little ink on Ewing. The reporters didn't ask Bresnahan why he pulled Ewing when he still held the lead and hadn't yet given up a run. Or if they asked, they didn't find the answer interesting enough to print. One account said simply that Ewing was relieved after he "began to get bumped" by the Boston hitters.[35] Another said he was yanked after he "developed a wild streak."[36] Considering he had allowed all of two hits and one base on balls, neither explanation is entirely satisfactory. Perhaps Ewing was hobbling from Sweeney's shot in the first inning. Perhaps, given his history, Ewing's arm was hurting and he simply couldn't continue. Or perhaps Bresnahan was already convinced Ewing had reached the end of the line and it only took seven batters to confirm that judgment. Perhaps the start was only a courtesy so the veteran couldn't say he hadn't been given a chance.

The next day, "Ancient Bob," as one St. Louis paper called him,[37] received his unconditional release.

Ewing headed home by way of Cincinnati, where he stopped off to watch a ballgame with Harry Steinfeldt. The homecoming must have stirred some odd sensations. Though the game was played on the same ground where Ewing had sweated and toiled through the best years of his career—the site of an abandoned brickyard where the Reds had played since 1884—the setting was new and strange.

Speaking at the dedication of the Palace of the Fans in 1902, Judge Howard Ferris had declared, "The ravages of time will make little or no change in the buildings that are now dedicated to the national sport."[38] In fact, despite the accolades that greeted the 1902 renovations, the ballpark where Ewing played most of his career quickly proved inadequate. The Palace of the Fans never had enough seats, especially not enough top-dollar box seats. Mushrooming automobile traffic soon overwhelmed the available parking space. The celebrated classical pillars merely spoiled the sightlines for those sitting in the grandstand. Moreover, the structure wasn't especially well built. By the time the stand had been in use five years, the city building inspector was beginning to complain of cracked girders and decaying supports.[39] Demolition work began in the fall of 1911, before the Reds even played their last home game of the season. In the end, the Palace of the Fans had lasted barely 10 seasons.

At the start of the 1912 season, the Reds had moved into a new home. Built at a cost of $400,000, the new park had seats for 20,696 spectators. On Opening Day, it had welcomed a record crowd of more than 26,000. In sharp contrast to the facility it replaced, the new park was noticeably lacking in architectural flourishes. Instead, the red brick exterior "meshed perfectly with the neighborhood ... [and] reflected the working-class surroundings."[40] Though occupying the same space, the new plant retained no recognizable trace of old League Park. The scene of Ewing's greatest triumphs was no more.

There was some sentiment for naming the new park in honor of Garry Herrmann. The Reds' president quickly squelched that idea and modestly chose instead the name Redland Field. In the mid-1930s, Redland would be renamed for the club's new owner and would remain in use until 1970 as Crosley Field.

BACK HOME, Ewing worked on the farm. He pitched a few games for the town team in Wapakoneta. And before long, baseball came calling with another chance.

Roger Bresnahan may have recommended Ewing to George Stallings, or perhaps Stallings filed Ewing's name away for future reference back in April, when he passed through St. Louis scouting for pitchers who might not be up to major league standards but might still be good enough to help him.

Stallings was a former major league manager and before that, had been a major league catcher briefly in the 1890s. Away from the ballpark, the native Georgian cultivated the manner of a courtly southern gentleman. On the field, he was known for his colorful language and many quirks and superstitions. He was a smart and innovative baseball man, one of the first managers to achieve noteworthy success by platooning with right- and left-handed batters. Back in the major leagues in 1914, Stallings would lead the Boston Braves from last place in mid-July to the National League pennant and a stunning World Series sweep over the favored Philadelphia Athletics, thereby earning himself a lasting place in baseball lore as the game's "Miracle Man." But in 1912 he was in the minor leagues, in his second stint as manager of the Buffalo Bisons in the Class AA International League. By mid-season, the Bisons were in seventh place and badly in need of pitching.

Stallings liked his pitchers well seasoned. In 1912 he tried eight former major leaguers. When Ewing arrived in Buffalo, the staff included his former Philadelphia teammate Fred Beebe and ex-Detroit Tiger Ralph "Sailor" Stroud, plus Phifer Fullenwider, a North Carolinian who had landed in Buffalo after being cut by the New York Giants.[41] Ironically, Stallings' most consistent winner was a 19-year-old left-hander, Charlie Jamieson. The team's other up-and-comer was Wally Schang, a 22-year-old catcher discovered on a local semipro team. Both Jamieson and Schang would eventually play in the major leagues into the 1930s—though in Jamieson's case, big league success wouldn't come until after he was converted to an outfielder.

Ewing encountered a number of familiar faces in the International League. Joe McGinnity, a frequent mound rival when he was with the Giants, was now manager and part-owner of the Newark club—and, at 41, still his own best pitcher.[42] Jack Dunn, who ruined Ewing's no-hit bid in 1903, was owner and manager in Baltimore. Thirty-nine-year-old Cy Seymour was playing the outfield (and still batting over .300) for Newark. Bill Bergen was catching for Baltimore and another ex-Red, Harry Gaspar, was pitching for Toronto. Two of Ewing's former managers, Joe Kelley and John Ganzel, were battling for the pennant as managers of the Toronto Maple Leafs and the Rochester Hustlers.

Some of these veterans, at least, still harbored aspirations of returning to the major leagues. Ewing certainly hadn't given up on that possibility. He signed with Buffalo on the condition that the club agreed to release him at the end of the season. If his performance in the last two months of the season turned some heads, he wouldn't be tied to Buffalo in 1913; he would be free to accept the best offer he could get—possibly, if all went well, a ticket back to the majors.

Ewing made his Bison debut on July 13. The game was in Toronto, where the ballpark was on an island in Lake Ontario, accessible only by ferry. Long Bob entered the game in relief of Phifer Fullenwider after the Maple Leafs scored seven runs in the first two innings. Ewing "and his wild-breaking spitter"[43] allowed only one run over the next seven, but he ultimately lost the game 10–9 in the 10th.

He beat Montreal 10–2 in his next outing and on July 23 he authored a six-hit shutout against Jersey City, out-pitching ex-Red Jack Doscher. But overall, Ewing was erratic. Used as a reliever and spot starter, he appeared in 12 games. He won five and lost four, but got touched up for 98 hits in 83 innings. George Stallings never did get his pitching sorted out. After a parade of Buffalo hurlers surrendered 37 hits in dropping a doubleheader to Newark, *Sporting News* correspondent Carl W. Chester declared that the "high-salaried … old major stars of the Bison staff look like has-beens."[44] Though Ewing wasn't among the offenders on that particular afternoon, the assessment applied to him as well. The team, a dozen games under .500 when Ewing signed, won more than it lost after his arrival, but still couldn't climb above fifth place.

The Buffalo club granted Ewing his freedom on October 7. No big league offers were forthcoming.

OVER THE WINTER, Ewing sent inquiries to several teams in the high minors. The best offer he got was a tryout with the Minneapolis Millers. The Millers were arguably the strongest minor league team of the time; if the road back to the big leagues didn't necessarily run through Minneapolis, it was at least a place where a proven major league veteran could collect a top minor league salary.

The Millers were owned and operated by two brothers, Mike and Joe Cantillon. Mike served as club president and Joe—a one-time major league umpire and former manager of the Washington Senators, for whom he signed Walter Johnson—was the field manager. Unlike most minor league operators, whose success depended heavily on developing young players who could be sold on to the big leagues, the Cantillons simply tried to assemble the strongest possible team every year and hoped to make money by winning games and putting fans in the seats. Typically their teams were loaded with famous old hands, aging but still able, and they had enjoyed outstanding success, winning three straight American Association pennants. When Ewing signed with Minneapolis, a small headline in *The Sporting News* announced that he was "joining [the] old men's home."[45]

But before Ewing could join anything, his plans were put on hold by the catastrophic spring floods of 1913. The deluge inundated large parts of Cincinnati, where the Ohio River overflowed its banks and put Redland Field under water. The story was much the same up and down Ohio's Miami Valley. Statewide, flooding was blamed for 467 deaths. Along Auglaize Street in Wapakoneta, 15 miles from Ewing's New Hampshire farm, rescuers in rowboats plucked stranded residents from second-story windows.

Ewing reached Minneapolis just as the season was beginning—just in time, that is, to miss both spring training and a brief smallpox scare that resulted in one player, pitcher Ralph Comstock, being temporarily quarantined in the local pesthouse.

Looking around the clubhouse, Ewing would have seen immediately that *The Sporting News*' assessment of his new club had some validity.

Among the Millers' regulars were infielders Dave Altizer and Jimmy Williams, outfielders Claude Rossman and George Browne, and pitchers Roy Patterson and Bill Burns—all major league veterans and all well into their 30s. Burns had been a teammate of Ewing's in Philadelphia and Browne, when he was a New York Giant, had been something of a nemesis. Out of the same mold, and also in the Millers' lineup, were two of the Delahanty brothers, Frank and Jim. Jim Delahanty had witnessed all stages of Ewing's career, from its beginning in the Northwestern Ohio League to its peak in Cincinnati, and now he was in at the finish.

Also on hand was Rube Waddell, the overgrown delinquent and former American League strikeout king. During his glory years with the Philadelphia Athletics, Waddell was one of the game's biggest stars and certainly its greatest character. Sportswriters never tired of retelling, embellishing and embroidering tales of the big left-hander's bizarre antics. Today, what a biographer characterized as Waddell's "incorrigible childishness"[46] might justify any number of diagnoses—manic depression, acting out, bipolar or personality disorders, narcissism.[47] Another modern view attributes Waddell's peculiar behavior to "either severe psychological problems or … at least mild retardation."[48] Whatever his condition, it was clearly exacerbated by alcoholism.

At 36, Waddell was three years removed from the major leagues. He had pitched for Minneapolis in 1911 and 1912. He had also made himself a hero in Hickman, Kentucky, where the Millers conducted spring training. During floods along the Mississippi River in 1912 and again in 1913, Waddell worked tirelessly helping to shore up the levee with sandbags, sometimes going days without sleep. Toiling for hours waist-deep in the icy water, he was a conspicuous figure, a shirtless white man towering above a sea of mostly black laborers.

By Opening Day, Waddell was in bed with a case of pleurisy, soon compounded by a hemorrhaging lung. Two weeks later, in no shape to pitch for the Millers, Waddell was demoted to the Cantillons' farm team, the Minneapolis Broncos—frequently called the "Little Millers"—in the Class C Northern League, where it was hoped he could regain his strength. But his health was broken. Bent double with coughing spasms between deliveries, he made his last attempt to pitch on July 20.[49] Nine months later, Rube Waddell was dead.

Ewing sightings are infrequent in the Minneapolis papers, but they trace a neat and succinct storyline. On April 16 the *Minneapolis Tribune* noted that the Millers' latest pitching acquisition "lobbed the ball over to the batters in practice" and, on the strength of that showing, opined that he "looks as though he still has an arm which will earn him a salary."[50] Four days later, a photograph taken during pre-game warm-ups showed Ewing "at play in the outfield" with teammates Bill Burns and Red Killefer.[51] At the end of the month, Joe Cantillon was said to be contemplating starting Ewing in an upcoming series with Columbus.

The start never materialized. A month into the season, Ewing still had not appeared in a game. On May 13—three weeks after Long Bob's 40th birthday and a year to the day after his last major league appearance—Mike Cantillon approached Ewing and asked if he was in shape to pitch. Ewing said he didn't think he was quite there yet. Cantillon, according to the *Tribune*, decided on the spot that if Ewing wasn't ready after a month with the team, he never would be.

"So the twirler was released," the reporter concluded, "and at this writing is in parts unknown."[52]

ENDNOTES

1   *St. Louis Globe-Democrat*, March 24, 1912.
2   *The Sporting News,* Nov. 30, 1911.
3   *Cincinnati Times-Star*, reprinted in the *Shelby County Democrat*, April 22, 1904.
4   Unidentified news clipping, September 1911.
5   *The Sporting News,* Nov. 30, 1911.
6   *Ibid.*, Jan. 25, 1912.
7   *Ibid.*, March 28, 1912.
8   Bill James, *The New Bill James Historical Baseball Abstract* (New York: The Free Press, 2001), p. 377.
9   Edward Mott Woolley, "The Business of Baseball," *McClure's Magazine*, Vol. XXXIX, No. 3 (July 1912), p. 250.
10   *Ibid.*
11   *The Sporting News*, Dec. 29, 1912.
12   *Ibid.*, Jan. 18, 1950.
13   *Sporting Life*, Jan. 20, 1912.
14   *St. Louis Globe-Democrat*, March 4, 1912.
15   *Ibid.*, March 8, 1912.
16   Completed in 1902, the West Baden Springs Hotel had 708 rooms rising in six circular tiers around an inner court 200 feet in diameter, culminating in a domed atrium 130 feet high. Amenities included hot and cold running water, marble bathrooms, telephones, steam heat and electric light. See the *St. Louis Times*, Oct. 31, 1917.

17 *St. Louis Globe-Democrat*, March 10, 1912.

18 *The Sporting News*, March 28, 1912.

19 *St. Louis Globe-Democrat*, March 12, 1912.

20 *Ibid.*, March 13, 1912.

21 *Boston Globe*, Sept. 6, 1911.

22 *St. Louis Globe-Democrat*, March 18, 1912.

23 *Ibid.*, March 24, 1912.

24 *Ibid.*, March 10, 1912.

25 *Ibid.*

26 *St. Louis Times*, March 21, 1912.

27 Indoor baseball was a variant of the game adapted for play in a gymnasium. Players typically used a smaller bat and a soft ball roughly twice the size of a baseball. See Dean A. Sullivan, *Middle Innings: A Documentary History of Baseball, 1900-48* (Lincoln, Neb.: University of Nebraska Press, 1998), p. 47.

28 *New York Times*, March 29, 1912.

29 Patricia O'Toole, *When Trumpets Call: Theodore Roosevelt After the White House* (New York: Simon and Schuster, 2005), p. 175.

30 *St. Louis Globe-Democrat*, March 29, 1912.

31 *Ibid.*, March 13, 1912.

32 *The Sporting News*, March 28, 1912.

33 *Ibid.*, April 18, 1912.

34 *New York Times*, May 8, 1912.

35 *St. Louis Star*, May 14, 1912.

36 *St. Louis Times*, May 14, 1912.

37 *St. Louis Post-Dispatch*, May 14, 1912.

38 *Cincinnati Enquirer*, May 17, 1902.

39 Michael Benson, *Ballparks of North America: A Comprehensive Historical Reference to Baseball Grounds, Yards and Stadiums, 1845 to Present* (Jefferson, N.C.: McFarland and Co. Inc., 1989), p. 101.

40 Greg Rhodes and John Erardi, *Cincinnati's Crosley Field: The Illustrated History of a Great Ballpark* (Cincinnati: Road West Publishing, 1995), p. 43.

41 Fullenwider never pitched in a big league game, but he went to spring training with the Giants in 1912 and pitched for them at the Polo Grounds on April 21 in a benefit game for survivors of the sinking of the *Titanic*. He worked three "very successful" innings as the Giants beat the Yankees 11-2; *New York Times*, April 22, 1912.

42 Iron Man Joe McGinnity continued to pitch in the minor leagues until he was 54 years old. In all, his playing career spanned 34 years.

43 *Toronto Daily Star*, July 15, 1912.

44 *The Sporting News*, Aug. 29, 1912.

45 *Ibid.*, April 17, 1913.

46 Alan H. Levy, *Rube Waddell: The Zany, Brilliant Life of a Strikeout Artist* (Jefferson, N.C.: McFarland and Co. Inc., 2000), p. 303.

47 *Ibid.*, p. 6.

48 Donald Dewey and Nicholas Acocella, *The Biographical History of Baseball* (New York: Carroll and Graf Publishers, 1995), p. 487.

49 By this time, Waddell had been dropped by Minneapolis and picked up by the last-place Virginia (Minn.) Ore Diggers. See Rich Arpi, "Rube and His Bears: A Short History of the Virginia Ore Diggers and the Team's Time in the Northern League," *The National Pastime*, No. 42 (2012), p. 22; and

Harry Brammell, "Tribute from Rube's Last Battery Mate," *The Sporting News*, April 9, 1914.

50   *Minneapolis Tribune*, April 16, 1913.
51   *Ibid*., April 20, 1913.
52   *Ibid*., May 14, 1913.

> "Every once in a while somebody asks me how many of the old trio are dead. I tell them we're *all* dead, but Chance is the only one who's buried."
>
> —JOHNNY EVERS, 1940[1]

CHAPTER 14

Final Innings

ACTUALLY, it wouldn't have been difficult to guess Bob Ewing's whereabouts in the hours after his release by the Minneapolis Millers. Ewing wasn't one to sit and sulk or drown his sorrows in a barroom. He drew his pay, packed his bags, and caught a train for home.

Ewing's conversation with Mike Cantillon took place on Tuesday. By Friday evening, he was back home in New Hampshire, Ohio. On Sunday afternoon, he took the mound for the same town team he had pitched for as an unknown farm boy in the 1890s. For several years now they had been called the Wapakoneta Reds, reflecting his hometown's allegiance to the big league club long associated with their hometown hero. "Scores and hundreds of friends" came to witness Ewing's return. What they saw as he effortlessly shut out a visiting squad from Findlay, a local newspaper reported, was "the same hardworking, clean and enthusiastic pitcher he has been for years in league ball."[2]

A week later he made another appearance on the local diamond. This time, with ample opportunity for appropriate arrangements, boosters mounted an official "Ewing Day" celebration. And this time, in contrast to the 18–0 rout of Findlay, promoters promised a real ballgame. The opposition would be provided by a well-regarded nearby town team, the Botkins Reds, led by their formidable left-hander, referred to in a Wapakoneta paper as "the famous Burley Peart."[3]

Nearly 600 people paid to see the duel. The first time Ewing came to bat, the game was halted so he could be presented with "a splendid grip-horn gold-mounted umbrella" with an engraved plate on the detachable handle.[4] Then, in the tradition of such "presentation speech" moments, he returned to the plate and struck out.

Once he got down to business, Ewing struck out 11 and allowed only three or four hits, depending on whose account one trusts. Even so, "Botkins hit the ball with greater regularity by far than did Findlay" and Wapakoneta's defense was repeatedly put to the test. With such old hands as Harry Eichler, Lefty Houtz and Whitey Guese playing behind Ewing, there were "several instances [when] swats that looked good for a couple of bases were pulled down."[5] When Ewing picked off a base runner to kill a potentially game-tying rally in the seventh inning, Botkins howled loudly—but to no avail—for a balk call. Wapakoneta ultimately prevailed by a 4–3 score, but even the local paper acknowledged "it wasn't a May Day picnic…by any means."[6]

After that, the old leaguer found himself in demand as a gate attraction for teams throughout western Ohio. The newspapers in Kenton started a drumbeat for a "Ewing Day" game there. Teams from Lima and elsewhere attempted to pump up their crowds by announcing—often in clear and total disregard of the truth—that Ewing was scheduled to pitch. What could have developed into a Bob Ewing farewell tour never took place. Long Bob had taken on the first Wapakoneta game "merely for practice,"[7] indicating he was keeping in shape in case an opportunity arose to return to professional ball. But, having been given his walking papers by four teams in a little over a year and a half, he soon accepted that baseball had decided it was time for him to retire.

Ewing pitched his last formal game in Bellefontaine, Ohio, on June 17, 1913. The occasion was the dedication of a new ballpark and Ewing agreed to do the honors for the Bellefontaine Greys against a collection of former minor leaguers who billed themselves as the Columbus All-Professionals. Ewing rose early, as usual, and worked five hours on the farm before knocking off at 10 a.m. to make the 20-mile trip to Bellefontaine. He took along his Philadelphia Phillies uniform, and it was good that he did. The uniform set aside for him by the Bellefontaine team proved laughably too small for the lanky pitcher.

From the moment of his arrival, the *Bellefontaine Examiner* glowed, Ewing "was the hero every minute."[8] Before a paying crowd of nearly

1,000, he banged out four hits, including two doubles, and drove in three runs. Even after shelving the spitball, which proved too much for the Bellefontaine catcher to handle, he struck out 12 and permitted only five hits. There was one embarrassing moment in the fourth inning when Long Bob was picked off second base on a hidden-ball trick, but that was soon forgotten as he cruised to a 6–3 victory. The *Examiner* pronounced it "as pretty an exhibition as was ever given on any baseball field."[9]

In the crowd was Bade Myers, a former Toledo teammate of Ewing's who was now managing the Canton Senators in the Class D Interstate League. Myers was sufficiently impressed to offer Long Bob a job. Ewing asked if he could sleep on it before giving an answer. At this stage of his life, Ewing had little enthusiasm for bouncing around towns like Steubenville, Wheeling and Zanesville on the bottom rung of organized baseball. He might have been able to fool bush league batters with some combination of spit and savvy, but there wasn't much in it for him, monetarily or competitively. For a 40-year-old pitcher, Canton was for all practical purposes as far removed from the major leagues as Wapakoneta or Bellefontaine. After turning the matter over in his mind, Ewing told Myers that before he could return to baseball, he would have to find two good men to fill in on the farm—one to work in the hay field and another to oversee the hog sale. "Those things come before baseball with me now," Ewing wrote.[10]

Ewing didn't miss much by declining Myers' offer. Barely a month later, with Canton in seventh place, the Interstate League folded.

Subsequent ballpark sightings typically found Ewing in civilian clothes, sometimes sitting with the players, "pulling hard on his cigar during the interesting moments of the game."[11] A story that he had broken his arm in an industrial league game in Lima was picked up by a national publication, but when a reporter tracked Ewing down, he insisted his arm was as good as ever and he hadn't been in Lima in two months.

AS TIME PASSED, Ewing settled into post-baseball life. He trained harness horses and bred hunting dogs. He hunted in season, often with his brother Maynard, the two of them spending contented hours together and hardly exchanging a word.[12] He farmed for a few more years, but by 1916 he had sold off most of his acreage. During World War I, he worked at a Lima plant that manufactured Garford "Liberty" trucks for the military. Among his responsibilities was organizing a baseball league for the factory workers.

In September 1915 Bob and Nelle's first child, a son, died shortly after birth. Two years later, when he was 43 years old and she was 36, they became parents again. Borrowing something from each parent, Nelle named the child Robert Hunter Ewing. She always joked that her son's initials came from the line score notation for runs, hits and errors.

Ewing's life after his playing days, comfortable and respectable, was typical of most of his contemporaries. A few of them, however, living up (or down) to the unsavory reputation under which baseball players labored when Ewing was starting out, came to sad ends. Poor Larry McLean, ever more relentlessly tormented by his demons, eventually drank and brawled his way out of baseball and was shot to death in a Boston saloon in 1921, at age 39.

At least four of Ewing's former teammates got caught up in the gambling scandals that rocked baseball in the wake of the 1919 World Series. Sleepy Bill Burns acted as a bagman for gamblers during the series and later emerged as the star witness for the prosecution in the conspiracy trial of the eight so-called "Black Sox"; out of baseball and beyond the reach of the commissioner's office, Burns escaped without punishment. Jean Dubuc, who admitted knowing about the fix and placing bets based on insider knowledge, became *persona non grata* in organized baseball for a time, but he slipped quietly back into the minor leagues in 1922 and eventually returned to the majors as a coach with the Detroit Tigers. Gene Dale, who had shared Ewing's brief sojourn in St. Louis, was banned from baseball in 1921 for his part in a Pacific Coast League bribery scheme.[13] Al "Cozy" Dolan, a rookie in Cincinnati during Ewing's last year there, was a coach for the Giants in 1924 when he was accused of attempting to bribe a member of the Philadelphia Phillies to dump a game. Baseball Commissioner Kenesaw Mountain Landis banned Dolan for life.

The Black Sox scandal also brushed up against Garry Herrmann. It happened after the name of one Philip Hahn of Cincinnati, referred to as "the betting commissioner," surfaced in grand jury testimony. Two days later, Herrmann acknowledged to Ban Johnson that he was well acquainted with Hahn. Herrmann was subsequently called to testify before the grand jury but prosecutors seemed to take pains not to ask him any potentially embarrassing questions; his testimony was inconsequential and there was no further inquiry into Herrmann's relationship with Philip Hahn.[14]

Cy Seymour, fated to play out a Ruthian drama writ small to the end, contracted tuberculosis while working in the New York shipyards during the war and died at 46.[15] Miller Huggins also lived barely into middle age. After a respectable playing career, Huggins achieved true greatness as a manager, winning six pennants and three World Series with the New York Yankees in the 1920s, but the little man who had dated Nelle Hunter before she became Mrs. Bob Ewing never married; when he died in 1929, Damon Runyon recalled him as a rather sad figure, "a solitary chap, with few intimates."[16]

For the most part, though, Ewing's mates seem to have enjoyed reasonably fulfilling lives. Several were baseball lifers who never retired. John Ganzel's career spanned more than 50 years, mostly as a minor league manager and executive. Andy Coakley coached 38 years at Columbia University, where his discoveries included Lou Gehrig. Hans Lobert, longtime coach, manager and scout, was calculated to have logged more years in baseball than anyone other than Connie Mack.[17]

Some accumulated considerable wealth, among them Clark Griffith, who became the owner of the Washington Senators. Orval Overall went into banking and, upon his death, was described as "the most opulent of the old Cubs."[18] Dummy Hoy, who batted leadoff for the Reds the day Ewing made his major league debut, saved and invested carefully and lived comfortably to the end of his long life; a son and a grandson became judges, and at age 99—recognized as the oldest living former major leaguer[19]—Hoy threw out the first ball for the third game of the 1961 World Series between the Reds and the Yankees.

A few of Ewing's teammates went from fleeting big league trials to distinguished careers in medicine or law.[20] Most seem to have used baseball as a steppingstone to middle-class respectability. Catcher Tommy Clarke owned a restaurant in New York City. Pitcher Jack Rowan delivered mail in Dayton, Ohio. Noodles Hahn became a government meat inspector in

By 1920 Bob Ewing had traded in his baseball flannels for a suit and tie to make a run for public office. He was elected to two terms as Auglaize County sheriff. *Photo courtesy of Charlotte Ewing-Preville.*

Cincinnati; in his 60s, he still suited up and worked out at Crosley Field, mingling with players who had no inkling that he was once the National League's preeminent left-hander. Former home run champ Fred Odwell went back to Downsville, New York, where, with a letter of recommendation from Garry Herrmann, he got himself appointed postmaster.

In March 1920, Ewing took over the Brunswick Pool Parlor. The Brunswick had been (and in time would be again) a popular Wapakoneta watering hole, but in 1920 its future was somewhat doubtful. The 18th Amendment to the Constitution had just taken effect, banning the manufacture, importation, transportation or sale of alcoholic beverages in the United States. If Ewing's new business was to survive the dry years of Prohibition, it would have to do so as a pool hall and tobacco shop. Ewing would hold a lease on the Brunswick for nearly a decade. But he also had loftier aspirations for his post-baseball career. He was about to enter politics.

Ewing's family had a long, if modest, history of public service. As far back as 1853, his maternal grandfather had been a justice of the peace. More recently, both his father and his brother had served as clerk of Goshen Township. His father-in-law had been elected six times as Auglaize County coroner and was acknowledged as an influential man in the Democratic Party.

The Democrats had controlled Auglaize County virtually as long as it had existed. For whatever reason, though, when Ewing decided to run for sheriff, he entered the lists as a Republican. His affiliation probably had little to do with ideological commitment or deep political convictions. More likely the underdog party put out some feelers and Ewing grasped an interesting opportunity. His complete lack of training or experience in law enforcement was not viewed as a particular drawback. Especially in rural counties, the perception was that there was little serious crime to be dealt with. The job of sheriff was seen as requiring mainly an honest, conscientious citizen with some common sense. An electable candidate needed little more than an upstanding reputation and some name recognition. That being the case, the sheriff's office presented an attractive employment opportunity for ex-ballplayers. At least six of Ewing's former teammates served as county sheriffs in Ohio and other states.[21]

In terms of reputation and recognition, Long Bob was the ideal candidate. His campaign was disarmingly artless. One-column newspaper advertisements announced:

There was a photograph of the old spitballer in suit and tie, and underneath, the words "Root for him to win his game November 2, 1920."[22]

Even in what was up to then a Democratic stronghold, Ewing's likability and personal popularity were considerable assets. And, unwittingly or not, he had picked a propitious moment to hitch his wagon to the GOP star. Riding the coattails of Ohioan Warren G. Harding's presidential landslide, Auglaize Republicans won every countywide office on the ballot except for a single judgeship where the Democratic candidate was unopposed. Ewing garnered a comfortable 54.6 percent of the tally, outdistancing his Democratic opponent by 1,046 votes.

One of the perks of Ewing's new job was a place to live, provided by the county. With the start of his term, Bob and Nelle moved into the jail, where she would serve as matron, feeding the prisoners and overseeing housekeeping chores. Ewing quickly got an indication of what he was up against. He hadn't been in office a month before he took a prisoner to New Hampshire to work out a financial settlement with his wife on a non-support charge. While in the village, Ewing had an errand to run, so the trusting rookie lawman left the prisoner "on his honor" at the barbershop, only to return a short time later and find that the bird had flown.[23] While Ewing fumed, the newspapers had a field day, especially the pro-Democrat *Wapakoneta Daily News*. He subsequently came in for more of the same treatment when his car, parked on the street in downtown Wapakoneta, was stolen practically from under his nose.

It wasn't long, however, before the new sheriff had more serious business to deal with. On November 21, 1921, Joseph Scott Kershaw, an unemployed veteran of the late world war, was shot to death in a boxcar on a freight train traveling between Lima and Wapakoneta. The only other person in the car was Harold Nierengarten, a 20-year-old bellboy at a Lima hotel. Because of uncertainty on which side of the county line the shooting took place, there was some question as to where the case should be prosecuted. Nierengarten was initially held in Lima, where he was quizzed for five days by a succession of interrogators, including Ewing. The suspect was ultimately charged in Wapakoneta, where the indictment for first-degree murder was described as "the first of its character in [Auglaize] county for many years,"[24] and lodged in Ewing's jail to await trial.

Notwithstanding the severity of the charge against him, and Nelle's presentiments about having an accused murderer under the same roof with her family, the former juvenile delinquent didn't seem a very dangerous or desperate character. Certainly the prisoner wouldn't have cut much of a figure among the brash and brawny ballplayers Ewing had associated with for most of his adult life. Described as "very slight in build...[and] delicate in appearance,"[25] Nierengarten had an oddly inert quality; the other bellhops at Lima's Argonne Hotel had nicknamed him "Statuary."[26] Still, the sheriff took extra precautions. Unlike Ewing's other guests,[27] Nierengarten was to be locked in a separate cell every night. While the other prisoners had the run of a common "bullpen" area during the day, Nierengarten was kept locked up most of the time. Ewing instructed the other inmates to look after their fellow boarder as best they could, fetching him a drink of water should he ask for one or bringing other requests to the attention of jail staff. And so a month passed uneventfully.

Then, a little after 7:30 a.m. on Friday, February 10, while Bob was in the basement firing the coal furnace and Nelle was preparing breakfast for the prisoners, the telephone rang. Nelle answered and a woman living about a block from the jail relayed the news that she had just seen Harold Nierengarten running down an alley.

For the next three days, "the countryside for a hundred miles in every direction" remained "in a furor of excitement."[28] The reward offered for Nierengarten's capture, dead or alive, quickly grew to $300; Ewing kicked in $50 out of his own pocket. A team of bloodhounds was called in to track the fugitive and Ewing grew haggard from lack of sleep. Thirty-six hours after the escape, the sheriff "was the picture of disconsolation." There were deep circles under his eyes and "his shoes and clothes were muddy from ceaseless tramping."[29]

Even as the search went on, investigators tried to figure out how the escape had occurred. First thought was that the 120-pound Nierengarten had somehow managed to wriggle through a "grub hole" by which meals were passed in to prisoners. That theory was discarded after an experiment demonstrated that even 4-year-old Bobby Ewing could not squeeze through the 5½-by-17½-inch opening. Ewing was initially convinced that Nierengarten must have had "inside help,"[30] but the other prisoners strenuously denied any involvement. Nelle complained publicly about responsibility for the escape falling on her husband, telling a group of Lima men, "You should have kept him up there where he belongs."[31] Suspicion fell for a time on a young woman employed at the jail as domestic help, but she too was quickly cleared.

The mystery was still unsolved late Sunday afternoon when a farmer collecting eggs in his granary near the rural crossroads of St. Johns noticed that a tarpaulin wasn't where he had left it. He gave a tentative kick and something moved underneath. Thinking he might be dealing with a possum, the farmer fetched a neighbor to help dispose of it. They lifted the tarp and came face to face with Harold Nierengarten.

The wanted man was a forlorn figure. He gave every indication he was glad that his bid for freedom was over. His feet were frostbitten and he shivered in the cold. For three days and two nights, he said, he had had nothing to eat or drink. Hiding by day and moving by night, he had crisscrossed the landscape on a confused course that carried him only six miles from Wapakoneta. While the neighbor ran to find a telephone, Nierengarten was taken to the farmhouse, where the farmer's wife sat him down by the glowing coal stove and fed him noodle soup.

Ewing didn't get to be in on the arrest. When the call came into the jail, he was on his way to Muncie, Indiana, to examine a man in custody there who was said to fit Nierengarten's description. The honor of bringing the fugitive back to jail fell to county Prosecutor Karl Timmermeister. Hurrying to the scene of the capture, Timmermeister arrived to find dozens of neighbors already gathered to gawk at the accused killer, who was being interviewed by two reporters from the *Wapakoneta Daily News*.

One thing they wanted to know was how Nierengarten had managed to escape. His explanation led to the unavoidable conclusion that he owed his 56 hours at liberty to extraordinary carelessness on the part of his jailers. Nierengarten said his cell had been left unlocked and the keys to an outer door left within reach. He simply looked for an opportune moment, then slipped down a corridor and out a window. Regardless who was directly to blame, the ultimate responsibility came down entirely on Sheriff Ewing.

THE ESCAPEE WAS HARDLY BACK in his cell before Ewing had another slaying on his hands. Two days after Nierengarten's capture, Ewing was urgently summoned to the village of Minster in southwest Auglaize County. When Ewing arrived, he found Charles "Red" Piening, a 48-year-old horse trader, in the custody of the town marshal and the community in shock over the death of the parish priest, Father Richard Schwieterman. After days of drinking moonshine liquor, Piening had fallen into hallucinations and become convinced, as he later testified, that specters were attempting to kill him. Schwieterman was called in hopes of calming the disturbed man. Instead, upon entering Piening's two-room shack, the priest was killed by a shotgun blast to the chest.

As best the boys in the press could determine, there hadn't been a murder trial in Auglaize County in 30 years. Now, on Ewing's watch, there were about to be two of them back to back.

When Nierengarten's trial opened on March 7, 1922, 500 people came out to witness the unfolding drama. A crowd had gathered by 5:30 a.m. in hopes of getting into the courtroom. Budding entrepreneurs soon found there were profits to be made in delivering water, soft drinks, fruit and sandwiches to spectators who didn't want to risk giving up their seats over the lunch break.

Those who got in were not disappointed. The trial climaxed with sensational testimony from the defendant. Nierengarten admitted shooting Kershaw, but told the jury he had been unable to stop himself. Ever since being struck over the head during a fight several months earlier, he said, he had been periodically seized by what he described as a sudden, overpowering "impulse to kill."[32]

By now, after more than a year in office and having dealt with two homicides and a jailbreak, Ewing was becoming more acclimated to his duties and comfortable with the routine. Even amid the highly charged atmosphere of the trial, there were moments of levity. At one point Judge Joseph D. Barnes called the noon recess and instructed Ewing to take the jurors to lunch.

"Rather unlucky, don't you think?" Ewing remarked, noting that would make 13 at the table.

"Well," the judge replied, "you don't have to eat."[33]

The jury deliberated 12 hours before returning a verdict of guilty with a recommendation for mercy. Nierengarten was spared the death penalty but was sentenced to life in prison without the possibility of parole.

Rumors and rumblings of another escape attempt had swirled during the trial. Ewing and his deputies, eager to avoid further embarrassment, maintained a constantly heightened state of alertness throughout the weeks leading up to Nierengarten's conviction and delivery to the state penitentiary. In one search of the prisoner's cell, Ewing—probably tipped off by another inmate—discovered two strips of iron, 15 and 18 inches long, bound together with muslin torn from bedding. Nierengarten had reportedly boasted that he "could knock Bob's brains down in his socks" with the improvised weapon.[34]

Piening posed less of a challenge to jail security or Ewing's personal safety, but he presented other complications for the sheriff to deal with. The defendant in Auglaize County's second murder trial of 1922 was a confused, frightened and pathetic figure. Piening was given to wild outbursts and sudden fits of bizarre behavior. At times he repeated the Lord's Prayer over and over, or cried out to God for help. During his arraignment, he lay on the floor in front of the judge and refused to get up. His conduct became so disruptive that Ewing and deputy Ed May had to carry him out of the courtroom. When they attempted to put him in Ewing's car to return to jail, Piening braced his feet against the door and pleaded, "Bob, kill me right here. I don't want to go in there."[35] Any time Piening was out of his cell, in court or on his way to or from, Ewing was never far from his side.

Crowds for the second trial were small at first, only gradually growing to rival those for the previous case. Nierengarten had alarmed the countryside with his escape and inspired a certain morbid fascination with his dark and lethal urges. Imaginative reporters even discerned unlikely flashes of "nerve and bravado" in his public appearances.[36] Piening, by contrast, was described during his trial as a mere "object of curiosity."[37] Most of the time he sat with his chin in his hands, staring at the floor.

Father Schwieterman's parishioners hired an additional attorney to help with the prosecution. A psychiatrist testified for the defense, saying he believed Piening's nervous system had been damaged by heavy drinking and expressing the opinion that the defendant was not responsible for his actions. Piening took the stand and recounted a "rambling story of his life," saying that "from childhood he was accustomed to drinking liquor."[38] Ewing also testified, saying that except for a couple of public outbursts, Piening had appeared "all right" the entire time he had been in custody.[39]

This time the jurors were out only seven hours. They returned a verdict of guilty with no recommendation for clemency. Judge F.C. Layton, setting aside the death penalty, sentenced Piening to life in prison.[40]

THE REMAINDER OF EWING'S TENURE IN OFFICE was relatively uneventful. He was narrowly re-elected for a second two-year term in November 1922. He devoted much of his energy to chasing bootleggers. That was close to a full-time job in Auglaize County. Years earlier, when Ewing's friends and neighbors had voted to make Goshen Township dry, the news startled Ren Mulford 100 miles away in Cincinnati. "When Bob Ewing lands in Redtown he'll have a talc to tell...that will make the gang's eyes bulge," Mulford wrote in *Sporting Life*. "...The idea of a dry spot in Auglaize seems incredible."[41] When Prohibition settled over the entire county as the law of the land, Auglaize fought back vigorously. Bootlegging became big business and "nearly everybody had their leg in it," according to one recollection recorded years later.[42] If it hadn't been owned by the county sheriff, the Brunswick Pool Parlor would have been a good place to find out where to get a drink. As it was, there were stills all over the county and drugstores where a Coke and green alcohol could be had for a quarter.

Executing warrants from local justices of the peace, Ewing dumped buckets and smashed barrels of illicit booze. He dismantled stills and confiscated booze-making equipment. Once in the vicinity of a still, it was often necessary only to follow his nose, tracking the powerful odor of fermenting mash back to its source. Never a drinker of the hard stuff, Long Bob nonetheless became something of an expert on moonshine liquor. After one bust, he and Ed May reported that "the liquor found ... was of a poor grade, being weak and water-soaked."[43] Moonshiners often could expect a year in prison, but in that instance the first-time offender got off with a $250 fine and $17.15 in court costs.

Weeks before the end of his second term, Ewing's routine as a country sheriff was disarranged by another headline-grabbing homicide. This one took place 65 miles to the southeast in Xenia, Ohio. On the morning of November 26, 1924, the day before Thanksgiving, two men argued heatedly on a downtown street corner. The men parted and started to walk in opposite directions. Then one turned, pulled a .38-caliber revolver and fired four times. Across the street, in his office in the Greene County Courthouse, Sheriff Morris Sharp looked up and saw the victim fall. As Sharp and a deputy ran to the scene, the shooter raised his gun in the air and surrendered. By the time the officers reached the fallen man, it was too late to call a doctor.

The dead man was Charles Mackrodt, a former security officer for the Pennsylvania Railroad. The shooter was Cliff "Tacks" Latimer, 46, a former ballplayer and sometime scout for the Cincinnati Reds and other clubs. Around the turn of the century, Latimer had had brief trials as a catcher with five major league teams. Most of his peripatetic career had consisted of an exhaustive tour of minor league outposts—alphabetically from Atlanta to York, Pennsylvania, and geographically from Norwich, Connecticut, to Denver and from Montreal to Montgomery, Alabama. In 16 years he wore 33 different uniforms, never spending an entire season with any club in organized ball.[44]

Those who knew Tacks Latimer were shocked. In unrefined baseball circles, he had always been regarded as a particularly solid citizen. When Latimer was in his early 20s, *The Sporting News* described him as "an earnest, ambitious player…[who] does not smoke, chew or drink."[45] Latimer didn't even like his nickname, which he said was hung on him when he was playing in Austin, Texas. "Tacks" was a sobriquet sometimes applied to players who were prickly or hard to handle, and the implication stung Latimer deeply. "I am the most quiet man in the world, and have never made trouble," he protested. "I was never fresh in a ballgame, either."[46] John H. Gruber, a longtime Pittsburgh sportswriter who had known Latimer when he was with the Pirates, seconded that impression. "In all his history," Gruber wrote, "nowhere can be found an instance in which he came in serious conflict with either umpire or fellow player, or manifested an unruly disposition."[47]

Latimer's good reputation was about all the defense had to work with in his trial, given that there were numerous witnesses to the shooting.

Several men "prominent in baseball"[48] were subpoenaed as character witnesses. The most prominent was Ewing,[49] though it isn't obvious why his testimony was particularly desired. Latimer hailed from the Cincinnati area and was a recognizable figure around the Reds' ballpark. But he and Ewing were never teammates and there is no evidence they were more than casual acquaintances. For five straight years, starting in 1898, Latimer spent part of each season in the same league with Ewing, but in some instances Latimer's stay was so brief that they never met on the field. Still, they knew each other, and to a defense attorney in need of a life preserver for his client, Ewing—an upright citizen and a law officer to boot—probably seemed as good a place to turn as any.

No record has been found of Ewing's testimony or that of any of the other character witnesses. Whatever they said, it didn't help. In court it came out that the slain man had been Latimer's superior before being fired from the railroad security force, a development for which Mackrodt blamed Latimer. Latimer contended that Mackrodt had threatened him repeatedly and fired two shots at him in the rail yard. At the time of the killing, Latimer said, he believed Mackrodt was about to attack him with a knife. The self-defense claim was a tough sell, however, considering that all four of Latimer's shots hit Mackrodt in the back. The only weapon the victim was carrying was a pocketknife, found in his pocket with its blade closed.[50]

Justice came swiftly for Tacks Latimer. The jury deliberated only three hours before finding him guilty of second-degree murder. All together, barely six weeks elapsed between the shooting and Latimer's delivery to the Ohio Penitentiary to begin serving a life sentence. At his sentencing, Latimer shook hands with the attorneys, prosecutors as well as the defense. Reiterating his claim of self-defense, he added, "I hold no grudge against anyone." He promised to be a model prisoner, in hopes of someday winning his release.[51]

In that, Latimer was as good as his word. Soon made a trusty, he spent most of his term in charge of the prison's main gate. He managed the prison baseball team, which played in the Columbus Municipal League. He also distinguished himself in attempting to stop a mass breakout by inmates, including Ewing's old friend Harold Nierengarten, in 1926,[52] and standing guard over terrified prisoners who were released from their cells during a horrific fire in 1930. At least 320 died in the inferno, some roasted alive in their cells by heat so intense it melted the locks before the doors could be opened. A newspaper account described Latimer standing guard through the night with a shotgun "while the fire licked above him."[53] The 1926 incident, when some credited Latimer with saving the life of the warden's daughter, stirred recommendations for clemency. His performance during the fire clinched the issue. On Christmas Eve, 1930, Gov. Myers Y. Cooper issued a full pardon and ordered Latimer's immediate release. He was a free man after serving less than six years of a life sentence. He returned home to the Cincinnati suburb of Loveland, where he died in 1936.

EWING DID NOT seek a third term as sheriff. By the time he stepped down, even the *Wapakoneta Daily News*, which hadn't deigned to mention his name when he was first elected, had kind words for him. Speaking of both Ewing and outgoing Prosecutor Karl Timmermeister, the paper commented:

> Both of these men…have had careers in public office that have been marked by uncommon incidents…as a result of which the officers in charge were in the limelight. Both are leaving office…with clean records and with the good wishes of those who have been in contact or associated with them.[54]

After leaving the sheriff's office, Ewing worked at an assortment of jobs. He continued to run the pool hall for a time (and was later employed there under the new management), operated Wapakoneta's movie theater and, after Prohibition ended in 1933, worked as a bartender. Between Bob's baseball savings and the resources of Nelle's family—including the house on West Auglaize Street that they inherited after her mother's death in 1935—they lived comfortably with few money worries, even during the Depression.

While Ewing had been preoccupied with political campaigns and the duties of sheriff, his former profession had been undergoing sweeping changes. The Black Sox scandal had precipitated the demise of the National Commission and led to the appointment of Judge Landis as baseball's first commissioner, with autocratic powers. On the field, Babe Ruth electrified and transformed the game by hitting 54 home runs in 1920 and 59 in

1921; in his first four seasons with the New York Yankees, Ruth alone hit 28 more home runs than the Reds had amassed as a team during Ewing's entire eight-year stay in Cincinnati.

Of greater interest to Ewing was the major leagues' move in 1920 to ban the slippery, elusive and much-reviled spitball. Exemptions were ultimately granted to 17 established hurlers who were deemed dependent on the pitch for their livelihoods. As a group, this last generation of spitballers effectively buried the notion that the delivery was hard on a pitcher's arm. Burleigh Grimes was 41 years old when he delivered the majors' last legal spitter in 1934. Red Faber, who said he took up the spitball after his arm was "nearly ruined…throwing curves,"[55] pitched for the Chicago White Sox until he was 45. Ageless Jack Quinn, who broke into the big leagues when Ewing was still with the Reds, was past 50 when he loaded up Cincinnati's last legal spitball in 1933.[56]

Once the cares of public office were lifted from his shoulders, Ewing got back into baseball in a small way. But the game he was involved in during the mid-'20s was far removed from the newly sanitized major leagues. As manager of the semipro Wapakoneta Reds of the Ohio-Indiana League, Ewing's experience harked back to his earliest days in baseball 30 years before. Like the Wapakoneta team Ewing had started out with, these Reds played Sunday afternoons against other town teams within a radius of 40 miles, drawing crowds that sometimes approached 1,000 paying customers. The lineup sometimes included Ewing Mahan, the son of Bob's sister Laura. It must have amused the old spitballer that here, beyond the pale of organized ball, spitball artists still loaded up openly and with impunity.

Ewing particularly enjoyed his 1926 team, which reeled off eight straight early victories to take a commanding lead in the standings. By mid-summer, it was clear nobody had a ghost of a chance of catching up, and the entire league—including Wapakoneta—was losing money playing games that were essentially meaningless. At the end of July, league officials awarded Wapakoneta the pennant and canceled the remainder of the schedule. Ewing proudly referred to his boys as "the team that broke up the O-I League."[57]

The league folded for good in 1927, closing the final chapter in Long Bob's involvement with baseball. In retirement Ewing followed the profes-

The 1926 Wapakoneta Reds made a shambles of the semipro Ohio-Indiana League. Bob Ewing (back row, third from left) was the team's manager; the batboy (front) was 9-year-old Bobby Ewing. *Photo courtesy of Charlotte Ewing-Preville.*

sional game only from a distance. He was still interested in sports, enough so to be among more than 100,000 fans at Chicago's Soldier Field on September 22, 1927, for the heavyweight championship boxing match between Jack Dempsey and Gene Tunney. Ewing and the rest of the throng were treated to a classic—the famous "long count" fight in which Tunney came off the canvas after a seventh-round knockdown to retain his title in dramatic fashion. But Ewing found less and less interest in baseball as a spectator sport. Attending the opening game in Cincinnati was an annual ritual for Nelle, who usually went with a group of friends. Bob's participation in these junkets was no more than sporadic.

If Bob had harbored any hard feelings about being traded away from the Reds, however, they faded once he was out of the game. Invited to Cincinnati for a gathering of old ballplayers to mark the National League's golden jubilee in 1925, he responded with a cheerful note to Garry Herrmann: "Will be glad to take part in the Big Celebration. Thanks...and I will see you on the 12th."[58] Ewing and two dozen other former Reds from as far back as the 1870s rode in a parade featuring six bands and a calliope. They were introduced before the game and treated afterward to "one of Garry Herrmann's own parties."[59] Jack Ryder wrote that Ewing still looked "as if he could go right out there into the box and fling them over in the same puzzling manner that he used to employ."[60]

Six years later Ewing returned to Redland Field again for a reunion of nearly 100 ex-Reds and other former big leaguers and, at age 58, he suited up and pitched an inning in Cincinnati's first old-timers game. The invitation generated quite a bit of excitement in the Ewing household.

"Bob...was so proud of that invitation that he carried it around in his pocket to show all his friends," Nelle wrote to the event's organizer. "Bob is looking forward to pitching on the big day and started in training today (August 16). I shall try to do my part in the cooking and dieting to keep him trim."[61]

The five-inning contest was a lark with more than 50 players shuttling in and out, switching positions and even teams. Ewing joined a pitching corps that included Cy Young, Mordecai Brown and two mainstays of the Reds' pennant-winning team of 1919, Hod Eller and Slim Sallee. Among Ewing's erstwhile mates taking the field was 69-year-old Dummy Hoy, who "showed that [he] could still go and get them in the outfield."[62]

One person who sadly wasn't there to enjoy the game, or the banquet afterward, was Garry Herrmann. After decades of rich food and high living, Ewing's old boss had passed away 10 days into the 1931 season at age 71, his death attributed to arteriosclerosis. Since resigning as club president and selling his by-then majority interest in the Reds in 1927, Herrmann—plagued by deafness and deteriorating health—had become increasingly withdrawn. At the end, the man who had been the life of so many parties became a sad and reclusive figure. He was also haunted by fears of financial insecurity. Unlike his mentor, Boss Cox, who had started with nothing and died immensely wealthy, Herrmann had spent or given away a small fortune. Though the Reds' new owners approved a generous annuity (later taken over by major league baseball) for Herrmann, he persisted in the belief that he was destitute. A year before his death, it was reported that he had applied to the International Typographical Union for a pension of $8 a week.[63] When he died, according to Lee Allen, Herrmann's estate amounted to only $800.[64]

The Sporting News headlined the passing of "baseball's great conciliator and father of [the] World Series."[65] The flag flew at half-staff at Redland Field and the Reds' game was postponed the day Herrmann was buried. More than 1,500 people attended his funeral, said to have been the largest ever held at the Elks temple in Cincinnati.

Herrmann's departure from the Reds' front office and his death four years later severed Ewing's last connection to the organization where he spent most of his career. One former teammate with whom he remained in contact was his old catcher and teacher, Heinie Peitz. After his playing days, Peitz managed and umpired in the minor leagues and served as a coach for the Reds and Cardinals, working especially with pitchers. He was a Cincinnati police officer for a time and, in later years, was employed as a "good will man" for a brewery. In 1942, a year before his death, Peitz was among several former ballplayers invited to be special guests at a "hot stove league" banquet that Ewing helped to organize for the Wapakoneta Elks Lodge.

Baseball didn't forget Long Bob, either. He was among the first group of former players presented with lifetime passes to all major league games. Veteran sportswriter Hugh Fullerton, as part of a series in which he named all-time teams for all 16 major league franchises, included

Ewing among his selections. Fullerton confessed some difficulty in choosing a squad from Cincinnati's long line of "freaks, comedians and wild men," but he spoke highly of Ewing, "who with bad teams was consistently good."[66] Ewing received similar recognition in the other city where he pitched longest. When Toledo fans selected an all-time team devoid of representatives from before 1911, local baseball historian Ralph Lin Weber took it upon himself to name his own "Ancient All-Stars" from the 19th century. His pitchers were Tony Mullane, who won 36 games for the Mud Hens in 1884, and Ewing.[67]

Ewing might never have been aware of that honor. For him, acknowledgement usually took more humble forms. Occasionally the mail would bring an autograph request from an aging fan or a young collector; Ewing always graciously complied.[68] Decades after departing the scenes of his baseball exploits, he still periodically turned up in the sports columns. As late as 1943, J.G. Taylor Spink of *The Sporting News*, reminiscing about baseball in the first years of the 20th century, made passing mention of "Long Bob Ewing, a crackerjack pitcher of the time."[69] Two years later, a note in the same publication acknowledged Bob and Nelle's 40th wedding anniversary.

The warmest remembrances were those shared with other members of the fraternity of old ballplayers. Ewing was a regular on the banquet circuit around west central Ohio. He rarely stepped up to the microphone, more typically being content to sit back and listen while others spun their stories of the game's good old days. But once in a while, the spotlight turned briefly on Long Bob. On one such evening, Ewing was among 400 people listening as Roger Bresnahan recounted the embarrassing afternoon when he struck out four times in a ballgame "for the only time in my life."

"And the Cincinnati Red who struck me out four times is right here in this crowd tonight," Bresnahan added. "Long Bob Ewing from Wapakoneta, Ohio. You wouldn't take a bow for it that day, Bob, you rascal, but you're going to take a bow for it tonight."

Perhaps Bresnahan's memory was flawed after more than 40 years, or perhaps he was embellishing the story a bit for Ewing's benefit. The reference clearly was to the game of August 18, 1903, when Ewing shut out the Giants on one hit, fanning Bresnahan three times. In any case, Ewing stood up and took his bow, beaming broadly.[70]

As it turned out, the gathering marked Roger Bresnahan's last public appearance. Three weeks later, the fiery old catcher was dead of a heart attack.

Ewing outlived his long-ago rival and teammate by 2½ years. Diagnosed with cancer of the rectum and large intestine, he fought the disease for 18 months before losing his final extra-inning battle. He died at his home in Wapakoneta on June 20, 1947, at the age of 74. His obituary in the *Cincinnati Post*, under a two-column headline, recalled Long Bob Ewing as "one of the [National] league's best and most frequent users of the now-outlawed spitball."[71]

His death certificate, under "usual occupation," listed "ball player."

Bob and Nelle Ewing share a common gravestone in Walnut Hill Cemetery near New Hampshire, Ohio. The circular engraving between their names features a baseball and a bat. *Photo: Lindsay Steiner.*

1   Frank Graham, *Baseball Extra* (New York: A.S. Barnes and Co., 1954), p. 15.
2   *Auglaize County Democrat*, May 22, 1913.
3   *Ibid.*
4   *Ibid.*, May 29, 1913.
5   *Ibid.*
6   *Ibid.*
7   Ibid., May 22, 1913.
8   *Bellefontaine Examiner*, June 18, 1913.
9   *Ibid.*
10 *Kenton News-Republican*, June 29, 1913.
11 *Ibid.*, Aug. 8, 1913.
12 Ewing earned a local reputation for his prowess as a quail hunter. Robert M. Nichols (1890-1953), a Wapakoneta native who became the shooting editor of *Field and Stream* magazine, said Ewing was mentioned among the best in "the little town ... full of wingshots." See Nichols, *The Shotgunner* (New York: G.P. Putnam and Sons, 1949), quoted in Rachel Barber, ed., *The Book of Wapakoneta* (Wapakoneta, Ohio: Daily News Printing Co., 2009), p. 283.
13 Dale was reinstated in 1941, long after his playing days. It is not clear whether he ever returned to organized ball in any capacity. Ray Nemec found this information in the National Association Bulletin (No. 6, 1941); Nemec, e-mail to the author, Aug. 27, 2004.
14 William A. Cook, *August "Garry" Herrmann: A Baseball Biography* (Jefferson, N.C.: McFarland and Co. Inc., 2008), pp. 248-53.
15 Just as his numbers eclipsed Seymour's in every other regard, Babe Ruth lived a few years longer, dying of throat cancer at age 53 in 1948.
16 *New York American*, Sept. 27, 1929, reprinted in Damon Runyon, edited by Jim Reisler, *Guys, Dolls, and Curveballs: Damon Runyon on Baseball* (New York: Carroll and Graf Publishers, 2005), p. 70. Baseball historian Leo Trachtenberg wrote that "Huggins led a lonely bachelor's existence," shadowed by a "frustrated longing for a family." See Trachtenberg, "The Travails of Miller Huggins," *Baseball History* (summer 1987), p. 58.
17 Lawrence S. Ritter, The Glory of Their Times: *The Story of the Early Days of Baseball Told by the Men Who Played It* (New York: Macmillan Co., 1966), p. 170.
18 *The Sporting News*, July 23, 1947.
19 The same title was inherited years later by Paddy Livingston, a catcher with the Reds in 1906. Livingston was 97 years old when he died in Cleveland in 1977, apparently Ewing's last surviving teammate.
20 Harry Wood, an outfielder in two games for the Reds in 1903, became a prominent Washington, D.C., surgeon. Catchers Philip B. "Peaches" O'Neill (eight games, 1904) and Si Pauxtis (four games, 1909) had long careers in law, O'Neill in Anderson, Ind., and Pauxtis in Philadelphia and Wilkes-Barre, Pa. Obituaries for Wood in the *Washington Post and Times Herald* and for Pauxtis in the *New York Times* made no mention of their baseball backgrounds.
21 The list includes former Reds Al Bridwell in Scioto County, Ohio; Dick Hoblitzell in Wood County, W.Va.; Ward Miller in Lee County, Ill.; Johnny Siegle in Champaign County, Ohio; and Ezra Midkiff, who played one game for Cincinnati on the final day of the 1909 season, in Cabell County, W.Va. In addition, Stanley Arthur, Ewing's catcher with the Toledo Mud Hens, held the office in Clinton County, Ohio, from 1917 to 1921.
22 *Auglaize Republican*, Oct. 28, 1920.
23 *Shelby County Democrat*, Jan. 28, 1921.
24 *The Lima News*, Jan. 5, 1922.

25   *Ibid.*, Feb. 11, 1922.

26   *Ibid.*, March 10, 1922.

27   There were three at the time, serving sentences for petty larceny, forgery and incest.

28   *Wapakoneta Daily News*, Feb. 13, 1922.

29   *The Lima News*, Feb. 12, 1922.

30   *Ibid.*, Feb. 11, 1922.

31   *Ibid.*, Feb. 12, 1922.

32   *Sidney Daily News*, March 10, 1922.

33   *The Lima News*, March 12, 1922.

34   *Sidney Daily News*, March 8, 1922.

35   *Ibid.*, Feb. 18, 1922.

36   *The Lima News*, Jan. 29, 1922.

37   *Wapakoneta Daily News*, April 22, 1922.

38   *The Lima News*, April 20, 1922.

39   *Wapakoneta Daily News*, April 19, 1922.

40   Piening served the entire sentence, but it wasn't long. He died in the prison hospital five months after being sentenced. Nierengarten, against the odds, lived to breathe free again. On Christmas Eve, 1954, Gov. Frank Lausche commuted Nierengarten's sentence to second-degree murder, making him eligible for parole. He was released from prison in 1955, at age 53, and lived at least another 10 years.

41   *Sporting Life*, Jan. 22, 1910.

42   Rachel Barber, ed., *A Celebration in Story: Auglaize County Since 1900 in the Words of its People* (Wapakoneta, Ohio: Auglaize County Sesquicentennial Committee, 1998), p. 115.

43   *Wapakoneta Daily News*, May 5, 1922.

44   Three years before his retirement, Latimer claimed to have a scrapbook that would document his participation in 1,080 professional games (*New Orleans Picayune*, reprinted in *The Sporting News*, Aug. 29, 1907). In several years of diligent digging, Ray Nemec of the Society for American Baseball Research was able to document only something more than 800 games for Latimer's entire career, 1895 to 1910. It seems likely that the player's count included exhibition games and stints with independent or semipro teams.

45   *The Sporting News*, March 31, 1900.

46   *Ibid.*, April 18, 1903.

47   Unidentified newspaper clipping, c. 1926, on file in the A. Bartlett Giamatti Research Center at the National Baseball Hall of Fame.

48   *Wapakoneta Daily News*, Dec. 30, 1924.

49   Also on the witness list was Stanley Arthur, Ewing's minor league catcher and more recently sheriff of neighboring Clinton County.

50   One startling aspect of the case is the light it sheds on the open operation and widespread acceptance of the Ku Klux Klan in the Midwest in the 1920s. Mackrodt's funeral took place at the local Klan Tabernacle, officiated by two local pastors, one identified in news accounts as a "Klan minister" and the other as "former head of the Klan" in Greene County. Evidence at the trial indicated that Mackrodt carried a grudge against the former head of the Klan and had threatened the life of the county coroner, holding them responsible for his expulsion from the organization. The same year as the slaying, Garry Herrmann received a letter from a Cincinnati pastor requesting designation of a "Klan Day" at Redland Field. The writer claimed a combined membership of more than 100,000 in Klaverns in southern Ohio, northern Kentucky and southeastern Indiana, adding, "The greater majority of this number may be counted as loyal Red fans and your club benefits by their patronage from day to day." See the *Xenia Evening Gazette*, Nov. 27, Dec. 1 and Dec. 30, 1924; and O.W. Baylor, letter to August Herrmann,

May 31, 1924. The letter is on file in the A. Bartlett Giamatti Research Center at the National Baseball Hall of Fame.

51   *Xenia Evening Gazette*, Jan. 5, 1925.

52   Thirteen prisoners escaped but were soon recaptured. Nierengarten joined the rush but failed to get past the gate. He went down with a slight head wound, probably from a shot fired either by Latimer or Warden Preston E. Thomas who, according to one newspaper account, were "shooting helter-skelter at the fleeing convicts" (*Columbus Citizen*, Nov. 9, 1926) with a shotgun and a .45-caliber revolver.

53   *The Lima News*, April 22, 1930.

54   *Wapakoneta Daily News*, Jan. 1, 1925.

55   "The Vanishing Spit Ball," *Baseball Magazine* (September 1922), p. 456.

56   Of the last eight legal spitballers, five pitched past the age of 40. Besides Grimes, Faber and Quinn, Dick Rudolph made his last major league appearance at 40 and Clarence Mitchell pitched regularly in the minors until he was 45. Of the eight, Urban Shocker's career ended at the earliest age, 37, but his arm remained sound to the end. His pitching days were abruptly ended by a heart ailment, which proved fatal a few months later.

57   *Wapakoneta Daily News*, Aug. 31, 1926.

58   Bob Ewing, letter to August Herrmann, May 29, 1925. The letter is on file in the A. Bartlett Giamatti Research Center at the National Baseball Hall of Fame.

59   *Cincinnati Post*, June 13, 1925. Lee Allen wrote years later that the party "was a dandy, although Prohibition agents turned out for the occasion and threw something of a damper on the post-game activities." See Allen, *The Cincinnati Reds: An Informal History* (New York: G.P. Putnam's Sons, 1948), p. 175.

60   *Cincinnati Enquirer*, June 13, 1925.

61   Unidentified newspaper clipping, August 1931.

62   *Cincinnati Enquirer*, Sept. 6, 1931.

63   Herrmann had maintained his membership in the union from his boyhood employment as a printer's devil. See *New York World-Telegram*, May 22, 1930, reprinted in Joe Williams, edited by Peter Williams, *The Joe Williams Baseball Reader: The Glorious Game, from Ty Cobb and Babe Ruth to the Amazing Mets* (Chapel Hill, N.C.: Algonquin Books, 1989), p. 37; see also *Washington Post*, April 26, 1931.

64   *The Sporting News*, July 6, 1968.

65   *Ibid.*, April 30, 1931. The references are to Herrmann as broker of the 1903 peace agreement and his later work on the National Commission to establish the World Series as an annual event after none was played in 1904.

66   *Ibid.*, Dec. 12, 1935. Fullerton's other Cincinnati pitchers were Tony Mullane and Ted Breitenstein from the 19th century and Hod Eller, whose career effectively ended when his shine ball was outlawed along with the spitball in 1920. Fullerton also tapped Ewing's teammate Tommy Corcoran at shortstop and Bid McPhee at second base. For catchers, Fullerton went with old-timer Buck Ewing and Heinie Peitz—bypassing Larry McLean, "who should have been one of the greatest of all, but never was."

67   Ralph Lin Weber, *The Toledo Baseball Guide of the Mud Hens, 1883-1943* (Rossford, Ohio: Baseball Research Bureau, 1944), pp. 298-99. The Ancient All-Stars also included Ewing's teammates Erve Beck, Bob Gilks and Skeeter Hartman. Lin Weber passed over Ewing's catcher, Stanley Arthur, in favor of Ed McFarland, who batted .389 for Toledo in 1894.

68   Responding to one such request from a man in St. Paul, Minn., in 1940, Ewing signed his name and added the inscription, "The pleasure is all mine." As of July 2001, the original penny postcard was in the collection of Paul Esacove of Van Nuys, Calif.

69   *The Sporting News*, April 22, 1943.

70   *Ibid.*, Dec. 14, 1944. The banquet took place in Kenton, Ohio, on Nov. 16, 1944.

71   *Cincinnati Post*, June 21, 1947.

> "Time rolls back when the
> players run to the *field*
> and the chants start
> in the *dugout*."
>
> —NELLE EWING[1]

CHAPTER 15

The Oldest, Most Loyal Fan

NELLE EWING BURIED HER HUSBAND in accordance with his wishes, with a baseball in his right hand, his ball glove on his left, and his cleats on his feet.[2] Nelle went on another 25 years alone.

A diminutive person with a formidable personality, she remained as well known in Wapakoneta, Ohio, as her celebrated spouse. She got along on her own in the big house on West Auglaize Street. Nelle never learned to drive, but that wasn't a problem. Her groceries were delivered, her doctor made house calls, and friends were always available to chauffeur her wherever she had to go. When she stepped out her front door, one of her granddaughters recalled, she was "treated like a celebrity everywhere she went."[3] She enjoyed traveling and maintained lively interests in many subjects, including history and archaeology[4]—and her nine grandchildren. But no interest overshadowed baseball. Nelle followed the Reds avidly. Waite Hoyt's radio broadcasts of Cincinnati games held her attention to the exclusion of everything else.

"When there was a ballgame on, you might as well not even go over there," said granddaughter Christine Frye Terkelsen. "She wouldn't talk to you; you weren't allowed to make any noise."[5]

Opening Day at Crosley Field was the occasion for an annual pilgrimage. Mrs. Ewing always organized a group of friends for the 100-

mile trip. She was a familiar figure in the box seats, often draped in furs against the April chill and invariably clutching the lucky rabbit's foot she always took with her to the ballpark.

Within a few years of Bob's death, Nelle was becoming regionally famous for her long run of consecutive Opening Day games. The string eventually extended more than 60 years, though it probably wasn't as long as some newspaper accounts would have it. She told two Cincinnati newspapers in 1953 that she was attending her 50th straight opener. By 1967, *The Lima News* calculated her streak at 65 games. Aside from the fact that those two tabulations don't match up with each other, they don't take into account several contemporary news articles in 1906-07 about Nelle's so-called "jinx" and her refusal to go to the park when Bob pitched.

Based on her comments at that time, she surely skipped the 1907 opener, when Bob defeated Pittsburgh, and resumed going to the opening game in 1908, after the jinx was broken—again, as documented at the time—in August 1907. Even so, the string continued into the early 1970s, spanning more than six full decades. She was introduced at home plate before the 1961 game, the same occasion when the first ball was thrown out by Bob's old teammate, 98-year-old Dummy Hoy.[6]

Over the years, Nelle was interviewed by numerous reporters, not only from the Wapakoneta paper but also from Lima, Dayton and Cincinnati. They always came calling around the time a new baseball season arrived. "Cincy's oldest, most loyal fan,"[7] as her hometown newspaper styled her, entertained them with stories from earlier days, observations on the contemporary game, and usually a look at the scrapbook in which she had documented her husband's glory days on the diamond. Her conversation was "spiced with baseball jargon."[8] Visiting journalists were likely to discover, 50 years after Bob's departure from the Reds, that Nelle was still irked by Cincinnati newspaper articles at the time praising the trade that sent Long Bob to Philadelphia.

Sometimes she shared recollections of Miller Huggins and other old-timers, but as the years passed she found that names from Bob's day meant less and less to her listeners. So she sang the praises of the modern-day Reds (center fielder Gus Bell and pitcher Bob Purkey were among her favorites), and offered assessments of the team's pre-season prospects. She was particularly prescient in 1961.

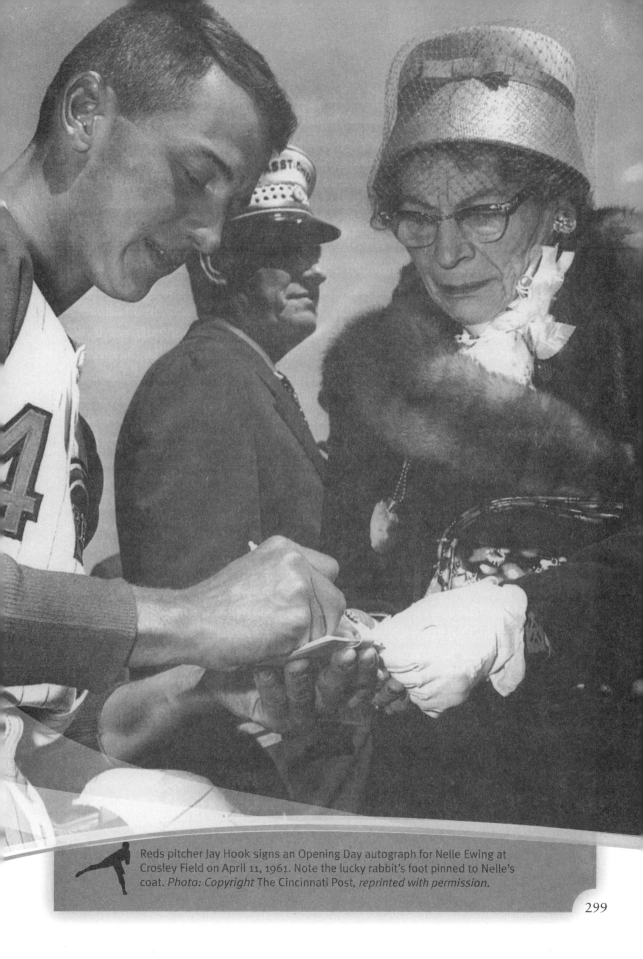

Reds pitcher Jay Hook signs an Opening Day autograph for Nelle Ewing at Crosley Field on April 11, 1961. Note the lucky rabbit's foot pinned to Nelle's coat. *Photo: Copyright* The Cincinnati Post, *reprinted with permission.*

"I think they will do well this year," she told the *Wapakoneta Daily News*. "With Gene Freese at third and Gordy Coleman at first, I'm confident that they can do it."[9]

Coleman was beginning his first full season in the major leagues. Freese had come to Cincinnati as part of a three-way trade in the off-season. They combined for 52 home runs and 174 runs batted in, helping the Reds to an unlikely pennant and their first World Series appearance in 21 years.

Some of her stories got exaggerated over time, whether due to Nelle's embellishments or misunderstandings on the part of reporters. Typical was the tall tale of the time in Boston when Bob supposedly hit the longest home run in the annals of baseball. In one telling, the ball sailed over the fence and into a nearby freight car, ultimately ending up "someplace down south after traveling hundreds of miles."[10] The fact, obscured by the passage of more than 50 years, was that Bob's swat was not a homer at all but merely a foul ball over the short left-field fence at the South End Grounds. The incident took place July 28, 1908, while Bob was in the process of cobbling together a routine 4–2 victory over the hometown Boston Doves, and was duly reported the next day in the *Cincinnati Enquirer*. "The longest hit on record," as Jack Ryder called it with tongue in cheek, "… went into the open door of a passing mail car, and did not stop until it reached the station, three miles away."[11]

Free agency hadn't yet hit baseball, so Nelle wasn't exercised about the salaries of modern players. She was, however, shocked by the youthful ages of latter-day phenoms such as Johnny Bench, who took over behind the plate for the Reds when he was 19—a full 10 years younger than Bob when he made his Cincinnati debut. It was unimaginable to Mrs. Ewing that such a child could be sufficiently seasoned to stand the rigors of major league baseball.

One recurring topic of conversation, not surprisingly, was the spitball. She seemed puzzled by baseball's decision to ban the pitch, and never missed a chance to express her disapproval. In time, a lot of people came to agree with her.

The possibility of bringing back the spitball was rehashed periodically throughout the 1950s and '60s. As the balance between offense and defense tilted more and more in favor of the batter, some baseball lovers grew nostalgic for the return of the low-scoring game of the dead ball era, or at least something closer to it. By 1950, Branch Rickey was pained to see "good pitchers, sound pitchers" routinely abused to the tune of three or four earned runs a game. "It's terrible," he told John Lardner. "It's saddening."[12]

The spitball was suggested as one possible answer. Lardner termed the revival of the spitter a romantic notion, but added, "many old-timers share that dream."[13] Some were former practitioners of the art, among them Ed Walsh, Burleigh Grimes and Red Faber. Over time, others signed on, too, respected baseball men. Besides Rickey, a short list would include American League president Joe Cronin, National League president (and later commissioner) Ford Frick, numerous managers and a smattering of former umpires. Some—Rogers Hornsby, Casey Stengel and Charlie Grimm, to name three—had endured the misery of trying to hit the pitch when it was legal, but they still thought its reinstatement would be a good thing.

Taking the other side of the argument were the venerable Connie Mack, longtime owner and manager of the Philadelphia Athletics, and Clark Griffith, who didn't like the pitch any better than he had when he was managing the Reds in 1909. Another holdout was Elmer Stricklett, Ewing's one-time teammate who played a significant role in introducing the pitch in the early 1900s. His obituary 60 years later said Stricklett maintained "until his dying day" that the spitball "was dangerous and hard to control."[14]

For a time, it seemed the preponderance of opinion favored the return of the spitball. A 1954 editorial in *The Sporting News* expressed sympathy for pitchers. "Perhaps," the baseball bible ventured cautiously, "the good old spitball is worth a revival."[15] Six months later, a *Sporting News* poll of 120 major league players, coaches, managers and executives found a clear majority, 64, in favor of bringing back the spitball and only 36 opposed, with the other 20 "on the fence."[16]

The debate came to a head in 1961, as Roger Maris and Mickey Mantle staged their epic chase for Babe Ruth's 34-year-old single-season home run record. When the season was over, Arthur Daley extolled the virtues of the spitball in a *New York Times* column that stated, "The ridiculous outbreak of home run hitting is destroying baseball's finely attuned checks and balances."[17] While the battle was still raging, the case for the spitball was succinctly summed up by Red Smith in the *New York Herald Tri-*

bune. Considering the plight of the beleaguered pitcher, Smith concluded, "It's high time the poor slob got a break."[18]

The question of lifting the ban came before baseball's rules committee twice, in 1950 and 1961. Both times the proposal was rejected with only a single vote in favor.

Legal or not, the spitball never went away. Many pitchers followed Ed Walsh's pragmatic advice: "Throw it and keep your mouth shut."[19] Suspected or admitted offenders throughout the Nelle's later years included Tommy Bridges, Joe Page, Preacher Roe, Whitey Ford, Don Drysdale, Lew Burdette, Gaylord Perry—and Nelle's favorite, Bob Purkey[20]—among numerous others. By 1963, Al Abrams of the *Pittsburgh Post-Gazette* reported that Burleigh Grimes had stopped campaigning for the spitball's restoration "because there are more spitters thrown now than ever before."[21]

Nelle watched all this with interest and claimed she could always tell when a pitcher was loading up. When her friend Jim Bowsher asked how, she smiled knowingly and replied, "You forget I was married to a spitball pitcher."[22]

NELLE'S STRING OF CINCINNATI OPENERS went on and on, surviving a broken collarbone (and son Robert's misgivings) just two months before the game in 1963, when she was 82 years old. She said the game kept her young, and she joked about drinking from the Fountain of Youth when she accompanied Bob to spring training in St. Augustine, Florida, in 1908. Attending the opener wasn't about maintaining a tradition, she insisted. "I'm going," she told a reporter days before the 1961 opener, "because I'm crazy about baseball and the Reds, and because I couldn't stay away."[23]

Nelle Ewing lived to see the opening of Riverfront Stadium, to meet Pete Rose and Johnny Bench, to root for the Reds in the 1970 World Series and to witness the dawn of the Big Red Machine dynasty. She died February 15, 1972, at age 91—having outlived her son and one of her nine grandchildren[24]—and was buried with her husband in Walnut Hill Cemetery near New Hampshire, Ohio. They share a common headstone decorated with a baseball and a bat.

The Baseball Days of Long Bob Ewing

Even Nelle's death, however, wasn't quite the end of the saga. Though memories faded with time, Long Bob's accomplishments were never completely forgotten. In 1998 Rich Wallace, president of the Shelby County Historical Society, wrote a story for the *Sidney Daily News* recounting Ewing's 1901 encounter with the Cincinnati Reds on the banks of the Great Miami River in Sidney, the game that opened the door for his major league career. Wallace's article launched an effort, spearheaded by Wallace and Dave Ross, to get Ewing inducted into the Cincinnati Reds Hall of Fame.

The honor finally came three years later. On August 12, 2001, nearly 100 years after that fateful afternoon in Sidney, Ewing and 1980s pitching star Mario Soto were installed as the 56th and 57th members of the Cincinnati shrine.[25] Three dozen Ewing relatives, including all eight of Bob and Nelle's surviving grandchildren, were in attendance at Riverfront, by this time renamed Cinergy Field. Following the ceremony, before a sunny Sunday afternoon crowd of 23,887, the Reds took the field against the Colorado Rockies and suffered a 7–6 defeat.

Between them, the two teams employed nine pitchers in a nine-inning ballgame. The Rockies used five in the last four innings. Long Bob Ewing, who completed 184 of his 228 starts in eight years with the Reds, would have been appalled.[26]

Bob and Nelle Ewing's eight surviving grandchildren take part in his induction into the Cincinnati Reds Hall of Fame at Cinergy Field on Aug. 12, 2001. From left: Connie Ewing Kantner, Cindy Ewing Stechschulte, Coleen Bowersock, Carol Hickman, Charlotte Ewing-Preville, Clifford Ewing, Christopher Ewing and Christine Frye Terkelsen. *Photo: Rebecca Gratz, courtesy of* The Lima News.

1   *Lima Citizen*, March 26, 1961.

2   Jim Bowsher, interview with the author, July 23, 1999.

3   Christine Frye Terkelsen, interview with the author, May 24, 1998.

4   Bowsher, *op. cit.*

5   Terkelsen, *op. cit.*

6   After the Reds won an unexpected pennant in 1961, Hoy was recalled in October, at 99, to do the honors again before the third game of the World Series. He died two months later, six months shy of his 100th birthday.

7   *Wapakoneta Daily News*, undated clipping, April 1961.

8   *Lima Citizen*, *op. cit.*

9   *Wapakoneta Daily News*, *op. cit.*

10 *Ibid.*, undated clipping, *c.* 1965.

11 *Cincinnati Enquirer*, July 29, 1908. All three of Ewing's major league home runs came in Cincinnati, and all three were inside the park. But the story of "the longest homer ever hit" lives on, being perpetuated in recent years by Greg Rhodes and John Snyder in *Redleg Journal: Year by Year and Day by Day with the Cincinnati Reds Since 1866* (Cincinnati: Road West Publishing, 2000), p. 159.

12 John Lardner, "Will They Bring Back the Spitter?" *Saturday Evening Post*, Vol. 222, No. 51 (June 17, 1950), p. 167.

13 *Ibid.*

14 *The Sporting News*, June 20, 1964.

15 *Ibid.*, Sept. 1, 1954.

16 *Ibid.*, March 23, 1955.

17 *New York Times*, Nov. 27, 1961.

18 *New York Herald Tribune*, June 8, 1961, reprinted in Red Smith, *The Best of Red Smith* (New York: Franklin Watts Inc., 1963), p. 125.

19 *The Sporting News*, Jan. 9, 1957.

20 Lonnie Wheeler and John Baskin are unequivocal about Purkey's use of the illegal pitch. "Bob Purkey gave it up in favor of the knuckleball," they wrote, "... and won 16 games with it in the pennant season of 1961, and 23 the next year." See Wheeler and Baskin, *The Cincinnati Game* (Wilmington, Ohio: Orange Frazer Press, 1988), p. 111.

21 *The Sporting News*, Oct. 5, 1963.

22 Bowsher, *op. cit.*

23 *Cincinnati Enquirer*, April 9, 1961.

24 Both Robert H. Ewing and his son Charles L. Ewing died in 1970.

25 Ewing contemporaries in the Reds Hall of Fame are Noodles Hahn (inducted 1963), Sam Crawford (1968), Cy Seymour (1998), Bid McPhee (2002), Dummy Hoy (2003) and Garry Herrmann (2008). Jake Beckley, who batted .325 in 879 games for Cincinnati between 1897 and 1903, has not yet been honored by the Reds, although he was inducted into the National Baseball Hall of Fame in 1971.

26 Years later, honors were still coming. On Sept. 4, 2011, in an article by John Erardi and Greg Rhodes, the *Cincinnati Enquirer* named Ewing one of the 100 greatest Reds of all time.

APPENDIX
Bob Ewing's Career
Pitching Record

YEAR	TEAM	LG	G	GS	CG	IP	W	L	PCT.	H	ER	BB	SO	SHO	ERA
1897	Toledo[a]	I-St	4	—	—	25	2	1	.667	15	—	4	10	—	—
1898	Toledo	I-St	42	—	—	349	25	13	.658	317	—	106	96	—	—
1899	Toledo	I-St	30	—	—	252	21	9	.700	243	—	67	80	—	—
1900	Toledo	I-St	33	—	—	290	21	10	.677	245	—	58	87	—	—
1901	Kansas City[b]	WL	31	—	24	251	21	5	.808	233	—	43	113	—	—
1902	Cincinnati[c]	NL	15	12	10	$117^2/_3$	5	6	.455	126	39	47	44	0	2.98
1903	Cincinnati	NL	29	28	27	$246^2/_3$	14	13	.519	254	76	64	104	1	2.77
1904	Cincinnati	NL	26	24	22	212	11	13	.458	198	58	58	99	0	2.46
1905	Cincinnati	NL	40	34	30	$311^2/_3$	20	11	.645	284	87	79	164	4	2.51
1906	Cincinnati	NL	33	32	26	$287^2/_3$	13	14	.481	248	76	60	145	2	2.38
1907	Cincinnati	NL	41	37	32	$332^2/_3$	17	19	.472	279	64	85	147	2	1.73
1908	Cincinnati	NL	37	32	23	$293^2/_3$	17	15	.531	247	72	57	95	4	2.21
1909	Cincinnati	NL	31	29	14	$218^1/_3$	11	12	.478	195	59	63	86	2	2.43
1910	Philadelphia[d]	NL	34	32	20	$255^1/_3$	16	14	.533	235	85	86	102	4	3.00
1911	Philadelphia[e]	NL	4	3	1	24	0	1	.000	29	21	14	12	0	7.88
1912	St. Louis[f]	NL	1	1	0	$1^1/_3$	0	0	.000	2	0	1	0	0	0.00
1912	Buffalo[g]	IL	12	—	5	83	5	4	.556	98	—	15	35	—	—
1913	Minneapolis[h]	AA				*(did not play)*									
Major League Totals *(11 years)*			291	264	205	2301	124	118	.512	2097	637	614	998	19	2.49
Minor League Totals *(6 years)*			152	—	—	1250	95	42	.693	1151	—	293	421	—	—

(a) Signed with Toledo Mud Hens, August 1897. (b) Signed with Kansas City Blues, February 1901. (c) Signed with Cincinnati Reds, Oct. 18, 1901. (d) Traded with pitcher Ad Brennan to Philadelphia Phillies for pitchers Harry Coveleski and Frank Corridon, Jan. 20, 1910. (e) Released by Philadelphia Phillies, Sept. 11, 1911. (f) Signed with St. Louis Cardinals, April 1912; released May 14. (g) Signed with Buffalo Bisons, July 1912; released Oct. 7. (h) Signed with Minneapolis Millers, April 1913; released May 13.

ABOUT THE AUTHOR

MIKE LACKEY is a retired newspaper reporter, editor and columnist. He has contributed to the *Dictionary of Literary Biography, Deadball Stars of the National League and Nine: A Journal of Baseball History and Culture.* He holds a bachelor's degree in history from Earlham College and has been a member of the Society for American Baseball Research since 1985. He lives in Lima, Ohio.

Photo: Craig Orosz.

BIBLIOGRAPHY

BOOKS

Achorn, Edward, *Fifty-Nine in '84: Old Hoss Radbourn, Barehanded Baseball and the Greatest Season a Pitcher Ever Had* (New York: Harper), 2010.

Adair, Robert Kemp, *The Physics of Baseball* (New York: Harper and Row), 1990.

Alexander, Charles C., *John McGraw* (New York: Viking Penguin Inc.), 1988.

Allen, Frederick Lewis, *Only Yesterday: An Informal History of the 1920s* (New York: Harper and Row), 1959 reprint of 1931 original.

Allen, Lee, *The Cincinnati Reds: An Informal History* (New York: G.P. Putnam's Sons), 1948.

Allen, Lee, *Cooperstown Corner: Columns from The Sporting News* (Cleveland: Society for American Baseball Research), 1990.

Allen, Lee, *The Hot Stove League: Raking the Embers of Baseball's Golden Age* (New York: A.S. Barnes and Co.), 2000 reprint of 1955 original.

Anderson, David W., *More than Merkle: A History of the Best and Most Exciting Baseball Season in Human History* (Lincoln, Neb.: University of Nebraska Press), 2000.

Angell, Roger, *Once More Around the Park: A Baseball Reader* (New York: Ballantine Books), 1991.

Asinof, Eliot, *Eight Men Out: The Black Sox and the 1919 World Series* (New York: Holt, Rinehart and Winston), 1963.

Axelson, G.W., *"Commy": The Life Story of Charles A. Comiskey* (Chicago: Reilly and Lee Co.), 1919.

Barber, Rachel, ed., *The Book of Wapakoneta* (Wapakoneta, Ohio: Daily News Printing Co.), 2009.

Barber, Rachel, ed., *A Celebration in Story: Auglaize County Since 1900 in the Words of its People* (Wapakoneta, Ohio: Auglaize County Sesquicentennial Committee), 1998.

Barrett. S.M., ed., *Geronimo's Story of His Life* (Alexander, N.C.: Alexander Books), 1999 reprint of 1906 original.

Beirne, Francis F., *The Amiable Baltimoreans* (New York: E.P. Dutton and Co.), 1951.

Benson, Michael, *Ballparks of North America: A Comprehensive Historical Reference to Baseball Grounds, Yards and Stadiums, 1845 to Present* (Jefferson, N.C.: McFarland and Co. Inc.), 1989.

Bernstein, Mark, *New Bremen* (Wilmington, Ohio: Orange Frazer Press), 1999.

Bevis, Charlie, *Sunday Baseball: The Major Leagues' Struggle to Play Baseball on the Lord's Day, 1876-1934* (Jefferson, N.C.: McFarland and Co. Inc.), 2003.

Blue Stockings to Mud Hens: A History of Professional Baseball in Toledo, Ohio, and Guide to the Toledo Professional Baseball Wall (Toledo, Ohio: Society for American Baseball Research), 1998.

Bowman, John, and Joel Zoss, *Diamonds in the Rough: The Untold History of Baseball* (New York: Macmillan Publishing Co.), 1989.

Boxerman, Burton A., and Benita W. Boxerman, *Ebbets to Veeck to Busch: Eight Owners Who Shaped Baseball* (Jefferson, N.C.: McFarland and Co. Inc.), 2003.

Bready, James H., *The Home Team: From Earliest Times to Last Year's Last Out – Here is How Baltimore Did* (Baltimore: privately published), 1979.

Brinkley, Douglas, *Wheels for the World: Henry Ford, His Company, and a Century of Progress, 1903-2003* (New York: Viking Penguin), 2003.

Browning, Reed, *Cy Young: A Baseball Life* (Amherst, Mass.: University of Massachusetts Press), 2000.

Burk, Robert F., *Never Just a Game: Players, Owners, and American Baseball to 1920* (Chapel Hill, N.C.: University of North Carolina Press), 1994.

Bryson, Bill, and Leighton Housh, *Through the Years with the Western League* (Des Moines, Iowa: Western League), 1951.

Carmichael, John P., *et al.*, *My Greatest Day in Baseball: 47 Dramatic Stories by 47 Stars* (New York: A.S. Barnes and Co.), 1945.

Carney, Gene, *Burying the Black Sox: How Baseball's Cover-Up of the 1919 World Series Fix Almost Succeeded* (Washington, D.C.: Potomac Books Inc.), 2006.

Chace, James, *1912: Wilson, Roosevelt, Taft and Debs – the Election that Changed the Country* (New York: Simon and Schuster), 2004.

Chadwick, Henry, ed., *Spalding's Official Baseball Guide, 1902* (New York: American Sports Publishing Co.), 1902.

Chadwick, Henry, ed., *Spalding's Official Baseball Guide, 1903* (New York: American Sports Publishing Co.), 1903.

Chadwick, Henry, ed., *Spalding's Official Baseball Guide, 1904* (New York: American Sports Publishing Co.), 1904.

Chambrun, Clara Longworth de, *Cincinnati: Story of the Queen City* (New York: Charles Scribner's Sons), 1939.

Clark, Dick, and Larry Lester, *The Negro Leagues Book* (Cleveland: Society for American Baseball Research), 1994.

Cobb, William R., ed., *Honus Wagner on His Life and Baseball* (Ann Arbor, Mich.: Sports Media Group), 2006.

Conner, Floyd, and John Snyder, *Day by Day in Cincinnati Reds History* (New York: Leisure Press), 1983.

Cook, William A., *August "Garry" Herrmann: A Baseball Biography* (Jefferson, N.C.: McFarland and Co. Inc.), 2008.

Cornell, James, *The Great International Disaster Book* (New York: Charles Scribner's Sons), third edition, 1982.

Cottrell, Robert Charles, *The Best Pitcher in Baseball: The Life of Rube Foster, Negro League Giant* (New York: New York University Press), 2001.

Crouch, Tom D., *The Bishop's Boys: A Life of Wilbur and Orville Wright* (New York: W.W. Norton and Co.), 1989.

Curran, William, *Big Sticks: The Batting Revolution of the '20s* (New York: William Morrow and Co. Inc.), 1990.

Curran, William, *Strikeout: A Celebration of the Art of Pitching* (New York: Crown Publishers Inc.), 1995.

Debo, Angie, *Geronimo: The Man, His Time, His Place* (Norman, Okla.: University of Oklahoma Press), 1976.

Derks, Scott, ed., *The Value of a Dollar: Prices and Incomes in the United States, 1860-1999* (Lakeville, Conn.: Grey House Publishing), 1999.

DeValeria, Dennis, and Jeanne Burke DeValeria, *Honus Wagner: A Biography* (New York: Henry Holt and Co.), 1995.

Dewey, Donald, and Nicholas Acocella, *The Biographical History of Baseball* (New York: Carroll and Graf Publishers Inc.), 1995.

Dichtl, William J., *Images of America: Ohio County, Ind.* (Chicago: Arcadia Publishing), 2001.

Dickson, Paul, *The Dickson Baseball Dictionary* (New York: Facts on File), 1989.

Dittmar, Joseph J., *Baseball Records Registry* (Jefferson, N.C.: McFarland and Co. Inc.), 1997.

Dorrell, Dillon R., *Mostly About Ohio County Folks* (Rising Sun, Ind.: Ohio County Historical Society), 1989.

Dorsett, Lyle W., *The Pendergast Machine* (Lincoln, Neb.: University of Nebraska Press), 1968.

Duren, Don, *Boiling Out at the Springs: A History of Major League Baseball Spring Training at Hot Springs, Ark.* (Dallas: Hodge Printing Co.), 2006.

Durso, Joseph, *The Days of Mr. McGraw* (Englewood Cliffs, N.J.: Prentice-Hall Inc.), 1969.

Dyer, Frederick H., *A Compendium of the War of the Rebellion* (Dayton, Ohio: Morningside Press), 1994 reprint of 1908 original.

Ellard, Harry, *Base Ball in Cincinnati* (Cincinnati: privately published), 1907.

Erardi, John, and Greg Rhodes, *Opening Day: Celebrating Cincinnati's Baseball Holiday* (Cincinnati: Road West Publishing), 2004.

Evers, Alf, *The Catskills: From Wilderness to Woodstock* (Woodstock, N.Y.: Overlook Press), 1982.

Evers, John J., and Hugh S. Fullerton, *Touching Second: The Science of Baseball* (Chicago: Reilly and Britton Co.), 1910.

Faber, Charles F., and Richard B. Faber, *Spitballers: The Last Legal Hurlers of the Wet One* (Jefferson, N.C.: McFarland and Co. Inc.), 2006.

Fields, Armond, *James J. Corbett: A Biography of the Heavyweight Boxing Champion and Popular Theater Headliner* (Jefferson, N.C.: McFarland and Co. Inc.), 2001.

Fleitz, David L., *Ghosts in the Gallery at Cooperstown: 16 Little-Known Members of the Hall of Fame* (Jefferson, N.C.: McFarland and Co. Inc.), 2004.

Fleitz, David L., *More Ghosts in the Gallery: Another 16 Little-Known Greats at Cooperstown* (Jefferson, N.C.: McFarland and Co. Inc.), 2007.

Fleming, G.H., *The Unforgettable Season* (New York: Holt, Rinehart and Winston), 1981.

Foraker, Joseph Benson, *Notes of a Busy Life* (Cincinnati: Stewart and Kidd Co.), 1917.

Foster, John B., ed., *Spalding's Baseball Guide, 1909* (New York: American Sports Publishing Co.), 1909.

Foster, John B., ed., *How to Pitch* (New York: American Sports Publishing Co.), 1912.

Gershman, Michael, *Diamonds: The Evolution of the Ballpark* (Boston: Houghton Mifflin Co.), 1993.

Gietschier, Steve, ed., *Complete Baseball Record Book* (St. Louis: The Sporting News), 2005.

Ginsburg, Daniel E., *The Fix is In: A History of Baseball Gambling and Game-Fixing Scandals* (Jefferson, N.C.: McFarland and Co. Inc.), 1995.

González Echevarría, Roberto, *The Pride of Havana: A History of Cuban Baseball* (New York: Oxford University Press), 1999.

Grace, Kevin, *Cincinnati on Field and Court: The Sports Legacy of the Queen City* (Chicago: Arcadia Publishing), 2002.

Grace, Kevin, *The Cincinnati Reds, 1900-50* (Charleston, S.C.: Arcadia Publishing), 2005.

Graham, Frank, *Baseball Extra* (New York: A.S. Barnes and Co.), 1954.

Graham, Frank, *McGraw of the Giants: An Informal Biography* (New York: G.P. Putnam's Sons), 1944.

Grayson, Harry, *They Played the Game: The Story of Baseball Greats* (New York: A.S. Barnes and Co.), 1945.

Helyar, John, *Lords of the Realm: The Real History of Baseball* (New York: Villard Books), 1994.

Hilton, George W., and John F. Due, *The Electric Interurban Railways in America* (Stanford, Calif.: Stanford University Press), second printing, 1964.

History of Cincinnati and Hamilton County, Ohio: Their Past and Present (Cincinnati: S.B. Nelson and Co.), 1894.

Hittner, Arthur D., *Honus Wagner: The Life of Baseball's "Flying Dutchman"* (Jefferson, N.C.: McFarland and Co. Inc.), 1996.

Hoie, Bob, and Carlos Bauer, *The Historical Register* (San Diego: Baseball Press Books), 1998.

Honig, Donald, *The Cincinnati Reds: An Illustrated History* (New York: Simon and Schuster), 1992.

Honig, Donald, *The Man in the Dugout: 15 Big League Managers Speak Their Minds* (Chicago: Follett Publishing Co.), 1977.

Howland, H.G., *Atlas of Auglaize County, Ohio, from Records and Original Surveys* (Philadelphia: Robert Sutton), 1880.

Hurt, R. Douglas, *The Ohio Frontier: Crucible of the Old Northwest, 1720-1830* (Bloomington, Ind.: Indiana University Press), 1996.

Husman, John R., *Baseball in Toledo* (Charleston, S.C.: Arcadia Publishing), 2003.

Ivor-Campbell, Frederick, ed., *Baseball's First Stars* (Cleveland: Society for American Baseball Research), 1996.

James, Bill, *The Bill James Guide to Baseball Managers from 1870 to Today* (New York: Scribner), 1997.

James, Bill, *The Bill James Historical Baseball Abstract* (New York: Villard Books), 1986.

James, Bill, *The New Bill James Historical Baseball Abstract* (New York: The Free Press), 2001.

James, Bill, *The Politics of Glory: How Baseball's Hall of Fame Really Works* (New York: Macmillan Publishing Co.), 1994.

James, Bill, John Dewan, Neil Munro and Don Zminda, *STATS All-Time Baseball Sourcebook* (Skokie, Ill.: STATS Inc.), 1998.

James, Bill, and Jim Henzler, *Win Shares* (Morton Grove, Ill.: STATS Inc.), 2002.

James, Bill, and Rob Neyer, *The Neyer/James Guide to Pitchers: An Historical Compendium of Pitchers, Pitching, and Pitches* (New York: Simon and Schuster), 2004.

Johnson, Lloyd, ed., *The Minor League Register* (Durham, N.C.: Baseball America Inc.), 1994.

Johnson, Lloyd, and Miles Wolff, eds., *The Encyclopedia of Minor League Baseball* (Durham, N.C.: Baseball America Inc.), 1993.

Jones, David, ed., *Deadball Stars of the American League* (Dulles, Va.: Potomac Books Inc.), 2006.

Jordan, David M., *Occasional Glory: The History of the Philadelphia Phillies* (Jefferson, N.C.: McFarland and Co. Inc.), 2002.

Kahn, Roger, *The Head Game: Baseball Seen from the Pitcher's Mound* (New York: Harcourt Inc.), 2000.

Karst, Gene, and Martin J. Jones Jr., *Who's Who in Professional Baseball* (New Rochelle, N.Y.: Arlington House), 1973.

Kavanagh, Jack, *Ol' Pete: The Grover Cleveland Alexander Story* (South Bend, Ind.: Diamond Communications Inc.), 1996.

Kavanagh, Jack, *Walter Johnson: A Life* (South Bend, Ind.: Diamond Communications Inc.), 1995.

Kelley, Brent, *The Case For: Those Overlooked by the Baseball Hall of Fame* (Jefferson, N.C.: McFarland and Co. Inc.), 1992.

Knepper, George W., *Ohio and its People* (Kent, Ohio: Kent State University Press), 1997.

Kohout, Martin Donell, *Hal Chase: The Defiant Life and Turbulent Times of Baseball's Biggest Crook* (Jefferson, N.C.: McFarland and Co. Inc.), 2001.

Koppett, Leonard, *The New Thinking Fan's Guide to Baseball* (New York: Simon and Schuster), 1991.

Kunstler, James Howard, *The Geography of Nowhere: The Rise and Decline of America's Man-Made Landscape* (New York: Simon and Schuster), 1993.

Leavengood, Ted, *Clark Griffith: The Old Fox of Washington Baseball* (Jefferson, N.C.: McFarland and Co. Inc.), 2011.

Lee, Bill, *The Baseball Necrology: The Post-Baseball Lives and Deaths of Over 7,600 Major League Players and Others* (Jefferson, N.C.: McFarland and Co. Inc.), 2003.

Levy, Alan H., *Rube Waddell: The Zany, Brilliant Life of a Strikeout Artist* (Jefferson, N.C.: McFarland and Co. Inc.), 2000.

Lewis, Allen, and Larry Shenk, *This Date in Philadelphia Phillies History* (New York: Stein and Day), 1979.

Lieb, Frederick G., *The Baltimore Orioles: The History of a Colorful Team in Baltimore and St. Louis* (Carbondale, Ill.: Southern Illinois University Press), 2005 reprint of 1955 original.

Lieb, Frederick G., *Baseball as I Have Known It* (New York: Coward, McCann and Geoghan), 1977.

Lieb, Frederick G., and Stan Baumgartner, *The Philadelphia Phillies* (New York: G.P. Putnam's Sons), 1953.

Lin Weber, Ralph E., *The Toledo Baseball Guide of the Mud Hens* (Rossford, Ohio: Baseball Research Bureau), 1944.

Longert, Scott, *Addie Joss: King of the Pitchers* (Cleveland: Society for American Baseball Research), 1998.

Lowenfish, Lee, *Branch Rickey: Baseball's Ferocious Gentleman* (Lincoln, Neb.: University of Nebraska Press), 2007.

Lowenfish, Lee, and Tony Lupien, *The Imperfect Diamond: The Story of Baseball's Reserve System and the Men who Fought to Change It* (New York: Stein and Day), 1980.

Lower, Andre, *Auditioning for Cooperstown: Rating Baseball's Stars for the Hall of Fame* (Lexington, Ky.: Baseball by Positions.com), 2012.

Lowry, Philip J., *Green Cathedrals: The Ultimate Celebration of Major League and Negro League Ballparks* (New York: Walker and Co.), 2006.

Macht, Norman L., *Connie Mack and the Early Years of Baseball* (Lincoln, Neb.: University of Nebraska Press), 2007.

Madden, W.C., and Patrick J. Stewart, *The Western League: A Baseball History, 1885 through 1999* (Jefferson, N.C.: McFarland and Co. Inc.), 2002.

Mallory, Jerry, ed., *Sol White's History of Colored Base Ball with other Documents on the Early Black Game, 1886-1936* (Lincoln, Neb.: University of Nebraska Press), 1995.

Mann, Arthur, *Branch Rickey: American in Action* (Boston: Houghton Mifflin Co.), 1957.

Mathewson, Christy, *Pitching in a Pinch, or Baseball from the Inside* (New York: Stein and Day), 1977 reprint of 1912 original.

Matthews, George R., *America's First Olympics: The St. Louis Games of 1904* (Columbia, Mo.: University of Missouri Press), 2005.

Mayer, Ronald A., *Christy Mathewson: A Game-by-Game Profile of a Legendary Pitcher* (Jefferson, N.C.: McFarland and Co. Inc.), 1993.

McConnell, Bob, and David Vincent, eds., *The Home Run Encyclopedia* (New York: Macmillan), 1996.

McGraw, John J., *My 30 Years in Baseball* (New York: Arno Press), 1974 reprint of 1923 original.

McGraw, John J., *Scientific Baseball* (New York: Police Gazette Publishing House), 1910.

McMurray, William J., ed., *History of Auglaize County, Ohio* (Indianapolis: Historical Publishing Co.), 1923.

Mead, William B., and Paul Dickson, *Baseball: The Presidents' Game* (Washington, D.C.: Farragut Publishing Co.), 1993.

Meyer, J.H., *Atlas and History of Auglaize County* (Piqua, Ohio: Magee Brothers Co.), 1917.

Military History of Ohio (New York: H.H. Hardesty, Publishers), 1885.

Miller, Zane L., *Boss Cox's Cincinnati: Urban Politics in the Progressive Era* (New York: Oxford University Press), 1968.

Mooney, Michael Macdonald, *Evelyn Nesbit and Stanford White: Love and Death in the Gilded Age* (New York: William Morrow and Co. Inc.), 1976.

Morrell, Parker, *Lillian Russell: The Era of Plush* (New York: Random House), 1940.

Morris, James McGrath, *The Rose Man of Sing Sing: A True Tale of Life, Murder and Redemption in the Age of Yellow Journalism* (New York: Fordham University Press), 2003.

Morris, Peter, *Catcher: How the Man Behind the Plate Became an American Folk Hero* (Chicago: Ivan R. Dee), 2009.

Morris, Peter, *A Game of Inches: The Game on the Field* (Chicago: Ivan R. Dee), 2006.

Morris, Peter, *Level Playing Fields: How the Groundskeeping Murphy Brothers Shaped Baseball* (Lincoln, Neb.: University of Nebraska Press), 2007.

Murdock, Eugene C., *Ban Johnson: Czar of Baseball* (Westport, Conn.: Greenwood Press), 1982.

Murdock, Eugene C., *Baseball Players and Their Times: Oral Histories of the Game, 1920-40* (Westport, Conn.: Meckler Publishing), 1991.

Murphy, Cait, *Crazy '08: How a Cast of Cranks, Rogues, Boneheads, and Magnates Created the Greatest Year in Baseball History* (New York: Smithsonian Books), 2007.

Myler, Patrick, *Gentleman Jim Corbett: The Truth Behind a Boxing Legend* (London: Robson Books Ltd.), 1998.

Neft, David S., Bob Carroll and Richard M. Cohen, *The Cincinnati Reds Trivia Book* (New York: St. Martin's Press), 1993.

Neft, David S., Bob Carroll, Richard M. Cohen and Jordan A. Deutsch, *The Sports Encyclopedia: Baseball* (New York: Grosset and Dunlap), 1976.

Newcombe, Jack, *The Best of the Athletic Boys: The White Man's Impact on Jim Thorpe* (Garden City, N.Y.: Doubleday and Co.), 1975.

O'Brien, John, and Jerry DeBruin with John Husman, *Mud Hen Memories* (Perrysburg, Ohio: BWD Publishing), 2001.

Okkonen, Marc, *Baseball Memories, 1900-09* (New York: Sterling Publishing Co.), 1992.

O'Neal, Bill, *The American Association: A Baseball History, 1902-91* (Austin, Texas: Eakin Press), 1991.

Orodenker, Richard, ed., *Dictionary of Literary Biography, Volume 171: 20th American Sportswriters* (Detroit: Bruccoli Clark Layman), 1996.

O'Toole, Patricia, *When Trumpets Call: Theodore Roosevelt After the White House* (New York: Simon and Schuster), 2005.

Overfield, Joseph M., *The 100 Seasons of Buffalo Baseball* (Kenmore, N.Y.: Partners' Press), 1985.

Pietrusza, David, *Lights On! The Wild Century-Long Saga of Night Baseball* (Lanham, Md.: Scarecrow Press), 1997.

Polner, Murray, *Branch Rickey: A Biography* (New York: Atheneum), 1982.

Portrait and Biographical Record of Auglaize, Logan and Shelby Counties, Ohio (Chicago: Chapman Bros.), 1892.

Powers-Beck, Jeffrey, *The American Indian Integration of Baseball* (Lincoln, Neb.: University of Nebraska Press), 2004.

Preimesberger, Jon, ed., *Presidential Elections, 1789-1992* (Washington, D.C.: Congressional Quarterly Inc.), 1995.

Pringle, Henry F., *Theodore Roosevelt: A Biography* (New York: Harcourt, Brace and Co.), 1931.

Pringle, Henry F., *William Howard Taft: The Life and Times* (Newton, Conn.: American Political Biography Press), 1967 edition of 1939 original.

Quigley, Martin, *The Crooked Pitch: The Curveball in American Baseball History* (Chapel Hill, N.C.: Algonquin Press), 1984.

Rader, Benjamin G., *Baseball: A History of America's Game* (Urbana, Ill.: University of Illinois Press), 1994.

Raitt, John E., *Ruts in the Road*, Vol. 2 (Walton, N.Y.: Reporter Co.), 1983.

Rasenberger, Jim, *America, 1908: The Dawn of Flight, the Race to the Pole, the Invention of the Model T, and the Making of a Modern Nation* (New York: Scribner), 2007.

Rathgeber, Bob, *Cincinnati Reds Scrapbook* (Virginia Beach, Va.: JCP Corp.), 1982.

Reach's Official Baseball Guide for 1897 (Philadelphia: A.J. Reach Co.), 1897.

Reach's Official Baseball Guide for 1898 (Philadelphia: A.J. Reach Co.), 1898.

Reichler, Joseph L., *The Baseball Trade Register* (New York: Collier Books), 1984.

Reichler, Joseph L., revised by Ken Samuelson, *The Great All-Time Baseball Record Book* (New York: Macmillan Publishing Co.), 1993.

Reid, Whitelaw, *Ohio in the War, Volume II: The History of Her Regiments and Other Military Organizations* (Cincinnati: Moore, Wilstach and Baldwin), 1868.

Reisler, Jim, *Before They Were the Bombers: The New York Yankees' Early Years, 1903-15* (Jefferson, N.C.: McFarland and Co. Inc.), 2002.

Rhodes, Greg, and John Erardi, *Cincinnati's Crosley Field: The Illustrated History of a Classic Ballpark* (Cincinnati: Road West Publishing), 1995.

Rhodes, Greg, and John Snyder, *Redleg Journal: Year by Year and Day by Day with the Cincinnati Reds Since 1866* (Cincinnati: Road West Publishing), 2000.

Rhodes, Greg, and Mark Stang, *Reds in Black and White: 100 Years of Cincinnati Reds Images* (Cincinnati: Road West Publishing), 1999.

Richter, Francis C., *Richter's History and Records of Baseball, the American Nation's Chief Sport* (Jefferson, N.C.: McFarland and Co. Inc.), 2005 reprint of 1914 original.

Riess, Steven A., *Touching Base: Professional Baseball and American Culture in the Progressive Era* (Westport, Conn.: Greenwood Press), 1980.

Riley, James A., *The Biographical Encyclopedia of the Negro Baseball Leagues* (New York: Carroll and Graf Publishers Inc.), 1994.

Ritter, Lawrence S., *The Glory of Their Times: The Story of the Early Days of Baseball Told by the Men Who Played It* (New York: Macmillan Co.), 1966. Also enlarged edition (New York: HarperCollins Publishers Inc.), 2002.

Ritter, Lawrence S., *Lost Ballparks: A Celebration of Baseball's Legendary Fields* (New York: Viking Penguin), 1992.

Robbins, Michael, ed., *Brooklyn: A State of Mind* (New York: Workman Publishing), 2001.

Robinson, Ray, *Matty: An American Hero* (New York: Oxford University Press), 1993.

Runyon, Damon, edited by Jim Reisler, *Guys, Dolls, and Curveballs: Damon Runyon on Baseball* (New York: Carroll and Graf Publishers), 2005.

Schechter, Gabriel, *Victory Faust: The Rube Who Saved McGraw's Giants* (Los Gatos, Calif.: Charles April Publications), 2000.

Schwieterman, Joseph P., *When the Railroad Leaves Town* (Kirksville, Mo.: Truman State University Press), 2001.

Selter, Ronald M., *Ballparks of the Deadball Era: A Comprehensive Study of Their Dimensions, Configurations and Effects on Batting, 1901-19,* (Jefferson, N.C.: McFarland and Co. Inc.), 2008.

Seymour, Harold, and Dorothy Seymour Mills, *Baseball: The Early Years* (New York: Oxford University Press), 1960.

Seymour, Harold, and Dorothy Seymour Mills, *Baseball: The Golden Age* (New York: Oxford University Press), 1971.

Silberstein, Iola Hessler, *Cincinnati Then and Now* (Cincinnati: Voters Service Education Fund of the League of Women Voters of the Cincinnati Area), 1982.

Simon, Tom, ed., *Deadball Stars of the National League* (Washington, D.C.: Brassey's Inc.), 2004.

Simon, Tom, ed., *Green Mountain Boys of Summer: Vermonters in the Major Leagues, 1882-1993* (Shelburne, Vt.: New England Press Inc.), 2000.

Sive, Mary Robinson, *Lost Villages: Historic Driving Tours of the Catskills* (New Delhi, N.Y.: Delaware County Historical Association), 1998.

Skipper, John C., *Wicked Curve: The Life and Troubled Times of Grover Cleveland Alexander* (Jefferson, N.C.: McFarland and Co. Inc.), 2006.

Smiles, Jack, *Big Ed Walsh: The Life and Times of a Spitballing Hall of Famer* (Jefferson, N.C.: McFarland and Co. Inc.), 2008.

Smith, H. Allen, and Ira L. Smith, *Low and Inside* (Halcottsville, N.Y.: Breakaway Books), 2000 reprint of 1949 original.

Smith, Red, *The Best of Red Smith* (New York: Franklin Watts Inc.), 1963.

Snelling, Dennis, *The Pacific Coast League: A Statistical History, 1903-57* (Jefferson, N.C.: McFarland and Co. Inc.), 1995.

Snyder, Brad, *Beyond the Shadow of the Senators: The Untold Story of the Homestead Grays and the Integration of Baseball* (Chicago: Contemporary Books), 2003.

Solomon, Burt, *Where They Ain't: The Fabled Life and Untimely Death of the Original Baltimore Orioles, the Team that Gave Birth to Modern Baseball* (New York: The Free Press), 1999.

Sowell, Mike, *July 2, 1903: The Mysterious Death of Hall-of-Famer Big Ed Delahanty* (New York: Macmillan Publishing Co.), 1992.

Spalding, Albert G., *America's National Game: Historic Facts Concerning the Beginning, Evolution, Development and Popularity of Baseball* (Lincoln, Neb.: University of Nebraska Press), 1992 reprint of 1911 original.

Spink, Alfred H., *The National Game* (Carbondale, Ill.: Southern Illinois University Press), second edition, 2000 reprint of 1911 original.

Spink, J.G. Taylor, *Judge Landis and 25 Years of Baseball* (New York: Thomas Y. Crowell Co.), 1947.

Stallard, Mark, ed., *Echoes of Cincinnati Reds Baseball: The Greatest Stories Ever Told* (Chicago: Triumph Books), 2007.

Stark, Benton, *The Year They Called Off the World Series* (Garden City Park, N.Y.: Avery Publishing Group Inc.), 1991.

Steffens, Joseph Lincoln, *The Struggle for Self-Government* (New York: Johnson Reprint Corp.), 1968 reprint of 1906 original.

Steinberg, Steve, *Baseball in St. Louis, 1900-25* (Charleston, S.C.: Arcadia Publishing), 2004.

Sterngass, Jon, *First Resorts: Pursuing Pleasure at Saratoga Springs, Newport and Coney Island* (Baltimore: Johns Hopkins University Press), 2001.

Sullivan, Dean A., ed., *Early Innings: A Documentary History of Baseball, 1825-1908* (Lincoln, Neb.: University of Nebraska Press), 1995.

Sullivan, Dean A., ed., *Middle Innings: A Documentary History of Baseball, 1900-48* (Lincoln, Neb.: University of Nebraska Press), 1998.

Sumner, Benjamin Barrett, *Minor League Baseball Standings: All North American Leagues, through 1999* (Jefferson, N.C.: McFarland and Co. Inc.), 2000.

Taylor, Tim, *The Book of Presidents* (New York: Arno Press), 1972.

Thomas, Henry W., *Walter Johnson: Baseball's Big Train* (Washington, D.C.: Phenom Press), 1995.

Thomas, Joan M., *Baseball's First Lady: Helene Hathaway Robison Britton and the St. Louis Cardinals* (St. Louis: Reedy Press), 2010.

Thomson, Cindy, and Scott Brown, *Three Finger: The Mordecai Brown Story* (Lincoln, Neb.: University of Nebraska Press), 2006.

Thorn, John, and John B. Holway, *The Pitcher* (New York: Prentice Hall Press), 1987.

Thorn, John, and Pete Palmer, eds., *Total Baseball* (New York: Warner Books), first edition, 1989.

Thorn, John, Pete Palmer and Michael Gershman eds., *Total Baseball* (Kingston, N.Y.: Total Sports Publishing), seventh edition, 2001.

Thornley, Stew, *On to Nicollet: The Glory and Fame of the Minneapolis Millers* (Minneapolis: Nodin Press), 1988.

Tiemann, Robert L., and Mark Rucker, eds., *19th Century Stars* (Kansas City, Mo.: Society for American Baseball Research), 1989.

Tolzmann, Don Heinrich, ed., *Festschrift for the German-American Tricentennial Jubilee: Cincinnati, 1983* (Cincinnati: Cincinnati Historical Society), 1982.

Tolzmann, Don Heinrich, *German Heritage Guide to the Greater Cincinnati Area* (Milford, Ohio: Little Miami Publishing Co.), 2003.

Toot, Peter T., *Armando Marsans: A Cuban Pioneer in the Major Leagues* (Jefferson, N.C.: McFarland and Co. Inc.), 2004.

Traxel, David, *1898: The Birth of the American Century* (New York: Alfred A. Knopf), 1998.

Trostel, Scott D., *A Brief History of Interurban Railways of the Northern Miami Valley* (Fletcher, Ohio: Cam-Tech Publishing), 1996.

Trostel, Scott D., *The Lima Route* (Fletcher, Ohio: Cam-Tech Publishing), 1998.

Voigt, David Quentin, *American Baseball: From Gentleman's Sport to Commissioner System* (Norman, Okla.: University of Oklahoma Press), 1966.

Wallace, Rich, *Voices from the Past* (Sidney, Ohio: Shelby County Historical Society), 2001.

Walsh, John B., *Atlas of Auglaize County, with Historical and Biographical Sketches* (Wapakoneta, Ohio: Atlas Publishing Co.), 1898.

Ward, Arch, ed., *The Greatest Sport Stories from the Chicago Tribune* (New York: A.S. Barnes and Co.), 1953.

Warner, Hoyt Landon, *Progressivism in Ohio, 1897-1917* (Columbus, Ohio: Ohio State University Press), 1964.

Westcott, Rich, *Philadelphia's Old Ballparks* (Philadelphia: Temple University Press), 1996.

Wheeler, Lonnie, and John Baskin, *The Cincinnati Game* (Wilmington, Ohio: Orange Frazer Press), 1988.

Wheeler, Sessions S., *Gentleman in the Outdoors: A Portrait of Max C. Fleischmann* (Reno, Nev.: University of Nevada Press), 1985.

Wiggins, Robert Peyton, *The Deacon and the Schoolmaster: Phillippe and Leever, Pittsburgh's Great Turn-of-the-Century Pitchers*, (Jefferson, N.C.: McFarland and Co. Inc.), 2011.

Wilbert, Warren N., *The Arrival of the American League: Ban Johnson and the 1901 Challenge to the National League Monopoly* (Jefferson, N.C.: McFarland and Co. Inc.), 2007.

Williams, Joe, edited by Peter Williams, *The Joe Williams Baseball Reader: The Glorious Game, from Ty Cobb and Babe Ruth to the Amazing Mets* (Chapel Hill, N.C.: Algonquin Books), 1989.

Williamson, C.W., *History of Western Ohio and Auglaize County* (Columbus, Ohio: W.M. Linn and Sons), 1905.

Witherspoon, Margaret Johanson, *Remembering the St. Louis World's Fair* (St. Louis: Plus Communications), 1973.

Wolff, Rick, *et al.*, eds., *The Baseball Encyclopedia* (New York: Macmillan Publishing Co.), eighth edition, 1990.

Wright, Marshall D., *The American Association: Year-by-Year Statistics for the Baseball Minor League, 1902-52* (Jefferson, N.C.: McFarland and Co. Inc.), 1997.

Wright, Marshall D., *The International League: Year-by-Year Statistics, 1884-1953* (Jefferson, N.C.: McFarland and Co. Inc.), 1998.

Wright, Marshall D., *The Southern Association in Baseball, 1885-1961* (Jefferson, N.C.: McFarland and Co. Inc.), 2002.

Writers' Program of the Work Projects Administration, *Cincinnati: A Guide to the Queen City and its Neighbors* (Cincinnati: Wiesen-Hart Press), 1943.

Zingg, Paul J., and Mark D. Medeiros, *Runs, Hits, and an Era: The Pacific Coast League, 1903-58* (Urbana, Ill.: University of Illinois Press), 1994.

ARTICLES

Anderson, David W., "Bonesetter Reese, Baseball's Unofficial Team Physician" in Brad Sullivan, ed., *Batting Four Thousand: Baseball in the Western Reserve* (Cleveland: Society for American Baseball Research, 2008), pp. 99-103.

Arpi, Rich, "Rube and His Bears: A Short History of the Virginia Ore Diggers and the Team's Time in the Northern League," *The National Pastime*, No. 42 (2012), pp. 19-24.

Bailey, Bob, "The Philadelphia Negro World Championship Series of 1903-04," *The National Pastime*, No. 24 (2004), pp. 91-94.

Bales, Jack, and Tim Wiles, "Franklin P. Adams' 'Trio of Bear Cubs,'" *Nine: A Journal of Baseball History and Culture*, Vol. 19, No. 2 (spring 2011), pp. 114-40.

Barra, Allen, "The Immortals," *American History*, Vol. 46, No. 1 (April 2011), pp. 56-61.

Betzold, Michael, "Turkey Mike Donlin: One of the 20th Century's First Sports Entertainment Figures," *The Baseball Research Journal*, No. 29 (2000), pp. 80-83.

Blau, Clifford, "John McGraw Comes to New York: The 1902 New York Giants," *The Baseball Research Journal,* No. 31 (2003), pp. 3-10.

Bonk, Dan, and Len Martin, "Bourbon, Baseball and Barney" in Walter Barney, ed., *A Celebration of Louisville Baseball in the Major and Minor Leagues* (Louisville, Ky.: Society for American Baseball Research, 1997), pp. 62-64.

Borst, Bill, "The Matron Magnate," *Baseball Research Journal*, No. 6 (1977), pp. 25-30.

Camp, Walter, "Our National Game – Save the Mark!" *Collier's* (April 4, 1899).

Campf, Brian, "The Man Who Won Big for Portland" in Mark Armour, ed., *Rain Check: Baseball in the Pacific Northwest* (Cleveland: Society for American Baseball Research, 2006), 22-27.

Cardello, Joseph, "The Parker Brothers and Other Cincinnati Oddities," *The Baseball Research Journal*, No. 24 (1995), pp. 21-24.

Carroll, Bob, "For the Hall of Fame: 12 Good Men," *The National Pastime*, Vol. 4, No. 2 (winter 1985), pp. 14-27.

Coyne, Kevin, "Ultimate Sacrifice," *Smithsonian*, Vol. 35, No. 7 (October 2004), pp. 72-82.

Daher, Naiph J., "The Spitter Hits the Trail," *Baseball Magazine,* Vol. XLVI, No. 4 (March 1931), pp. 441-42, 472.

Davids, L. Robert, "Bud Fowler, Black Baseball Star" (1989), in Jim Charlton, ed., *Road Trips: A Trunkload of Great Articles from Two Decades of Convention Journals* (Cleveland: Society for American Baseball Research, 2004), pp. 23-24.

Davids, L. Robert, "John (Bud) Fowler: 19th Century Black Baseball Pioneer" and "The Contribution of Black Players in the 19th Century" (Frankfort, N.Y.: Society for American Baseball Research), July 25, 1987. Pages not numbered. Articles in a booklet compiled for the dedication of a memorial to Bud Fowler.

Deane, Bill, "Normalized Winning Percentage, Revisited," *The Baseball Research Journal*, No. 34 (2005), pp. 3-4.

Dorward, Jane Finnan, "Island Baseball" in Dorward, ed., *Dominionball: Baseball Above the 49th* (Cleveland: Society for American Baseball Research, 2005), pp. 15-18.

Edelman, Rob, "Baseball, Vaudeville, and Mike Donlin," *Base Ball*, Vol. 2, No. 1 (spring 2008), pp. 44-57.

Edwards, Owen, "Down but not Out," *Smithsonian*, Vol. 42, No. 5 (September 2011), pp. 36-37.

Fisher, Randy, and Jami N. Fisher, "The Deaf and the Origin of Hand Signals in Baseball," *The National Pastime*, Vol. 28 (2008), pp. 35-39.

Gagnon, Cappy, "The Debut of Roger Bresnahan," *Baseball Research Journal*, No. 8 (1979), pp. 41-42.

Grace, Kevin, "Cincinnati's King of Diamonds" in Mark Stang and Dick Miller, eds., *Baseball in the Buckeye State* (Cleveland: Society for American Baseball Research, 2004), pp. 25-28.

Grace, Kevin, "Sporting Man: Garry Herrmann and the 1909 Cincinnati *Turnfest*," Cincinnati Occasional Papers in German-American Studies, University of Cincinnati, No. 3 (2004), pp. 1-31.

Greenberg, Glenn P., "Does a Pitcher's Height Matter?" *The Baseball Research Journal*, Vol. 39, No. 2 (fall 2010), pp. 51-56.

Griffith, Clark, "25 Years of Big League Baseball," *Outing*, Vol. LXIV, No. 1 (April 1914), pp. 36-42.

Griffith, Clark, "25 Years of Big League Baseball, Part II," *Outing*, Vol. LXIV, No. 2 (May 1914), pp. 164-71.

Griffith, Clark, "Why the Spit Ball Should Be Abolished," *Baseball Magazine* (July 1917), pp. 371 and 390.

Hamann, Rex, "Ballparks of Toledo: 1897-1955," *The American Association Almanac*, Vol. 3, No. 6 (July/August 2004), pp. 1-38.

Hamann, Rex, "Kansas City's American Association Ballparks, Part 1," *The American Association Almanac*, Vol. 4, No. 3 (summer 2005), pp. 1-31.

Holli, Melvin G., "Toledo's Golden Ruler, Samuel M. Jones," *Timeline*, Vol. 17, No. 4 (July/August 2000), pp. 40-51.

Holway, John B., "Cuba's Black Diamond," *Baseball Research Journal*, No. 10 (1981), pp. 139-45.

Jackson, Frank, "Crossing Red River: Spring Training in Texas," *The National Pastime*, No. 26 (2006), pp. 85-91.

"Jim Corbett Playing First Base," *Baseball Research Journal*, No. 12 (1983), pp. 184-87.

Karger, Gustav J., "George Barnesdale Cox, Proprietor of Cincinnati," *Frank Leslie's Popular Monthly*, Vol. LVII, No. 3 (January 1904), pp. 273-*ff.*

Kermisch, Al, "From a Researcher's Notebook," *The Baseball Research Journal*, No. 28 (1999), pp. 141-43.

King, Steven A., "Rusie for Mathewson: The Most Famous Trade that Never Happened," *Base Ball: A Journal of the Early Game*, Vol. 6, No. 2 (fall 2012), pp. 83-101.

King, Steven A., "What Inspired 'Take Me Out to the Ball Game'?" *The Baseball Research Journal*, Vol. 38, No. 2 (fall 2009), pp. 57-58.

Kirwin, Bill, "Cy Seymour," *The Baseball Research Journal*, No. 29 (2000), pp. 3-13.

Lamb, William F., "A Fearsome Collaboration: The Alliance of Andrew Freedman and John T. Brush," *Base Ball: A Journal of the Early Game*, Vol. 3, No. 2 (fall 2009), pp. 5-20.

Lardner, John, "Will They Bring Back the Spitter?" *Saturday Evening Post*, Vol. 222, No. 51 (June 17, 1950), pp. 31, 167-70.

Macht, Norman L., "Sunday Baseball" (2003), article written for the annual convention of the Society for American Baseball Research.

Marcus, Alan I., and Zane L. Miller, "From Bummer to Boss: Cincinnati's George B. Cox," *Timeline*, Vol. 4, No. 4 (August/September 1987), pp. 16-31.

McAdam, D.J., and Harold Jacoby, "The Menace in the Skies," *Harper's Weekly*, Vol. LIV, No. 2786 (May 14, 1910), pp. 11-12, 30.

Meaney, P.A., "Who Invented the Spit Ball," *Baseball Magazine*, Vol. X, No. 7 (May 1913), pp. 59-60.

Miller, Richard, and Gregory L. Rhodes, "The Life and Times of Old Cincinnati Ballparks" in Dottie L. Lewis, *Baseball in Cincinnati: From Wooden Fences to Astroturf* (Cincinnati: Cincinnati Historical Society, 1988), pp. 25-41.

Moses, Ralph C., "Bid McPhee," *The National Pastime*, No. 14 (1994), pp. 48-50.

Murphy, Joe, "The Sunset Years of Joe McGinnity," *The National Pastime*, No. 21 (2001), pp. 20-22.

Oremland, Barbara, "The Silent World of Dummy Hoy" in Walter Barney, ed., *A Celebration of Louisville Baseball in the Major and Minor Leagues* (Louisville, Ky.: Society for American Baseball Research, 1997), pp. 49-51.

Park, Edwards, "Pictures of a Tragedy," *Smithsonian*, Vol. 29, No. 11 (February 1999), pp. 26-30.

Rosciam, Chuck, "The Evolution of Catcher's Equipment," *The Baseball Research Journal*, Vol. 39, No. 1 (summer 2010), pp. 104-22.

Rose, Ed, "Pop Kelchner, Gentleman Jake, the Giant-Killer, and the Kane Mountaineers," *The Baseball Research Journal*, Vol. 41, No. 1 (spring 2012), pp. 46-52.

Schmidt, Ray, "Eddie 'Smoke' Stack," *The National Pastime*, No. 17 (1997), pp. 121-24.

Selfridge, Anna B., "The Road to Liberty: B.A. Gramm, Lima, and the 'Liberty' Truck," *The Allen County Reporter*, Vol. LVIII, No. 2 (2002), pp. 49-125.

Shieber, Tom, "The Evolution of the Baseball Diamond," *The Baseball Research Journal*, No. 23 (1994), pp. 3-13.

Simon, Tom, "Sherry Magee, Psychopathic Slugger" *The Baseball Research Journal*, No. 30 (2001), pp. 53-58.

Skinner, David, "Havana and Key West: José Méndez and the Great Scoreless Streak of 1908," *The National Pastime*, No. 24 (2004), pp. 17-23.

Soderholm-Difatte, Bryan, "The 1906-10 Chicago Cubs: The Best Team in National League History," *The Baseball Research Journal*, Vol. 40, No. 1 (spring 2011), pp. 12-24.

"Spit Ball, The," *Baseball Magazine*, Vol. VIII, No. 4 (February 1912), p. 84.

Stang, Mark, "A Grand Gathering: Cincinnati's First 'Old-Timers' Day" in Stang and Dick Miller, eds., *Baseball in the Buckeye State* (Cleveland: Society for American Baseball Research, 2004), pp. 37-38.

Steinberg, Steve, "Cardinals' Opening Day, 1912," *Gateway*, Vol. 25, No. 3 (winter 2004-05), pp. 46-53.

Steinberg, Steve, "Horace Fogel: The Man Who Knew (and Talked) Too Much," *Base Ball: A Journal of the Early Game*, Vol. 6, No. 2 (fall 2012), pp. 33-50.

Steinberg, Steve, "Matty and the Browns: A Window onto the AL-NL War," *Nine: A Journal of Baseball History and Culture*, Vol. 14, No. 2 (summer 2006), pp. 102-17.

Steinberg, Steve, "The Spitball and the End of the Deadball Era," *The National Pastime*, No. 23 (2003), pp. 7-17.

Suehsdorf, A.D., "Frank Selee, Dynasty Builder," *The National Pastime*, Vol. 4, No. 2 (winter 1985), pp. 35-41.

Sunday, Rev. W.A. "Billy," "All-America Baseball Team," *Collier's* (October 1908), in Tom Meany, ed., *Collier's Greatest Sports Stories* (New York: A.S. Barnes and Co., 1955), pp. 39-42.

Thorn, John, "Henry Chadwick," *The Baseball Research Journal*, Vol. 39, No. 1 (summer 2010), p. 122.

Tunney, Gene, "My Fights with Jack Dempsey" in Isabel Leighton, ed., *The Aspirin Age, 1919-41: The Essential Events of American Life in the Chaotic Years Between the Two World Wars* (New York: Simon and Schuster, 1949), pp. 152-68.

Trachtenberg, Leo, "The Travails of Miller Huggins," *Baseball History* (summer 1987), pp. 48-60.

Twyman Bessone, Lisa, "He Didn't Hear the Roar," *Sports Illustrated*, Vol. 66, No. 21 (May 25, 1987), p. 20.

Vaccaro, Frank, "Origins of the Pitching Rotation," *The Baseball Research Journal*, Vol. 40, No. 2 (fall 2011), pp. 27-35.

"Vanishing Spit Ball, The," *Baseball Magazine* (September 1922), pp. 455-56.

Woolley, Edward Mott, "The Business of Baseball," *McClure's Magazine*, Vol. XXXIX, No. 3 (July 1912), pp. 241-*ff*.

Young, Dick, "'The Outlawed Spitball was My Money Pitch,'" *Sports Illustrated*, Vol. 3, No. 1 (July 4, 1955), pp. 18-21 and 60-61.

NEWSPAPERS

National publications: *Sporting Life* (Philadelphia), *The Sporting News* (St. Louis).

Albany, N.Y.: *Times Union*.

Anderson, Ind.: *Herald*.

Atlanta: *Constitution*.

Atlantic City, N.J.: *Daily Press*.

Bakersfield, Calif.: *Californian*.

Baltimore: *American*.

Bellefontaine, Ohio: *Examiner*.

Boston: *American, Globe, Herald, Journal, Post, Traveler*.

Buffalo, N.Y.: *Courier, Evening News*.

Butte, Mont.: *Montana Standard*.

Chicago: *American, Chronicle, Daily News, Inter-Ocean, Journal, Record-Herald, Tribune*.

Cincinnati: *Commercial Tribune, Enquirer, Post, Post and Times-Star, Times-Star*.

Cleveland: *Leader, Plain Dealer*.

Columbus, Ohio: *Citizen, Evening Dispatch, Ohio State Journal*.

Dayton, Ohio: *Daily News, Journal*.

Fort Wayne, Ind.: *Journal-Gazette*.

Kansas City, Mo.: *Star, Times*.

Kenton, Ohio: *Daily Democrat, News-Republican*.

Lima, Ohio: *Citizen, Daily News, News, Times-Democrat*.

Little Rock, Ark.: *Arkansas Democrat, Arkansas Gazette*.

Los Angeles: *Times*.

Marlin, Texas: *Dispatch*.

Minneapolis: *Tribune*.

New York: *Evening Post, Evening Telegram, Herald, Journal, Sun, Times, Tribune, World*.

Orlando, Fla.: *Sentinel*.

Ottawa, Ohio: *Putnam County Sentinel*.

Philadelphia: *Evening Bulletin, Evening Telegraph, Evening Times, Inquirer, North American, Press, Public Ledger, Record*.

Piqua, Ohio: *Daily Call, Leader Dispatch*.

Pittsburgh: *Press*.

St. Louis: *Globe-Democrat, Post-Dispatch, Republic, Star, Times*.

St. Marys, Ohio: *Evening Leader*.

Salt Lake City: *Salt Lake Herald*.

Sidney, Ohio: *Daily News, Shelby County Democrat*.

Springfield, Ohio: *Daily News*.

Toledo, Ohio: *Bee, Blade, Commercial*.

Toronto, Ontario: *Daily Star*.

Urbana, Ohio: *Daily Citizen*.
Van Wert, Ohio: *Times-Bulletin*.
Wapakoneta, Ohio: *Daily News; Auglaize County Democrat, Auglaize Republican*.
Washington, D.C.: *Herald, Post, Post and Times Herald, Times*.
Wilmington, Del.: *Evening Journal, Every Evening*.
Wilmington, Ohio: *News Journal*.
Xenia, Ohio: *Evening Gazette*.

HALL OF FAME FILES

The author has consulted files from the A. Bartlett Giamatti Research Center at the National Baseball Hall of Fame in Cooperstown, N.Y., on the following persons: Bob Ewing, Jake Beckley, Bob Bescher, Ad Brennan, Al Bridwell, Brownie Burke, Andy Coakley, Tommy Corcoran, Sam Crawford, Jim Delahanty, P.H. "Cozy" Dolan, Mike Donlin, Bud Fowler, John Ganzel, Whitey Guese, Frank "Noodles" Hahn, Topsy Hartsel, August "Garry" Herrmann, Dick Hoblitzell, Fred "Lefty" Houtz, Al Hueneke, Miller Huggins, Grant "Home Run" Johnson, Joe Kelley, Cliff "Tacks" Latimer, Frank Leary, Paddy Livingston, Bill McCarthy, Larry McLean, Bid McPhee, Fred Odwell, Orval Overall, Claire Patterson, Heinie Peitz, George Rohe, Bob Rothermel, George "Admiral" Schlei, Jimmy Sebring, Cy Seymour, Johnny Siegle, Bob Spade, Harry Steinfeldt, Jake Weimer and Bill "Barney" Wolfe.

INTERVIEWS AND CORRESPONDENCE

Bowsher, Jim, interviews with the author, July 23, 1999, and April 7, 2004.
Bryan, Harry, interview with Fred Zint, undated; courtesy of Fred Zint.
Dickson, Paul, letter to the author, Oct. 15, 1999.
Ewing, Bob, letter to Nelle Hunter, March 11, 1905; courtesy of Charlotte Ewing-Preville.
Gutmann, William J., interview with the author, Oct. 18, 2002.
Hoie, Bob, letter to the author, Jan. 26, 1999.
Lauer, Steve, letter to the author, Nov. 17, 1997.
Nelson, Winifred Ewing, telephone interview with the author, March 14, 2001.
Nemec, Ray, e-mail to the author, Aug. 27, 2004.
Terkelsen, Christine Frye, interview with the author, May 24, 1998.

WEBSITES

Ancestry.com
Baseballhall.org
BaseballLibrary.com

Baseball-Reference.com
EH.net
IBDb.com
Indo.com
Mapquest.com
MLB.com
Newspaperarchive.com
Retrosheet.org
SABR.org
Westegg.com

INDEX

292; shin guards, 183-84; with Giants, 59, 85, 191 (note 71), 193, 246, 255